The Private Diaries of

Alison Uttley

Author of *Little Grey Rabbit*
and *Sam Pig*

The Private Diaries of

Alison Uttley

Author of *Little Grey Rabbit* and *Sam Pig*

Edited by Denis Judd

Authorised biographer and author of
Alison Uttley: the Life of a Country Child

Foreword by Ronald Blythe

REMEMBER WHEN

First published in Great Britain in 2009 by
Remember When
An imprint of
Pen & Sword Books Ltd
47 Church Street
Barnsley
South Yorkshire
S70 2AS

ISBN 978 1 84468 040 5

A CIP catalogue record for this book is
available from the British Library

Typeset in Ehrhardt
by S L Menzies-Earl

Printed and bound in England
by MPG Books Group
in the UK

Pen & Sword Books Ltd incorporates the imprints of
Pen & Sword Aviation, Pen & Sword Maritime, Pen & Sword Military, Wharncliffe
Local History, Pen & Sword Select,
Pen & Sword Military Classics and Leo Cooper.

For a complete list of Pen & Sword titles please contact
PEN & SWORD BOOKS LIMITED
47 Church Street, Barnsley, South Yorkshire, S70 2AS, England
E-mail: enquiries@pen-and-sword.co.uk
Website: www.pen-and-sword.co.uk

Contents

❧ ❧

The Taylor Family

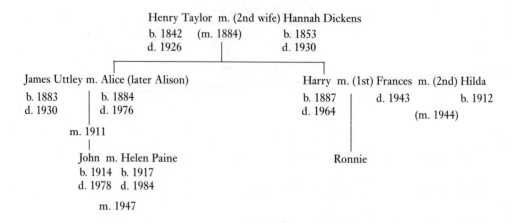

Henry Taylor m. (2nd wife) Hannah Dickens
b. 1842   (m. 1884)   b. 1853
d. 1926   d. 1930

James Uttley m. Alice (later Alison)
b. 1883   b. 1884
d. 1930   d. 1976

m. 1911

John m. Helen Paine
b. 1914 b. 1917
d. 1978 d. 1984

m. 1947

Harry m. (1st) Frances m. (2nd) Hilda
b. 1887   d. 1943   b. 1912
d. 1964   (m. 1944)

Ronnie

The Uttley Family

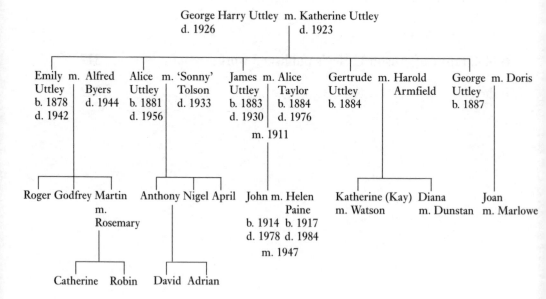

George Harry Uttley m. Katherine Uttley
d. 1926   d. 1923

Emily m. Alfred   Alice m. 'Sonny'   James m. Alice   Gertrude m. Harold   George m. Doris
Uttley   Byers   Uttley   Tolson   Uttley   Taylor   Uttley   Armfield Uttley
b. 1878   d. 1944   b. 1881   d. 1933   b. 1883   b. 1884 b. 1884   b. 1887
d. 1942   d. 1956   d. 1930   d. 1976

m. 1911

Roger Godfrey Martin   Anthony Nigel April   John m. Helen   Katherine (Kay) Diana   Joan
        m.   Paine   m. Watson   m. Dunstan m. Marlowe
     Rosemary   b. 1914 b. 1917
                                                d. 1978 d. 1984
                                                  m. 1947

Catherine   Robin   David Adrian

Alice Uttley, nee Taylor, changed her name to Alison to avoid confusion with her sister-in-law, Alice.

Dedication

To
Alison Uttley

Prolific Author

Compulsive Housekeeper

Inquiring Mind

Spinner of Tales

Thanks, Permissions and Acknowledgements

M y first thanks go to the Society of Authors, the Trustees of Alison Uttley's Literary Estate and Fiona Shoop of *Remember When Books* for their belief in this project and for their support as it developed. I am especially grateful to Elizabeth Haylett-Clark, of the Society of Authors, for her friendship and wise counsel at a number of points. I also owe much to the helpful staff of the Manuscripts Reading Room at John Rylands University Library, Manchester; to the Ashburne Association, Manchester University, for some important financial assistance; to my skilful and extraordinarily accurate typist, Malini Maxwell-Hyslop, and to all those who have given encouragement and help in any fashion as this project has unfolded – especially my wife Dorothy, who not merely kept reacting with enthusiasm to every extract from the Diaries shown to her, but who also helped me solve most of the word processing problems I encountered.

I am particularly grateful to Mrs. Sheila Griffiths, of the Ashburne Association, for acting in effect as an invaluable Assistant Editor when it came to checking the Diary entries – a task in which Dr. Elizabeth Healey also played an invaluable role. Both gave me important moral support as I laboured from the foot hills of the project to the summit. It was, after all, a matter of reducing the Diaries' total word length of over six million to a compact single volume of some 120,000 words – enough to give the sanest of editors some sleepless nights.

The text is reproduced with the permission of the Uttley Trustees and of John Rylands Library. The pictures in the book are reproduced with the kind consent of the John Rylands Library, Faber, Denis Judd, Ben Judd, Dorothy Judd, Antony Paton, the Trustees of Margaret Tempest's Literary Estate, Giles de la Mare and the Estate of C.F. Tunnicliffe.

Foreword
by Ronald Blythe

D enis Judd's perceptive, but sparing, use of Alison Uttley's *Diary* in his memorable biography made me long to read more of it. For what lay outside or beyond that beautiful prose of her books? When Virginia Woolf wrote her diary, usually just after tea when the day's work was done, she dropped her artistry, so to speak, and scrawled the day's happenings with no thought of spelling and punctuation, letting the pen rip. Alison Uttley, however, does no such thing. These private pages have a similar elegance to that finely constructed autobiography in many volumes, which was her life's work – that is why parts of the *Diary* are so disturbing. Her pen was not made for some of these happenings.

So many years have passed since I read her books and wrote about them, that I had to go to them again to discover if my admiration had been justified. Was she a gentle rural belletrist of her time and nothing more? That is not to denigrate this kind of country writing, for it has its genuine place in literature and continues to give pleasure – and information. However, these small narratives which stretch from the Thirties to the Seventies, whilst packed with the social attitudes of the period, are still wonderfully readable. She meant to last. In *Wild Honey* (1962) she wrote:

> *The artistic quality which is called style is a gift of the gods, a birthright which will come into being without extraneous help, although that help may quicken the seed and bring forth the flower earlier. The seed may whither if the art is never put into practice or it may stay alive as a power of appreciation, a critical faculty with no practical expression. Style cannot be taught, but it can be influenced and assisted at its birth. When it comes into being it is a personal attribute of the writer's, unique as his own character.*

Thus, Alison Uttley speaks for herself, both in that miniature output of big ideas and in her toil as a diarist. Her books are inventories of small much-loved possessions. Many of these 'small things', such as her father's farm, are also great things. Her often-returned-to account of Castle Top Farm in the Peak District, belongs to the best English rural writing. For example, although she was born into the agricultural depression, she was able to write about those years with neither a false lyricism nor the black realism of a Mary Mann. She is saying, 'This is how it was when I was a little girl' or how it was when she was a growing girl, i.e. the arrival of the handsome Irish mowers. The published *Diary* will make the reader return to, or discover anew, these scenes. They are where cultivated plants and 'wildings' grew together in the high windy garden, and where most of the furnishings in the old farmhouse were 'hand-ons' and not purchases.

It was not so much her university education – though rare for a woman then – that cut Alison Uttley off from her traditional farming roots, but what she read – science. This was the time when a scientist could know all science, or most of it. The discipline and the 'poetry' of this learning, created in her, qualities which prevented any kind of woolliness when she was writing about *The World of Animals, Country Crafts* or *The Village Shop* – topics which only a first-rate writer could deal with, if slush was to be avoided. She is a kind of hard or tough sentimentalist, ever anxious that the little things which come together to constitute the great things in life, do not fall from sight. This understanding, of course, came from her knowledge of science in which it is the atom that rules. It was something much talked about in her youth. A popular novel of her childhood was Marie Corelli's *The Mighty Atom* (1896). Whilst praising 'style', Alison Uttley's work is about the true nature of often minute possessions. It is evangelistic in wanting the reader to recognise and love the minutiae which are his and his alone, and the real basis of his existence.

In a marvellous essay in *Secret Places* (1972) she describes 'Falling in Love with Mathematics and Physics', and how she thought of nothing else . Although she was to think of many other things – some of them tiny – the intellectual discipline of the exciting Edwardian lecture-room remained with her. It gave her delicate writing body and space, taking it out of the good, if conventional, essay-writing of her time, and lending it something special and difficult to describe. She never sought to return to her native countryside. She listed what she could remember of it. Instead, she lived in villas in small towns after student digs in Chelsea. Like most women writers – and few men – both her books and her *Diary* are fascinating about the pounds, shillings and pence of domestic existence. For years, she was an author of slender means, and the social historian will have much to go by.

It was early in her career that *Little Grey Rabbit* appeared, joining that adored, humanised animal population of the first half of the twentieth century; Peter Rabbit, Ratty, Mole, Mr. Toad, Winnie-the-Pooh, Tiger Tim, Orlando the Marmalade Cat, and many other beloved creatures. Alison Uttley seemed not to share their warmth, and indeed, appeared to be chilly and difficult even. She had a kind of genius and such people are complex.

But never in a thousand years, could one have imagined her tragedy, or rather the tragic fate of the two men closest to her. Thomas Hardy allowed for happenings of what he called 'Sophoclean properties' to occur in his small world, and was blamed for it. What happened to Alison's husband and son, throws all our concepts of her out of kilter. Thus, one reads her *Diary* with a renewed admiration for her work, and a tense interest in her personality. It has been impeccably edited by Denis Judd. Only he could have balanced her brilliance as an essayist with her 'nature'. It will join the ranks of writers' confessions, the tale of a cool and philosophical woman, who for the most part didn't get on with many people; who was highly professional, intensely dedicated to her craft, but far more complex than those who read her – young or grown-up – could ever have imagined. We are what we are, is what her *Diary* says. It is eloquent, and of course, stylishly written. Yet, a great sadness runs through it, like one of those Derbyshire streams which reflect the visitor's mood.

Ronald Blythe
Dr Blythe is one of our most distinguished and best loved writers about country life, the British countryside and English literature. His books include *Akenfield: Portrait of an English Village, The Pleasures of Diaries, Private Words: Letters and Diaries from the Second World War, Word from Wormingford, Talking About John Clare* and *Out of the Valley.* His latest books are *Field Work* and *Outsiders.*

Books by Denis Judd

Balfour and the British Empire
The Victorian Empire
The British Raj
Posters of World War Two
Livingstone in Africa
George V
The House of Windsor
Edward VII
Someone Has Blundered:
Calamities of the British Army During the Victorian Age
Palmerston
The Crimean War
Eclipse of Kings
Radical Joe: A Life of Joseph Chamberlain
The Adventures of Long John Silver
Return to Treasure Island
Contributor to The Queen; a Penguin Special
Prince Philip
The Evolution of the Modern Commonwealth
(with Peter Slinn)
Lord Reading
Contributor to Foundations of the Welfare State
George VI
Alison Uttley: The Life of a Country Child
Jawaharlal Nehru
Contributor to Victorian Values
Further Tales of Little Grey Rabbit
Empire: the British Imperial Experience from 1765 to the Present
Editor of A British Tale of Indian and Foreign Service:
The Memoirs of Sir Ian Scott
Contributor to Fin de Siècle
The Boer War
(with Keith Surridge)
The Lion and the Tiger: The Rise and Fall of the British Raj

The Diaries of
Alison Uttley
1932–71

Introduction

Born on a Wednesday, amid a great snow storm, Alison Uttley's life, like the child in the old nursery rhyme she loved so much, was full of woe; but at the same time she had far to go, was loving and giving, and certainly worked hard for a living. Her life encompassed more than ninety-one years, from 1884 to 1976. She was born when the great Liberal leader, W.E. Gladstone, was leading his second reforming administration, and while the Dervish host was closing in around the besieged and doomed General Gordon at Khartoum. When she died, Margaret Thatcher was an inexperienced leader of the Opposition and still to unleash the 'Thatcherite Revolution', and Britain, bereft of its empire, and uncertain of its future role, was half-heartedly established as a member of the European Economic Community.

Alison Uttley journeyed far in other ways, not least from her humble origins at Castle Top Farm, high up and overlooking the Derwent Valley in Derbyshire, to an enviable status as a profoundly admired writer of rural belles-lettres, and a best-selling and greatly loved author of books for children. Even within her chosen profession, she voyaged as daringly as her creation Penelope in *A Traveller in Time*, moving deftly from the imaginative worlds of *Little Grey Rabbit* and *Sam Pig*, to her books of essays – clear-eyed, provocative and nostalgic. From fairy tales, to finely fashioned autobiographical works, such as *The Country Child*. From magic and nursery rhyme, to studies of place and time, and dreams and space. From two novels for adults, to a few plays for children, and a host of stories, articles and reviews. She even published a cookery book, *Recipes from an Old Farmhouse*, as well as *Buckinghamshire*, a history of her adopted county.

By any standards, Alison Uttley was richly gifted and prodigiously productive. Raised in rustic simplicity, trained as a scientist, widowed tragically and obliged to earn a living for herself and her son, she achieved the fame she craved and the security she needed, by the heroic exertion of her chief talent – that of an instinctive, extraordinarily gifted and compulsive writer. She was in her mid-forties when she began to write, bringing to what became her life's work an unquenchable curiosity, a fine mind, a sensitive spirit and, despite bouts of depression and despair, an unshakable resolve. Her appetite for knowledge was unbounded and remained with her to the end of her life.

Mrs. Uttley's best selling status as an author was based on a few, relatively simple formulae – the vivid recollection of a vanished rural England for the pleasure of the nostalgic and curious reader; the creation of several closely-knit and wonderfully described communities of animals, in which the real world was mixed with magic, and in which some danger and suffering was contained by the security and goodwill of the wider community, and the writing of many precise and thoughtful essays that sparkle even more brightly with the passing of time.

Her success was, however, achieved at the cost of much pain, for herself and for others, as she relentlessly pursued her objectives. Indeed, the writer Penelope Fitzgerald was to describe her as 'a self deluding romantic...and a compulsive housekeeper, patching and jam-making in an heroically untidy kitchen.... it is impossible not to think of her as a sorceress, a story teller whose tales were produced only at mortal cost.'

Often kindly, thoughtful, loving, and a provider of merry company and stimulating friendship, she was, however, also capable of being domineering, scornful, harsh and calculating. Very few were able to measure up to the demands she made of them. Her husband committed suicide (driven to it by Alison's nagging, or so his relatives believed). Her only son lived in some fear of her all his life and her daughter-in-law disliked her intensely. Most of her relations were set aside as unworthy and her friends often found themselves in disfavour. Several of her domestic servants were abruptly dismissed.

Even within the world of publishing, she was not always easy to work with, and although she almost invariably delivered a highly polished and properly considered typescript, she was a shrewd businesswoman capable, on occasion, of digging in her toes very firmly. She was moreover, fiercely competitive with any other authors who seemed to overshadow her. She developed a deep aversion to Enid Blyton who, by an unhappy quirk of fate, lived not far from her after she settled in Beaconsfield in Buckinghamshire. Alison's diary entries sometimes drip venom when, for instance, she describes at the fishmonger's 'a woman ogling [*the shopkeeper*], her false teeth, her red lips, her head on one side as she gazed up close to him... the Blyton, photographed and boastful!'

She also quarrelled bitterly and persistently with one of her most famous illustrators, Margaret Tempest, who had helped so successfully to create the characters in the *Little Grey Rabbit* books. The essence of the disagreement, over who had truly created the characters that inhabit the pages of the *Grey Rabbit* books with so much grace and distinction, reflected Alison's own high self regard and her steely determination to protect her literary and financial interests.

Ironically, or perhaps inevitably, Alison herself could not always come up to her own high standards. She often felt 'unworthy' or 'dull and stupid'. She confessed amazement that her books should sell in such vast quantities, and she was able to recognise the havoc that she could wreak among those she loved, through the assertion of her powerful personality . Although she generally managed to keep her guilt at bay, the crushing depressions, psychosomatic ailments and chronic insecurities that beset her, bear witness to much internal anguish. She was often very lonely and self pitying.

Her almost desperate desire to assert her view of the world not only made her a singularly overbearing person, but also led her to eliminate much of what she found unpalatable or inconvenient from her published writings. What she has left behind, in books like *The Country Child, Ambush of Young Days, Country Hoard* and many other works of autobiography, is the censored version of her life – a sort of Alison in Wonderland. For example, the unwary reader would have no idea that she had a younger brother, Harry. He simply becomes a 'non-person' in Alison's autobiographical works. So powerfully did Mrs. Uttley project her version of her life that, hitherto, everyone who has attempted to write about her, has swallowed it whole and then obediently regurgitated it.

Fortunately, Alison had the integrity, or possibly the vanity, of the true artist when she left posterity another account of her life in her unpublished diaries. These run to thirty-nine volumes and are packed with the most detailed and intimate information. Although, externally, her life may seem to have been rather prosaic, the diaries reveal an internal world of great passion, where self-confidence and uncertainty, pride and self-pity, joy and anguish, are intermingled. For the first time, therefore, the revelations contained in her diaries make it possible to put Alison's long and triumphant career into accurate perspective.

The diaries are bound in hard covers and mostly, Alison writes on one page for each date. She makes her entries in blue ink, in a flowing, but often small, hand. Occasionally, there are small sketches, lists of Christmas presents and now and again, a postcard, or some other momento. Almost every year is fully recorded, although there are very rare occasions when she ends a year a few months early, or writes skimpy entries – lapses deriving almost always from feelings of unhappiness, depression or despair. The diaries, with all their close observation of nature, their intensely felt emotions, their vivid accounts of the struggles and triumphs of an ambitious woman writer, and their remarkable picture of life in Britain over the course of four decades of momentous history, are a completely absorbing record.

Not all of it makes for comfortable reading: there are half-truths and evasions to confront. Choices have to be made between Alison's different accounts of events. Her intense, jealous, and apparently incestuous passion for her son John, has to be honestly assessed, as does the claim that she drove her sensitive, war damaged husband to kill himself. There are many other vagaries of her behaviour to be scrutinised and assessed. Patterns soon assert themselves – a chronic failure to find satisfactory long-term home helps or gardeners, for example; a robust sense of her worth as a writer – though sometimes tempered by panicky self-doubt – a frequent tendency to be bitterly disappointed in friends and acquaintances; a passionate love of the passing seasons, the natural world and of the deep traditions of the English countryside, of culture and scientific inquiry, and much, much more.

There are also a bewildering number of paradoxes that the diaries help to resolve. Mrs. Uttley idealised her country origins, yet was stimulated and excited by the cities and towns she lived in and visited. She was trained as a scientist at Manchester University, but believed in fairies all her life. She was an Edwardian suffragette and read bed time stories to Ramsay MacDonald's children, yet ended her days as a staunch Conservative. She was intrigued by dreams, even writing a book *The Stuff of Dreams*, but shied away from any deep self-analysis.

Of course, these paradoxes and contradictions, and her confused, passionate and often contrary emotions, are simply a part of the whole. In the end, it is perhaps a relief to know that she, too, like most of us, could be mean and rude and selfish, just as she was often charming, warm-hearted and constructive; that she changed her mind, sometimes stuck too resolutely to her guns, was capable of prejudice and sometimes failed to suffer fools gladly. Certainly, it makes her a far more interesting person to try to understand, and also goes a long way towards explaining why so much of her writing deals with communities that are able eventually to resolve problems and tensions, and with social structures that are based on reassuringly traditional, mostly rural and seasonal, rhythms and patterns.

This intimate, hidden and sometimes shocking, record of Alison Uttley's long life, by no means diminishes her, either as a person or as an artist. As we seek to make sense of the new millennium, the nostalgic appeal of Alison's writing, deeply rooted in her late-Victorian childhood in rural Derbyshire, may prove an irresistible tonic for the jaded, over-stimulated, computer-zapped imaginations of today.

It is easy to see why this could be the case, for in these sparkling, sharp, diamond-bright, yet also dreamy stories, there are no soulless tower blocks, no bored and distracted au pairs, no lurking paedophiles, no violent and terrifying videos. Instead,, there is adventure, magic and good-fellowship; a world where small dangers are encountered, but also successfully navigated, and where, more often than not, well meaning individuals rally to the cause of the community – even though they may puzzle, mutter, and scratch their heads before deciding what to do for the best.

Above all, the considerable achievements of Mrs. Uttley's authorship were built upon a dazzling creativity, and upon her capacity to write beautifully. Despite the turmoil and the pain of so much of her private life, these foundations are as solid as the rocky Derbyshire farmland from which Alison sprang so many years ago.

The Uttley diaries are a unique record, not only of an extraordinarily creative writer, but also of the British countryside and of Britain itself, as it declined from superpower status to its current weight in the international community. During Alison's life, the Empire was on the way out, and the Welfare State was on the way in. The strength of the Royal Navy declined, but the condition of the people improved; post-Victorian morality gave way to the 'swinging sixties'; men lost their monopoly of the political franchise, and women not merely got the vote, but in 1979, were to be represented within 10 Downing Street. The nation's external enemies were defeated, but a host of internal conflicts sprang up instead; the beauties of the British countryside and its wildlife were still appreciated, but ecological issues became more pressing, and climate change suddenly seemed more than a distant, faint rumour.

These beautifully-written diaries provide us with a privileged insight into nearly half a century of personal and national struggle, change and achievement. They fully deserve the wider readership that their publication will now bestow.

The Diaries of Alison Uttley are so rich in description, detail and comment, that the process of selecting the extracts contained in this single volume has often been difficult – though always enjoyable. As with all condensed versions of a much larger body of work – which in this case means producing one volume from Diaries covering thirty nine years – the problem has been what to put in and what to leave out.

In the end, I have tried to give as comprehensive and vivid a picture as I could of Mrs. Uttley's life and work within the space allotted to me. Inevitably, it has been a matter of personal judgement, although I hope that my experience as Alison Uttley's authorised biographer has enabled me reasonably to separate the wheat from the chaff. Of course, there were many occasions when I have deeply regretted leaving aside some fine piece of writing or a telling description. What remains does, I believe, represent an accurate and absorbing account of the life of a truly remarkable writer and person.

In order that readers might have some appreciation of how a complete version of the Diaries might have looked, I have reproduced 1932 – the first year that Alison kept a record – in far fuller detail than most other years. Nonetheless, I am confident that in each year that follows, the essential qualities of the writing, and the feelings expressed are faithfully represented.

I have reproduced Alison's Diaries as accurately as possible, despite her sometimes indecipherable writing, and with blemishes and inconsistencies of style included. Where it has seemed helpful to the reader, I have used square brackets to ensure clarity of meaning or to identify a particular person, place, event or publication. The copy editor has further rationalised some aspects of the writing.

At the end of this book I have provided a full list of Alison's publications in order that the reader may delve further into her remarkable output as a writer, but also as a useful measure of her extraordinary creativity.

One final point. When she married James Uttley in 1911, the former Alice Taylor, realising that her husband's elder sister was also called Alice and that there would now be two Alice Uttleys in the same family, decided to re-name herself Alison Uttley. Whether one sees this as an act of vanity or of prudent good sense, it meant that the author celebrated in these Diaries was known as Alison Uttley for over three quarters of her long life.

Denis Judd
Authorised biographer, *Alison Uttley: the Life of a Country Child* and author of
   Further Tales of Little Grey Rabbit
Trustee of the Alison Uttley Literary Estate
Professor Emeritus, London Metropolitan University

> *I always felt I was a changeling child,*
> *a bit of fairy got into me at Castle Top.*
>
> Alison Uttley, Diary, 7 April, 1963

1932

15th January

We cycled to Dunham Massey. The beech trees were silver against the pale blue sky. Sunshine and light flickers of cloud. It was four o'clock, and a dimness was rising, dusk coming slowly up. An old woman in a blue shawl leaned over a cottage gate and watched us. A little girl with fair curls and blue eyes, holding a box which said 'Somebody's sausages' in her hand stood staring on the cobbled road. Chaffinches and robins flitted along the bare hedges. The great leafless trees in the middle of the village. Dusk came and we hastened back. Up the path nearer home we saw four black old women, witches with strange umbrellas on their shoulders, waddling silently along. They were roadsweepers, ancient men with long coats, and brooms on their backs.

17th January

We stood under the great beech trees in the park and watched a procession of deer thread their way across the paths from the deep wood on the left to the open space on the right, where hay lay scattered by the domed barn. Antlered stags led, in single file, and after them came the does with little baby fawns, all about the same distance apart, about sixty of them. Their shadows drifted on each others' mottled sides, their steps were light, and the sound like the moving of leaves by a little wind. I tried to feel like one of those little wild creatures, to imagine its thoughts as it moved so gracefully and unconsciously along; but all I could get was a feeling of comfort in the presence of the other animals, a sense of comradeship, no loneliness where others were so near.

20th January

We have been to see 'Helen'. Exquisite and delicate, with the absurdities of Menelaus thrown in for laughter. Helen was beautiful in her gossamer dress and blue cloak and her little quaint hat studded with gold, when she ran off with Paris. Menelaus was at his most nonsensical when he went to Knossos in his bowler hat, with, a big patterned ribbon, carrying a carpet bag and a hot-water bottle with the monogram M.. The stolid audience gaped and clapped feebly.

21st January
John is having breakfast in bed. He sits, or rather leans, against a pillow with his head on the top rail, just under the two little Raphael angels. His top button is undone, his sleeves up, and he contentedly nibbles the toast, tea, ham, porridge, and toast, in the pale blue breakfast things on the fresh blue cloth. Books and a little carved bear, a mouse and a wristwatch lie by the bedside. A crumpled blue collar, and a soiled handkerchief are on the chest of drawers. He glances at me, with whimsical twitches of his mouth, and loving amused eyes. Professor Alexander at tea. Kind brown eyes and a great forehead, soft long beard. Grey shirt and tie. He looks rather tired, his cheeks pale, but they get more colour as he kindles in conversation!.... We feel refreshed and vivified by his presence, and before he went I suddenly leant forward and gave him a kiss. I felt touched by his tiredness and his greatness. 'How sweet of you to feel so affectionately towards me' he murmured.

24th January
[*A description of the violinist Kreisler*]: Greying hair, firm tread, erect carriage, eyes looking straight ahead, brave and proud. Whilst waiting to begin, he moved his head and body in unison with the music, so that he was one with the rhythm even before he put the violin to his shoulder, and brought out the lovely notes. He was cheered and encored, and returned again and again, bowing stiffly, walking smartly.... Four times he played to us... in deep notes like a cello, then higher, then so high that it was like the music of the stars, ethereal, exquisitely fine.

29th January
In Dunham Park. The elm trees have lavender in their trunks, presaging the purple flowers so soon to burst from their twigs. The silver birches are rosy-pink, twigs and trunks alike. There is nothing more lovely than a grove of silver birches in winter. The company, the intimately talking company of rose-silver trunks, slender and straight, with tiny delicate twigs, so fine that beyond them all a massive beech trunk shines out through the mist of all those boughs like a green and grey light from beyond. I leaned against my oak tree, and had a little prayer. I felt its affection and its strength. I put my lips to a warm red bud of a lime tree, it seemed humanly alive. It was so lovely in the winter sunshine. Nature seemed to speak to me. There was a smell of growth, a smell of Mimosa, which filled me with happiness. This is the first day I have felt that vitality and joy of living which I possess so intensely. It seemed to wake up with the sun in the wood.

1st February
St. Bridget's Day. As I walked along the misty road tonight, the lamplighter came with his long wand to light the lamps. I asked him how he did it, and he showed me a trigger which

he pressed, which compressed the air in the long hollow wand and sent a little petrol up with the oil flame at the top, so that a jet of flame came out and lighted the gas. The wand looked very fascinating, bright and shining, with the little cage of fire at the end.

3rd February
I am listening to Mussorgsky's St. John's Night on the Bare Mountain. He never heard it, and I feel that his wraith is leaning slantwise in the air, hearkening to it, far away. Tiny wild dances spin up and down, twirls of the witches, with little cries, and all the time there is the steady rhythmic pulse of motion, unceasing, troubled! The whinnies of the witches' mares.

5th February
[*Alison mourns her dead husband on his birthday*]: My darling's birthday. I took flowers, snowdrops, violets, and scarlet anemones to his grave. It was all very still, and I could hear him speak to me. 'Little Bimbo, I love you. I'm all right, dear,' and I told him too that we are 'going on', loving him always. I told him John was a lance corporal [*in the school cadet corps*]. I put a few snowdrops from my drawing room bunch among his, telling him about the room, the sounds and the scents and the feel of the writing table; and I brought back a few violets which had lain on his cross.

7th February
Prints of heavy horseshoes on the soil by the plough land, freshly turned up. The path is covered with the ovals, with the nail marks deep in the soil. Piles of hedge trimmings lie in the fields, the faint pale green parallel curves where the roller had been. A flock of peewits wheels in the air and settles on the field. I sit under an oak tree with a tangle of branches of wild rose by me. A little thorn tree grows by my side, with an oak leaf impaled on one of its thorns, swinging like a little weathercock. Why is there something rather frightening about a torn ragged coat hanging on a hedge in winter? It always startles me.

10th February
Snow today, a fine covering of gleaming white over the trees and gardens and roofs. When I ran downstairs in my bedroom slippers and dressing gown to open the door I saw it through the little window, and I shouted with joy. It is lovely and fresh, and I felt full of energy. I wrote again part of the fairy tale for *My Magazine*.

11th February
Last night I dreamed that the Queen [*Queen Mary*] and little Princess Elizabeth came to stay at Castle Top. The Queen sat quietly in a chair, looking about her, and I remembered to call her Your Majesty. Little Elizabeth ran about the farmyard asking questions, holding my hand, as I showed her where the hens slept. Grannie was there – so delighted and honoured, and I tried to stop her from telling long family histories, but to treat the Queen simply. They came for the night.

15th February

Why does L'Arlesienne move me so terribly? They are playing it out of tune, but it makes no difference.... I see the tower at Arles, the stones of the street and the cafe, and the little garden where we sat eating melons and grapes, among bits of the Greek theatre like a stone quarry around us. But my mind runs to that boy, demented with love, to his parents, to the old man, sitting in the corner, the honour of his house lost. Blow, blow, thou winter wind, sang someone this morning – a wonderful song, which always goes to my heart. I feel it is Castle Top; they must have felt like that about so many whom they helped, yet there was no bitterness, only the acceptance of man's ingratitude.

A Vision

I can see my father sitting; at the kitchen table holding; my book [*The Country Child*] in his hands. He holds it a little way off as he reads carefully through has spectacles, with the light of the lamp falling on his clean shaven face. He holds it with both hands.
'Has our Alice written this? What a deal of writing!'
'Take care, Dadda, don't dirty it,' says Mother.
'I *am* taking care,' he asserts sturdily. Then he reads and all is silent.
'We didna have two mares called Duchess and Diamond.'
'Diamond was a horse'
His blue eyes shine.
'Hers got the Irishmen's names wrong.'
'She shouldna say this about me.'
'It's made up, Dadda, it's a book, made up.'
'Well, her's made it up wrong,' but he looks very proud, then he turns to the corner and looks at the binding, the index, the author's name.
'Windystone Hall! Hey it's Castle Top right enough.... Who'd have thought it?'

25th February
A memory

I have a memory of long ago. One fine day I went to Holloway with my mother. We walked through the wood, up the long long hill, past my music teacher's, the house that always made me feel a little sick, I detested it so much.... Then we climbed up a stony path and walked round by a window, through a gate to a little house where lived my old Nurse. She always exclaimed with delight when she saw me – we seldom went however. My mother unpacked her basket with its bottle of cream, its eggs and snowdrops, or tea-roses, and I *believe* there was at times a little bottle of brandy hidden away for the old lady. Usually there was potted meat and brawn. She sat by the fire, sometimes smoking a clay pipe, and this thrilled me more than anything. I was quite, quite certain she was a witch. I liked her, and kissed her thin cheeks. She had a hooked nose, and a few hairs on her lip, a moustache, very faint but very extraordinary.

6th March

[*She describes walking back to her cottage in Kendal with her son John*]: The dark road. Orion came out from behind a bank of cloud. Then all was covered with snow cloud again, but still my planet glowed. The lamp in the scullery window was a guide on which I fixed my eyes, as I thought of Castle Top, of climbing the hill with just one thought, opening the door and rushing in, stamping my feet, to the blazing fire. Dear Castle Top!

10th March

There was a slip of a moon, like a horn, a thick curved hunting horn, or a finger-nail, or the horn of a celestial cow, dropped in that blue and gold field. Nowhere could I see my star. Then suddenly I saw it, in the south west, quite near the lovely moon. Ten black rooks flew across, just missing the moon. I knew I had seen perfection; it was one of those moments, always to be remembered.

12th March

This morning the illustrations for *Moonshine and Magic* came – very delightful. I love Diana in the moon mountains and the Tinker under the tree with his box. William Townsend is the artist. I wonder what he can be like? How strange to be studying my stories and thinking of them and working on them.

13th March

In church. 'Yea, though I walk through the valley of the shadow of death.' And now I know what that means, for I have walked there, and it isn't a dark valley, dry and clean, but a black valley between great rocks, with pitchy, inky water which washes off on one's feet. It is cold and sickly and terrible, and as one nearly drowns there is nothing to cling to, not a stick or a helping hand. Overhead is dark too, and no stars shine. I drift and then struggle for life, then drift, then fight against that horrible flood. Then after a long long way, a little star peeps out, to hide behind the clouds, and then comes again. So one goes on, with hope and despair, but one rejoices to have fought back the water, that strength has come from God to get through at the end.

15th March
A Dream

John and I with James in the middle sitting on a wall at Castle Top, in hot sunshine. James's sleeves rolled up. I leaned across and laid my face on his bare arm. I saw the veins, the hairs shining, the ruddy healthy colour and I kissed it, and I smelled the smell of his dear flesh. I knew suddenly that death shadowed him. 'You won't do it, darling, will you?' I asked, and he laughed aloud, and kissed us both. 'As if I would, when I have my two dears,' said he. Alas! I awoke with aching heart, puzzled and grief-stricken.

11th April

The loveliest thing in the house is its sunlight, splashing its bare walls. There is a Cubist picture here, a circle, intersected by a parallelogram, with squares and oblongs, all in different tones of grey, black and white, with faint rippled lines, and then a dazzling band of light below with a lily leaf and lily shadow. Across the ceiling are long narrow bands, curving like a rainbow, – everything shimmering, scintillating, like water in the sunshine.

19th May
A thrilling day at Old Trafford. I sat alone by the railing, enjoying every minute – the grass, the air, the speed and rhythm of the game, the brilliant batting of Paynter, the lightning fielding of Chapman. It was a tense, record making day, high scores, and a win by nine wickets. I felt happy, and as I glanced around at the people I saw such joy on those plain amid ugly faces, all enjoying it.

27th May
[*A visit to her sister-in-law, Emily*] Emily in tweed frock with silk collar and front, groaned over the weather and garden. I looked at the flower bed and said how well it looked. She nodded her head and moved continuously in a nervous, irritable manner when she talked – yet she was very cheerful after her Torquay holiday where, she was at great pains to explain, they stayed in cheap rooms near the gasworks. There is no atmosphere of peace in that house. I get weary, too, through her incessant movement and fidgeting. I watched my words carefully, and did not talk of writing, of relations, of money, keeping to the safer subject of books.

6th June
Lost my pound note, or so I imagined, though now I doubt it, and missed my silver spoons and forks. I felt ill with worry and anxiety, as I sought through drawers and boxes and trunks. It spoilt the day, – nearly, for after tea I suddenly cheered up and felt it didn't matter in the long run. Life is better than money - it's no use to worry. The silver will turn up I pray, – if not, I have lost it.

8th June
At the Lancashire v Hampshire cricket match.

Man: There's Hampshire going to field.
Girl: How do you know which is which?
Man: By their caps.
Girl: But they all have the same dark caps.
Man: No, they are different.
Girl: How slowly the bowler walks!
Man: He's going back to get ready to bowl.
Girl: They don't run!
Man-:   Give them a chance (after three balls).
Girl: A maiden over? What's that?
Man: (Apologetically) Not very exciting yet.
Girl: (Emphatically) It isn't.

12th June

A meadow full of buttercups, with daisies down below, an embroidery thickly patterned. An old man said, 'A field of flowers,' and I replied, 'Soon they will build over it.' Alas, this is probably its last year. Beauty goes, yet it will live as long as I live, that field of flowers, and I will put it in a tale sometime.

20th June

Went to Manchester, dusty and dirty after Sunday. Paper in the streets.... Crowds of slovenly ugly women in Piccadilly going into the C and A shop, pushing and jostling, pawing the garments. It was quite nice to escape into St. Anne's Square, but I had to meet packs of people in Market Street. I hated Manchester, with its vistas of dirty scum-covered canals. Even inside the best shops there was emptiness and stupid, vapid young women.

4th July

Sometimes I feel like someone on a raft, hurrying down a rapid stream, carried I know not where, and I stare at the banks as I pass. Once I used to grab an oar, and steer first this way and then that, but now I drift on, uncaring. This house is a refuge for me. I even feel glad that there will be no holiday, and I can sit and dream as my raft goes on.
Night. A real mother of pearl sky at 10 o'clock. In the East a purple cloud, pansy-coloured, strange red-blue-purple. In the West a green sky, pale green with lines of pink and deep rose, then a lovely, a heavenly blue, and drifting over all these bands of colour were pale smoke grey clouds, the softest loveliest grey of a dove. Deep down a radiance of gold. Never have I seen a more lovely sight than this vast shell of luminous colour.

5th July

Emily's letter, offering seven pounds in such a grudging way, after having told me how Alice [*Uttley*] works, and hinting that I do nothing.... How bitter is the heart of charity! How I hate to take it. Oh Mother darling, how you must have felt! I could hear Mother today, when I read the letter and stood in my bedroom. 'Don't take it, Alice, be independent! You'll manage without it. *And I will.* Please God'. I *will* carry on and manage. That's the last of them, Emily, George, Alice and Gertrude, all selfish and cruel, and Emily weak. Let me never be confounded. Let me never give way. Let me rise up and fight till I die. The things of the spirit they shall not spoil. I will keep my dreams and my imaginings, my clouds and flowers and sunshine and shadows.

15th July

Lunch at the Croquet Club with Lady Crossley.... But, and here let me confess, I think all the people I dislike, the well-fed, unimaginative, snobbish women of Bowdon were there.... I felt really frightened and overwhelmed, – eager to escape from a nest of fat spiders. God, keep me free from that life, that outlook, those people. I can't get ever it, I am disturbed, troubled, by those curious glances. I have read again the charming and cheering appreciation which came this morning from the *Atlantic Monthly*.

16th July

On Thursday I returned from Manchester with fivepence ha'penny, and I have got to make it last, living on cheese and an occasional egg. Cynthia [*her home help*] and I had an omelette made of one egg today, and I had cheese for supper, and Sunday's dinner will be similar. Twopence for the Observer, twopence for a lettuce, and one and a half pence left for Monday. I am reading again *The Renaissance* [*an article of hers*] –it is good, and pleases me, and bits of the new book delights me too. Yesterday morning I wrote the little tale of the *Ballet Shoes and Ploughboy Shoes*, – an Andersen touch I think – inspired by a tune I heard on the wireless.

20th July

I feel terribly happy. I feel immortal, and part of the wind and rain and sun. The sky is exquisite blue, with dim white clouds, so soft they look as if a puff would dissolve them. Against them wave the trees, golden in the sunlight, reflecting, moving, dreaming. A little gold dab floats on the ceiling, and... lights and shades flutter through the room. It is one of my moments of fountain joy, when the spring of my heart bubbles up *in spite* of the sadness of life.

21st July

Evening, dusk falling, little shadows creeping across the room. On the piano the brown jug: of flowers, a red rose, blue delphiniums, yellow and white and green, and the brilliant orange carpet and black flowered curtains. A jolly fire darting flames up the chimney.... My papers are on the oval table on the hearthrug, and Hamish [*her Scottie*] asleep. The canary singing and the wireless playing some air. Outside all is green, with a grey sky, chill and dull. All day, on and off, I have been writing, copying pages of the book. I went to the Coopers, talked to old Mrs. Johnson, and returned feeling rather depressed, – poor, a nobody! How absurd of me, when I have a sacred fire burning in my heart.

27th July

The River. Water-striders, little oarsmen jerking along the liquid surface.... A dry rustling, and the coat of a weasel shines with reddish lustre among the comfrey. A frightened water rat tumbles down like a brown ball, dives with a plop and shoots across with his muzzle splitting the surface. A moor-hen paddles across, black, distinguished, hesitant. The kingfisher, a blue arrow. Reed-warblers, busy, restless. Winter sun, a light fall of shells from buds long before the leaves come; a row of poplars enveloped in luminous vapour; a red fire broods over the tops of the elms; grey catkins hang from aspen branches; little oblique tunnels in the soil; moths appear at night. In February a bird, chaffinch or greenfinch, will isolate himself from the band and return to his old haunt. Birds have become pairs. In Africa, birds are preparing to leave. The black caps are going to leave the mimosas, the orange trees, to come and pick the ivy-berries in our bare woods. Among the olive trees the white wagtails follow the narrow furrows turned by the Arabs' plough. In the oasis, along the streams, the swallows chase the flies, and the willow-warblers flutter their wings under the date trees. All are preparing to leave the Mediterranean for the North.

2nd August
[*Alison, is visited by gipsies*]. A little ringletted child came with an old wrinkled brown, woman, selling buttons and pins. I gave her a chocolate Father Christmas. Her eyes sparkled as she held out her hand – such an unexpected joy in a hard world..

17th August
John cutting the hedge, I writing my book.... The tent is up, chairs are outside for our meals. There are more roses than anything, and I think they are the best flowers to grow. No more annuals for me. Tea in the garden on the newly cut grass, – and such a tea! A gargantuan tea such as Castle Top loved, prawns and radishes, and jam, and walnut bread and cake. We sat in the corner, near the rose trees, and the sun shone and the wireless next door poured out jazz dances, and we laughed.

27th August
A visit to Midsummer Hill. We climbed through the bracken to a smooth hilltop, with the dyke surrounding it. One felt the presence of the ancient people, looking out over a distant country little changed since their own time, except for the absence of this village. All round were woods, hills, bracken, and far away, the great rounded Malverns, and the distant Cotswolds. We looked for arrow heads and spears in the loose stones of a barrow.... Bumble bees flew low down, skimming the grass. A stonechat sat on a rock near, butterflies hovered. There were little groups of twisted hawthorn. and holly, and bare jutting: rock.

15th September
Joy! *Moonshine and Magic* came. The big parcel lay in the hall; John met me as I came from Manchester to carry my things, and tell me the news. We undid the knots, eager and thrilled, on the drawing room couch. Bright colours peeped out from the brown, and we cried 'Oh, Oh! How lovely!' Such a gay charming book. I love it, the cover, the size, the coloured pictures and my own dear stories. I read some again and adored them.... the book is lovely, and it will make a thousand children happy, I hope. Bless it! I gave it a kiss, and prayed a prayer for it.

17th September
We rushed off to Manchester, and went to the Rylands Library, – a gem in dark Manchester. Silence, books, marvellous jewelled books, illuminations, manuscripts, and all those alcoves with chairs and tables ready for the student. A marvel of a place, a secret heart in this busy street.

20th September
Alone again for the Autumn; sitting by a little fire, for cold weather has suddenly come. A tiny frost this morning, icy hairs, mists and sweet Autumn smells. Last night John and I walked up the road and looked at Orion among the glittering stars... I felt like a child in a story.... Today we rushed about all morning, and John went. We had a great hug and a kiss

in my bedroom, bless him. At the station he was shy and diffident, peeping over the heads of three other fellows. I felt lost and lonely.

25th September
A Dream. She was held in her lover's arms, and she knew she was spied upon. He was a young schoolmaster, and she hardly dared give him her lips, for a dog came rushing, and a maid said, 'She's coming, the game-keeper's wife has seen you, and has brought him to see.' As they stood kissing, ghosts around them, ghosts of people a hundred years ago, Anne sobbed 'Don't, don't, I am frightened, let me go,' to her lover. Then she broke away and ran out into the dark, just as the keeper's wife and the man came in. They didn't catch sight of her face, they knew someone had been with the young man, and they went out after her....

27th September
I took Hamish for a walk in the park, and when, nearly home met Lorna Johnston, who with, solemnly ugly face waylaid me. She had seen my book [*Moonshine and Magic*], and read the shadow story. It had no ending, it wasn't like a child's story. She didn't know how a child would like it. None of the stories had endings, 'if you will allow me to say so,' she continued. Had there been reviews yet?.... I felt squashed completely – and even Eleanor Graham finds the pictures 'difficult'.... Writing some pages of my book, which has progressed today. I like it. I have felt so clearly the hayfields at Castle Top, the flowers, cricket, and that young girl on the threshold of life, eager for all experience.

6th October
Read about Miss [*Florence*] Nightingale at Lea Hurst, her favourite country home when she was a child. She, too, saw the invisible world when she lived there in 1850. Father would be a little child; he used to say his father knew her quite well.

11th October
'And now we will play [*the*] Sonata in A Major, opus 1 by Handel.' I sit by the fire in a grey checked skirt, white blouse, green cardigan and green slippers, with the typewriter in front of me, and papers open at Chapter Five of the book [*the manuscript of The Secret Spring*] which causes me many pangs. I wonder if people will like it, and whether scientists will scoff, and what will happen. But I must go on, and get it done. All afternoon I have written, with rushes out to the kitchen, to make green tomato pickle.... My domestic sense is satisfied, I have inherited domesticity. I could run a big house with all the stores – but I shouldn't like it.

13th October
On Expectation
No, I don't expect, I just go on, and if my books are a success, it will be unexpected bliss, but I never expect. If we manage, if we go on – splendid! Today I slipped into Chester Cathedral for a little prayer, and I nearly cried, for I felt it all so keenly, the people who *have*

cried to God there.... A deep purple thunderous sky, and a park of gold leaved trees.... and a stream, and some long-horned shaggy cattle, a bridge across a moat on which ducks swam and the white arch of a gate into a wood. These I remember.

14th October

Gertrude: [*Alison's sister-in-law*] sent a cruel letter, accusing me of lack of courage, hurting me terribly.... I haven't written to her for ages... I always refer to darling James, for they never mention him, I want them to say 'I often think of dear James and his sweetness and love,' but they don't. The whole letter is on the theme of 'you have no courage, you don't face things,' yet I feel that it is quite untrue. I have started again, and have happiness and joy in life. I don't want to forget my dear one. I must break away from the Uttleys, they lack something, a facing of facts, they must throw blame on, or decry, someone.

20th October

The Vincent van Gogh Exhibition. Vivid and vibrant pictures, which thrilled and exhilarated me. How I loved them! I even adored the bent brass bowl and the potatoes, and the pair of old boots – Oh, I did adore those old boots, and the landscape.... the boy cutting corn.... Also that little pear tree growing in the back yard, it was alive, I had a word or two with it, and the great bunch of irises in a pot, and Arles with irises in the foreground. It was queer how I loved them. A chestnut tree in flower, with a limestone wall I loved. There were only two I didn't adore – a portrait of a woman and a chair. The green chair was 'it' alive, but the other was just fantastic and makelike. It's the curious way I have of seeing things, *alive*.

21st October

Interviewed by a dark young man from the *Manchester Evening News* – a nice simple youth whom I liked. He whipped out his notebook and scribbled.... when I said I got my inspiration from little things I saw, children, a cockerel on a steeple. I showed him my Moon Marble, which he liked. When I said I was Mathematical, and had taken Physics honours, he positively leapt. Just what one would expect, said he. I looked astonished. Why? said I. Dodgson was a mathematician, said he, and he wrote *Alice*. He was quite thrilled at discovering an 'Alice' hidden away in Bowdon. Poor little Alice, so lost and so small, alone in that looking glass land, with no escape from it, going on forever in magic.

25th October

Morning. I have just come down late, after breakfast in bed, still sneezing and snuffling, and pale, sore throat and aching upper lip. As I entered the drawing room, some smell, that of half burnt sticks brings back the little drawing room at Didsbury before John was born. There is that boredom and 'in the hands of fate' feeling, the future so terribly unknown, for James had resigned his job, and had to get another, we had to leave our little house, my baby would be born, in a few months. I was sick and ill and Manchester's heavy atmosphere pressed on me, I felt I had no friends there, Castle Top was far away, the Uttleys took no notice, not realising our awful difficulties. Their thoughts were on Alice K's marriage, and

Gertrude, on Emily and her maids... so from them we had no help. God! How despised and rejected I was. Yet I was sustained by the thought of the coming life, bringing hope. Night. Retreat to bed, after a day by the fire, typing, reading Swinburne and Matthew Arnold for my book. Thirteen and a half pages I have typed today, a record, struggling on, tired and throat aching yet carried away by the thrill of physics, and the effort to tell of one's joy in that world of science, a world I still love fiercely.

28th October
A most impertinent and patronising article about me in the *Manchester Evening News*. All day I felt sick at being called 'a kindly woman' who lives in a house in the 'Higher Downs' and the rest of it. I wrote a wrathful letter to the paper, but that doesn't help, the die is cast, I must brave it out. One ought to keep clear of newspapers as of the law. I felt so unhappy that I thought I must leave here and go to London, where one is not questioned and stared at. It's taken the fun out of things, and it has given the horrid Bowdon people a chance. Now they really must think I am a rotten writer, – and it makes me afraid of my new, intimate book. Well, before it is published there will be a year. I hope my financial position will better, and perhaps I shall be bolder. I made John parkin, and sent it with his scarf, and two apples, and *The Shropshire Lad*. God help me.

5th November
A great bonfire in the grounds opposite, golden sparks, long flames roaring up; against the beech trees with a sudden flash of gold which, seemed to throw the shadows of the trees on the fog which fills the air. Blue lights and fountains fall from the sky, sudden flickers and bangs, shouts of children, and hisses of fire. In a garden I saw a little table, a father letting off fireworks in the dark, the children excitedly hopping around, all silhouetted against the fog by the green and red lights from Roman Candles. Little Bimbo sitting in her chair, listening to Jack Payne's band, her foot beating time, her face smiling – absurd infant! The book, chapter twenty, on the typewriter, going quite gaily just now, full of excitement, feeling that lovely time of College again.... I am feeling thrilled; over my writing, and over the prospect of seeing John next week. How I loved Meteorology and Mr. Simpson! He was so inspiring and enthusiastic. I still feel that fire burning within me, the fire of life. 'Always remember there's a new day,' – Jack Payne's band!

13th November
Sunday at Sedbergh [*where John was at school*]. The wind is East, icy, sharp, and it carries my hat boldly across the fields. John looks up at me to see if I am respectable enough to go to school, my hair is untidy, my hat awry. I struggle to become presentable before I sit in John's study. 'A kiss' I demand when the door is shut, and John kisses me softly lest the boys should hear.

26th November
Lovely music on the wireless. Suddenly a woman's voice, affected, loud, said 'I'm going to

read you a poem of Robert Bridges. She began. 'I will not let thee go.' I turned it off. Oh James, darling, darling, darling. It was *our* poem, and you *have* let me go. Did you forget the stars, the moon, the flowers? I *cannot* let thee go.

1st December

I welcomed the new month, the month I love, with a kiss.... In the park after lunch. Fir trees with flakes of pink bark, green edged, as if outlined with a faint brush dipped into [*the*] vivid lichen around the base of a tree. Immobile they stand, but the silver birch moves slightly in a tiny haze, so that it looks, like a bunch of summer grasses. Rooks caw and fly overhead, in twos and threes with a continual call they beat the air. 'Are you there? Is this the right way?' they seem to say conversationally, as they flap their way along the skied road to their treetops.

8th December

Cavalcade this afternoon. I was thrilled! and exalted, and swept away by the force of it, the movement through time.... from a little girl of fifteen, just had my Birthday at Castle Top, Boer War, death of the Queen [*Victoria*]. Then the gaiety of London, my marriage in 1911, and the War and parting. 'If you were the only girl in the world.' I cried a little during the war, the futility, but one goes on, it was magnificent. I felt it was England, just as my own little farm and country experiences are England, the land I adore.

13th December

In London. Walking through Russell Square, with my eyes on number 24 [*the offices of Faber and Faber*], feeling rather nervous. Wait in the little room, and then shown into Richard de la Mare's room. He came forward, staring very hard, pale, thin, with moustache, slightly aggressive and distinctly curious about me. 'I am sorry to say that our reader's report [*of The Secret Spring*] is not favourable.' I felt more contemptuous than disappointed. I know it is good.... I kept cheerful, and laughed, and told him of John, asked his baby's name. She is called 'Tillie,' and some strange long name. He promised to read the book, 'if I have time.' I really felt rather sick about it. I went to the National Gallery and had a chat with the lovely old people there, who told me they had a thousand times worse things to contend with. There was an old woman by Rembrandt, and a man.... and a family. I talked softly to them all, winking back a tear when I felt very sad, and they all looked kindly at me. Now one couldn't talk to some of these modern pictures, could one?

14th December

Just come in from a walk by starlight with Hamish. Orion said it wasn't, fair, and the Moon was perturbed when I told him. Orion wanted to throw a dart at Fabers, but it might have swept away the whole of London. So I just laughed up at that stormy sky and felt happy again.... A reviewer said, 'The born writer of fairy tales is as rare as a rose at Christmas; one discovers both, with surprise and delight. Mrs. Alison Uttley is such a discovery.' Oh my! Now that, is a lovely comparison, and gives me the greatest pleasure, because it has a magic quality.

17th December

Here I am – my birthday – my thoughts running back to Castle Top, and the little girl born there, one cold winter's night – anxiety, hot water, racing feet, and the excitement of the arrival, and sorrow, I fear, that I was a little girl instead of a son and heir – only momentary sorrow, I hope! I got a birthday kiss from G.L. [*her friend Gwladys Llewellyn*], and a letter from John enclosing my only present, a tiny thimble fit for a baby hand, and two kisses, dear child.

24th December

Christmas Eve. After tea we sang carols, and listened to *The Yeoman of the Guard*. The house decorated last night, with holly and ivy and laurel, and a great bough of mistletoe which hangs from the lamp. The stairs have trailing sprays of ivy, and little red bells and yellow balls, and a 'tree' of laurel at the foot. There is still [*a*] rose left from the garden, but I bought some white lilac for one of my Christmas presents. John decorated the little tree, it looks prettier than ever, with bells at the bottom and a bird at the top. Goodnight, little house. I am going to fill John's stocking.

30th December

The sixth day of Christmas, and the days have flown by, like misty birds carrying letters and poems and songs and little talks by the fire on their wings. We have had walks through the park, by tall grey trees, which took on a blue colour in the slight fog, where a thrush sang like spring, and the deer walked, and blue smoke beat down from the lodge chimneys against the fragile leaf buds. The world outside goes on – we have made a gay little world indoors with our holly decked walls and our flowers.... I am so thankful for this spot in the spinning world, in the great stretch of ether. I read [*astrophysicist Sir Arthur*] Eddington in bed last night, [*on*] the beginnings of the Universe, and to John I read part of it aloud this afternoon before I went to make mince pies in the kitchen.

1933

12th January

I have been ill for a fortnight, lying in bed with influenza, but I am feeling quite jolly in the pretty room. I have come down to a peaceful room, seemingly cut off from the world, with [the] canary, the red glowing fire, and John who slips in and out smiling. Lately I have slept well, and when awake, I have had a seraphic feeling of happiness, a sensation of bliss which I connect with lying in the Parlour Bedroom at Castle Top, years ago, when I arrived and was cosseted after a stormy term or difficulties and discomforts in lodgings. No news of books or scholarships – there is an atmosphere of waiting and listening, not hoping, but prepared for whatever may befall.

20th January

John has gone!... We talked of this important term, with scholarships, of my writing, my anxiety because I have only seven pounds left in the bank, and there are his school fees and no prospects of books this year. He has been so good, I terribly want to help him to make up for all he has lost. This term I want to write two or three 'stories', to sketch out an animal book on the lines of *The Wind in the Willows*, to try to start a novel, and to put into order the *Little Pigs* book, beside writing for *My Magazine* and the children's papers. I must do some work each day. Things are desperately low now that I have to draw on capital, and I must earn some money to carry on. Besides, I am only really happy when I am writing, so I will try to begin tonight.

22nd January

I walked in the snow.... to Bollington. The old park keeper told me that once he saw seven swans fly across.... Dear Professor Alexander came, in his big top coat and soft white hat, a dear figure standing on the doorstep. I told him about my book. He said that there are other publishers. He advised me to write to Mr. Faber, asking about the fate of the book.... We talked of John and sending him to Oxford. He said 'there is another university', nodding his head in the direction of Manchester. He may be right. How charming he is, a darling man, a genius.

29th January

The lights faded and I rushed off to bed. How dark darkness is. I remember not long ago thinking of the darkness of space and getting quite horribly frightened.... I went to church with Mrs. Johnston, and was happy, that *safe* feeling again.... I felt [that the sermon] had a special message for me.... [I went] to Lady Crossley's after tea, and had a private talk about [Alison's financial] affairs. Lady Crossley is so kind, she would be horrified if she knew how much I have to scrape, it is really very funny. I have nothing left and should draw my last £7 tomorrow…. A wonderful sermon on 'The peace of God which passes all understanding' – those words I felt were a special message to me.

4th February

I went for a walk with Miss Hackforth, she thinks I am a staunch Conservative and a Church woman. I feel astonished, I who am the greatest vacillator in all things…. We talked a little of religion, verged on capital punishment (where I was silent) kept off Russia, and I saw nothing of the beauties of trees and fields.

5th February

[*She goes to the cemetery to see her husband's grave*] which had a brown bowl and four pink and white tulips from an unknown, perhaps from George [*Uttley, James's brother*]. It was very neat and quiet and I had a little prayer. I always fear he moves as I approach, and half raises himself. 'I am so glad to see you darling'. Oh, Bimbo, why did you do it? You had a lover, and a sweet son, a house, private income, a job, everything one would wish. I am trying very hard to forget, to be brave, to be someone else.

10th February

'The Renaissance' came back and '*Lace in the Wood*' was returned yesterday. It is disappointing for '*The Renaissance*' is the best thing I've ever written, it would make me despair if I wasn't an optimist. I have had so many ups and downs, so I think of the solid rock of the earth down below with the bright stars above and nothing matters. Yesterday… the feeling of long ago when I walked there [*a road in Hale*] came on me. I used to feel 'lost' in the world, nobody wanted me. I had quarrelled with Castle Top – I don't know why – Southbourne [*home of James Uttley's parents*] was hateful, that I was there on sufferance with J [*James*] at the War. Alice K and her husband came in each day in luxury clothes, snubbed me, snubbed John, and Mrs & Mr Uttley seemed infatuated with their success in life, their dinner parties and the invitations, and all the time the War went on, and I felt lost, no home, no-one to love me, no money, no place even where I could cry. I know what it is to be outcast, and I was that fifteen years ago, it's as clear as today. Then I thought of this charming house and the nice little tea table and the wireless and John loving me, and I felt so thankful, for I did have those years after the War with J, and he might never have returned from France.

11th February

Two more manuscripts returned! I am blessed, and no letter from R de la Mare, as I expected, I knew he would not write. I was a bit depressed about the manuscripts, not about Fabers, that was expected…. I worked hard at my housework…. scurrying around. I bought a bunch of white narcissi at the market to cheer myself up for my rejections. It made me feel I am not a good writer. *The Little White Ass* and *Homework* came back, and my work is good. But I don't care, I'll go on and struggle.

13th February

A charming letter from John, with news of his Third XV colours…. I tidied up James's records. I found a yellow curl of John's hair, which I put in mother's locket. And little notes from me. Somehow my notes to James touch me more than his to me, mine are so young and trusting and innocent, – poor child. I had a good cry, it brought it all back. At night Mars red and Jupiter blazing white.

1st March

Emily came, the most successful visit I have had…. I told her what a lot John does for me in the holidays, and she said 'It is a good thing for a boy to have to do house work'. [*Alison, however, finds fault with this, interrupting her sister-in-law, and telling her:*] That's what some people say – 'It is excellent for you not to have to pay income tax, and delightful for you don't have my worry with servants. It is a good thing for your boy to do housework all the holidays, and good training that neither of you can have any new clothes or go to the theatre. It is very healthy to have no meat, and so on.' I get sick of this.

3rd March

Breakfast in bed as usual to save the gas fire…. Started to write and finish Chapter 4. It is a jolly little book…. Miss Hackforth asked me if I listened to Vernon Bartlett on the radio. Aren't you interested in humanity? *No*, said I, I don't care if it's wiped out – I hoped that would shock her. She *did* look amazed. Confound it, but she isn't as bad as Emily. These Liberals with their Nonconformist consciences bore me stiff.

2nd April

Lovely darling April has come. I ran down to open the door to let her in yesterday.

15th April

Professor Alexander said he wanted to finish the proofs of his new book because he wanted to give some of the royalties for John's education. The dear man.

30th April

A dream last night. James sitting low by a table, I leaned over and he drew me down to his arms and kissed me. Our lips clung as if he was drinking life, – there we clung in a long, passionate beautiful kiss, never moving. John, I knew, was near, but I did not see him, although I wondered what he thought. I awoke happy with the feeling of the kiss on my lips.

3rd May

Glorious news, a Kitchener scholarship for John of £110 a year…. Now I hope we can manage. It makes a difference between comfort and difficulty…. Tonight after playing cards, we sang all the lovely old songs.

4th May

A dream. I sat on the sand with people and introduced James, who looked very jolly. I whispered, 'He's dead, really'. James sat down at my side, and I tried to explain to them. We turned and he was not there, to the lady's horror and my grief but he had 'gone back'.

5th May
I am all alone for jolly little-big boy has gone back to school. This morning we were hilarious as we dressed, chasing after each other, lying in wait. John sat in my bed at 8.15 and we read the congratulating letter from Professor Alexander. I saw him off from the gate, after long clinging kisses, when he reminded me of James. Then I gardened for over three hours, hard.

6th May
Felt tired. There was nothing to eat and no money left, so I took pence from the money box.

13th May
Cleaned up the awful kitchen, [*with Cynthia, her home help*]. Mrs Hogg called. I told her the fate of the *Secret Spring*.... I feel at home with the people of Altrincham. The house is so charming [*and*] clean that I keep peeping into the rooms with pleasure.

14th May
I suddenly go to the Downs Chapel to hear a preacher...who used to inspire James. I felt icy-hearted, but am warmed by the gospel of the Prodigal Son....[*Later*] I listen to the radio, on Christianity and Communism.... All life is interesting, whether slaves or free, Communists or not. Life is marvellous.

15th May
I have been looking at last year's diary. I am much more happy now, partly because of John's scholarship, partly because of not seeing Emily, or having to ask for money from George [*Uttley*] or anyone.... I had a great washday.... The garden is a dream.

16th May
Some day! Rushed off to Manchester. Called at the stockbrokers... invested £100 in War Loan, and drew out £30 from savings. I had my hair waved. Slippers too dear, couldn't afford 16/lld, – returned to put £10 back in bank again.... felt I had drawn too much. I began to write at home. I did ten pages. I have enjoyed living in my Guy Fawkes chapter [*to be part of A Traveller in Time*].

25th May
Cricket, Lancs v. Kent. A grey day.

6th June
A happy day. Breakfast in the sunny garden, then gathering flowers. I felt.... I could spend days outside, if there was no wireless next door, but that boring noise drives away the joy. I

see Jupiter and Mars very close, almost touching.... I water the garden, and stagger about with the buckets full, feeling like a dairy girl or a servant at Castle Top. It is quite natural to me to carry four buckets.

7th June

Depressed tonight. This morning *Tim Rabbit* came back. I felt.... I could never ever manage to write. Doubts assailed me, as I tried to write a little but I couldn't. I was irritated by Lady C[*Crossley*] at the cricket... she *would* carry the bag.... We dithered. It was all a stupid business, all due to deafness. I cheer myself up by picking some flowers & thinking of John. What will it matter in a thousand years? But I was happy watching the cricket.

17th June

I lay awake in the morning wondering whether to teach little children, and how to supplement my income now I get nothing accepted. I tried to write last night, but the result wasn't *magic*, not as I want it to be.

19th June

Great storm in the night.... I called Hamish upstairs to let him lie under my bed. Poor thing! Slept brokenly. [*In the morning there was*] a nice letter from John, about the poem. 'I bet no other mother sent an original poem to her son!' I finish the *Silver Tree*, a charming little tale, but it took hours. Tonight I have been typing *The Renaissance* again. I am quite certain it is excellent.

29th June

A strange thing, I took Walter de la Mare's *Motley* from the shelf, and read some poems. Suddenly I came across a tiny photograph of soldiers, and I hunted again and found a letter from James, an exquisitely beautiful little love letter. I turned to the beginning of the book 29th June 1918, exactly fifteen years ago to the day.... I had the letter a few days later, and slipped it in the book and there it has lain till now. He speaks of our great love, and our joy in John, and our sweet life together. It is like a voice coming out of space. Beloved, darling, I do love you always.

21st July

The nice story of the Hedgehog in the cornfield returned. It is very depressing. I have lost all ambition. I am sure that some of the stories are beautiful, but nothing happens, and I get poorer and poorer. I have one shilling and ten pence for the weekend, and an empty larder. I keep Cynthia on, but it is for companionship. Alone I should lose all heart.

6th August

Music [*on the radio*] can give me an exhilaration and exquisite happiness beyond anything else, beyond poetry, beyond human love. They played *Lady Greensleeves*, and I cried, it made my heart ache, not with happiness, but with the forgotten things.... I will always try to remember the dead, to make them live again. Cynthia went, and I felt uncomfortable and sad.... I did some typing, darned a pile of stockings, and have enjoyed the day.

10th August
My wedding day, I forgot, I'm glad to say, till this afternoon. Tea at the Snells, [*but I feel I am looked down on by a woman*] who had been at Newnham [*College, Cambridge*] and [*had*] taught for 23 years at St Paul's School.

11th August
Once more *Tim Rabbit* has come back. Now I shall keep it till after Christmas. Poor little chap. His legs are tired running up and down to London to a dozen publishers. I am glad I am not spending a pound a week on wages and food for Cynthia. [*She describes her new routine*] ....all work is done by 10. 30.... Down at 8.00, breakfast at 8.10. A cheque from *New World* [*magazine*], and a charming letter from John.

6th October
Sitting in the dark listening to the wireless, John reading Wodehouse's last book. The canary swings on its perch. My open work box with a pile of socks. John sits there in James's old suit, his face half smiling with amusement, his eyebrows dark lines.... This is our last night together before [*John goes up to*] Cambridge. It is wonderful that our dreams come true. I am so happy for John. The big trunk is packed.... John has cleaned James's cigarette case, my present of long ago.

22nd October
To church in the morning. The quietness of the service helps me. Sometimes I pray, sometimes I dream, or a lovely word catches my attention, and I feel exhilarated. Today it was the shadow of God's wings.

28th October
'...fighting in Jerusalem' just came through on the wireless. 'Russia is giving Turkey five fighter planes as a birthday present'. Another returned manuscript from *My Magazine*, which is closing down, a loss for me, for they paid well. There is the acceptance of *Peter Peter* from *New World* [*magazine*]. I sit by fire, and finished off *The Fir Tree* and *Tom Tit*. I posted it to *New World*. I ought to have written more but I feel wretched.

31st October
I enjoyed having Harry [*Taylor*] and Frances to dinner.... Tomorrow they are going to my dear Castle Top. I sent it my love. I felt glad to have them here, relations, my nearest blood relations and it is as if mother was with us smiling & listening.

1st November
A jolly beginning, for there was a letter from Mr. Collins, the publisher, telling me how

much he likes the *Grey Rabbit* books, and saying he will continue publication. I felt on air, elated, happy, and I read the new Squirrel story and found it entrancing, one of the best.

13th November

I went to Lady Beattie's for lunch. I was terribly tired…. We always get on to armaments. I said 'death isn't the worst thing' and she didn't agree. I subsided. John is reading Herodotus at Cambridge.

21st November

There was a letter from Margaret Tempest with roughs of the new book. John has joined the machine gun platoon – Oh why!…. I arranged all the pictures of the new squirrel book, and typed a few pages slowly…. Going down to Altrincham…. and see a poster 'Inquest on a shot councillor. Widow's story!' It makes me sick with the thought of the woman's ordeal, the gloating of the people over the tragedy.

25th November

To Manchester to meet G L. [*Gladwys Llewellyn*] We went to a tiny shop kept by a smiling Jewess, looking at trays of old jewels. We were like two children among a lot of toys.

7th December

What a day. Slipped & hurt my back. Tomorrow [*John*] comes home…. I haven't finished my book. I have done three quarters of it, 147 pages. Last night I dreamed James came into my room….and said 'I have changed my things all ready, darling', and kissed me. The sweetness of the kiss woke me up, such a loving kiss. I feel as if James and John were one nowadays.

17th December

Nobody remembers my birthday, as does Gladwys. She is a staunch friend. [*She describes going to church*]…. I prayed for my mother who bore me at Castle Top… I can't stop weeping on my birthday night. I feel worried about kind people's offers of help. I want nothing except to be left to manage in my own way… & now comes the interference of Lady [*Boyd Dawkins*]. I feel the old misery when Emily and G were helping. I want to do Cambridge alone. That would be a triumph…. I won't submit. I cannot tell everything, I, who am so secretive.

1934

(I will look unto the everlasting hills, from whence cometh my strength).

9th February

My heart sank…. Gollancz have returned *Winged Chariot*. I feel quite downhearted for three minutes. Then I cheered up and remembered when *Cuckoo* came back. It isn't *reviews* I dread, but rejections! I waited for the parcel…. It was my journal…. so there may still be a chance.

10th February

A charming letter from R[*ichard*] de la Mare [*of Faber*] 'I wonder when you are going to write a successor to *The Country Child*? I do wish you would think about it, and see if you can't plan another book.' …Also a nice letter from *The Lady* [*magazine*] after two and a half weeks of displeased silence.

19th February

[*She has a disagreement with Miss Hackforth*] She thinks I am joking when I state my point of view, approval of Nazism…. A succession of visitors…. Margaret Tempest has sent the rough of a lovely advertisement…. The death of the King of the Belgians. I keep thinking of the sadness of the Queen.

25th February

Pale milky sky with a white moon. Black boughs of pear trees with fresh buds already forming. Light on the yellow chimneys and red brick of a distant house. In the room the wireless plays Liszt, a lightning ripple of notes. My tea tray with the flowered teaset, and the important hot water jug, stands waiting on the chest of drawers, beside a vase of incomparable anemones, a bowl of oranges and bananas and John's photograph. On the mantelpiece more anemones…. and John's grey jug of violets. The photograph of Castle Top. The funny laughing picture of John, silver cups, the box of matches, and blue china treasures from Castle Top's double-bedded room. Above them the St. Francis picture, and the adoration of Richard II. A medicine bottle and glass, and a box of tablets – a full complement.

1st March

A jolly day, darling March, for I felt a lot better. I got up after lunch and wrote *Twenty Four*

Tailors.... [*Various people called*].... A charming letter from Eleanor Graham. *The Country Child* is *the* book for February for the Junior Book Club. 'You will get recognition in time,' says she.

11th March

I do believe in God, but he is a great Spirit, and the god of universal worship, not only the god of Christianity.... A reading from the *Death of Socrates* [*on the radio*]. Tears fall down my cheeks.

13th March

Last night I thought of my sweet little mother newly married 50 years ago.... How pretty she must have been, and how simple and wide eyed, and timid and brave, and how she prayed to God to help her do the right, and be a blessing. It was so real, I could feel it...and now they are all dead except one, and she I don't know.

16th March

Today I finish *Lion and the Unicorn*. A triumph, for I have done it feeling ill.... Soon John will come home, only one more day by myself.

23rd April

I lay awake last night, worried about my nose, and my future. Dr. Hughes suggests six weeks holiday. Dr. Cooper says an operation is necessary.... What should be done? Richard Tauber singing [*on the radio*]. He gets to my heart.

25th April

I must write down my devastation. *Blue Ribbons* came [*back*] at 10 o'clock, and at 12 o'clock came *Cuckoo!* Two rejections in one day. Talk about depressions – I felt pretty sick. Let's hope I shan't see *Winged Chariots* tomorrow!... (NB It came on 9th May!)

27th April

I worked on the owl story & finished it roughly.... Lady C[*Crossley*] came, – was alarmed that I am touching my capital. What else can I do? At last a letter from Frances [*Taylor, the wife of Harry*], the first since January, no apology. She speaks of cattle sickness at Castle Top.

6th May

Great wind in the night. It is quite a delicious sensation to feel the bed wobble. I posted off *Wise Owl's Story* and *Grey Rabbit's Party*. I think they are both very jolly, full of delicious jokes, which made me gurgle as I wrote them. Hamish has two great big blisters. [*N.B. Wise Owl and Party accepted 16th May.*]

24th May

I met [*in Devonshire*] a black haired Manchester woman who has been telling me of her son in Manchester & Heidelberg. Poor thing. She is a most repulsive looking creature.... Today has been the loveliest day in the world. 'God save the King' plays the band. England is safe, and rich, and happy. All evil is forgotten in the beauty of the day.

11th June
[*Her first meeting with William Collins, in London*] He is a dark haired young man who reminded me of Harry when he was young. Diffident, and charming and gay and careless. I liked him very much. Mrs. Collins, a charming little person.... Mr. Collins asks me to write a story to fit in with some illustrations he had. Also asked me to write a long animal book, about a dog or something.... I saw illustrations at Collins, and gave him my nursery rhyme book. I telephoned Nelsons, where I was told that my book was accepted.... I rushed round to tell Eleanor Graham.... I went to the National Gallery.

2nd July
Wash day. And then to the Sussex match [*at Old Trafford*]. [*Maurice*] Tate's magnificent bowling.... Florence [*her home help*] gave notice. Again! This awful business with maids.

17th July
A queer day! Eleanor Graham returned my manuscript saying it had no climax. Quite true, alas. I packed it off to Mr. Bell's, sick of it.... I had my hair waved.... [*Florence*] has broken my balloon woman! I felt furious and told her I am glad she's going.... John has a bursary of £20, thank God.

20th July
I saw G.L. [*Glwadys Llewellyn*] off in Manchester. She looks very tired. I offer to go and help in the school if ever she wants me to. I walked in Manchester, and felt dazed by all the people.... I went to the new library and read Child Psychology.... [*At home, there was*] a letter from [*a Mr*] Baird, Amherst College, Massachusetts, asking for permission to quote the *Country Child* in his book. I looked through the *Country Child* and adore it. My dear Castle Top.

24th July
A delightful day, without a maid. John 'untied' the house while I washed and dressed.... Then I went shopping...and John did his Greek. [*After tea*] we read over *Wise Owl's Story* and corrected the suggested pictures of Margaret Tempest, and then rattled on about books.

1st August
I finished *Sons and Lovers*. It is too rambling and not quite 'true' enough for me: the mother is too harsh with the drunken father.

7th August
Cuckoo Cherry-Tree came home again, so no luck with my two Castle Top books. I am

depressed, but not unduly. I feel so thankful to have the *Country Child* and *Moonshine* [*published*]. I thought I would never have anything taken.

8th August
I heard from Heinemann that the *Grey Rabbit* books are to be translated into Swedish and broadcast. Hoorah! I always wanted to be broadcast. I wish it brought in some money, though. I was so thrilled that I forgot to put tea in the teapot. *Grey Rabbit* must do this in one of the tales! I went to watch cricket with John, Lancs. v Derbyshire. I wanted my own county to win.

23rd August.
Last night John was very sick after tea….he is very brave, never makes a fuss, so I never know when he is ill. We had a fire to cheer up a cold day. I wrote some pages of the first chapter of my novel, and another character, a gamekeeper, comes in. I couldn't keep him out.

1st September
A glorious morning. I slept well, and felt jolly at a new month…. A great shout from John over some trivial thing with the vacuum cleaner upset my nerves. I had a good cry. I drank a little brandy in a time-honoured way by ancestors, for shock.

4th September
Tea at Lady Crossley's…. I feel depressed because my Squirrel [*Goes Skating*] book hasn't come out yet. I want the money. No news of the Swedish translation. No news of *Cuckoo* [*Cherry-Tree*] (probably been rejected), nor of the nursery rhyme book. Nothing I write seems any good, and no cheque from Faber's for royalties. I drew £21 from the bank for our holiday, a terrible sum for us.

2nd October
John and I scurried off to Manchester, I in my new blue felt hat. 'You look hot-stuff', said John. We drew out £25 for expenses. I am sick of Manchester….I would like to escape far away to another part of England.

7th October
9.15 pm, the wireless playing Strauss. The news of a great rebellion in Spain [*led by Franco, and beginning the Spanish Civil War*], many dead….strange and terrible events. G. L. came at the weekend. We walked through parks, and back by Dunham golf links. G.L. looked so fresh, her hair so lovely and long and brown, now she looks younger than I. She is a dear. We talked of books.

8th October
Orion in the east, at 5 am. [*She describes John going off to Cambridge*] We had our little prayer, most beautiful and helpful, and a great kiss as he left the house. When the train went I came

sadly home, dawdling through Altrincham, loath to reach the lonely house…. All day I struggled slowly and glumly. Hamish waiting faithfully for me.

10th October
No letters so I got on with my work…. Then Hamish & I tramped through Altrincham, – a dog fight…where I smote the attacker with my umbrella. Then I paid my wireless bill, which I could do because I have had no maid…. In the afternoon, a sweet letter from John, thanking me for my gay companionship, *and* the returned *Cuckoo*! How sad I felt. Dent sent it back…. It *is* good. Well, off it goes tomorrow…. It's strange, I can get nothing accepted nowadays. I simply do nothing, *Cuckoo, Blue Ribbons, No Ordinary Rabbit* – all wandering about.

19th October
Last night I was wakened by a little strange thumping sound, – it was some rose petals falling from a vase on the mantelpiece. I sat up and grinned at myself in the glass. What a light sleeper! A princess!

22nd October
No letter from John today, – so I feel anxious about his sprained arm…. Today Kathleen [*the new home help*] came, energetic and pleasant…. We washed table cloths…. W[*Winnie*] Armitage comes in a new, bright blue car, and took me to the Regal to see *Empress Catherine*, with [*Ingrid*] Bergman. She is the most exquisite and lovely creature…. We had tea in the Regal café. I felt appalled by the atmosphere of it, the ugly suburban women…. But the tea was fine.

25th October
In the morning the piano tuner came….the first time in four and a half years…. I was enthralled when it is finished, and get music out of the oak chest and play. It was delightful to touch the piano again. I didn't go for my usual walk, but sat by the fire *enjoying* life. A great fire, a cosy chair, roses in the vases, my knitting, Hamish by my side. I felt carefree, a curious feeling which I only get in winter, – as if I were on an island. This is St. Crispin's Day, – which no man should forget. I am listening to a Haydn Symphony….knitting, the wind roars.

1st November
Snow falling nearly all day. I went to the Free Library, and recommended *Squirrel* [*Goes Skating*]. I found they actually knew my books, and had them in stock, which cheered me. A nice cheque comes for November, but I am so low I ought to do without a maid this month to manage. It is the only way to save for Rates and for John's [*school*] fees which I owe. Tonight is All Souls' Night, when the dead are allowed to return. I hope that my little mother and father are happy – I feel they would be at Castle Top, as I would [*be*] myself and all my ancestors. Our hearts are there, loving that land most passionately.

9th November

A most stirring speech from the Prime Minister [*Ramsay MacDonald*] at the Lord Mayor's banquet, brave, courageous and inspiring; referring to the country's efforts for peace, for a reduction in armaments, for international help.

16th November

I have just listened to Winston Churchill on the causes of war. A solemn warning of our fate if we don't arm to protect ourselves. It is terribly true, and fills me with fear.... my darling John is just twenty. Churchill wants a first class Air Force. I hope his prophetic words are listened to. A letter from [*Mr.*] Munro at Heinemanns, saying they are rushing two books into print, out by the end of the month! Joy! Especially if it means royalties. I am so glad I went to see Mr. Evans when I was in London and talked about it. Every time I have been in London there has been something good. I have written several pages of the novel, but am no nearer the denouement. I cannot bear H.G. Wells's autobiography, and am taking it back.

19th November

At last I rest, and it is such bliss I must describe it. Fires, washing and ironing, curtains etc., then mopping the floors, tea and washing up. It is now 7.30 and I sit by a lovely fire in the bright room. On the little table on my left are various balls of wool I am trying to 'compose' into a scarf. By the fire, on my right is a basket of logs. The piano is wide open, all gleaming in the light. Yellow chrysanthemums in front of the little mirror, dark red ones from my garden in front of The Little Street, and tawny ones on the mantelpiece. My work basket lid lies on the rug, and the basket of wools lies on the table beside the many balls. I wearing beige jumper and skirt, and a gold lace I have devised criss-crossing up the front, so that I am gay.... I feel too tired to write tonight. I just bask by this fire, loving the warmth and the nice room.

20th November

What a day! A letter from Heinemann's saying they don't intend to pay royalties! I was dumbfounded, angry.... when I think of the money they have had from my books, and here I am laying fires, carrying heavy buckets of coal.... I have only two shillings left [*after shopping*]. Tonight I wrote to Mr. Collins and Mr. Munro [*at Heinemanns*]. [*But*] I put the wrong address on the Collins' letter, and had to wait by the pillar box for half an hour in the cold. At last the postman [*arrived*] and let me change the address to 48 Pall Mall.

29th November

The wedding day of Prince George [*son of George V and Queen Mary*] and Princess Marina [*of Greece*]. I sat by the fire with the wireless to hear the broadcast. Only England could combine such grandeur & such simplicity. It all made me adore England, my own England.... It made me think of Mother and Father too. Yes, I am un-fashionably patriotic, but so are most people at heart.

1st December

I have been thinking sadly about Mother, what we might have done for her, but it all comes back to the problem of James. No man can serve two masters. Poor little darling, I think she was happy. I loved her so much but I could never fit in with her, or show my love…. I feel lonely and depressed.

6th December

Margaret Tempest's pictures [*for Wise Owl's Story*] are quite good, one or two excellent. Owl looks a nice creature, but there aren't enough of him.

7th December

[*A letter*] from Sheldon Press, making an offer for *No Ordinary Rabbit*. They want other books later on, but I can't see my way to it, for I fear it would spoil my series. But I am glad they think so much of *No Ordinary Rabbit*, for I love my wild child Tim.

13th December

I am annoyed that Harry hasn't given me the names of the field I wanted [*at Castle Top farm*]…. All day I felt queer, as if I'd lost something. It is *Cuckoo* [*Cherry-Tree, which had been rejected the day before*], my incentive has gone, I can't write…. I might as well burn all my manuscripts and enjoy reading.

17th December

[*John's birthday*] I worked hard, dusting and sweeping, and got John's breakfast, and then, when he called, went up for a birthday kiss. How happy I feel with him here!

28th December

Prof. Alexander came to tea, his kind brown eyes and lovely curly beard, and his grey shirt, and grey tie half slipping down, his grey suit, and cold fingers as he clasped my hand and kissed me delicately. We talked of Shakespeare, – of the missing words in the last sonnet, or of emendations that are 'forced'…. He said he had learnt most of Horace's *Odes* by heart, and much of Goethe and Heine in his youth. His favourite Shakespeare was *Love's Labour Lost*.

1935

1st January
Letters, dividends, a PC from Emily telling us the sad news of Aunt Liz's [*Uttley's*] death. I hurried off by bus to Brookfields, and saw Nora and Maud. They tell me of Aunt Liz's struggle against death. 'Don't let them bury me, I'm not dead yet'…. Poor darling, she wanted comfort before she crossed the icy river. Other relatives came. They talk of James's grandmother, who lived with them for years, his grandfather, and the snobbery descending to George Harry Uttley and his girls.

2nd January
Aunt Liz's funeral…. Now she has gone, another link with James, for she admired and loved him and always spoke so nicely of him…. At night we went to Lady B-D's [*Boyd-Dawkins's*]. Who would be there? I gasped [*at a Bradford Grammar School boy who talks as if he was at Eton*]…. Lady B-D asked [*Alison and John*] whom we know. We said 'Nobody. We are apart. We don't want to know people, it is much more fun'.

9th January
The Kitchener committee are paying John's medical fees! I'm so thankful. We went to Wilmslow. The Uttleys talked of the great strain of Christmas, the expense. Godfrey [*Emily's son*] rough looking came in. Emily chided him….hinted he was mentally unsound, very cruel.

15th January
Resolutions and Review of Work
Unpublished, *Cuckoo*, already sent to many; *Tim Rabbit*, half accepted by Sheldon Press; *Nursery Rhymes*, which Collins have had for seven months.
1. I must write one fairy tale a week to add to my collection, which I want to send out in the spring.
2. Once a month, send a tale to the NW [*New World*] magazine.
3. Once a week, write a story or sketch for a book of country tales.
4. Each day write about six pages of novel, revise and rewrite and revise again.

24th January
[*The manuscript of Cuckoo Cherry-Tree is returned with the comment that it is too old for children and too young for grown-ups*]. How true! That is my fault. I live a fairy tale, in-between life, dangling myself on the rail between the flowery fields of childhood and the arid plains of grown-ups.

5th February

Poor James's birthday…. Emily sent 2/6 for a little memory present. Her heart is good. A kind thought. I posted *Wee Willie Winkie* to Routledge. It is quite nice I think. I am not writing, I feel tired with housework.

7th February

Great joy…over £8 of interest from Lewis's [*bank*]. Travelling on the bus…I reprimanded a boy for spitting. Really, these Lancashire people are the limit.

17th February

I hurried off to church, – got the 39 Articles! Dull hymns. Then Miss Hackforth arose…. so I followed. My dinner [*was*] all burnt in the new oven.

18th February

I thought how much I would like to live in Devonshire. Here the cars roar up & down…dirt blows in…& the people are all 'gentry'. I am dejected that John's letter didn't come, but I lose myself in writing. I have written twenty pages of Susan [*the successor to The Country Child, published in 1937 as Ambush of Young Days*].

26th February

A brilliant day of sunshine, glorious shadows, blue sky. I bought 2 little azaleas at Woolworth's. Everywhere was lovely, the market with its trays of red, orange, yellow and purple tulips, its primulas and boxes of the first primroses, its hyacinths and narcissi, and pretty china stall and all the fruit…. I like my room, shut quietly here, the falling fire, the clock, the wind. It is peaceful at night like this – in the daytime people come and cars whizz past and there are too many disturbances, dogs and smoke, things impinging on me.

2nd March

Joy! The BBC accepted six stories I sent. I am delighted!…To be broadcast all over England…. to children everywhere.

7th March

I went to *Treasure Island*, tramping along the dirty dusty road, among poor people and dirty paper, to the Regal. A lovely film, which filled me with excitement, so that I relived the joys of childhood. Came home, to no fire, but a jolly house, so I lighted the drawing room fire, and took Hamish out. The lilac is marvellous still.

8th March

A curious day of loneliness. I did my work, changed my library book, and sat down by the fire at ? to 12.0 to write more nursery tales. It was cold and dreary outside, a gloomy wretched day, but it changed and the sun came out for an hour or two. The buds on the pear tree are big, like white marbles on the dark boughs, and the cherry is covered with little bunches of knobs. Almond blossom full out, and the bed of yellow crocuses are lovely. I lunched off soup, and then had a little nap and wrote again. After tea I made up a big fire and went to *The Camels are Coming*, which made me laugh and cheered me. There was a lovely picture of the Hague, and another of Exeter. Oh Devon! I feel that must be our future home. The dust and noise of cars racing past here, and smoke at the back are getting me sick of Bowdon.

10th March

I dreamt about being in a chariot with a prince, & I found a marvellous field mouse. The prince and I both adored it and he said, 'I want you to be the mother of my children'. I worried how I should keep cats & dogs from killing the mouse before he is grown up.

24th March

Last night's dream.... James was with me.... I knew something terrible was going to happen.... 'You'll have to die in September.' 'No, I shan't,' he laughed.... Then I sleep again and dreamed we stood by a passage, an entrance to a house on a cliff. 'It's Elizabethan,' I said.... In the passage was a flight of steps. The doorway had an overhanging cornice deeply carved painted bright green, a marvellous and gorgeous colour.

24th April

To Manchester, to look for a blue coat. My first lunch [*there*] except by invitation for 5 years. I feel rich for no reason, the sunshine, I think, and carelessness. I went to the film of the *Bengal Lancers*.... It was marvellous.... I wept.... I came out looking stern, trying to hide my tears.

25th April

Joy at a cheque from Collins for nine pounds fourteen shillings for royalties [*for Squirrel Goes Skating*]. 3,400 sold before December 31st. I rushed off to pay bills. The money is nothing to people like Mr Collins, but to me it is great riches.

19th May

I have listened for hours to the wireless – glorious *Prince Igor* music & then *Richard II*. The play astonished me.... I wept.... I was quite tired with emotion.... T. E. Lawrence is dead.... a Genius. English people don't realise, they and their anti-war [*feelings*]. A happy day, I have spoken to no-one.

21st May

[*A description of going to Clitheroe*] ....thowing away my cares ready to enjoy myself. I think of John's Classical Tripos [*finals examinations*] beginning on the 25th May. I pray for him.

8th June

A good meeting with Mr. Collins [*in London*], he is very enthusiastic, praising my books. He says I have sold 5,000 copies…. We talk of our children. We suggested *Rat* and *Grey Rabbit's Party* for next year.

11th June
I went to meet Mr. Dwye Evans [*at Heinemann*], who says they have printed 3,000 copies of *Little Grey Rabbit* and the sequel, and sold 1,500 of each. He didn't know about Tim Rabbit, but would let me know. I liked him…. To dinner with E[*Eleanor*] Graham. Her book is taken. She was very sweet and encouraging, and kissed me. I sat curled on her bed.

17th June
John has won his oar! [*at Cambridge, for rowing*]…. Heinemann sent an invitation to their At Home. The first time I have had that honour!

24th June
John has a Second [*Class Honours Degree*] in his Tripos. I felt overwhelmed. I blamed myself for giving him too much housework. It may change his life, – he can't get into a great school now [*as a teacher*]…. It's a blow. I suppose it isn't important, – far more important he should be loving and brave.

30th July
The Story of Mole [*Moldy Warp, the Mole*] and *Tale of a Rat* [*The Knot Squirrel Tied*] both accepted and delighted in by Mr. Collins. I am so glad. Some day I may get a small income from these tales.

2nd August
[*She describes her sad parting from John as he leaves on a voyage to Canada.*] I felt an awful ache…. & I will be alone for a month. I wanted to kiss him goodbye [*in his cabin*], but was shy, so we only kissed hurriedly on the dock, with many dockers passing.

8th August
I took a letter from the box and opened it as I went into the garden for breakfast. Imagine my amazement when I saw a cheque for seventy seven pounds from Fabers, mostly for *Moonshine and Magic*, that darling book! Oh joy and thankfulness, and I didn't forget to thank God. I want to buy John a blazer, and for myself a picture of Van Gogh's, and I shall pay my bills and get straight. I bought a 4d ice to celebrate.

10th August
My wedding day, – I prayed for James. Fabers tell me that Whitman Publishing Co (USA) have taken *Moonshine and Magic* for £100. Great news…. It will get me known in America. *M and M* is my best thing. The BBC like my stories, several organisers have asked for them…. I told Lady C[*Crossley*] the two pieces of news . She said 'You know I don't like children's stories'. Really she snubs me.

16th August
Lady C says 'I could not bear the rabbity stories'. Really, I am sick of this patronage. I swear I won't mention any of my books to her again. I dislike this patronage... [*She struggles to listen to The Lion and the Unicorn on London Regional Radio.*] I crouched on the floor, turning and pressing feverishly, and got it, but I had to hold the knob all the time. The tale sounded delightful I thought.

19th August
War with Abyssinia seems inevitable... Mussolini decided at the beginning... I pray England will keep out of it.

30th October
[*She gets ready for a visit from her sister-in-law, Alice Tolson.*] I prepared thoroughly, the brass and copper shining everywhere, a big fire. I dressed in my very best blue dress, – for I determined I would not look the shabby down-at-out relations whom she despises.

13th November
Late last night.... I finished my book of personal memories, 18 chapters typed and revised in 18 days, very hard work.... I went to the Missionary Bazaar. Mr. Potts spoke of the black man as being one's brother, & I looked round and knew that even the white man isn't our brother.

27th November
I posted off my autobiography *Give us This Day*.... I have written it in one month, during August, retyped it, a chapter a day for eighteen days (Christmas, PS. It was accepted.)

9th December
What a day of housework.... I hope Emily won't come tomorrow, – I invited her in a mad moment. Tomorrow is the Varsity [*rugby*] match, he [*John*] is in Hampstead with Dick May.

20th December
Faber have accepted my *Give Us This Day*, to be published on the same lines as the *Country Child* not earlier than July next year. I was thrilled when John brought me the envelope at 1.00 am, when he came back from the BBC dance at Manchester with the Gillow girls. I will perhaps have a hundred pounds or more to help us on our frugal way. I think about how I worked on the book.... It's grand to be rewarded for that great effort. I began to write it properly and retype and arrange on Oct. 26 and finished it on Nov. 12th, in 18 days. A record of hard work. So all my childhood games and fancies, the fields and woods of dear Castle Top, my father and his stories, my mother and her sweetness, will be told to the world. Another thrill is a cheque from Lady B-D towards our Christmas expenses. I list my blessings: five pounds from Lady B-D, two pounds from the Holmes's, a suit from Lady C. My book accepted, the most important thing in the year.

24th December

We listened in the firelight to the lovely carols from King's [*College, Cambridge*]... I am feeling miserably ill, coughing all night. I can scarcely swallow.... All the good things I cannot eat... Last night came a letter from G[*Gertrude*] saying that her daughter Katherine has *not* won any scholarship! I am glad, they need snubbing by Fate, they think they are so brilliant, and they can afford to pay. It will be a blow to G's pride, she was quite certain she would get one, so were the others of her family.

25th December

At 10.20 am I am sitting in bed, surrounded by gifts.... John is washing up, looking after me.... The drawing room is gay with the holly, decorated by John after I went to bed last night, and the mistletoe surrounding the lamp is the prettiest bunch I have ever seen.... John has been a marvel in this illness of mine, helping me and cheering me. I write it down, this special Christmas of 1935. At night we sang carols.... a lovely time, I only humming, my throat was sore, J singing with a deep rich voice.

~ *1936* ~

3rd January
Once again we managed alone [*without a charwoman*].... John is out tonight, gone to see Miss Henderson, whom he met on the boat [*on his recent trip to Canada*]. La! La! I sat down & retyped parts of my book. I do not want advice, so much. I met a jolly family...Isobel (6).... had bought nearly all of my books with her Christmas money.

7th January
A pile of letters, one from Mr. Collins suggesting I write a Christmas tale for 1937...one from Mrs Jackson [*a potential home help*] saying 'my husband won't let me come', one from Miss Walker inviting John to a dance at the week-end, one from Professor Alexander.... I went into Manchester & bought socks for John, stays and knickers and notepaper for myself, no extravagance. Crowds of women buying silk nighties, – they alarmed me, so rich & painted.

12th January
Professor Alexander [*who is 77*] says that any multiple of seven or nine is a dangerous age.... Miss Chase's has a bad review of her book in *The Observer*, – she has [*written*] nothing vile, so is badly criticised.

18th January
Today.... a parcel.... A collection of *Little Grey Rabbit* toys.... I am thrilled...adorable. George V is very ill, and Rudyard Kipling is dead. What glorious hours Kipling has given me.

20th January
'The King's life is drawing peacefully to its close', said the wireless a few minutes ago, – and all the hearts of the country and Empire are aching.... I knew, I felt it, – and oh I feel as grieved as if it were my own father. It brings my father's death to me.... It is so sudden, we feel bowed down under the grief of it. Never before have I felt like this over royalty – Queen Victoria, I was a child, confused and frightened, [*for*] King Edward [*VII*], I was a young eager woman, just engaged, and now I am getting old, and I feel the devastation and grief of our King's death.... It makes me feel my loneliness more, the King has been a lodestone for me, a beacon.

21st January
[*She gives descriptions of the death of King George V.*] I have been filled with grief, very lonely. The grief of all England seems to float over the land. The air was desolate. I admired [*Prime Minister Stanley*] Baldwin [*who*] has given a wise & moving address.

28th January
[*The day of George V's funeral*] ....so ends a great King.... twenty-five years, the middle portion of my life, marriage, war, John's birth, our houses and life, J[*James's*] death, our struggles.... I thank God for it.

31st January
A busy day (but when am I not)... I went to see Maude [*her friend who lived at Timperley*]... I sat in her 'lounge' for about ten minutes before she appeared, – I was amazed at the ugliness. Silver wallpaper (!) with all her pictures and trashy watercolours, – a really common room, half-nude girls holding bowls, a tall vase with imitation tulips... I mentioned John at Cambridge... 'All our men were Cambridge.' says she... Maude's bedroom was rather appalling with its satin quilt and the common look overall... Thank God I live in Bowdon instead of Timperley.

1st February
I engaged a stout woman to come as a daily, so large I fear she won't be able to do the work. These young girls are no good.

8th February
I type up an old *Grey Rabbit* story, then cut up oranges for marmalade. I went to tea with Mrs. Johnson. Her horrible [*son*] Billy came in and says [*of Alison*] 'Who's this old woman?' He is possessed of a Devil, I think. An amazing devil of a child.

9th February
Bed last night was exquisite; cosy, warm and the nicest place on earth! I lay enjoying it. I sent off the *Tim Rabbit* stories to the BBC, – but not much hope... An experiment.

10th February
A wild night, such terrible gusts that I could not sleep.... I thought of the safety I used to feel safe at Castle Top – here I feel nervous during storms, for these walls are not like those at home.... The daily woman can't [*come to*] help, so I started my big day's work.... Today [*the toys of*] Hedgehog, Mrs. [Hedgehog[and Fuzzypeg arrive – sweet.

13th February
The [*toy*] hedgehogs arrive on the doorstep, so I send them off.... *Peter Peter* came back from the BBC, – they have taken a microphone copy.... I don't mind the housework as long as I haven't to dress well and entertain.... I enjoy my writing and revising, I like my gay lunches and teas, and the big fires, and Hamish and the canary are sweet companions. I like my embroidery, too, I find it quite exciting; and then the thoughts of darling John.... I have ordered a chair from Fortnum and Masons!!

27th February
A new moon in the evening.... I bowed to it, disguising my obeisance, sending a little

prayer. Does anyone pray to the moon now? I thought of Castle Top & how we looked at all this beauty.

29th February
Leap Day. A day…. of varying fortunes. It started brilliantly with a letter from the BBC, accepting 5 *Tim Rabbit* stories, a feather in my cap, and a cheque in my pocket. Later the wireless has gone horribly wrong…. No letter from John…. Is he ill? I implored him to read my tale & return it…. The revised *Squirrel* [*The Knot Squirrel Tied*] came, very nice indeed…. I can't stand the icy winds nowadays.

2nd March
Sweet letter from John…. with the manuscript. Frances [*Taylor*] writes, pleased with John's photograph, which gave them much pleasure. I went to the Sixty club. The atmosphere of wealth and snobbery sickened me. I put on a disdainful face & stared back. [*Gerald*] Herd spoke, praising present day Science, prophesying, amazing his audience…. His loud voice made me feel sick. I now long for London, and to escape from this monkey house of Bowdon.

9th March
War clouds are looming. England will support France and Belgium if they are invaded. Just the same as in 1914. It fills me with horror. These treaties are our doom. England should keep clear, as Quintin Hogg [*Conservative politician, later Lord Hailsham*] said.

19th March
Each night John and I sit upstairs, I in bed, he by the fire, and we have Ovaltine and talk…. I have had an invitation to Mr. Collins' cocktail party at the Carlton for 26th March. Honour!

20st March
I had my ordeal, – being interviewed by the Altrincham Council, for [*the*] derating of my house. I sat on a long form with several men, and the kind oldish man by me chatted about what I ought to say, and what points I should make, – the age of the house, the deterioration of property, the smoke of the flat-chimneys. I was called to a big room where a semicircular group of men sat and a great fat old man on a dais in the chair. He said: 'Mrs. Uttley? Of 13 Higher Downs? What have you got to say about your house?' Then I made my speech, loudly and boldly, and they asked questions, of the rates of 14 and 15 (which I did not know). I told of the flats and the smoke. 'When the wind is in the East?' interrupted one man. 'It usually is in the East,' I retorted, and they laughed. They gave me my request, rateable value £45, assessed for rating purposes at £35. I was delighted, for I had not expected it.

3rd April
The house…. prepared for sweep who never came. Why do sweeps play these scurvy tricks? [*She dismisses Annie, her home help*]. Why? Rudeness, said I…. I am glad that she's gone.

12th April
[*Describes going to Easter Sunday service with John*].... a nice friendly feeling in church. Tonight we listened to Dick Shepherd's broadcast service.... The day after tomorrow we go to the Cotswolds, I shiver to think of it! It's so warm and cosy here, we two together. The change will do us good.

24th April
John.... has the offer of a post, Classics master at Newcastle Grammar School. Should he go for it?.... Should he should throw away a scholarship of a hundred and ten pounds a year to take 'a certain job'. Should he go to the ugly industrial North? I said no, but left it open. Dear John, I hope he makes the right decision. I went to Manchester to see the Chinese Exhibition. I enjoyed it very much.

26th April
Awakened Sunday morning by hammering at 8 am.... two men putting a roof on a house nearby! Oh Bolshevism! All the neighbours must have been swearing at being wakened up.

9th May
GL came. Lady B-D invited us to dinner to GL's chagrin. 'I won't talk politics', [said she] and was horrified that a clergyman would be there. I persuaded her.... It was a delightful evening...and we came home rolling with laughter.

11th May
Mr Collins doesn't like the pictures, doesn't want to do a Babar book.... He longs to see the Christmas tale, so I have sent it. I write a fairy tale for Deborah Collins (*aged six*).

21st June
John has a second, 1st Division, very good indeed. I feel most relieved as I thought it would be Division 2. A knock on the door & there stood Harry [*her brother*]! I was pleased to see him and brought him in to lunch. We talked [*of*] my plans for moving, of the sale of Castle Top and of my wish to move.... The news of my books astonished him, although he thought I was making a pile of money! They all think books bring in lots of money.

2nd July
[*She agrees a valuation of her house value.*].... £1000 & I think very fair. I felt at once I did not want to sell the house.... I love it so much.... a darling old house, and my own.... The manuscript of *Give Us This Day* [published as *Ambush of Young Days*] came back for correction. I read it with admiration. Was I tactless this day? [*in her negotiations with the valuer?*]

25th July
I went to see Pantiles [*the house she was thinking of buying*] again. They asked me to decide at once as someone else wants it.... Eventually John telephones yes. I felt frightened and

horrified about buying a fourteen hundred pound house with no money. All our savings in the Halifax Building Society would be gone in one swoop. I told John 'I ought not to have bought a house after seeing it only the day before', I said.

3rd August

I disagreed about Neville Cardus [*the writer and Manchester Guardian journalist*] with Lady C[*Crossley*] saying he's bigoted about music and cricket. Lady C was so incensed that she put down her ear trumpet.

6th August

I discover that I last went to Emily's on the 4th October 1935.... so I have had a most welcome rest. Tomorrow I have to make my abhorred visit.... Today came the proofs of *Candlelight Tales*, a lovely book. [*At night*] the wireless playing lovely Mozart, I think [*of*] inanimate life, feeling at one with nature, feeling strangely happy and sad together.

9th August

[*Her Silver Wedding Day*] I tried not to think of it, for such things bring pain, but I looked at James's photograph and saw the extreme delicacy and sensitiveness of his face, too frail for this world's turmoil.

15th August

Another wasted day.... the house takes up too much of my time.... My possessions are too many....I sat in the garden.... Sometimes I think 'Why write? Why work?' but then I feel dissatisfied. I *must* go on and produce and use my talents, which have been hidden all these years.

30th August

John found my [*book title*] in the Shakespearian sonnets.... *The Ambush of Young Days* [*with which she proceeds to entitle the typescript of the book provisionally called Give Us This Day*].

3rd September

Turned out the box room.... I came across John's baby boots.... and James's service tunic, which I kissed. At night I unlocked the chest with thousands of love letters [*from James*] How glorious they were! They brought such pain and ecstasy and misery I thought I would die as I read them. Death seemed desirable, I felt again the pangs and love of long ago, the loveliness of London, and our meetings.... One telegram told me that he had two hundred less twenty five [*pounds*] and if he had two hundred we could have been married!...[*I recalled again*] the worries of poor James haunted by failure.... [*In the end*] I burnt thousands of love letters, for I must not keep them.... it was best to burn them, but it made me very sad.

1st October

I was thrilled to be asked to act as a judge with Neil Bell in the children's essay competition in the *Children's Encyclopaedia* for Collins. I feel most flattered, and as I dressed I felt elated by the unexpected excitements of an author's life.... I went to the Art Gallery in Manchester and looked at a lovely cornfield, which cheered me up. Manchester was full of dirt and lots of Jewesses with red lips.

3rd October
I was delighted with Margaret Tempest's pictures for *Rat* [*The Knot Squirrel Tied*], it is one of the nicest books MT has ever done. Today a dozen copies of *Grey Rabbit's Party* came, so I [*have*] a houseful of my own books.

28th October
Met John at Marylebone.... we went off happily together, laughing and gay, to Beaconsfield. A glorious day, sun shining, the woods golden, the houses charming. We fell in love with several, and felt that we should like to live there.

30th October
[*She goes to London to see Mr Collins who was*] full of praise, one thousand copies of *Grey Rabbit* sold a month, and numbers going up. He wants me to write an older, longer book, which could have a sequel. I thought of *Anne of Green Gables*. I must try. [*She goes on to Chelsea to see Margaret Tempest*] She was just the same, her cold voice, her pale eyelashes and her cold eyes, her schoolmarm manner. I was glad to get away.

31st October
I went to a bookshop where there was a display of *Grey Rabbit* books, and I was given the author's book to sign. On my page was AP Herbert, Henry Williamson, etc.... I felt so flattered, and so surprised at the honour. Really I am not conceited, just filled with amazement, at the wonder of writing, and the help it had been.... I found the pictures of the National Portrait Gallery really alive.

2nd November
[*Back in London*] I was excited by my visit to Eleanor Graham. How vivid and exciting she is. I felt so happy with her.... Mr. Collins is full of praise for *Candlelight Tales*.

29th November
A dream. I was in an unknown, lovely green country, with great trees. Sunny Tolson [*her dead brother-in-law*] comes towards me. I held out my hand, astonished, to welcome him. He looked handsome, young, his face was fuller than in life, his eyes looked kind, he had lost the look of anxiety and worrying.... 'How are you?', I asked? 'I am well and happy but I *had* to come and see my sons' he replied. 'Yes, of course' I answered, 'they are nearly grown up. John is here. Would you like to see him?' He said 'Yes'. John came and I told him of John's career. He [*Sunny*] was brown and radiant with health, as I never saw him in life. There were sounds below. I knew the boys were there. He went to meet them, to talk for a few minutes before he went back. He was full of vigour, health, happiness as never in life.

3rd December
[*The Abdication crisis breaks*] today's papers are full of a great crisis, not referred to by name in the DT [*Daily Telegraph*] which is most discreet, but people say it is the affair of the King and Mrs. Simpson. With wars in Spain, and Germany and Italy rearming and threatening, and Russia counter-arming, and sending Communists all over the world, and now this blow to England!...I think that the Bishop of Bradford is wrong to attack the King, why can't he be quiet? Poor Mr. Baldwin. And poor Queen Mary!.... I went to see a film of *Rhodes of Africa*, most thrilling, but for the first time in my life I sympathised with Kruger [*President of the Transvaal before the Boer War of 1899-1902*].

11th December
The King's brother becomes George VI. We feel bewildered, people talk of nothing else. I felt more cheered as I saw the pictures of the new Queen and the jolly children. For happiness on the throne, a united family will make a great difference to England.... I realise that he [*the former King Edward VIII*] will never know happiness, he has renounced all for that awful woman [*Mrs. Simpson*], and she will never give him joy, and he will feel longing for his home, his castles, the royal parks, the wonderful traditions he has cut away.

18th December
It is nearly midnight. I have been sorting out chapters [*of her future novel High Meadows*] trying to fit my crossword puzzle of a novel. I don't know what to think of it – there is so little plot, yet many books have no plots. However, I have made some kind of form – if I had nothing to do but write I would finish it.... I got a nice letter from cousin Cissie, saying she remembers my birthday. Wonderful after forty years. I sent her the *Country Child*, for she says it is out of print.

31st December
John [*holding up the book, Inside Europe*] says, 'I'll tell you Hitler's four aims,' and we laugh, for we are in a giggling mood, because I've been looking at him and trying to make him look at me.... It has been a lovely Christmas.... I've not cared about the Uttley family. I felt I have cast off their shackles, which have fettered me for over 20 years – no visit to Emily this Christmas, no writing to George, no annoying long letter from Gertrude, except a few words, ignoring her hints and her curiosities. Only through escape can I find myself and become myself once more, living in flowers and trees and dreams, and in my writing, in nice ordinary people, unselfconscious and without belittlement. So the New Year approaches, bringing with it unknown destinies.

1937

3rd January
[*In church*] I thought of the hypocrisy of practised religion… At night I did the *Rat* book, working hard, pasting pictures.

5th January
A dream. John and I and several strangers…. see a flock of birds, dazzling whiteness. They [*the birds*] swept down, icy cold & human…. as cold as outer space. I said 'Angels! So they are real!'

6th January
All Hallows Eve. We took down the holly, the laurel…and burn it. I think of the shortness of life…. I sent off the book *No Ordinary Rabbit* to Nelsons. It is strange that such an original book hasn't been taken. In any case, I have made £30 from it, from the BBC and *New World* [*magazine*].

7th January
John has gone off to Manchester to meet his friend [*Geoffrey*] Healey…. I must write down my plans for work. *Ambush of Young Days* will be published, also *The Knot Squirrel Tied*. I must write a new *GR* book, *GR and the Robin*, perhaps, or *GR and the Speckledy Hen*. I must retype the 4 Pig stories, and send them to the BBC. I must finish *Patty Verity* [*her first novel, to be published as High Meadows*]. I must try to write another country book, on people I have known, country types and places.

12th January
John went back to Cambridge. I wakened him and we put our arms round one another and played the game of the tiniest squeak, just as we did when he was a baby…. We had our prayer before he went, and the long embrace of mother and son.

23rd January
A parcel came when I was washing up. I held it to me, for I knew it was *Ambush of Young Days* at last. I decided to finish my work, but my heart sang as I carried the coal and made fires, as I turned my bed for luck, as I swept and dusted. At last I was ready and untied the string…then I sat on the couch and took out the lovely book, bright green jacket with a beautiful woodcut of a horse under a tree, a grey book. I read the flattering notices of this, and of the others. It made me very happy to think of little Alice and dear Castle Top coming into their own. I went out to do the shopping [*noticing*] ugliness everywhere.

24th January
I thought of Dr Johnson's dictum: 'The man who is tired of London is tired of life'. An odd thought strikes me. We shall get no letters in the grave.... It has been an odd day, for last night I awoke filled with terror about my book. Perhaps I am worried about reporters coming, prying people. But this is silly. It is a beautiful book.... [*Where I am living*] is so ugly and wrong. I must always be brave.... so Mimbles.... Be brave!

28th January
The publication day of *Ambush* [*of Young Days*]. I drank its health.... at lunchtime. I realised that it is the first book written since I have been alone, and published, because I did the C.C. [*Country Child*] before 1930. John has sent a charming note wishing for its success. I typed and revised the four Pig stories.... It's amazing how long it takes for these things.... I listened to the Brahms *Symphony*.

29th January
No cheque yet [*from Faber*] for *Ambush*, so I took my last 10/- note from its hiding place.... No sign of *Ambush* anywhere [*in the shops*], & I say nothing at all.

30th January
The cheque for *Ambush* came, to my relief.

1st February
A new month, a very important one for me. A letter from Mr. Collins, – a request from Germany for a translation of some of the little books. I am most thrilled. I went to [*WH*] Smith's, and other shops, and paid old bills with my new money. I met Mrs. Harrison, 'How young you look, how rosy,' I exclaimed & she blushed, – & I knew it was rouge!... I ended my day by typing a story, *Sledging*.

3rd February
[*She does not think it is a good idea for John to accept a teaching post at*] a great aristocratic school.... I knocked it on the head, because I don't think he would be happy, even if I could spare him, and I should be too lonely and desperate without him.... I wrote a Cock and Bull tale [*before lunch*].... I wrote a long letter to John.... After lunch I slept for an hour, [*a*] most blessed sleep.

5th February
Poor James's birthday. Emily wrote me a nice letter, with 2/6 for flowers...I am glad there is a cross over the grave.... This afternoon a lady came to see the house. She seemed charmed with it...but my head ached, for I do love this house.

8th February
[*She reacts angrily to several reviews about her new book, and is especially angered by a review*

in the Sunday Times, saying there was insufficient plot]: I was infuriated, it was so unfair…. I wrote a scientific study of youth, with no love story or divorce, or eavesdropping conversation…. A pouring day, torrents. I saw a pile of *Ambush* in Smiths, but I was too wet to say anything. A charming letter from John…. 'Wyn Lewis [*his friend*] has been reading it [*Ambush of Young Days*] & enjoyed it very much…. In Hall…. he started asking chaps what they remembered of their early childhood.'

10th February
Lady C[*Crossley*] sends me my third copy of the hated review [*in the Sunday Times*] I felt it was the last straw…. I had thoughts of Lady C reading it, and I wept as I, Cinderella, took her cinders from the grates and made the fires. I am not well, I am on edge, frightened, hunted, feeling like a wild little creature with a pack of dogs after me, and the dogs are those Bowdon women with their brown faces and hats and clothes and affected voices and supercilious stares. I am feeling irreligious these days.

12th February
I went to Ashburne [*Hall*] to see a play. I sat by Miss Conway [*a member of staff*] and her sister. The play, *The Two Mrs Carrolls*, was extremely good, a lovely young heroine with bare legs and thighs and back, – rather a shock for Miss Conway.

13th February
Frances writes to tell me that [*Aunt*] Lizzie died two years ago. So ends that great tragedy, which for more than 50 years has haunted me. Now I shall never know the old secrets, she is the last of her generation, the last link with the past. She has suffered and has paid for her wrongdoings.

14th February
I slept till eleven o'clock. It is the sleep I have been needing for some time & my anxiety [*over the critical reception of Ambush of Young Days*] is past. I feel normal again…After lunch…I suddenly saw a review of *Ambush* [*in her newspaper*]. The reviewer …so kind, so sensitive. Bless him! He has cheered a lonely one.

17th February
Emily is coming today. This morning a letter from Frances, – all coming on Saturday. I have suggested she let me have the musical box [*from Castle Top Farm*] No, she won't. How glad I shall be to escape to the south [*of England*], with none of them to make me unhappy…. Emily and Frances, and the Johnson family…. It is these uncongenial people…. A charming letter from a lady thanking me for the *GR* books. [*During her visit*] Emily says, 'Why should we bring children into the world to be cannon fodder?'…. Very true, said I, and I suggested 'Why should we bring children to be killed by motor cars?' That was much better. Poor Emily, we might have been such friends.

18th February

Two lovely reviews.... I wrote to the financial editor of *The Observer*, signing myself Perplexed, asking about my shares.... I typed several pages.... The proofs of *Rat* came. W[*Winnie*] Armitage and Mrs. Muir bought *Ambush*. It *is* kind. WA. is a darling, one of the best people I know.

21st February

Yesterday Harry [*Taylor*] told me that Morton had been enquiring about me and wanted the names of my books. 'He is very rich now', says Harry. It gives me a pang of memory for the great boy whom I once liked, because he was quiet and strong – but he was a *duffer*! Tonight I write a *Fuzzypeg* tale. Walter de la Mare makes me think of my dreams; he writes them, I dream them.

4th March

More praise for *Ambush*. This morning I was thinking of how *Ambush* is never shown at Smiths, so I decided to tackle them. The manager was disarming. He said he had sold seventeen. He told me how his children love them, quoted bits. 'Snaps of dialect are always good', he said. He tells me a Cumbrian dialect tale.... He will have a Collins show if it can be arranged, so I wrote to Mr. Collins.

5th March

Today I have been typing the new Fuzzypeg [*Fuzzypeg Goes to School*], looking up flowers and trees and thinking of phrases. I like it very much, and think it will do for Mr Collins, but John must read it first.

9th March

[*She is upset by Frances telling her about the sale by the Coxon's of Castle Top Farm*] Again my heart aches, I dare not think of it, it is too vivid. I cannot bear these disasters at my darling Castle Top. I feel I would like to rush there and spend a thousand pounds making it all beautiful once more. Poor Coxon's I am sorry for them and wish I could help them.... What a topsy turvy world it is, there seems to be no permanence in it, like I felt at my home.... I was very tired typing, trying to disentangle the confused tale of Patty's lovers.

10th March

Last night I broke my glasses as I pulled them off.... They cost six shillings to mend. I got a pair from Woolworths to use while I wait – they cost a shilling.... [*In a second-hand bookshop*] I bought *My Lord Fish* by W de la Mare.... Then to *Murder in the Cathedral* – when Emily came and sat in front of me! She said she had enjoyed *Ambush*!.... The play is half divine and half devil, – the devil a modern man.... sneering at religion.... flippant jargon. That was ugly and spoiled the latter part of the play.

16th March

John is coming tomorrow, bless him. The sad news of Sir Austen Chamberlain's death [*elder son of Joseph Chamberlain, and formerly Foreign Secretary*] – a shock for England. There have been terrible floods near Cambridge, I wondered about John. I have typed fourteen pages [*of High Meadows*], and felt I was in the hayfields at High Leas, and then I remember and life seems so full of cares. No money, no reviews, no anything, – but John coming helps and cheers me.

20th – 28th March

Several happy events: eleven thousand copies of *GR* books sold up to Christmas, and a fat cheque which was stuck in the letter box and not found till later, from Collins. The BBC has taken the four stories of the *Little Pigs*. [*There is*] a lovely review of *Ambush* in the *Oxford Times*.

1st April

The lady who liked the house returned….She offered a thousand pounds. I said one thousand and fifty. I do hope she'll buy it. *GR* is going to the Paris International Exhibition, and Mr. Collins has…accepted *Fuzzypeg*. He likes it very much. So there I am!

2nd April

LM [*Lily Meagher*] comes and reads with me the new book I am working on, much altering and criticism. It is terribly confused, not fit for anyone to read. LM suggests that Patty ought to marry Jim Crossland. This surprises me. I feel this is the solution. We worked till nearly midnight. I felt so happy and Patty would be happy with him.

4th April

I was in great pain all night, – LM helps me to do some of the work. We finished the book. Now I can retype about 100,000 words. After LM went, I wrote part of a *GR* play to cheer myself up. I went to the Coopers. I showed Harry [*Dr. Cooper*] my sore knee. His wife snubs him, how patient he is. James would have exploded like a powder magazine.

30th April

A letter from Mr. Stewart with the manuscript of *Tim Rabbit*, which I want to correct. He says 800 of *Ambush* have been sold. I felt quite depressed over the low number. Miss Chase writes, saying she likes *Ambush* and wants to mention it to her American publisher. I sent a copy off to Macmillans, New York. Then I felt depressed, [*but*] then a miracle happens. In the *Tim Rabbit* parcel I find a note from Mr. Faber to Mr. Stewart: 'EEF [*Enid Faber*] reports favourably on this. She says also that AU seems to have staying power, and is likely to go on to increase her reputation and is therefore worth sticking to.' A feather in my cap, and encouragement for a lonely Mimbles. It makes me want to write more and more.

16th May
A dream of Castle Top. Then of Gertrude's house, from which I flee. Harold [*Armfield, Gertrude's husband*] comes calling me. Harold says will I be friends? I say not while Gertrude is there. I look at John who was waiting, John hating Harold...both of us hurrying to escape the baleful house.

20th June
[*She agonises over the right choice of partner for Patty Verity in the novel she is writing, High Meadows*]
'Oh Patty Verity, do you want to marry Martin Dunkerley or not?'
'No, I don't. I want to stay home and hide at the farm.'
'Yes, you'd better. There's a warm fire in the grate, P. V. And happiness, and here it is icy cold and no fire.'

18th July
John has gone off camping with [*his friend*] Healey. We had a long loving kiss before he left. I worked on the book on and off all day, reading and revising. I want to finish before the end of August. 22 long chapters means 44 days at half a chapter a day. I can do it in 30 days.

23rd July
I was cheered up by a share certificate from L Sugden, we have 3,588 pounds between us. I can't really take it in. J's future fortune. I was typing all day. In one day a small fortune (on paper), two postal orders, and a tale is broadcast. I *ought* to be happy, but I am feeling very lonely.

24th July
[*She comments on the first day of the Test match in Manchester, in the rain*] Brave men! I have typed all day, working on the *Fair* chapter. What a task is a book, but you have to do it quite alone. And I get so little profit. £30 for *Ambush*, which was months and months of work. No fame, no money, no notice taken, but I feel happy when I am writing, and it helps me along. How lovely to get encouragement!

30th July
Here I sit in the kitchen most depressed. This morning came a parcel with my *Cock and Bull* stories. They have been voted upon and lost. I wrote them well, and it is a loss of eighteen guineas, which I needed. Then another blow – John's car broke down...so he had to pay for a long train journey. Also I was so looking forward to my crumb....I feel my courage ebbing, my knee is painful and I am alone. But I must struggle on. My story of the *Performing Pig* is on the wireless.

31st July
Such worry and anxiety, – no letter from John all day. I wept in bed last night for a long time, and again tears fell this morning. I felt deserted and forgotten. However, I pulled

myself together, and carried on, did the housework slowly, and then typed on and off for hours...I keep thinking of Gabriel and Jim and Patty Verity, and of the flowers and beauty, and those fields come to my mind with intense reality.

1st August
I slept well in spite of my sadness. *The Observer* mentioned *Ambush* as one of the best books of 1937. How pleased & gratified I felt to be mentioned with all those other real authors, and I am the lost lonely and sad one. It is like a brilliant ray of sun in my heart. I have just finished chapter eleven of my book about haymaking, the milking and harvest supper.

3rd August
The King [*George VI*] is expected at John's camp [*the Duke of York camp for boys from all social backgrounds*]. He wears an open-necked shirt, – jolly fellow. I think George VI is better than Edward [*VIII*] more sensible and nicer.

8th August
LM [*Lily Meagher*] puts on the wedding garment [*from Alison' store of clothes*], of pale blue satin, and walked about with the train on the grass, very charming, she looked so young, and quite pretty. If the book is done, I will dedicate it to her, she has been such a brick.

13th August
[*She receives Margaret Tempest's draft illustrations for Fuzzypeg Goes to School*] more adorable things, which pleased me very much. She *is* good. I am sure the book will be lovely.

15th August
I finished the book (*PV*) at 8.00 pm. It is good I think. But there are some loose ends to tie up. About three weeks work. In a fortnight I will have the book ready for Fabers, corrected. I want to do some children's tales, [*and*] perhaps a new *GR* book. Also try an historical book.

22nd August
I am feeling a bit better, but am terribly tired after the six weeks of terrific strain. I am wondering how much royalties I shall get [*from her various books*], I think not very much. Fabers lost on *Candlelight* [*Tales*]. Heavens! Nobody knows how little I get.

23rd August
No letters. I have written to Lyons for some chocolates to cheer me up.... [*She describes the advertisement to sell her house that she is putting into the Manchester Guardian*]: Small detached house of character, excellent condition. Two large receptions, five bedrooms, many cupboards, pantry. Power, gas. Quiet road. Garden. Ten minutes to station. One thousand pounds.

29th August
All day I have been living in the past thinking of mother, and her wonderful courage and

splendid character, her unselfishness, and great overwhelming love, love which would have faced death for any of us, I felt very sad and lonely and wanted her back again. And I felt that James had somehow faded from my thoughts, and mother had taken his place, and she is the one I have always loved more than all the world. Then I wept for her and felt very lonely. Then I thought how pleased she would be that we have carried on, that John has been to Cambridge, and got his degree, that I have written books praising her. And she would have been glad that I have given pleasure to so many little children, I think how she worshipped and adored children…At night I wrote a rough draft of a *GR* tale.

1st September
There are several things I expect: proofs of *Tim Rabbit* with pictures (*they came on October 26th*) the new pictures of *Fuzzypeg* (*11th September*), a cheque from Faber (*October 3rd*), a cheque from Collins (*September 2nd*), books to autograph (*1st October*), the result of the new book (*accepted 27th November*), and the publication of *Rat* (*6th September*).

2nd September
John is not coming. I had to work hard to restrain my tears…. he is going to Cambridge to see the Appointment Board, for he has no post yet. Poor boy…. But a parcel comes with the *Knot Squirrel Tied*, to be published on the 6th September. Lady C sends a fish pie and a great bunch of lavender. So I have many pleasures, but I want to share them with John…. People did not come to view the house.

21st September
[*Margaret Tempest writes*] incensed at my criticisms of the *Fuzzypeg* book [*illustrations*] – and rightly so. I was stupid to criticise when they were done. She had spent three months over the paintings. So I wrote back, rather apologetic, but I feel rather uncomfortable.

26th September
John has just gone…. We had our prayer, beautiful and comforting, for which I am profoundly thankful. It is wonderful this bond between us. Then we kissed, long passionate kisses of mother & son, and I thought of James, and thanked God for John to comfort me…. I think John has special qualities, a love of the beautiful…. which other people I know don't have.

30th September
I had a knee massage for ten shillings and sixpence, but I noticed [*the masseur's*] greasy hair, and felt a bit squeamish…. I am told that the Duke of Gloucester is tactless, and only talks of polo and horses, and that he can't distinguish one Northern town from another.

25th October
John says that [*there*] are other candidates for the Marlborough [*teaching*] post. Mr. Collins says I may help at the children's room at the [*Sunday Times Book*] Exhibition. I can't get in

at the Regent Palace Hotel in London. I will have to go to the stuffy old Shaftesbury again. Bother!

26th October
A day of such beautiful sunshine…it seems a perfect world….I am pleased with the proofs of *No Ordinary Rabbit*. Eight small bottles of Burgundy arrive. A bargain (5/-) & a refresher for a faded & tired person.

27th October
The manager of Smiths looked happy that I will be putting one of his [*dialect*] phrases in my next book…. I bought chocolates (Oh!!) for a shilling…. I was moved by the tragic tale in John's copy of Anthony Babington [*the organiser of the Babington plot and the inspiration for her novel A Traveller in Time*] came. It is a tragic tale.

1st November
Good news. John has the post [*teaching history*] at St. Lawrence's College, Ramsgate…. I went to vote in the municipal elections…. I finished the book tonight.

8th November
To London, to the Shaftesbury Hotel. John joined me there for the night. On 10th November I move to the more comfortable Regent Palace. I never want to return to that place [*the Shaftesbury*]. I went to the *Sunday Times* Exhibition…. I met Rose Macaulay and Walter de la Mare. He was smiling and very charming, so that I quite loved him, as I do Professor Alexander. I complimented de la Mare on his writing. I didn't know what to say to Rose Macaulay.

27th November
Great news, the country book [*High Meadows*] is accepted! I opened the parcel containing complimentary copies of *No Ordinary Rabbit*, and assumed the other parcel was of a rejected manuscript. I agreed to cut it down in length by sixty pages. It will keep down the price. I will do anything to get it published. I am walking on air. I will dedicate it to LM….I started to type the final version of my new book, called *Thackers* [*to be published as A Traveller in Time*]. I must do a chapter a day for sixteen days to finish it.

10th December
Fabers will republish the *CC* [*Country Child*] in the spring, and put it in the Faber's Library. Glorious! They will give me an unrequested extra royalty of ten per cent on the first two thousand…. Not that I have ever reached such numbers. The book to be called *A Country Tale*.

11th December
I finished *Thackers*…sixteen chapters in a fortnight, long chapters too. I wanted to finish it so I can turn to *A Country Tale*. I think the ending of *Thackers* is weak.

15th December

I sent off *The Secret of Thackers* from Bowdon.... I always feel romantic when I post a new book.... The black astrakhan muff came.... It is adorable. Other presents came.... I feel quite rich, extravagant, and rather guilty when I remember that my bank balance is nil.

17th December

My birthday. I ran downstairs to find my letters....GL's with a book token for 7/6, which delighted me.

24th December

I overheard in the market someone say 'Have you ever noticed the stars aren't what they used to be?'.... Holly, a scrappy piece 3/-.... I was amazed. So we bought none.... John decorated the room.... mistletoe over the mantelpiece.

31st December

This has been a good year, with many blessings. Oh dear New Year, bring us health and good fortune, a new house and lovely surroundings and my nice books out. Bring happiness to dear Castle Top and help to Harry. Take care of us, God, in the future.

❦ *1938* ❧

2nd January

I feel refreshed with the sweetness of sleep and dreams.... I am reading Churchill's *Great Contemporaries*, – a magnificent book.

4th January

Today, John went to Alsager looking very nice. He will be in a jolly house with no housework.... I am tired of this house, and all the work and turmoil, and long for a little modern house with a tiny easy kitchen. I feel I am marking time, waiting for spring and a new house. This year the *Country Tale* and two *Grey Rabbits* will come out, bringing me sixty pounds for the lot, but I hope for royalties too. I want to write a book of country characters or short stories for Faber, & the draft of a novel. Also to put together a book of fairy tales.

12th January

I arrived at the dentist's, a young woman was reading *No Ordinary Rabbit*, and *Rat* lay on the table.... I think I have enough children's stories for two books of tales, but what will I send to Faber? I do not know.

20th January

John left for Ramsgate [*and his new teaching post*] this morning.... We had our prayer and a long kiss goodbye. I couldn't sleep last night thinking of his going, and then I dreamt a wild dream of being all alone in the world, with no roots, no home, a kind of lost dream, I wandering in a great city.... The new book is to be called *High Meadows*, a nice name, although I liked *Green Grows the Holly*.

31st January

I felt troubled today over John's letter. He isn't happy, the work is too hard, he says he is exhausted and in a state of collapse.... The school he doesn't like, the staff cliques.... and the feeling too religious, – altogether he is sick with it. I feel anxious lest he overdoes himself struggling against the odds.... Poor darling, I think of him all the time.... I typed eight pages of *Mrs. Mimble*.

3rd February

I feel in a panic last night and couldn't sleep.... I thought of the Insurance & being summonsed [*for not paying her insurance stamps*]. A paragraph in the papers? When I slept I had a lovely calm dream.... It gave me courage.... There are thirteen tales & I've called it

Christmas Comes but Once a Year. I sent it off to Faber with hope…. Orion is over this house now.

5th February
Darling James's birthday. I love him always, poor child, tossed by the world – yet with so many blessings, I cannot understand why he didn't face life, and battle on. When I think of the trials and difficulties, a million times worse than any of his, of my parents, and my own difficulties too. It must have been his father's fault…. £10 from the bank came, so I have started to pay bills.

10th February
I can't get going on my new book yet. Last night I dreamt about a play called *The Three Sisters*. Then on 10th Feb. I see an article on the play in the DT [*Daily Telegraph*].

12th February
Shopping, housework, – but at a quarter to four I went off to the parks and caught them at their best, a glory of colour with the sun and a blue sky and rosy clouds and gold clouds across it. Everywhere was golden, and blue and the trees were exquisite. I felt it was the perfection of beauty as I walked under their great branches with their long boughs against the dark blue and I watched the colour before me. Then I turned home and saw the full moon in the S. East, but before I got home the moon had deepened and become gold but no stars were out. When the sun set the moon lost the gold. I noticed how the buds of the beech trees lie nearly in one plane and the spruces with their fine points were like Christmas trees. Snow was now in the air and it was very cold. Two swans with necks stretched up by the blue lake, and a moor hen walking in the grass. I stood a long time listening to a robin in a silver birch, and after each little song he went a little higher in the tree. I answered him, and we had a long duet. Then it began to sing near and it was delightful.

21st February
[*Anthony*] Eden [*British Foreign Secretary*] resigns! It is absolutely staggering, a crisis over Italy. Eden won't agree as much as [*Prime Minister, Neville*] Chamberlain wishes…. Lady C comes bearing gifts, how kind she is! I am writing a tale, the Kiss, dreaming of that girl of long ago. Now I wait for Chamberlain's speech before going to bed. John…. says how much he enjoys my letters – I am glad for I spend much time & try to make them entertaining. Then Chamberlain [*on the radio*], 'what price Austria?' Austria, bagged by Hitler, becoming Nazi.

24th February
A parcel came…. My heart sank – the returned manuscript of the *Fairy Tales*, I thought…. It was the proofs of the first six chapters of P[*Patty*] V[*Verity*]. Most thrilled to see it in print, and the lovely leafy oblong round each chapter heading. They [*Faber*] are the most artistic and excellent publishers, they spare no pains…. My cold seems worse…. but the

book cheers me. I welcomed the wireless boy joyfully, and give him my letter to John and the proofs to post. Then came Mrs. Gillow…. who did my shopping. Bed at 9 with whisky, lozenges, and Emily Dickinson's poems!

1st March
[*I find*] the chapters of *High Meadows* from Fabers on the doorstep. [*Also*] terms for a boarding house at Haslemere, a dividend of £4.10.9. from the Orion Commercial Trust, the first for seven years. Joy! A review of *No Ordinary Rabbit* from New Zealand. Lord Arnold has left the Socialists, – praise be. And the Left Book Club fills me with horror, this propaganda of Communism.

7th March
A letter from GL answering questions about *High Meadows*, so I mean to wire for the MS and alter it. Tonight I found more mistakes in the proofs. A busy day with Mrs. J[*Johnson*] scrubbing…. and I fretting about under the roof. Gladys Johnson invited me to the Sixty Club. When I found it's Vera Brittain, I refused absolutely, – that conceited creature.

28th March
Lunch with Eleanor Graham who takes the MS of *Thackers* away. Earlier, Mr. Collins had said that *Thackers* would not do in its present form, too difficult. He was very charming and kind…He said he would give me plenty of work if I was nearer London. He was delighted over *High Meadows*.

1st April
We walked in the woods. John picked bluebells, and gave them to me and we kissed. At home on the 1st April, there was a cheque from Collins for forty two pounds. Good! A cheque from Faber, on 30th March, five pounds only.

11th April
I called on Mrs. Norton. 'Russia's revolution is all wrong because the wrong people are at the head.' I don't argue, but I felt rather Communistic…. *High Meadows* is to be published next Thursday.

16th April
I got £30 for *High Meadows*, and Faber request a girls' story, but only offered me three guineas! I ask you! [*There is*] a review by J D Beresford in the *Manchester Guardian*, saying I am not a novelist, and the book is 'terribly old-fashioned'…. I am dead tired…. John's friend Howarth comes tonight. John expects everything and gives so little, I feel miserable.

17th April
I was tired and ill when I wrote yesterday but today I feel different. Howarth talks too much. We had a great argument. John and I hold the fort against pacifism, the *Manchester*

Guardian, and this hatred of Italy. I was given new strength on Easter Day by Holy Communion.

19th April

A man came and demonstrated the Electrolux carpet shampoo [*machine*].... John dug the garden. I resented a sneering review of my book in the *Telegraph* (by [*Malcolm*] Muggeridge). They say all the characters are stock figures, but they were my father, my mother.

22nd April

The great drought continues....I hunted out some little tales for the fairy book for Fabers. E Graham says three guineas is preposterous, I should get twelve guineas for six thousand words, and must demand it from Faber. Reviews [*of High Meadows*] some flattering & then not so good. Last night the Edmondsons came...I admired Mrs. E. with her exquisite cobwebbed stockings.

26th April

LM leaves in the morning. [*The Chancellor puts*] Income Tax up by six pence, – what a blow. This will bring down my tiny income. I went to Mrs. Harrison's funeral, the first I have been to apart from my own family.... John and I burn my college notebooks, – maths and physics. I received a scathing review from *John O' London Weekly*, but I only laughed. Well, it *is* very sweet, but I enjoyed doing it in these days of suicide and miseries of rape and filth. However, I don't care a hoot.

29th April

Mr. Stewart [*of Faber*] tells me that the Junior Book Club has taken 200 copies of *High Meadows* for May. Tonight I started the new *Thackers* book, and did seven and a half pages.... Margaret [*Edwards*] says there is never a sign of *High Meadows* in [*WH*] Smith's.... I am doing a vendetta, not going there ever again if I can help it, I am so angry with them.... I burned piles of papers, John's dear letters from school...manuscripts of books, thousands of pages, in preparation for [*the*] removal.

9th May

I saw the first swallow.... I am tired, and depressed by an awful review in the *New Statesman*. I wonder if I could ever write decently – [*I*] am embarrassed with my awful reviews.

14th May

I worked like a jolly slave.... I cleaned out the ottoman, and filled it with things to give away. All afternoon & evening I have been writing, with an interval to burn old college notebooks, and letters. I read sweet letters from James, from mother, from Auntie Alice. I must go to bed, I feel queer, not knowing when and where I live, out of time, partly with doing the sixteenth century tale, partly with reading Mother's letters. There was a darling letter from me to James, when I told him that I had dreamed we were married, and we lived in a tulip, our house in the flower, and we climbed the stalk to get to it. How mad he must have thought I was! I found lovely, sweet letters from him, the darling one.

19th May
I am tired out with housework and writing. Professor A[*Alexander*] came, with his grey beard now quite long, grey scarf…. Professor A thinks that King Edward VIII's queer streak may have been the Stuart stock in him. Would his relationship with Mrs. Simpson last? He spoke of his own death. I say, we'll have lots of talks in the other world, but he says no, he will disintegrate, we kissed two or three times. I felt I would never see him again. I felt like it's parting from my father, or James going to the War.

24th May
A letter from Mr. Stewart, seven hundred copies of *HM* [*High Meadows*] sold. Quite good in five weeks. It is in America being judged, but I have no hopes.

25th May
What a calamity! At breakfast….I hear a grinding and clicking. Jaw dislocated! Mr. Whiteley [*a physiotherapist*] put it right, but it doesn't feel right…. I can't laugh or eat, or yawn.

27th May
I worked at revising the last chapters of *Thackers*….I have been invited to join the D. C. Watt [*Literary*] Agency. I think it is a good plan.

28th May
I went to see [*Dr.*] Harry Cooper, as Whiteley wasn't in. Cooper was horrified that I had been to Whiteley – he's a quack! Your jaw wasn't dislocated….

29th May
I came across smiling photographs of mother…. they touched my heart…. My neck is painful, I am trying to see Whiteley…. Goodbye Downs House – the roses are coming out.

3rd June
I went to Beaconsfield, but the houses are very dear.

6th July
Mr. Hill the solicitor says I ought have more knowledge of it [*the house she wants to buy*]. Was there dry rot?...I felt rather depressed but I do not think the house is a bargain in any case.

9th July
I ought to be bold and take the house [*her future home in Beaconsfield*]. The house costs £1,475, and I have £1,100 in the Halifax, £550 in Lewis's, the balance is £175 for lawyers'

fees, removals, etc. It should be all right. There is another forty pounds coming this Autumn, too.

11th July
GL urges me to take the house. John is delighted it's been offered to us…. So we shall try to get the house, it has been settled for me by these dear friends and by John.

14th July
The contract for *Rainbows and Robins* came. I went to Manchester [*but before seeing Professor Alexander*] I went to Kendal's & there frittered money away. I lack control in a sale. Professor A very tired, thinking of death…. I think that the treatment of the Jews has cast a deep shadow over him. He talks of a meeting with the exiled Emperor of Abyssinia…. I looked around wondering whether it would be the last time I see Professor A. I kissed him…. and said goodbye again at the door.

20th July
The house is ours, Aberdavon [*to be renamed Thackers*] is ours! I signed the contract with equable feelings, but with many a qualm. I think we can manage and I think we shall love it, but it is a terrific outlay for a penniless couple like John and myself…. We had to take the plunge and get away from Bowdon, to more sunshine, and for me to be nearer to John, and to have London not far away. To escape from these uncongenial people and dirty old Altrincham. Yet I love Downs house, and I hate to leave W. Armitage…and not to have LM so often, or to see darling Prof. A and Mrs. Johnson. The die is cast, and I must move forwards with no backwards glance.

21st July
To Ashburne Hall [*for a reunion*] where I met Miss [*Maude*] Parkin, rather stout, although she was always largely made, her eyes bright… her smile sweet, just the same as she called me 'Alice Taylor', and swept away the years, so that I was the slim young girl who worked at Meteorology and she was the lovely Vice-Warden in her blue silk frock and red roses.

31st July
To the Armitages for 'supper'. 'Isn't it a strange thing…that we have made a mess of India, Egypt and Palestine', said Mr. Armitage. I disagreed…. This running down of England taints him [*but*] a dear man.

11th August
Great thrills. A sweet little lady came, fell in love with the house, and took it! No sneers at the fireplaces or picture rails…. She [*Miss Duckworth*] will take it on a four year lease.

16th August
John's dear letter came [*from Germany*]. 'I am largely confined in speaking to Heil Hitler,

Good Morning and Thank You.' Dear child. I think of giving the contract for removal to somebody who can do it cheaper…. The plumber comes, and only charges two shillings for the job. A gipsy blessed my lucky face, but they bless everybody.

24th August
John came home. He tells me how he drove through Germany with the Union Jack and the Swastika, but in France the Swastika was torn off by somebody…. I told [*him*] how Miss Duckworth has sent a wire saying she won't sign the lease. I feel happy today…. John and I did a great turn-out of drawers, sorting clothes for the unemployed.

29th August
Serious war news. Czechoslovakia and Germany in peril of war…A wild terror sweeps over me when I think of John, that darling boy. But I must trust God….A great star shines in the East. I saw the new moon & made my fervent wish.

3rd September
Fuzzypeg Goes to School came today, – to be published on 5th September. A sad letter from Professor A saying goodbye. I feel it's like a rock going…. I felt such regrets [*about moving*].... I think of lovely days, James, John and I playing games in [*this*] room, feasting, laughing, dancing around the table when my Squirrel, Hare, and Little Grey Rabbit [*The Squirrel, the Hare, and the Little Grey Rabbit*] was taken.

8th September
A letter from darling Professor A. saying that we must not come and see him, he cannot say goodbye, he would break down…. How I love him…. Harry comes…. and he tells me that people go to Castle Top and ask to look over it, having read *Country Child* and *Ambush*! I was horror struck. I always ask to remain unknown…. I feel Harry never offers to do anything for us, but just accepts [*everything*] as his due.

13th September
My Professor Alexander has died. I have just heard on the wireless. It's the day of mother's death, too.

14th September
A devastating day…. War very near, Hitler menacing, the navy mobilised…. A handful of letters with kind words on losing my darling Professor A.. Goodbye, Downs House, where I have had much happiness.

16th September
To the [*new*] house, walking in and rather frightened, everything looking smaller, but clean and we liked it, and I loved it. John was enchanted…. [*he*] took me into the garden & kissed me happily.

23rd September
War seems imminent. Hitler and Chamberlain did not meet today. In England people are reviling Chamberlain. It seems as if there is no escape.... It will be the end of all things. I must not think of it, it is a nightmare.... I walked to Beaconsfield, it looks a nice welcoming place.... The manager in [*WH*] Smiths promised to show my books.

28th September
I was cheered by a parcel with six volumes of *Mustard, Pepper and Salt*...There is a respite of 24 hours before war breaks out. All England feels a chance to discuss again [*to solve the Czechoslovakian/Munich crisis*]. Hope is raised. Tears came to my eyes.

30th September
At 1.45 am [*news of*] the peace signed between Britain, Germany.... Thank God. The news has swept over the world. No war. All the terror and foreboding of a terrible slaughter past.... I stood outside tonight and saw ten searchlights, flashing across.... Our prayers are now answered, millions are saved. I felt dazed and tired, not knowing where I was.... I felt so thankful, so happy, so joyful that my darling John is safe.

3rd October
The man came to put linoleum in the kitchen, a surly creature.... so I took no notice & treated him with equal contempt.... I feel friendly to all.... I am trying to make friends with the house, to make contact.

14th October
[*A BBC radio broadcast of The Country Child*] brought tears to my eyes, I remember so vividly my home and parents, the fields, lanes, our road down the hill – the horses straining and all the difficulties my parents faced.

18th October
What a day! E Graham's letter says that frankly she does not like many of the tales in *Mustard, Pepper and Salt* they are not worthy of me, and [*she*] will have to criticise adversely! I *told* Faber not to put them in, but they would do so. Now my dear book is in the soup, just when I want the money.... The electric kettle fizzed & went off with a bang.

19th October
A blow: *Thackers* [*to be A Traveller in Time*] is rejected [*by Collins*]...There was a nice letter from W.A.R. Collins, but he said the characters were not [*distinctive*] enough and not enough action. So that's that! But I didn't repine, for now I have gone back to my first love, the first edition [*version*], and I am reading it with pleasure, and shall try Faber.

10th November
To London.... I went to the unknown soldier's grave & wept.... I put a cross in memory of

James in the Garden of Remembrance.... Then to the National Gallery & to the Medici Gallery, where I spoke boldly of my books, and they suggested I write a book about rabbits.

11th November
[*She describes her garden in Beaconsfield*] the beech trees waving gently, irregularly, some lower branches moving violently as the rain catches them, the high boughs swaying softly. Now a roar of wind in the trees. The lawn looks very green, and one dandelion stands upright. The two cypresses guard my doorway, and they don't move at all.... [*Mrs. Gurney*] swept in. When she found I wrote [*there was*] a brightness in her eyes.... She talks of sex and Radclyffe Hall, Germany, the pogrom of Jews...I feel dazed.

21st November
To London again. I met E[*Eleanor*] Graham.... Then to the Book Fair where I got in for Norman Angell, but I do not like him. Angell claims that Facism is democracy because the people will it. But it was all talk, confusing.

28th November
I found a good review in the DT [*Daily Telegraph*], referring to me as an author loved by thousands of children. It warmed my heart... The gardener is slackly working....I must rid myself of him.

24th December
11 o'clock, the lovely long room decorated with holly and ivy, the little Christmas tree on the green cloth of the dining table set for breakfast, holly over the brass in the chimney corner, mistletoe over the picture over the fire, the room in shadows and the big lamp lighting the piano. We had a jolly day, and loved the party at the Helliwells, with all those boys. Tonight we sang carols. The holly and the ivy, O little town, till we froze with the cold. The Helliwells, crackers and Christmas cake, a game of darts, all those boys, four brothers.

31st December
[*Alison and John do some gardening*] John planted 4 miserable specimens [*of*] rose trees. I must not buy plants from advertisements. I made a great fire with wood [*in*] the lovely room with 'Hare' in the corner of the couch. I feel thankful for the house, and my books.... the pictures, and all the blessings we have had. It's been a splendid year. I hope next year will be another good year, with books written and work done.

～ *1939* ～

12th January
When I got home last night, I found the parcel of *Thackers* [*later to be published as A Traveller in Time*] and this, added to my tiredness, was the last straw, – I felt quite ill. I opened it, and saw to my astonishment that they liked the book. They make certain suggestions, good ones which I shall try to carry out. So now it is up to me to finish the book well, for it is the darling of my heart.

17th January
John and Dick Frost went off early to town, and I was left alone to write a masterpiece. Did I write it? No, I had to go to the coal place, and sweep it up, and put nails for the tools, and hang up the forks and rakes. Then I did the laundry, and ironed it, then I darned, and it was ten o'clock at night! A dull rainy day – not one of my best efforts. But the little electric fire came, and the new electric kettle. And I had a very hot bath, and washed my hair.

21st January
I stayed indoors all day, except when I fetched in the coke, for it poured in torrents. Tonight there was a gleam of sun in the West, a finger of light, very cheering. I finished reading *The Squire*, by Enid Bagnold, a fine book which I should have been proud to have written – but never could I do such clever work. It brought back my own bliss before John's birth, my own deep content and safety ... the welcome to a new life. I have been writing odd bits for the novel, but tomorrow I must work at *Thackers*.

25th January
One of those blissful moments of beauty. Snow falling, the little fir trees heavy, branches drooping in curves with thick folds of snow. On one of them perched an exquisite chaffinch, so fresh, so lovely, swaying there, peering in at me by the fire.... This is the most astonishing day, snow everywhere at dawn, and it has never ceased, so that it is piled up against the doors, and the window sills are thick with it.... The beech trees are like frosted frozen trees, still and white, the oaks covered with bunches of white roses. The sky grey and the never ceasing flakes drifting down, large and feathery and silent. Birds flutter past, and a blackbird drops its fan tail on the snow.... Now a robin shouts at me from the same spot, and actually peeps in the window, calling me, but when I put out food it was gone. In the distance, trees are grey feathers against the pale sky.

26th January
In London I had a fourpenny soup which warmed me, and then I went to Collins. Miss

Tempest in moleskin coat and green hat and dress, her high, haughty loud voice dominating the room, sweeping over everybody, going on and on with such insistence. I just sat back and let her. She is a humourless bore, seldom does a smile come, her eyes cold and hard, and I watched her mouth moving, not listening to the words.

29th January
I read *The Observer* leader, and it put me in a panic of war, it was so serious. Hitler to speak tomorrow, and the last time he spoke brought such foreboding and threats. Spain for Franco. Italy against France, and we shall come in on the side of France.... The other Czechoslovakian reason was poor, no-one felt anything but horror, but if this is forced on us we shall fight. So I've been thinking once again of war.

26th February
I lay thinking how happy I was, with John in the next room. I got up at nine o'clock, dressed, lighted the fire, did the room. Then I called John, and we had a nice lazy breakfast. Sunshine everywhere, very beautiful, all golds and oranges. We went through the Hogback woods, and back across the fields. The hazels hanging in golden catkins, making a forest of colour in the brown beeches and red dogwood.... John has enjoyed it, I know, he said it felt really like home, and to me it had that feeling, – there was the comfort and the ease and the happy carelessness. I enjoyed every minute. He gave me many kisses in the hall before he went, the dear child. And so I thank God.

7th April
At night heard that Italy had invaded Albania. War imminent. The world torn asunder. There seems no escape from War. We go on, enjoying each moment as if it is the last. I never think of a month ahead, or of summer, or autumn, but accept the moment, thankful for it, with the world falling in pieces around us.

16th April
A lovely day. I went out with Hamish to see the woods. The cherry trees and blackthorn are lovely. In the distance I thought I saw three rounded woods, silver birch, bronze green, larch, pale bright green, and beech a golden brown. Violets out in blue drifts down the lanes. I got branches of cherry and blackthorn for the house. Some bluebells are out in the garden. Stitchwort under the hedges, and the hawthorn grey.
I heard [*on the radio*] the Tutenkhamen trumpets blown for the first time in three thousand years – I thought the ghosts of the Egyptians would rise up and flood the air, moving in astonished ranks, millions of them.

26th April
I slipped away from the house and went over the fields, for it is divine.... I picked some pink crab-apple blossom, and two open arums, marvels with their green leaves. I wanted to talk to them. Then I looked for cowslips, and stood under a great cherry tree, for I heard the

sounds of planes. Thirty-five flew overhead, high, in three groups, a wonderful sight, and the rooks flew lower down, cawing.

1st June

This morning an apologetic letter from Margaret Tempest, and an agreeing letter from Collins, very conciliatory. So I have won the tussle [*over illustrations*], but I do feel rather cross about it. I nearly always give way, and this is the first time I have insisted upon my rights. I feel fed up and angry with Margaret Tempest.

3rd June

To Clevedon, to see Lady Astor's grounds. The vast Italianate house with terrace and colonnades covered with creepers and roses on the terrace below. The storm seats, like Italian ones, in the wall across the grass. Then another terrace, all fine grass, with box beds in geometrical, shapes and cat mint filling them with purple mist. Far away an exquisite view of the curving Thames, under a wood side, all framed in an arch of trees…. We went down to the Thames where it poured through lawns, and we saw a Judas tree in full flower… We went into a closed garden, with rose trees, and walls, and another garden, with beds of flowers, a glorious red single peony, and masses of anchusa.

12th July

Ballet – Schumann's *Carnival*, most lovely, and the Columbine in white with scarlet roses. Harlequin most agile and delicious, and Pantaloon with white waving arms. Papillon in black-edged wings of white. Paganini thrilled me. The ghosts and wraiths, in black, and some in white, rising around him, and arms appearing at his fiddle, and sprites in purple dancing wildly, and rival musicians working horribly.

23rd July

On the night of the 22nd I dreamed I was through time. I met a woman in a high dark ruffed dress, who told me she had been a servant to Mary Queen of Scots. I compared our time with hers, showed her flowers and moving grass in a book…. telling [*their*]…. names. I remember 'Lady's Tresses' and 'Lady's Mantle'. The light was clear, radiantly lovely, and I felt it was more real than reality. I lay awake thinking of it, it was a dream-within-a-dream. In five minutes it faded.

24th July

Mars shines red as fire in the south. It is only thirty million miles away, the nearest approach. Glow worms shine green in the garden. The moon is new. Green woodpeckers calling. At dawn I saw the grass glittering, as if beaded nets were thrown over it.

22nd August

Racing against time, as I wanted to go to a cricket practice…. I got there to find a kind of match, with dirty little boys, and the ugliest charwomen, all shouting and playing. I was put in eleventh, and left to sit for two hours, so I suddenly said 'I shall go in next'. I got three runs, and was caught. Then I sat again, boiling with impatience, against the futility. Nobody fielding or bowling.... one awful female lying on her stomach with fat bare legs, another with a pinched ugly face scoring and mixing it all up. So I went out to field against my own side, bowled an over, got a wicket, and returned home in a dudgeon!!!

24th August
The war news very bad, so I laid in a stock of provisions and made black blinds from my rolls of paper. Mrs. Bates [*her home help*] got the ladder and we sealed up the landing window with black paper. All day, on and off, I worked at darkening the house. Also I got ready the guest room, emptied the drawers, and prepared for the slum children [*her term for evacuees*].
It is all terrible, and frightening, but the thought of John, and the danger to him, remains with me all the time. Strange to say, I have lovely dreams, but when I wake up I lie wondering what is the agony, and the thoughts come back, WAR again. Lord Halifax [*the Foreign Secretary*] broadcast his speech to the world. Russia has joined with Germany.

25th August
Well, war is coming. It is amazing. How does England feel? What about all the soft backsliders? Will they stick it out? Will they all pull together? I am thankful I am down here, and not at Bowdon. A telegraph from John to say he is returning. I am very glad. This is what I feel. Life has been good.... Now comes a struggle, and courage and willpower and strength must help us to bear it.

29th August
War will probably begin today, so we will enjoy our time and go off to Stratford-on-Avon. So off we went in the open car, in the sunshine, under the bluest sky, through green lanes, and cornfields, past the old house at Woodstock, and the great palace of Blenheim, past thatched and stone cottages, all lovely. Then the thrill of seeing Stratford, and thinking of Shakespeare walking along those lanes.

1st September
Germany invades Poland.

2nd September
Waiting, all darkened.

3rd September
War declared today at eleven o'clock. We heard at 11.15. It is like a nightmare. But the sky was blue, and the clouds white, and the trees lovely. We gathered berries and red leaves. Four little children, evacuated, came to tea. Now it is a bad time. I cannot write.

7th September

We snatched a day out of Time, a glorious day of sun, and went to the Cotswolds. It was so beautiful I do not know how to describe it. Golden stone in heaps by the roadside, great beech trees, golden walls and haystacks, and cornfields.... To Lower Slaughter, with its stream, running among old houses, old men sitting on a form under a wall, children paddling, all in the sunshine. Thank God for this day and for John's companionship.

3rd October

I heard a car, and Mrs. Palmer and her son John came.... She went on, asking questions, 'What do you think of the war? Do you think we ought to make peace now? My friends do, they say we shall all be starved. It is better to make peace than for everybody to be starved. Do you know there is no bacon? Russia is a wonderful country. They are educated now. It's the first time we have been afraid of them. Don't you think we ought to be on their side?' She got very aggressive, accusing me of speaking with no knowledge of Russia.... 'We could do without Christianity', said she. 'We want Communism'. Then I said what Communism meant, what Bolshevism was. We were quite hot when we heard a car, and she rushed out and got into her car without shaking hands. Never again will I see her.... She is the most aggressive woman I have ever met. Her conversation is one series of questions, and point blank contradictions of what one says.

4th October

A delightful Jacket for *A Traveller in Time* came – Penelope riding in her finery. A nice blurb too, and a good advertisement of my books. I ran down early, and opened up the house to sunshine. What a lovely world it is! Flowers and beauty, but all the time this awful dread in the background. Today I have been dreaming, gathering flowers, slowly doing my work, picking up sticks, and making a jolly fire.

11th October

Last night I dreamed that Father and James came to see how the Earth was. Father was clear and bright, smiling, happy, in his best top coat and hat, walking about so much I feared he would be very tired. He sat on a form and ate two great hunks of bread and butter, about three inches thick, and when I protested and went to cut dainty slices, he shook his head. I knew he liked the taste of bread, earthly fare, and he was relishing it. He didn't speak but I knew his thoughts. He and James were at a service, like King's College, sitting in a radiant glory of light, and I was in the shadows outside, watching, listening to the lovely music. I knew how much they enjoyed it. I knew too they had to go back. I wanted to sit by them, but couldn't.

14th October

[*She calls on Katherine Wigglesworth*] A lovely picture. Mrs. W, her cheeks like red apples, in her bright red and blue and green overall, holding little Bill in her arms, his head pressed to her cheek, and arms around her neck, and Jane holding on to her skirt.

19th October

Letter from Eleanor Graham, saying she has read part of *Thackers* and likes it 'quite a lot', which is damning. She went on to say that parts were lovely, then I wrote some unpolished poor stuff. Very critical, and I think unjust. She says I ought to have written it again and improved it. Considering that I have already written it four times!.... Never mind, I will never ask her opinion, or show her any of my work. She says she wishes someone could bully me into 'doing my best'.... A jolly letter from Alec Buckels [*the book illustrator*] yesterday. Pictures all done. He says that his family say that *Sam Pig* has demoralised them! I love *Sam Pig*. Now Eleanor Graham will adversely criticise it.

21st October

We do not fight for Poland. This is no war about a map. This is a war to enable individuals to live in freedom. This tyranny must be abased. Caesar was a conqueror, and he extended Roman law. Alexander spread Greek civilisation. What does Hitler bring! Torture, concentration camps, secret police, religious persecution. Only the defeat of Hitlerism can defeat the dark shadows over the world.

30th October

The Staffords [*her adult evacuees*] came. Oh goodness, how disappointed I was to see a frowsy old woman, in satin blouse and high heeled shoes, as different as possible from what I had expected. I liked the daughter, plain but good hearted and kind, and sensitively quick. The mother bored me nearly to tears. Cups of tea she wants, and such a fuss. I suggested scrambled eggs for tea, and she added 'and potted meat'. Such a greedy old thing, the antithesis of her daughter. She asked for the oil stove, and groaned, 'Two things I want I can't have, my cup of tea in the morning, and my oil stove at night.' Because we couldn't get the oil in the dark. She grumbled at everything. She never said she liked the lovely room, she only grumbled at its coldness. Never a word about the lovely embroideries, and colour and furniture. Blast her! What shall I do, and how shall I get out of it? Her first words when she went into my pretty bedroom: 'I have been through *hell*.'

31st October

This is All Souls Eve. The stillness, the quietness, ominous, as if all the ghosts were awake, moving in the air, and listening to England. So still we feel that snow is somewhere, but the trees are golden and green.... A bonfire across the woods sends drifts of smoke, which refuse to rise. They pass horizontally along the branches, then speed in a vapour, then move like grey dust.... A breeze touches the fringe of the wood and the edges of the trees move up and down. All Souls' Eve. The souls of all I love are out. I want to say to them, 'Take care of John. Ward off the evil'. 'Take care of England!,' I say to the myriad host of spirits. Help us in this time of stress.

2nd November

Joy, the new book *A Traveller in Time* came, in its pale blue cover, a pretty yellow jacket. I opened the packet on the couch, thankful to be alone while I welcomed it. All afternoon I sat reading it, and enjoying it afresh. A gleam of sunshine, and I got a few minutes of happiness. I went out for a tiny walk with Hamish in the morning, the air so sweet.... I gathered a nosegay, two red rosebuds, a yellow snapdragon, a love-in-the-mist, and arranged them in the silver vase.... Flowers and my books have been my pleasure.

9th November
Publication Day of *A Traveller in Time*. It is a great thrill that this book, which has had so many vicissitudes, should be safely launched in a brave blue jacket and yellow dustcover, with excellent print and paper and all. How nice it looks, bless it! But I had a returned manuscript from the BBC, who find my four tales unsuitable. A letter from the *Derby Evening Telegraph* asking for an autobiography and photograph, which alarms me. I struggle to write this, in a turmoil of 'Can I do anything? Sure? Here's some milk left. I don't want so much. What shall I do with it? Shall I put it here? Or here?' and so on. I am driven dotty by these continual questions [*from Mrs. Stafford*] about nothing.

14th November
Joy! A really delightful review in *The Observer* by Humbert Wolfe. It begins, 'Here are three beautiful books, of which the first, by the least professional of the three authors listed, is the nearest approach to literature. Mrs. Uttley.... with *A Traveller in Time*, addresses herself to a wider and wilder world' . Oh dear Humbert Wolfe, thank you for that word wilder. True, those are the ones whom I write for.

15th November
A grand review from *The Times*, calling *Traveller in Time* beautiful, and exquisitely done, and magic. The whole book has the rich quiet colour of country England, that was once merrie England, and is good to recall. Also a rather stupid one from *Time and Tide*, where the reviewer tries to be funny. These women reviewers in *Time and Tide* are always silly. This one is quite cheaply rude to Masefield in the same article. I felt very happy and did my work.... Now the old woman has come into the drawing room. I refuse to talk to her, she lies in wait with her foolish chatty tongue, 'Is it raining? I don't think it's raining! Too bad! Too bad to rain! It's actually pouring! Take your umbrella, darling, don't get wet, darling. Open your umbrella now darling', she says to her daughter of forty-five, whom she always calls Miss Stafford to me.

17th November
Still raining, a misty day with only the sparrows cheeping and the cocks crowing. I took Hamish round and back through the wood, and I gathered sprigs of ivy and picked up sticks. Purple toadstools in the wood, and bright moss, and rust red leaves underfoot. These people [*the Staffords*] went out too, – to visit the shop and buy two tins of sardines! They never go to the country lanes.

19th November

Summertime ends and clocks are put back. I didn't sleep – overstrained by these people, and I got up late. Work done, then off for a walk to the Hogback woods in the sunshine. The bracken, like carved brown wood, stiff and lovely, the colour of earth, not yet bent and broken. The woods bare and beautiful, the moss shining green. I saw a crimson spindle tree in a copse. I got branches of yellow gorse, which now fill the green vase. A fuss at lunchtime. I had cooked lamb and vegetables with mint sauce, pastry for us and rice for Mrs S. When she saw the pastry, she wanted some. 'But you told me you never eat pastry,' I said, surprised. 'Oh yes I do. I love it, but you never ask me,' she retorted. I was dumbfounded. She is a liar. She is greedy and common.... Well, this is the last night, living in this hell, and tomorrow she will be gone. Thank God. I am sorry for all those who have uncongenial women in their houses. Sunday. Ah! The sun setting behind violet woods, the sky clouded, trees snowed over with Traveller's Joy.

26th November

Another great ship sunk. Chamberlain is speaking, keeping up our courage. 'We are constantly thinking of you', says he to our sailors. 'The safety of these islands depends on the watchfulness of our seamen, as it did in the days of Elizabeth'. A fine call to courage and endurance. I felt rather depressed today, stupid, slow and tired. The wind blew a hurricane last night. It burst the doors of the garage. I tried to screw it up, but couldn't, as I struggled on a little stool with screws and screwdriver, with the wind lashing the door against me. The most lovely moonlight night, pure white and clear as day. Clouds racing across the sky...fleeting over the moon which tinges them with red orange, a lovely colour. The moon herself surrounded by a halo, which is not covered by these rushing veils of cloud.

30th November

Russia invaded Finland today, bombed it and set towns on fire. So the EVIL THING goes on. In *The Countryman* there is a war symposium, asking people what recreations they take. I should say I read Shakespeare's sonnets and Walter de la Mare's *Anthology*, and all the old things. I garden, and walk in the woods. Earth makes me forget.

1st December

There is no present, – past and future are one. In dreams your mind moves freely through time. One moves outside the limitations of the present moment. Past, Present, Future are co-existent. We can see them all spread out before us in dreams. A sleeper lives through events yet to come, – his mind is not moving in the here and now.... If a man's mind moves in the future, the future is co-existent with him. The priestesses of Egypt used to learn to dream, and in dreams they sought the vantage points where they could look out over all time.

9th December

Charming letters, one from Caroline Lejeune, telling me she hadn't enjoyed a book [*Traveller in Time*] so much since she was sixteen.... and asking me to write a sequel, to finish the love story of Francis. One from Miss Dobson, who says she was at Lady Manners' school, and am I Alice Taylor? She knows Lea, Dethick, and all my countryside. This afternoon, reviews, – rather sniffy in the *New Statesman*: 'She has told the tale prettily'. How damning they are! But the review was amazing, sneering at everyone, especially Arthur Ransome! I got off quite lightly.... a letter from Lady Crossley, also sneering at *A Traveller in Time*, as I had expected.

13th December

Cycled to: Beaconsfield with letters, and all John's names for sewing on his clothes – Lieutenant J.C.T. Uttley. Darling child. To WH Smith's, where there was no sign of even one of my books, either in the shop or in the window, but I didn't ask. I *must* not care at all, but let my books go. I cannot suffer the snubbing of these Smith's book sellers.

18th December

I have just washed my hair, and I am sitting by the fire after listening to Churchill's broadcast on the sinking of the *Graf Spee*. I came down at 8 a.m. and listened to the wireless this morning. John's letter, some reviews, quite good, a lovely one of the *Four Pigs* in *Books of Today*.... the best I have had of the Pigs. Tonight I hurried over my cake-icing, which took all afternoon, and the big washing, to listen to the broadcast of the *Four Pigs*. I sat in the hearth itself, close to the logs, and I felt I could write another tale at once! But no time. I turned out all the blue dresser drawers, nails and rubbish, such a mess. I covered the little jam pots and did a great kitchen tidying.

28th December

John came down dressed in his officer's uniform and two stars, looking very smart and handsome. I feel better today, more able to face this parting. I had made the fire, and the room was jolly and the breakfast table pretty. We had our prayer, and I thank God for uniting our prayer together, which few mothers and sons have now. It is really a wonderful bond. Then away we went in the car, with the long tin trunk. Frosty air, and snow falling. We had to wait for the train, in the cold, and then John got in a first class compartment with other officers, and I said goodbye. He was shy on the station, and he talked little, nervous I thought.... Snow falling all day, I did some washing, and then wrote letters. It is very quiet, the earth chill and bitter, grey, with the moon hidden. I am going to bed early, for I feel lost without my darling boy. Please God, take care of him and bring him safely back to me.

1940

3rd January

This year I want to write either a book of fairy tales, or *Pig* stories continued, or both. Also to clarify the short stories, and make two volumes, one of *Country Child* tales, the other of stories. There is that novel hanging in the air, and what about a sequel to *Traveller in Time*? I must work now each day and get something done, really finished. So each day to keep myself at the grindstone I will write down what I have done. Really I am lazy. I want to dream, and I must work.

13th January

Awful review, very first bad one, written by a Turpin, reviewer to the *New England* weekly, saying that *Traveller in Time* is fake rustic and all the country parts impossible, the furniture was bought in Kensington and the farm supported by Argentine Dividends, no imagination or reality and had I read *Cold Comfort Farm*. I saw red, wrote to the editor telling him how I knew every stick and stone in the story, that I was a farmer's daughter and knew what I was talking about.... Rather a hasty letter. I wish I had done it again after a night's sleep but I couldn't rest till I had let off steam.

26th January

[*The BBC have asked her to write a programme about Hans Christian Andersen*] I cannot tell you how proud and happy this made me feel. I thought of the little girl at Castle Top, reading Hans Andersen, and now being asked to write about him.

25th February

[*John has just returned to military service after leave*] It has been a lovely weekend, the feeling of John in the house, his attitude always intrigues me. I love his acceptance, the careless happiness, yet the careful attention he pays – never a word against any body, always jolly and charming.

15th March

Mrs Bates brought the child, & I took him for a walk…. I couldn't work till they had gone. Then I finished the tales and tonight I posted them *GR*'s *Wash Day* and *Water Rat*. I prefer *The Washing Day*, it is a delightful tale. I chuckled as I wrote it, and it should lend itself to good pictures. I hope Mr. Collins will like them. Now I've written the broadcast of Hans Andersen and these two tales. Next I must type the *Pig* stories, then get to the real work, the book. If I stick to it I may do the *Pig* book by the end of next week.

18th March
[*Collins have asked her to allot each illustration to a particular page in her forthcoming book* Moldy Warp, the Mole] I loathe doing this, it isn't fair to do it all from the MS. So I just raced over it and got it done ready for posting tomorrow.

22nd March
Packet from Faber, royalties only £10.7.0. Rather a shock as I expected twice this.... Also the contract from the BBC.... I have been alone but happy with all the flowers in the wood and the garden.... The birds singing.... and I... thought of that Good Friday long ago.

26th March
I am definitely lowbrow, touched by the delicious inborn sentimentalism of England, as contrasted with the hard-boiled highbrows whom I am quite tired of [*like*] Gertrude.... A letter from Ronnie [*Taylor, her nephew, Harry's son*] in the USA. 'Although America is a wonderful place I wouldn't change it for England at any price.'.... I typed the *Boat* story, it is not very good.

27th March
After my work was done I sat in the porch and read the *Scrapbook of Katherine Mansfield*.

28th March
I finished the last *Sam Pig* tale & I like it.... I feel quite sick of the 4 little pigs, and don't want to write any more animal tales yet awhile.

4th April
The gardener pruned the roses & rolled the lawn & I piled up the load of wood.... I felt angry with [*her home help, Mrs. Bates's*] short note saying she could not come any more so I wrote very nicely back to her.... I went to High Wycombe by bus [*for*] the first time.... Grubby women with market baskets got on, they looked like chars, not country folk.... M Tempest wrote, charmed by the two [*Grey Rabbit*] tales wondering how I think of them [*Little Grey Rabbit's Washing Day* and *Water Rat's Picnic*].

5th April
Went to London.... London was not warlike, although there are many soldiers about. I went to see [*the film*] Pinocchio & sat through it twice to get the details.... It was fun to get my cycle & ride home [*from the station*] in the cool wind.

9th April
Germany [*has*] invaded Denmark and Sweden.... I cycled off to B. I passed the plant shop...I bought a lot. The real war is very near, but we can only go quietly on. What should I do if the Germans landed? Poor Denmark! But why didn't Denmark resist? Gardening is the most soothing thing.

12th April

Battle is still raging, will Holland be attacked? I can't work or settle to anything. [*She hangs some pictures*] The Breughel is over the bookcase and the L. Knight over the couch. And a Paul Nash in my bedroom. Tomorrow John comes.

6th May

To London after much vacillation. London was wet but jolly. I did the whole day, not counting clothes, on six shillings and three pence.... Home is lovely.... The war is going badly, sometimes in London I felt ill with horror.

10th May

Belgium and Holland [*were*] invaded during the night.... I wonder if the cuckoo sings when bombs fall?.... I think of darling John, he may be sent off now, for we are helping these stricken countries.... Chamberlain resigned.... a great, noble and religious man. A cruel fate.

20th May

When I opened John's letter each movement of my hand.... seemed important, linked with letter.... His unit is preparing to face the invasion. I don't really want Miss. Hackforth to visit me. Mrs W arrived with a great armful of bluebells. We discussed the German invasion plans of England, thank God we are ready.... I hope people are keeping an eye on the Armfields. [*Gertrude Uttley and family*]

21st May

If the Germans come marching through here, I shall have to fly.... on my cycle perhaps, and I can't ride more than 2 miles, but it would help to have it. I wonder if one ought to hide one's silver, or what one ought to do. Darling John, – I wish I could see you to talk this over, I feel rather lost in this world.

23rd May

Germans at Boulogne.... We have been discussing flight if the Germans come from London. Should I bury my silver in the garden? [*Sir Oswald*] Moseley has been imprisoned, and an MP. Today a letter from Gertrude asking for John's address – I shan't send it as she is Fifth Column.... I think of Castle Top as a stronghold which would fight.... Darling John.... I long to speak to you.

28th May

The King of Belgium has acted traitor. Oh God!.... I had a vision of a lion roaring, with the jackals in the background.... like Gertrude. I had a letter from her attacking England.... [*She is*] Communist, advocating it.

5th June

What exciting days! I have had no time to fill in this diary. The B.E.F. evacuated [*from*

Dunkirk].... Thought of nothing else.... I met Angela Thirkell at Mrs. Heaton's.... I've written two fairy tales for *Child Education*. [One about] *The Old Woman & the Little Red Hen, T.R. and the Fairy*.

12th June
Cheque from the BBC, for £25.6.0, thank God...Letter from Faber's...no mention of advance for *Sam Pig*. Went off to see Mr. Collins in London. I gave Mr. Collins the typescript of *Sam Pig*. He was very encouraging [*about my books*]. Asked me to do a country book for him & said I ought to get an advance for SP.

16th June.
Germans rushing through France. Two million refugees homeless. I can't bear writing this Diary, it is all so like the end of the world.... Faber offer me twenty pounds advance for *Sam Pig*. He had forgotten.

17th June.
France's given up the struggle & we are alone.... Ireland will be taken next.... [*It will be*] a taste of being really conquered for Ireland. America still aloof. Nothing will bring her in.

18th June
[*Churchill's speech*] 'Let us brace ourselves to our duty. Upon this depends the survival of Christian civilisation. We will do our duty and so bear ourselves that if the British Commonwealth and [*its*] Empire lasts for 1,000 years, men will still say, "This was their finest hour".' What a leader! Inspired and magnificent.

22nd June
France has signed her freedom away & deserted us. Last night I saw a light at [*her neighbours the Lanigans*] breaking the blackout. Very nice letter from GL, says she thinks of the valour of the White Horse, – so do I.... Churchill is a worthy successor of King Alfred.... E Graham [*says*] she is [*working*] at the Board of Trade.... letter writing is most difficult.... I began to write *The Scholarship*, writing helps me a lot.

18th July
[*A Traveller in Time is bought by Putnams in the United States*] Oh joy!.... 250 dollars advance, and ten per cent against five thousand, twelve & a half per cent to ten thousand and fifteen per cent afterwards. Isn't that wonderful news! I am filled with gratitude and thankfulness, not for the money, nor the fame, but just to know that people over there will read about *Thackers* and *Penelope*, and all my thoughts and love and dreams.

25th August
Eight hundred German planes came over yesterday. We heard the sirens. LM went back. I felt so lonely when she had gone. [*She describes the visit of her sister-in-law, Alice Tolson*] She

asked whether John was a Communist. I say no!.... I guessed her family had done something or other. They are a disgrace & would help the Nazis.... I think of Gertrude.... Gertrude calls herself a Communist to attract attention!

30th August
[*On the radio*] Pianist playing Coleridge Taylor, aeroplanes droning with the... sinister moan of Germany.... Walter de la Mare's 'Anticipation' which I have been reading with such joy.... Oh, world, how lovely you are! I am feeling all this beauty so intensely. I hope heaven has such rapturous moments.

1st September
I came down in the night [*because of air raids*].... guns firing, bombs falling, & planes roaring over.... Eighty seven planes shot down.... Corrected the proofs of *Sam Pig*.

19th September
[*She refuses to accommodate two Czech Jewish refugees*].... a man & his wife. Mrs. Wilmott [*the Billeting Officer*] was rather insistent. But I had seen the girl with red painted lips, the man like an East End Jew, a couple I disliked intensely, the man avoiding military service, the two out for their own fun. Their air was most repulsive, I wondered who would take them in, rich and rotten they looked.

20th September
John's letter at last, – & a jolly one. I didn't wake till 9.10.... Poor Mrs. Foster had rung & fetched Mrs Wigg to see if I was alive!.... The Women's Institute Hut has been given to refugees.... Such anger.... Then people called for rooms, sent by Mrs. Wilmott! Blast her!

5th October
It seems wonderful to have this house to show to Harry & Frances. When I think of ten years ago and my difficulties, I am thankful to God for the miracle. I remember wondering [*about*] ways of livelihood – to let rooms or to have a little school? I never thought I'd do so well.... I think my mother would be thrilled to see me in this house.

25th October
To Walter de la Mare's.... The drive, & I felt conscious of the trees as inspiration on the way.... Mr de la Mare, smiling, small, sweet-faced coming to see me across the room. The fire flickering in long flames.... We talk of autobiography and childhoods, and first memories, and a child's impressions of grown-ups, flowers and smells and colour.... We spoke of Prof. A. and of words I talked of his [*Walter de la Mare's*] poetry. I asked him to come to tea, and he said he would. Oh joy.

1st November
Walter de la Mare came to tea. All morning I worked like a first class char.... He was so

nice, so pleasant. He loved the room, knew some of the pictures.... I showed the book, which he knew. He has St. Fortunata too, a 14th century saint he said. He loved the wood and the quietness. We talked of ghosts in houses, I showed him pictures of Castle Top and told of our candles. He told me of a house where he refused to open his eyes because he would see a ghost and then how he wanted sleep and was so tired. He said he would like to write more notes for *Come Hither!* We suggested a story.... He asked to see a photo of John and to borrow *TinT* [*Traveller in Time*]. I gave him *Ambush*.... We talked of illustrators, the woman on the Dream book. We talked and talked....

9th November

As I walked this morning I kept singing 'Oh the Holly and the Ivy', [*and*] scraps out of *Traveller in Time*. I felt happy as I walked along, nobody there, and all the lovely woods and farms with men throwing turnips in a heap in the big barn, and hens running into it to eat in the straw.

1st December

A new month, – I face it with odd feelings. We feel more confident, but the future is awfully unknown. This is my month....Posted two tales to Mr. Collins, *G R's Birthday* and *Hare Joins the Home Guard*.

2nd December

I cycled to Beaconsfield & paid bills.... After lunch I went to Old Beaconsfield for wool. [*I heard*] a mother and child speaking of *GR*, so I told them who I was and they were suitably thrilled. So was I, for it was jolly to find my friends in children with pointed wool caps and little red faces.

4th December

Determined to have my cracked tooth out.... caught the bus to High Wycombe. It was out in a jiffy. It was cold & wet & dirty in High Wycombe.... I put a blue pocket on my new nightie. Charming. I started a quite unexpected book, *Country Memories* [*published in 1943 as Country Hoard*]. I ought to be writing the *Sam Pig Tales*.

11th December

London. A gloomy day with drizzle & I noticed London had suffered.... St. Martin's [*has*] holes in [*its*] windows. [*I went in and thought it was*] like a service a thousand years ago, with [*the*] Danes invading.... I went to Liberty's where I bought a chair for fourteen guineas.... I looked at fur coats but I resisted.... I came home... worried I had spent too much.

13th December

A letter from John at last.... Mr. Collins loves *Hare and the Home Guard*, and wants to publish it next year. I am delighted, for I wrote it half as a joke.

25th December

Christmas Day over.... A lovely day of fun. Then Rosemary Helliwell came, all smiles & fur coat.... She began to lecture on the iniquities of England, the good news of the German people. We boiled over.... we went at it hammer & tongues.

27th December

Frances and Harry's present [*to her*] a pair of painted candles. Oh why do they waste their money on such rubbish. No mention of the new book I sent, of the 10/-. They have no gratitude. I really will never send them one of my books, or any money, for they don't deserve it. They are the only ungrateful ones I know.... Dream on the 25th December, with a dark-clothed figure [*prophesying what would happen*] in 1941 and 1942. I realised I could do nothing to change the plans of the future.

31st December

Another day of ominous quiet.... gardened.... I did a great pile of ironing.... Letter from Harry this morning, thanking me for the cheque. A nice letter. I love him far more than he loves me...The newspapers tell of the great raid on London.... O please God help us in this coming year to defeat the terrible enemy.

~ 1941 ~

1st January
I... looked over the country, and prayed for England.... I wished the house a Happy New Year, & I think it was glad. Letter from John.... very loving. He told me how he enjoyed his Xmas parcel.... He said he sang in the choir at the Church Parade.... [*He hoped that next Christmas*] we should be at 'our little Thackers....' The Wigs [*Katherine Wigglesworth and her twin children*] came to tea... great excitement.... I played nursery rhymes to them. All the stars are shining.... The room so beautiful with holly & rosehips & scarlet & green candles.

12th January
Afternoon, seated by the fire, wireless playing the Emperor Concerto, marvellous. Had Mrs. Gray to dinner.... she is quite nice.... Now I shall write out my duties for each week on Sunday. This week four complete *SP* tales, two complete *Fairy Tales*, one country sketch, and six pages of a new book. There, Bimbo! See what you make of that, and blush for shame if you don't do it. [*She resents the soldier's wife billeted on her*] At night the smell of fried potato exhausted me.

17th January
[*A review of Ambush of Young Days says that she has not lost the 'poetic vision of childhood'.*] I have not, but I do find life difficult at times, – alone I can do it, but strangers with no 'vision' are as disconcerting as strangers to a child, and I behave childishly too, and do foolish things, unworthy. I want a steadying influence then, – a mother to help me, a son to help me, for John has much more wisdom than I have, bless him. I don't think one can have great imagination and great wisdom. Can one?

19th January
Yes, they are gone.... [*the billeted soldiers*] How glad I am.... Alone in the house.... the loneliness and peace.... I realise I put an invisible ring around me at certain times.... [*Captain W*] says he is a psychologist – alas I do not like psychologists. I feel they make the theory and put things into it.

31st January
I feel I could write a life of Mary Q[*Queen*] of S[*Scots*]. I feel that I know her, but I am half frightened, as if she [*Mary Queen of Scots*] lived now...I got more than my ration of meat at Beaconsfield.... I got a great welcome at the Wigs. There is no-one like Mrs. W.... I have been writing, two scenes of the play, *The Murder of Darnley*, it may be too frightening. This week I must finish the play, finish correcting proofs in ink, putting in all the wretched proof reader had taken out.... I hope February will bring us victories.

3rd February

An awful review of *Ambush*.... [*By*] a woman, of course. She called me a horror.... [*She asks*] did I never lie when I was little?... never steal or cheat? Alas I did all those things.... I should have got such thrashings I shouldn't have survived, I think.... I went to the films and saw *Hunchback of Notre Dame*. It was worse than the review, [*Charles*] Laughton pulling awful faces.... Now for nice things: a sprinkle of snow, lovely, and the woods and garden most beautiful. A jolly fire.... LM sent the little book on Mary Queen of Scots.... An excellent lunch.

15th February

At last John's letter came.... all leave is postponed, they are moving south. 'Things are getting very hot.' A delightful letter which cheered me. Last night I felt ill.... but slept soundly and recovered. [*Rhoda*] Power [*of the BBC*] approves my broadcast script [*of Hans Christian Andersen*] but wants the third scene altered.

1st March

Such joy! John appeared unexpectedly at lunchtime.... I talked of Mary Queen of Scots of course. At 2. 30 he went away. But his coming has brought brightness.

22nd March

I am shocked. John wrote to say he has volunteered for the RAF. He has been accepted. He wants to do something active in this War.... I am stunned by the news, yet not really upset, somehow it seems a part of life.

8th April

[*I sent*] 13 tales to Faber, 10 to the BBC.... Cheque for £99. 2. 0 for *GR* books on April 1st. About twenty thousand sold. It seems a miracle.

10th April

I was washing up after lunch [*when*] a camouflaged lorry stopped outside – and I saw John's scarlet cap. I was thrilled! He told me about the RAF. He was pressed into it.... We talked and were so happy.... We kissed goodbye in the hall, – Ah John, I love you dear child. At such moments I feel his great love for me.... Greece invaded.... Yugoslavia fighting.

19th April

Fabers say that *Farm on the Hill* is to be published 24th April at seven shillings and sixpence.... A nice lace blouse comes.... I had a terrific clean up.... The news is bad every day. I think of the garden, it helps me like a prayer. [*The*] radio playing New World Symphony. I am sitting here in my long blue hostess dress, Hamish at my feet rolling in ecstasy, as I pet him.... Guns roaring.

23nd April

Shakespeare's birthday, St. George's Day. My new book *The Farm on the Hill* comes. It is one of the most exciting moments of life, to open a parcel containing a newly published book. What colour will be the cover? How will it look? This is a war book, a plain jacket with big lettering, but the book has a cover the colour of the *Country Child*. It is very nice, I have been dipping into it, welcoming it with a little ache in my heart for that girl of long ago. Heavens! How clearly it comes back to me! I could write a dozen books of memories! So here I sit by the fire, – which I lighted in celebration – and the book lies on the chair near me, and all the room is looking at it.

30th April
I am sitting in the new green arm chair.... a bowl of cowslips and some violets. The fire crackling.... All day... very busy but never a word of any book done.... I oiled my bicycle, lawnmower and locks of house.... I did the criticisms of the pictures of *Hare and the Home Guard* which MT sent today.... new moon, very lovely.... I bowed to her.

1st May
A lovely May Day but now the sirens are wailing. Today my chief pleasure was going to pick cowslips.... A cheque [*only £6 from Austin Reed*].... I wished I had help with the heavy work [*in the garden*].

25th May
Last night we heard the battleship *Hood* was destroyed. It is terrible. Crete holding out, but there is an ominous feeling, disaster's wings are beating.... I made cakes for John but the oven was stupid and the cakes a failure. I cycled to [*Beaconsfield*] and listened to the speeches on the [village] green, Sir W. Jowatt on England's fight for freedom.

27th May
John came on leave. He came on a motor cycle. I thought he was a girl... he was soaked.... [*She asked*] Mrs Wig [*to go to the local W. H. Smith's*] trying to get him [*the manager*] to stock my books.... he refused. No demand! 'Now if it was Miss Enid Blyton's books! They sell marvellously. Do you know her? She is a charming woman. Here is her photograph.' Mrs Wig, 'She looks rather harassed', – as she looks at the awful picture of a vulgar curled woman.

10th June
I was so cold that I got a chill, for I had cast my clout. I was icy & a pain in my back.... letter from LM saying Russia and Germany are combining to attack India.

11th June
Many jolly things.... Sunshine and loveliness.... I bought unrationed meat in [*Beaconsfield*].... MT sent the rest of the lovely pictures... and took my awful criticisms quite well.... I went to the film *Our Town* & was much moved by it.... The girl in it is like me at that age.

4th July
[*She spends £2 on having her hair permed in Beaconsfield*].... a wicked waste of good money. I hate it, but it has to be done with my mop.

15th July
Darling mother's birthday. It has poured with rain this St. Swithin's, too.... I went to B, got such provisions. It wasn't like wartime.... Tonight a broadcast on P G Wodehouse. Amazing. The strongest indictment of him.... a traitor. England is lost for him forever.

20th July
The poppies in the glass jug, crinkled petals delicate and beautiful, the crinkles making the beauty, longways and crossways as they are packed in their box. Some of them have many petals like a ballet skirt. The thick gold sepals, like a wall, guarding the green box. Tall grasses, with branches, and twigs and firm brown 'leaves' at the ends, hairy stalks and buds and perpendicular hairs, pointed and fine. The jug on the table, yellow snapdragons, purple phlox, cream rose, orange marigold and purple sebaea, & a bunch of red roses and one of white. An orange tawny rose on the mantelpiece repeating the colour of the picture. White love-in-the-mist in the glass jug. On the piano lilac delphiniums.... Desparate. If I [*could*] I would sit in the sunshine for hours on end. And why not?

27th August
To London to see R de la Mare [*at Faber*] about pictures.... He receives me glumly, his face cold.... Little sniffs of annoyance. I don't care. I hurried off.

3rd September
As usual a busy day, a special... clean ready for John, yet not really expecting him.... [*I went*] blackberrying in the wood beyond my little gate.... Great joy, the BBC... will do [*my*] tales of [*Sam Pig*] beginning... October 13th. So that will help financially.... [*Listened*] to 'No Longer Alone' – the wireless talk [*about the second year of the war*]. Amazing & terrible & wonderful.

11th September
To Old B[*Beaconsfield*] to see the clocks and little desk I decided to have the nice clock [*for*] £11.... At night we had our party.... Dr Wigglesworth [*husband of her friend Katherine*] came late & was his usual dry, cold, rude self.... a detestable man.

28th September
Harry's birthday. I think of those days, when Father was up the filbert trees, and Harry was born, to the great joy of my father and mother. No wonder I wasn't of much account. I wasn't worth it, I realise that now.

29th September
So tired I can hardly write…. Mrs. George [*her home help*] did the floors…. I vacuumed the rooms…. Harry writes that he has sold CT to somebody who will care for it.

2nd November
Apart from Mrs. Lanigan [*her next door neighbour*] shouting at me through the door, I have been alone all day. I think Mrs. Wigg might have come – her husband is at home, and the nurse…. Oh fool – do cheer up and be brave!! Laugh at yourself. There! I'm gay again.

13th November
Great joy, two parcels with thirty books arrive. The newly published *Sam Pig Goes to Market*, and the four little two and sixpenny books. All very pretty and attractive.

14th November
Preparing for the lady who was coming [*with a view to renting a room at Thackers*]…. I was staggered when I saw her. Common, like a barmaid…. [*Alison tried to put her off*]…. The house was cold (*I heartily agreed*)…. She is not living with her husband. I wouldn't have her if she paid £3 a week…. £25 from Fabers, bless them.

This is the last entry for this year.

1942

1st January

Peeping through the blue curtains at the new year. Misty grey light. I received cheque, letter from LM and reviews, a nice beginning, and I had tea & toast & butter, honey & an apple. I did the fire, swept, dusted, got in coal.... & then gardened. I planted 12 raspberry canes, transplanted gooseberries, & tried to plant apple trees but I couldn't dig the holes. Then I raked up loads of leaves, and worked till 1.0. Cooked lunch, sausage rissoles, potatoes & apples, – & then the young man from the wood came with his load.... I gave the young man & the little boy each a piece of barley sugar. I ironed a big pile of clothes, p. cases, hankies etc. Then Mrs. Dobell & Timothy came to tea.... I showed Tim John's early drawings.... We talked of books, of the *Book of Discovery*, & of *Odysseus*. At the end, I gave him [*Hare Joins the*] *Home Guard* which quite took away his breath. I wanted to write but letters, washing up, supper etc., have taken all evening. It has been a nice friendly day, a happy day, the room lovely with its holly branches and the little tree and my thoughts of dear John.

4th January

Up earlier than usual, & I would have slept on, but George [*the*] gardener coming. He arrived & began to dig holes for the apple trees. I went out and we decided on the places.... I standing listening while he told me of Christmas dinner.... about the Free French [*troops*] who came a few days later, with a pheasant and champagne.... In between I rushed in & shot vegs into pans & into oven in a reckless way.... A lovely day, not a bit lonely, with apple trees and good thoughts...

12th January

This afternoon a very nice fan letter from a Miss Bain of Edinburgh who had read [*The Farm on the Hill*] and found in it the eternal truths of life.... Off to B, to get my 1¹/₂ lb shallots for spring planting. I got 2 eggs (from Uruguay!).... Finished writing the *Singing Kettle* tonight. I shall not go to the Polish Ballet. I don't want to go to London in this cold weather, it is such fun at home.

31st January

The news is very bad, – 100,000 Japs assaulting Singapore.... Benghazi taken too. Retreat everywhere. I have felt very sad. I have kept up my spirits by thinking of little things.... a robin in the snow.... Please God, help us in February, help us to keep Singapore & to push on.

26th February

Lovely letter from G.L. about my writing.... John has been to Bowdon [&] seen the

Parkers, Gilloes, & Edwards, stayed with W[*Winnie*] A[*Armitage*]. I am so glad, it is a lovely & comfortable house. What a hostess she is! A marvel. Cleaned the brass & all the silver, quite fun. I haven't done it myself for a long time & didn't I make it sparkle!

1st March
The first of March. Each month seems so laden with the unknown & ominous travail. It is queer. So the people of past ages must have felt.... Well today I am wearing my blue frock & feeling happy to welcome John.... John came at 4 o'clock.... in his captain's uniform.... I make a fire in J's room, – he first had to carry the peacock butterfly hibernating in the chimney to another room!

26th March
Eureka! A cheque for £297.10.2 from Faber! Such sales as I have never known, I was quite staggered.

27th March
To London, in my brown coat, & scarlet dress.... I went to see Mr. Collins.... He said he could sell 100,000 books if he had them. He showed me a delightful poem on *Hare* etc by a child, & another child's remark 'Goebbels won't let the Nazis come now because *Hare* will stop them'.

1st April
I went to the post singing loudly in the wind, & suddenly a man came round the corner. I was silent, embarrassed [*but*] he took up the song as he passed. A friendly world.... I typed a little, I don't want to do any more of *Cuckoo Cherry-Tree*, I'm sick of it. I think I will start *Sam Pig* tomorrow.

4th April
Then to B.... Mrs. Wig in front of me in the queue, – we didn't speak.... After tea I went... to the Dobells, where I told Mrs. Dobell of my hurt and grief from Mrs. W, and my opinion that she is out for the main chance, cruel. Really Mrs W is trying to get Mrs Dobell, as she has a large house & money.

9th April
Off to High Wycombe in pouring rain with [*my*] typewriter.... Home to coffee & lunch by the fire, I was frozen.... After lunch I looked again at the MS & then cycled in rain & wind to B with the parcel, duplicates etc.... Came home had tea, & the sound of steps in the kitchen. It was John in battle dress with.... Mortimer and a batman come for tea & the night. It *was* fun .... A houseful.... Two cruisers lost. *Cornwall* & *Dorsetshire* in the Indian Ocean, bombed by the Japs. They are devils incarnate, I fear them.

19 April
Waiting for John! He is engaged to Dorothy Parker! Telephoned to tell me, to say he was

bringing her. My first reaction was deep surprise.... Well, I am sure he has chosen well, he would for he goes underneath mere skin to character, and I hope Dorothy has strength & character. I only remember a pretty girl. This is a critical moment. I feel intensely for John, his future, his all, bless him.

21st April
I wrote to John, asking him if he had truly considered his engagement to a girl he didn't know, a contract for life. Why hadn't we seen more of her before? It was a careful letter, I restrained my anxieties.... But she is sweet & charming & perhaps pliable – & perhaps he wants somebody who has not his own tastes. Well I did the shopping, & worked hard all day, I finished by final revision & I posted *Country Hoard* to [*Mr*] Stewart at night.

2nd May
Tonight I feel depressed and furious with myself, with talking about the engagement to one and sundry – to Mrs S.... Then, when she went, I seemed to see those two... figures, John radiant, with his arm round Dorothy.... I felt I had betrayed them. Oh God, I love them so much. Perhaps this revulsion of my own horrid selfishness will cure me. I have been mad, & now I shall be sane. Now I shall trust God, & think no more of my own loneliness.

24th May
To Church, cool, quiet, I sit near the front. John's banns were read out. It was strange to hear & very exciting. I am filled with deep joy mixed with all kinds panics and agonies, & joys again. When I get into John's mind I find such goodness & sweetness & bravery & love, my heart aches for him. He is still the little child I knew, the one who cheered me with loving arms when James was at the front. I recall too vividly. I get back with such poignance [*sic*] it hurts.

1st June
I awoke feeling unhappy because this is the month of separation from my John.... Excited over the great raid on Germany & over growing strength in the air.... Oh June, do let it be a happy month. Oh June, my darling darling June.

5th June
To London, I bought a lovely cherry dress for the wedding [*after*] hesitating a lot over it – & a wine hat & wine shoes to go with the last year's blue frock if I should wear that. A bit confused, undecided over dresses, – 10 guineas is a lot.

16th June
I got home at 2.0 & was boiling coffee for lunch when Mrs Dobell phoned, to tell me that Mrs. Wig went there last night & had a long talk [*about*] me. She was very sad that we have 'parted', & wanted to see me again, & would willingly apologise for her husband's rudeness(!!!) and had I mentioned it to Mrs Dobell. Oh dear. We had such a talk on the phone. Really I don't want to see Mrs Wig or renew her acquaintance. It wearies me.

2nd July

Well tragedy & misery & unhappiness have swept over us, and I am not going to put it down. Let me remember gay things.... Not since James's death have I suffered like this. Today, Thurs, a vile letter from [*Mr.*] Parker, speaking of John's ancestry as if there were some horrible blot, sneering, asking why *knowing what I did know*, I didn't stop the engagement, for John after a lifetime of obedience would obey me.... I feel I would like to hurl the Parker family to perdition.... Well, I will fight Mr Parker. I will write again.... I was so happy writing my books, gardening, & living here till John brought that girl into my life. Now I do nothing but write letters & letters & letters. Oh dear! Courage, Mimbles. Keep on trying!

6th July

LM said that John had told her that my love and courage had kept him firm & helped him through.... a letter from Dorothy.... She is a nice girl. I had always liked her but she is not the right kind for John.

9th July

Up early, work done & off to the vet with Hamish to be trimmed, dragging the little dog along, bless him. I 'snooped' raspberries from the wood [*of her neighbours, the Lanigans*] & felt frightened that [*Mrs.*] Gurney [*another neighbour*] had seen me!

16th July

Listening to *Midsummer Night's Dream*, sweeping the kitchen. I felt transported back as if it were the XVIth century, & a girl sweeping then..... Put £75 in John's war savings for 100 units.

29th July

Boiling over! ....I met Mrs Gurney on way to post, she asked inquisitively about John & I told her a little, being careful. *Then* I put my foot in it, asking if I could help her with her bazaar & give something for it. I said I had seen a notice, but it was rather *muddled* & would she tell me about it. Then she let fly in her usual way, because I had said muddled & she [*had*] printed it.... I said about 20 times a noisy apology determined to stop her flow.... I said again I was sorry. I came away boiling & burst into tears! Women! I loathe women!.... Now for lovely things the exquisite pictures from Tunnicliffe & his nice letter....

9th August

Gandhi arrested. Riots in India. A stab in the back for us, for China & Russia. A letter from Mrs Wig (!) lying in the hall, not very tactful, but she says 'We have kept away with the greatest sadness because we felt that after Brian had been so rude we should only distress you by asking you here'. It is no use, I can never see them see them to talk freely now.

10th August

My wedding day. At 12.0 just at the time when James stood by my side bless his noble glorious heart, I thought of him, & I remembered so vividly he seemed to come alive. He is waiting for me.... wrote to Mrs. Wig, saying I should remember her with affection.

24th August
To Ulverston & to lovely old Brown How [*a cottage*].

27th August
Sitting in a wood by a little roaring stream. The water making two songs, one a low rich tone as it curls and whitens under the.... wall, the other light as it drops round the stones. The wall is raised on a pillar of stone, with flat slivers of rock spanning the water & wall built on the top. The centre rocky pillar divides the stream which swirls aside & then joins again by a holly tree. There is a flowing cascade & smooth round 'falls' of clear water. Grey stones with silver dried moss and knobbed lichens & tiny fringed ferns.... 2 large brave spiders spinning webs in the bracken. Ferns trailing their fringes in the water, down at the edge, burnet growing in the stones in the water, wild strawberries cascading down the slope.... stones hidden and the deep cushion of moss and from it rise the trunks of silver birch and rowan. Behind are a tall larch tree.... Over the top of the stream's wall there is a great crag with four peaks, purple against the silver blue sky.... and dark wine heather.

28th August
By Coniston Lake under a great four fold oak, which grows at the water's edge. The lake reflecting the pale blue sky, and the deep green slopes of wood & moorland. A cornfield, a yellow triangle, has its counterpart in the water, above it the rounded trees in a dense wood, varying greens, with rock faces & silver birch and the rocky heights where... grass & bright green bracken grows. Crows flying by the water's edge, 3 men in a boat under the wood across the water.... 2 swans diving & shaking their white feathers, with long necked reflection, & a grass hopper cheeping, a bird tweeting, and the sound of a water fall. Bees humming, & again the sound of the swans preening their feathers. A fish plops, a robin sings a roundelay.... High in the sky a swift wings like a curling fish. The long reflections come across the water to this shore. Fish leap high. Now I sit close to the water on the tongues of grey rock, with its little shelves & crevices filled with fern & saxifrage and moss.... the little shingly beach, & the boat drawn up. The curve of the bay, the brown pebbles in the water, the shoals of fish. Two little 'capes'.... and then a far cape, & a high green hill. Above it the dim ghostly shapes of the mountain. Two butterflies fly over my head, down to the water. The shapes of ripples. The shining, changing edge of the land reflection, the gold of the cornfield. Clouds in the water. The barn. High stone walls with a great beam across & beamed ceiling, wooden floor, little window high in the wall overlooking rocks and trees, a sheep feeding, a rabbit playing.

29th August
Thunder last night. Full moon. Lightning. We walked up the opposite hill to a farm & sat in the kitchen, the saucepans & lids on the wall. The brass tap. Lunch under the wall. The

bent hawthorn leaning over. The fir trees in the hollow. The green grass of the bog and the exquisite moss and pearly Flowers of Parnassus.

31st August
[*The cottage at Brown How*] whitewashed with vertical stones in jams over the curved windows. Four tree trunks hold up the little porch roof.... Pink hydrangea on the left, red and yellow snap dragons, marigolds, cornflowers, asters, snap dragons on the edge of the green slope. A grassy slope leading to the barn, edged with rock, & a big rock on the ground at its base. Diamond paned windows, casement. Roses on porch, & cream standard rose in the grass. Silver lambs' ears among the grey rocks. To the left... a great sycamore at the iron gate. Bird table with ferns at the foot, & heather roof.... A seat by the door, another against the dairy wall. A clump of lamb's ear, all ruffled with wool like the silky skin of a calf and tall seeding flowers. Pansies everywhere, & forget-me-nots, & marigolds & lichen & stone crops. A white butterfly goes past & settles on a scabious. Ferns in the rocky border by the doorway.... Steps outside to a bed room. Pink cranesbill in the stones, cracks. Between the barn and the dairy is a view of the lake, blue, with a cornfield yellow beyond it. Trees up the hill, moss & rocks beyond reaching to the sky. A real fairy tale cottage is this.... 5 windows upstairs in a crooked row.... 4 down. One to the little house door.

1st September
The loveliest day imaginable, clear as heaven, every peak, every field glittering with colour and light. Old Man [*a mountain near Coniston*] very near. We talked to a farmer who told us the names of the hills, – the ranges before us. In the afternoon.... a tea party with Mrs. Tempest & shrieking child, & another woman & 2 girls, very boring.

22nd September
Last night (this morning's really) dream, – frightful. I lay in bed in a large room – a castle? John in bed across the room, others sleeping near.... Then I saw 2 enormous birds, cawing fiercely. They flew down and peered through the glass; one part of window open, & a bird flew in. I was filled with awful fear. It was black, fierce, baleful. It flew over my bed, & I knew it was going to pick out my eyes. I tried in vain to wake the others & couldn't. I could move no limb, I lay enchained in terror.

28th September
Harry's birthday, poor Harry he is 55, & his wife incurable. We have both had deep sorrow...& later I met Mrs. Wig & Jane in Boots.... My broadcast tonight, *The Three Brothers*. A good story, it went very well.

30th September
The war news is bad, Stalingrad directly pressed.... [*the*] Germans threatening raids & raids.

1st October

Letter from Stewart saying that a *Traveller in Time* was being considered by Films, the option wanted till a year next Nov. Omnia film. Mr Rolland the manager. *Cuckoo* can't come out this year, but I am overjoyed about *T in T.*

7th November

This morning a letter from the [*Beaconsfield*] Council say they were taking the woman [*Alison's lodger*] away. At night I spoke to her, – she denied making complaints, said she wanted to go because the way was long & rough & dark, and her friends were at B – but I had made her happy & comfortable. She seemed quite grateful.... M Tempest sent pictures for [*Grey Rabbit's*] 'Birthday'.... Great victories in Libya all this week, very cheering.... have slept and slept.

25th December

And a lovely day it has been.... I opened my 2 remaining parcels.... Out to tea with the Young husbands.... Tonight I had my Xmas dinner of pork.

30th December

The thrilling news in the paper of Charley Potts' bravery in Libya... he got the Military Cross on the field of battle.... Income tax £79, & house tax came, terrific sums for me to pay.... Tonight I have been reading through the new book.... I've done nothing to it for a month.... Then try to do *Sam Pig* in Feb & *Fairy Tales* in March.... rough copies only.

31st December

Snow in the night.... I got stamps & a W.S. certif. [*War Certificates*] for 25 units for John.... Sensible carpenter with his bag & his boy. He put a wooden ledge on the bottom of the outside WC to keep water off.... Two letters this afternoon.... so the chief billeting officer, Dr Myers, has had a dressing down & well he deserves it.... I think of John and his deep love and devotion, & I think of God in whom I put my trust. The end of a year of anxiety, of pain, of bitterness, of triumph , of flashes of happiness, & tomorrow a New Year begins.

∾ 1943 ∾

1st January
New Year's Day. A wet dark boistevons morning.... In bed... I opened [the] letter.... & it was a cheque for £300 from Heinemann for me and MT, remuneration for the sale of *GR* books! I was absolutely amazed.... They must have sold colossal numbers. I am delighted they have at last recognised our share in the business. A royal New Year's gift.... Very tired, after the cooking, & I slept by the fire. Pouring rain nearly all day, but a brilliant burst of sunshine which was like a fire in the room, lighting up the walls the yellow vase of jasmine.... I have done no writing of my book, but I must begin and work hard at it and finish the first draft this month of Jan. Then do *Sam Pig*: Feb draft only, & *Fairy Tales* in March, & then revise & do *Tim Rabbit* tales.

3rd January
A better day, for the sun shone gloriously, and the frost sparkled. The wet roads dried up, frozen, all the pools frosted over.... & off with little Hamish. It was exquisite, the woods, the green trunks of the beeches, the brown leaves & ice – & I noticed each leaf had its mid-rib & vein white with frost, lines drawn on them as they lay underfoot. The mist under a wood had shadows of the trees solid in it, a curious effect I can't understand. Lovely, mysterious. The trees in the wood near Penn, silver, vital, exciting – a hedge of quick thorn and ash, with garlands, bracelets of big red berries festooned over them, in a careless beauty that was breath taking. I was enraptured. On I went, & there were 2 little holly trees in a bit of hedge, scarlet with berries, most exquisite, like fairy trees. A tree of catkins in another hedge with the sun on them, & the blue sky beyond. The faint white clouds, circling over, the faint blue, the sun. Oh God . How lovely it is. I sorted sheets for Russia in the afternoon.

13th January
[*She goes for a walk in the woods*] Then off I went with Hamish, for the sun shone in a lovely day. We went through the wood, & I thought of tales I might write. Every tree, every jolly thing reminded me, so that my mind was brimmed with stories.

14th January
Letter from John, the most depressed I have ever received absolutley browned off, all in a muddle.... Poor darling, I wrote to cheer him, saying '*Courage, mon brave*'.

27th January
[*Tchaikovsky's*] *Concerto*, for Piano most glorious, the one which has a sudden turn which wrings my heart, as it changes its key so magically.... Letter... from M Tempest saying that

Heinemann have confessed to Collins the [*GR*] books [*are*] too profitable to sell to them. That's why we got the money. Great news of Churchill meeting Roosevelt in N Africa [*the Casablanca Conference*].

30th January
John wrote.... but he has been asked to be Adjutant to the colonel & he has accepted.... letter from C.S. [*Charles Stewart*], saying that they are all glad to have a *SP* book on the way.

31st January
Wild stormy day, so I stopped in bed all day – not that I wanted to do so, but I did it as a precaution, like a dose of medicine.... Later I worked at *SP*, finishing a tale. Now only one to be done. A dream, half-forgotten, (dreamt on night Jan 30-31) – of going into a great old [*Roman Catholic*] C church, it must have been a long time ago.... In the church I saw a black skinny hand under a stone... shadowy hanging, moving, I asked what it was, I recoiled from it. Three captured Devils he told me.

2nd February
MT's pictures for *GR*'s *Birthday* which I thought were poor. Spend evening criticising & making suggestions – 4 pages of them. She also sent *lovely* pictures of her own for her own little new work, all from the *GR* books. It is sickening.

8th February
A nice review of *Candlelight* [*Tales*] in *Books of the Month*.... Then off to B, to Old B for groceries.... I got marmalade.... & miracles, some real sausages for I just happened to be there when the sausage van drove up.... I began my typing of the *SP* tales, 12 tales, it should take about twenty-four days, 7 should be done this month, earlier if possible.

20th February
John [*has*] gone to stay the night with Peter and Rosemary Palmer.... Cycled to B.... to the butcher, where I asked him if there was any liver or kidney. None. 'Not even a little tiny bit?' I asked making a hollow with thumb & finger. 'Not even a tiny tiny little bit' reflected the butcher, holding up his finger & thumb & everybody laughed.... Notice of the Penn Club [*a local organisation*] came, but I know nobody, none of these famous ones, & I won't join it.

22nd February
London.... Called at Fabers, & John met Stewart. It was pleasant & CS seemed glad to meet us. He said 18,000 *Candlelight* and 17,000 *Starlight* sold to date, – a merry talk. Then to meet M Tempest, lunch with her at Grosvenor Place.... LM sends four eggs by Reg. Post.

5th March
Publication day of *Country Hoard*. It came in the afternoon, I went to the door, hands black with cleaning but I hoped the post girl wouldn't notice. However she stared hard, & later on

I found a smudge on my face! So now I've put a mirror in the kitchen! It's not seemly for an author to take in her works with a black-leaded face. A lovely little book is *Country Hoard*, & my mother would love it, bless her.

11th March
To London, – Mrs Lanigan introduced me to Miss Collins, GKC[*Chesterton's*] secretary & companion, on the station…. St Paul's…. the dome immense in the ruins. I was staggered at the devastation…. Then to Trafalgar Sq, where a Halifax bomber hung onto Nelson's Column.

13th March
Opened a letter from Tunnicliffe, very nice. Then casually opened a packet & it was my royalties, – with £1,090. I was staggered completely, could hardly believe my eyes… £200 was the utmost, my wildest hopes. It is quite amazing & very wonderful, – I think of my small beginnings, my timid efforts all alone with no-one to give advice. I feel very grateful and humble…. Did my work, feeling queer, I'm not used to having any money…. If mother and father were alive how I would help them! I must send something to [*Harry*] and Frances. Over 82,000 books sold.

18th March
To London…. To [*Mr.*] Collins, – saw him only a minute in his little room, as he rushed off to a meeting at 12. p.m. He congratulated me on *CH*…. Then off to lunch at Green Lizard, – with Scottish people at the table, to whom I talked – & shopping. I tried on fur jackets, couldn't decide. Then saw an exquisite gold blouse £7.10.0 & bought it. It's a preposterous price, but it was so lovely, it suited me…. I saw *Sam Pig* everywhere, in windows, & I waved to him, & smiled at him…. I scuttled home…. Found a letter from John with congratulations on the money…. This morning as I dressed I saw a figure in white overall in the far distance. 'That's the farmers wife coming with 6 eggs for me' I said to myself – & I laughed at myself…. It *was* the farmer's wife. She held out a bag. Six eggs. It was most uncanny.

31st March
Today the contract for *Sam Pig at the Circus* came with Stewart's letter asking about broadcasts…. I felt rather ill & sick again…. Hamish's little foot swollen with a cyst, he came to me & lay very close for comfort…. I feel he knows what I think, & we talked together. It might be better if we were all dumb…. Well goodbye, March, it has been a nice month, lovely sunshine, & very unexpected wealth.

9th April
A succession of excitements, – GL's charming letter telling me of the effect of my books, – spring water, full of water lights, cold clear… is the very first picture had come to her mind. Bless her. I cycled off to B…. I got sweetbread [&] ox-cheek from the butcher, & a whole pot of quince conserve…. for John's old rations…. Then I called at Browns. I looked again at the little Bible box, & a carved set of shelves, & behind stood a fine oak cupboard whose

price I never ventured to ask. 'This is only 18.10.0' said the girl.... I cycled home thinking of it very excited, measured the space, & phoned for it. I am delighted about it, it is just what I've always wanted.

12th April
A green day, spring has thrown her cloak all over the country.... Two lovely reviews [*of Country Hoard*].... The *Western Mail* under the heading 'Wordsworth Quality'.... 'To this...enchanted country girl'. Ah! that was me! Thank you Oh God!

13th April
Frances died on Saturday, the 10th, I heard from Harry this morning. Poor little thing. He will be so lonely, he has depended on her.... I suddenly decided to go to London.... Earlier the oak cupboard came.... I went by bus to John Barkers.... I chose a squirrel cape £46.10.0, very nice, – after trying on moleskin, & various furs. This suited me the best.... I went to St. Martins to pray for H and F. Then racing home.... John's letter.... Also [*one from*] M Tempest who doesn't like the Tunnicliffe drawings! It shows how inartistic she is. He is a real artist, she is very poor. Orion in the West, a half moon.... & the sky filled with planes that have been droning over for hours, at even distances, such a roar.... I think of Rotterdam. It is truly terrifying.

18th April
A dream. I was lost in black space, lost in time, in outer darkness. A terrible agony. And I called & called screaming, 'Mama. Mama, Mama'.... I noticed I had used the childhood word 'Mama' in my agony. A lovely review of *Country Hoard* by A A Milne in the *Sunday Times* today.

21st April
Letters from John & W de la Mare.... At Wilkinson's [*the fishmongers*] I was watching a woman ogling [*the fishmonger*], her false teeth, her red lips, her head on one side as she gazed up close to him, – suddenly he turned to me and to my surprise introduced her, Enid Blyton! The Blyton, photographed and boastful!....

4th May
All the ironing to do, the piano tuner here. We talked on conductors, – he didn't like Beecham or Sir Adrian Boult, but he praised Alec or Alan something, a poor Jew-boy from Mile End.... John's letter. Hurrah! Saying he is coming on leave next Monday. Letter from child's mother asking if *Rat*'s child is boy or girl, & name?

9th May
John came this morning at 9.45, – rather thin & pale.... He told me his momentous news. Embarkation leave... I feel sick with fear, yet I know the time must come. At last it has come, but I must be brave.... He spoke of Dorothy [*Parker*], & again I felt hurt.... sudden sweep of Anxiety. She is not the kind to make him happy. I think of that family and that disease.

18th May

John has gone, I hardly slept last night. I feel stunned. I think of his dear face, – as I kissed it as if it was half hidden in the bedclothes, and we made our old baby squeak.... then we had our prayer. I wept. Then we played the old song, – holding arms; I cannot write about it. It is all too sacred.... I pray he will be spared for many years to make others happy as well as me....

4th June

Dreamt of walking down a steep cobbled path, with green hills opposite.... I gave a tug by mistake to my pearl necklace & it broke, pearls dropping.... Such a busy day. Letter from Stewart saying 6,000 *C Hoard* sold which is very good. *Cuckoo* [*Cherry-Tree*] coming out soon.

10th June

To London (I always look forward to & I enjoy it).... I bought a blue hat, a little turban, at Dickins and Jones.

24th June

A year ago today, – I still feel wretched & ill when I think of the misery and agony of mind [*when John's engagement was broken off*]. That wonderful escape to Scotland.... I have been thinking of Shakespeare, and reading lines.

25th June

Off to London, – & what a jolly day it was! John's photograph is excellent.... Then I walked to Dover St & in a window I saw a silver tea set, handmade silver, plain, copy of a Georgian set. They told me, £21.... But I've got very little money in the bank, – I've put so much in war savings.... I went to see *How Green is my Valley*. It is very good. I wept. The father in it is like my own father.... Most moving.

28th June

A lovely review by S P B Mais (what a joke!). 'All unknown to me, this Derbyshire girl was a near neighbour of mine & of my own age.' Well, I don't think I should have liked him if I had known him. 'She is a born writer, with a peculiar gift for conjuring up a scene in a phrase. She recalls her own childhood as vividly as if it were only last week' says he. True, O how true nobody knows but me.... I typed scraps of new essays.

12th July

Then I dressed in my blue silk frock & cycled off to dinner at Miss Collins to meet [*the actress*] Margaret Rutherford. She looks about 60, but I don't suppose she is that, a nice face, keen clever mind, fair hair faded & light, & fluffy.

15th July

Cycled to B & got liver, corned beef, sponge-cake. I felt very rich.... Wrote some pages of 'I *wanted to learn*' for the BBC after hearing Naomi Michison's talk. Why do these people always pretend school taught them nothing?

28th July
Sitting at end of garden. Heavenly…. 3 woodpeckers were flying down & they saw me. Two veered into the wood, the third sat on a bough nearly overhead, squawking and staring. Sunlight on its head & shadows of twigs, barring it, its green the colour of the leaves in sun, almost invisible. They are waiting for me to go. It is so lovely, the sky blue, the hedge very green and lively against it, the house like a fairy tale, its roof greenish brown, a shadow over it, – a white butterfly flying across, long shadows on the lawn, a tall pink hollyhock at the corner and a mass of lavender & the little apple tree with yellow & red fruit on the left of the house, the two pointed trees, soft dark green like velvet, shadowed, the wood pile which is flecked with sun and shadows of the overhanging creepers. Leaves floating up & down in the breeze…. Today old Mr. Norris came smiling and hobbling along the road, with straw wheaten ears, the 5 plait, the 3 plait, & his Staffordshire knot (2 plait) 5 plaits for horses' heads & tail trimmings. He began to tell me about a circus at High Wycombe.

29th July
To London…. talked to Mrs Miller & that woman who never wears a hat even to go to London, who always has immaculately waved greyish hair & a society smile…. In the train I talked to a young soldier, 19, from Halifax…. In London, I walked up Regent St, to Lizard which was closed. Then to P. Robinsons for lunch, & it was awful. The first really poor lunch I've had in London…. I went to Harris & looked at the exhibition of furniture, an Eliz chest for £58…. I was glad to get home to this lovely little house which awaited me eagerly.

10th August
I never remembered this was the anniversary of my wedding day…. After lunch… went to Legion Hall to the…. recital. I enjoyed both singing, playing, especially the Schubert songs.

24th August
Letters from BBC, Jean Sutcliffe saying how glad she is she can have the tales, somebody else is writing about the cheque for *Sam Pig*! Little Sam is getting up in life!… [*Cousin*] Sissy wrote a dear letter but so superlative it makes me squirm, so flattering, but she means it…. The Tintagel Hotel can take me on Oct 1 for a fortnight, 7 guineas a week, so I hope to go…. E Graham phoned, & asked to come out this weekend. It will be very nice to see her after all this time…. Cheque from Sugdens, £94. [*and for*] John £31.

29th August
Somehow I felt discomfort today, not quite happy with Eleanor [*Graham, who is staying with her*]. I felt that she disapproves of me – but why?… Let me now say, how pretty she is, 47 years old, her charming face, her pretty lips…. she seems to get more charming.

31st August

A lovely day. Up early [*to go to London*].... To the... gallery, where I saw an exhib of early water colours. A glorious Turner, of Devon, blues & greens £250. I wish I dare buy it!! ...Oh I forgot to Medici, when I saw a Sampler, most beautiful. I asked the price, expecting them to say £10, & it was only £3.10.0. So I bought it. Then I looked in many shops, & went to Kensington, where I got the plaques (4 pounds) & the statue [*a statue of a girl*], £7.15.0. I still feel uncomfortable about the big price. Such a weight.

1st September

I lay worrying about the statue, whether I should keep it. Today I saw the arm of the child is broken and mended, so I decided not to keep it, phoned to London.... Later came the registered parcel from Tunicliffe, with the lovely altered pictures.... I am filled with gratitude to him.... The postman, the dry-as-dust one, whom I've always disliked, stopped me as I took, paid & began to talk, saying how he had looked forward to Churchill's speech last night.... It was interesting to see the postman become human. I felt happier today, with the pictures of Tunicliffe, for I hated to criticise them. He took it so nicely.

3rd September

Italy invaded.... John, my darling, I pray that you are safe.... I felt rather sick, tired but I managed to carry on.

7th September

I wept a few tears in the night, of sadness & loneliness, and this morning there was a letter from John.... I went off to B walking to the station, carrying the statue of the girl, to be returned. When I got to London I went first to the shop, – the horrible woman, contemptuous & rude, refused to take it. She accused me of breaking it myself.... So I walked out.... When I got home I was quite cheered up. The statue is really a lovely thing [*and*] I must deal with its broken arm. I think the statue is glad to come back here & not live with that vile woman.

15th September

I have felt very anxious. The fighting is very desperate at Salerno.... This morning a letter from John, written on Aug 16.... He says, 'As I lay on my little camp bed on the deck last night one expat on the saxophone started up and suddenly everyone started singing, it was great fun. On the whole, I am not finding the life too bad, very boring at times, uncomfortable, unpleasant occasionally but there is a lot of humour in it, interesting sights, new experiences, so I know you won't worry about me.... It would be marvellous to be sitting in the front [*garden*] in a deck chair reading the paper and sipping a glass of Framlin's Double Elephant.'

22nd September

The last letter I opened this morning, – which I thought was a pamphlet.... It was Faber's royalties for £1,268... I was quite amazed [*and*] bewildered at getting so much even in the autumn, more than last Xmas....*Country Hoard* has put up the profits, – but 'what a lot of money'.... I feel staggered. I took up the hall rug & beat it to let off steam & I bought some cider to celebrate.

25th September
Missing. I cannot write the words. God help us both. Oh John, John, my darling John. Can you read this? Oh John, I love you. John, Missing on Sept 9. Please God let him be alive. Please God help us.

28th September
Last night I dreamed that John is with me, smiling & happy.... 'I'm missing,' said John. 'I have to go back to the Germans'.... George came & cut the hedge.... He is a nice man. I have been sorting out tales for the BBC, *SP* tales. I cannot read or write or sew or listen to the wireless, – but I manage to go on.

1st October
A letter from the War Office [*about John being missing*], no news.... but it was a nice human letter, referring to ' your son'. A very kind letter from George Uttley.... & one from Harry at last, very nice too.

5th October to 26th October [*Holiday*]
At King Arthur's Castle Hotel, Tintagel. I was too lost and bewildered and tired to write a diary, except a few notes. It was beautiful beyond words, and I lived in a strange dream. I said the prayer to St. Jude always. I prayed on the little stone seat on the cliff the first day of discovery, and on the last day too. I prayed in the hollow of the rock... which became a temple to me.... The green water, the slanting strata the rock, black, cream, heavy grey with green tufts. The caves, 3 of them under the Castle. White gulls, catching the sunlight and shining like light. Clouds above horizon, grey & silver white. Clouds now fantastic, a whole set alike, of dragons, or rearing horses, or turrets, – round the horizon.

10th October –
Sitting on a rock.... A little root with grey threads, & green rosette of leaves growing in a tiny pocket of soil. Cream coloured bags of seed pods, like empty purses lying in it. It is sea campion. The threads like spiders of grass, – stone crop... grey hairs of lichen. Witches had those on their chins I think. All along the cracks of the rock, between the leaf thin strata are grey-green lichen, some with grey pearls, some with inky spots. Sea pinks and faded brown heather and blue scabious. The sea below a milky green. Jackdaws flying across.... From a window [*sketch of bird*]. Pearly eye with black iris. A feather on its beak. Dove grey back, flank, the feathers ruffled like silk in the wind. It fell softly, padding like leaves falling as it walks up & down the hedge by the window. Rainbows. The loveliest I've ever seen. Rainbow, bright on the sea, the water deep and indigo-grey, white foam round the rocks, yellow gorse, & pale grey walls, red bracken & rushes, bright green grass. A marvel of beauty.

26th October
Catching the train. The Polish soldiers who got in, one sat by me, his nice face & white teeth. I said I was honoured to have a Polish soldier by me. He didn't understand. 'Russians are Treacherous,' said he. 'My country, it is not a lucky country.' My heart ached as he said this.

29th October
John is safe! Thank God. Tonight a phone message from Capt Jock-de-Gooseynd [*the War Office*] saying that John was a prisoner in [*a military hospital in*] Germany.

6th November
Glorious! I saw John's writing on a pc, when I went down at 9.a.m. for letters. I rushed upstairs with it 'My dearest Mimbles'. I felt so overcome, so joyful. All the world looked different. I noticed the colours of the rosy hawthorns with their hips. He said he was captured in Italy, near Salerno.... cycled to Old B. & got the lustre jug.

7th November
I was wakened at 2.0 by a noise – probably the wood falling, but I came down with the sword drawn – telling myself to be brave for John's sake.

12th November
Great joy. John's letter came this afternoon, the first, the sweetest letter. 'Be brave, my dear, and not too downcast, it might have been worse.'.... Sent 1 guinea to the Earl Haig Fund [*for soldiers and their families*] at B.

25th November
A lovely letter from Margaret Rutherford about *T in T* this morning. She says 'It is sheer inspiration the whole thing. It has delighted & entranced me from start to finish.'.... She ends, 'What an infinity of life is in its pages'. Those last words I like the best. They are what I tried to give. The infinity of life. £5.18.0 from Fabers, from Nelson's for sale of a few books! Very poor, but it was out print a long time.... In every town & every village in England there live those insufferable women. Mrs. Bakewell.... the set of 'superior people' whose voices & noses are the same.... I must forget them & never get mixed up in them.

28th November
I feel rather lost. Nothing to look forward to. For the end of the war seems such a remote thing. It must be quite a year if not more.

6th December
Sam Pig at the Circus lay in the letter slit, with a letter from [*Charles*] Stewart [*her editor at Faber*] saying the [*book*] binders had made the book too small, & my name had to be cut off the jacket. Did I mind? So I phoned but it was alright, the 10,000 copies are all bound, he

said. He asked me to go to a film, *Jane Eyre*, private view, on Dec 16 and stay the night....
Then I had tea & went to see *The Man in Grey*. I really didn't like it.... But it gave me idea
for beginning & end of [*the prospective film*] *T in Time*.

9th December
Invitation to *soirée* for Prisoner of War relations at the British Legion. I refused. I expect
it's one of those upper classes for lower classes dos, with Mrs Bakewell in it.

13th December
[*I*] talked to Mrs Squire who said her husband got Whisky 12 bottles a year! And I used to
be shocked at Castle Top having about 3! Little did I know the way of the world.

17th December
Slept well. [*after seeing Jane Eyre with Mr. Stewart*]. Heard cries Mummy, Mummy, & then
Daddy, Daddy, & footsteps to the little boy's room.... Later I called him to my room, played
a game & told a tale. Breakfast of wheat kernels, kedgeree & toast.... A noisy meal.... I asked
if he [*Mr. Stewart*] would arrange for me to meet Miss Noble, the film producer.... Then I
went & bought a fur jacket for 75 1/2 guineas. I feel a fearful spendthrift about it.... So this
is my birthday, waking up at the Stewarts, an honour indeed, going into London, having a
gay time.

25th December
But such sad news, poor old Emily [*Byers, née Uttley*] has suddenly died. Poor Emily, she
has had a sad life, always depressed, always wanting more. She was the best of them,
devoted to James.... I hoped to see her again.... Well, I have had a nice Christmas, cheered
by the other letters.... I went to church.... Then nice dinner of roast duck.... Singing carols,
writing to John.

26th December
I was so tired in bed last night I was alarmed at myself. I could hardly lift my arm.... My
heart aches for them [*the troops*] and those in England they love.

31st December
[*She was annoyed when my guests arrived for lunch at 11. 30!*] So I asked them to go for a little
walk... What a year!... [*My*] strength came from God and marvellous music in my distress....
my income soared beyond my greatest dream.... Oh God give us fortitude & kindness, &
bring my darling [*John*] safely home. Amen.

1944

1st January
I enjoyed entertaining Miss Collins to lunch…. This year I must do *TR* tales (half done), *Fairy Tales*, the novel, – all partly done. Perhaps *SP*. Can I? Yes. [*By early 1945, TR and the novel were done*]…. I can hardly look ahead for this year, because John's in prison.

10th January
I went to B…. I paid for the cupboards at Browns, and bought a tiny table at Woods…. Nice review of *Country Hoard*. I saw the film *Watch on the Rhine*…. I worried that John is captured by those terrible Nazis…. I wept in agony at photographs of Germans sinking our ships…. The waiting would get me down if I didn't keep doing things.

12th January
Worked at…*GR and the Weasels*. Finished it in the morning. Then typed the whole tale in duplicate, 13 full pages & finished late at night. I got so intrigued, I just went on. Parcel of books comes from Windsor…. [*some are*] historical books for John…. No wonder John is fascinated with history…. Very cross letter from R de la Mare about Nancy Innes [*the illustrator*]. Very nice letter from Mr. Stewart, – he's a dear.

15th January
Miss Collins gives me books from G K Chesterton…. I cooked a good lunch, I haven't been eating much recently…. George moves the fruit trees, making me think the lawn is turning into an orchard.

22nd January
[*People in Beaconsfield*] were talking of the air raid. There is a new invasion near Rome by Fifth Army. I am very excited by it.

26th January
The newspaper was stuck in the gate, so I must eat my solitary breakfast without my early morning pleasure…. [*She comments on*] MT's lovely paintings for the *GR* book, although I don't like the fox.

31st January
Still no letter [*from John*]. I mustn't get into that letter habit. It is nearly two months since John wrote. I am tired to the skeleton within me…. Goodbye Janiver, with your frowns.

1st February
Great joy, two letters from John. My heart is singing.

4th February
[*She goes to London*] to the BBC. There is snow, so I can't wear my fur coat. [*She meets*] Janet Quigley at BBC. I read the trial script well. I refused to read it on the Woman's Page…. Miss Quigley's pet project. What a brick to drop! I promised to send a criticism of the Woman's Page to Miss Quigley. Then to the Royal Academy…. to the Yugoslav Exhibition…. to Harrods.

15th February
I slept well and feel better…. A nice letter from Miss Jones at Faber, but who is she? George the gardener says that for a working class family they have read more books than any in England…. I had an inspiration over the [D-Day] invasion date, the Ides of March (12th or 15th March).

20th February
I went to church in my new fur jacket. [*There was*] a nice sermon [*and*] prayers for the PoWs. Seventy-nine bombers are missing after a raid on Leipzig. I saw lights over London…. The all-clear at 10.45. Bed!

26th February
I was delighted with a letter from John, who has found *Country Hoard* in the camp library. [*Mr. Charles*] Stewart [*of Faber*] offers me one hundred pounds advance for [*The Adventures of*] *Tim Rabbit*, very good. He is glad my fairies are the *dangerous* kind…. Collins offices have been bombed. Have books been destroyed? Mr. Stewart asked me if I could look for somewhere for Mrs. S and little Charlie to stay in B? Mr Dowsett [*estate agent*] says perhaps I should sell Downs House, as it is not worth more than five hundred pounds now. I liked his philosophy. Tea with MR [*Margaret Rutherford*].

28th February
Judith has turned up to ask if I would take in a French woman [*who has been*] bombed out…. She would want breakfast. I said [*she*] would have had to look after herself. I said there was no clothes press, – that anyone who came would have to be simple & not expect lots of hot water. You see these young women leave the hot water running & drain it off…. So she went away, – I felt rather sad to refuse… but these people never fit in.

1st March
A happy March, darling John boy. I expect you thought of me today. I'm thinking Invasion [*of France*] will start on 5th March…. I called to see MR & had a most interesting talk…. We talked of Shakespeare's genius…. I wonder if ever again in human history will such a genius arise? Perhaps in Russia.

4th March

To the Bedwells [*neighbours*] for tea, Mrs. B says that Kat[*Katherine*] Wigg has done many accurate drawings for the British Museum....I don't believe it. Another lie. A mediocre talent.

9th March

I called on MR. A hundred thousand miners are on strike. I feel in a fool's paradise, for the world is all wrong. Yet I love things, even a flower or a wisp of smoke, or a blade of grass makes me happy.

15th March

Planes roaring over at night. The men finished decorating. I give them each two shillings. It is a very nice white room. I was outraged at only thirty six pounds from Collins. Mr. Collins is too bad. I stand in a fish queue with Angela Thirkell, talking of John and her boys..... Florence de la Mare loves the *GR* books.

21st March

A letter from Gore Graham, he recounts again how John was captured. The terror seizes me again. The Brains Trust is very good, with no women, thank goodness. Women can't get over their self-consciousness. They think all the time they are different from men, and resent it.

22nd March

I am very glad that Harry has remarried, to Hilda. She 32, he 56. I hope they will look after Ronnie. I am worried that Fabers was one of the publishers [*recently*] bombed. My marmalade is delicious.

28th March

Joy! Two letters from John. The second letter begins 'My dearest Mimbles'.

31st March

A sailor tells me he has read *CC* six times. A cheque [*came from*] from the BBC for the *Grey Donkey*. I spring-cleaned John's room.... I am very anxious about the War, sometimes I think it's the end of civilisation.

3rd April

The BBC want two more tales for June. I cried over a mother who has lost her son in the War.... I feel guilty about living in luxury. I must do more. I worked at the pictures of *GR and the Weasels*.

10th April

[*She describes in great detail the death of Hamish.*] O, now he is dead. I stroked him a long

time, as he lay on the blanket before the fire. I was going to have him in my room tonight....
Never have I loved a dog as I love Hamish. I've said a prayer to God to be with him.... I feel
so lost & lonely & sad.

21st April
I am delighted Faber tell [*me*] the Australian Broadcasting Commission want to broadcast
SP tales. Hoorah! [*But Mr.*] Stewart only asked one guinea per thousand words, it ought to
have been more.

17th May
No [*trip to*] London, [*so*] I stayed in bed in clean linen sheets. I feel unhappy when I
remember the millions of people who would like to be as comfortable and safe as I am. I
have nearly finished the novel [*When All is Done*], fifteen chapters done, five or six more.

19th May
A frost again.... Tonight I have been out with cloths & papers.... covering up the plants.
Sad news on wireless. 47 airmen officers tried to escape from Stalag Luft III & were shot in
April.... I think of their parents, waiting for letters & then getting this awful news. It makes
me feel sick.... I found a dead blackbird... so I buried it, in a grave lined with bush leaves....
such a lovely bird.

25th May
Big guns practicing.... I dreamt that John was stunned. To hold him in my arms was
bliss.... I was thrilled with [*the*] old oak cupboard, and polished it.

6th June
The day of [*the D-Day*] invasion. I am exhilarated and aghast. Many planes flying across.
The woman I buy Defence Bonds from is cold and hard.

19th June
I detest [*Nancy*] Innes pictures from Faber, an awful Hare.... I sent off seven tales of *TR*
for the BBC, and the pictures to Faber. I wrote a cross letter to the BBC, saying that they
are trying to influence children so that they think no generation was any good till they
adorned the world with their presence.... is it true that this year of grace, 1944, is the height
of civilisation? Tractors on the ploughland & tanks on the battlefield? It is a Nazi theory
that only this generation is any good and all else must be scrapped.... Look at us, gods with
electric light and neon light and water laid on, all invented by those people who lived in
candlelit days.

22nd June
A noisy night [*with air raids*] so I got under the piano!.... I phoned to Eleanor and invited
her. She came by the 3 [*pm*] train, in her blue coat and hair net (*which I dislike*) on her hair.

I am in my hairnet.... Cheques [*arrive*] from the BBC and from Child Education. EG said that Stewart has refused permission for Puffin to reprint [*Alison's*] books. I am secretly glad.

23rd June

Lovely letters.... I was shocked at being invited to lecture for only two guineas and expenses, my goodness! A letter from [*Charles*] Stewart saying he has refused to let *SP* go to Penguins, because it would spoil their sales. I agree.

26th June

It is horrid that Faber's have been bombed in Russell Square.... I call a doctor to examine my [*painful*] knee. MR is going to recommend *T in T* to Elstree [*Studios*].

2nd July

For some reason I feel happy. Was it the sleep and the dream, when I forgot the war? I pick some nice delicious fruit from my own garden... [*She receives*] a prodigious income tax demand of two thousand five hundred pounds. I am reading Russian books, and getting very pro-Russian.

12th July

The scent of limes goes to my heart.... A letter from George Uttley saying Alfred dead and Jamie is missing. He says that Emily and Alfred had had no pleasure out of their retirement. I can't understand it.

16th July

I was so tired and depressed that I stay in bed till nearly one o'clock. [*Then*] I lay in the garden reading Spencer's *Faerie Queen*.

17th July

I was staggered by letter [*from Robert Hale, publishers*] asking [*her*] to write a book on Buckinghamshire. I would enjoy doing it. But the wretched [*possibility of*] billetting is worrying me.

22nd July

The Council say my [*billeted*] girl must stay.... I wrote a letter of criticism to the BBC.... Faber don't want me to do a book for Robert Hale [*Buckinghamshire*], I should spend longer on their books.

31st July

[*Mr.*] Stewart sends me *Songs for Christmas*. I sat down at once and played them. I am waiting for the girl to go out.... I tell the police that the silver teapot [*is*] missing.... Actually it was behind a cushion!

20th August
I typed my play [*Little Grey Rabbit to the Rescue*]. I get so thrilled, so caught in poetry and books, if only I had somebody to look after me, I could do so much.

23rd August
Paris is taken, how wonderful. I called out the news to two French boys. I told Mr. Garvin [*G. L. Garvin, the writer and journalist*] that John is reading his life of GK Chesterton, he seemed very pleased. Rumania makes peace with Russia.

6th September
I have got the musical box in working order again, a great triumph, for I have often tried. I sat there with brush & bit of silk & removed oil for about 2 hours trying to get the spindle to work. Then I screwed & unscrewed over the spindle, [*slowly*], very hesitatingly it began to turn. How charming it is! Merrily going now. A queer day again, glorious sun. I cycled to B for nothing much. Met Mrs. Wig & invited her for tea…. I am glad I've made friends again, but I must go slow…. The [*publication of*] *The Spice Woman's Basket* [*a book of fairy tales*] is postponed to Sept 15…. Fighting for Calais & Boulogne now. I'm all anxious & restless, cannot work or [*do*] anything for this excitement that fills my heart.

16th September
Mrs Sibbring [*her newly appointed typist*] was typing all morning. It shows how much I do myself if I can keep the typist going all week. I took back a 45/- hat which I had out twice & refused, although I like it.

17th September
The invasion of Holland this afternoon. Planes roaring over all morning & in such droves it was deafening, a 21 after 21 [*squadrons*], successions of them. At ¼ to 4 the programmes interrupted with the big exciting news, & one thought of those men, their supreme test, dropped by parachute among enemies. How brave they are, how marvellous. I've been praying for them, thinking of them. Now it is dark & I wonder how they feel, those separated from companions in a strange country…. [*She is delighted with an article by*] A L Rowse criticising Shaw's book…. That awful old man is like a god in this country, & his tongue is so sharp & acid…. Rowse is honest. [*But*] I think he is conceited about his own powers…. On the wireless a letter written by a Russian soldier to an Allied soldier…. it was simple, & good…. At the end of the last war I prophesied that in the next war, Germany would be on our side. Russia the enemy.

18th September
Mrs. Sibbring suggests [*pay of*] three shillings an hour…. She really is a find…. A great spider ran across the floor. Oh dear, like a mouse.

21st September
Off at early light to Tintagel…. I am annoyed that the taxi man overcharges me… Back to same hotel and same bedroom.

28th September
John Edward [*son of a friend*] has been killed. I wrote a comforting letter…. A glorious letter from John…. Faber royalties drop by a thousand pounds, no paper, I suppose. I bought a ring, my last extravagance for many months. I cooked a goose for dinner.

12th October
An income tax demand, a thousand pounds, and I have got nothing to pay it with. John O'London's [*Weekly*] have a query about names [*of bird etc.*] in my books – I am blessed if I know myself!

13th October
Letter from Collins, very nice, asking for a new tale, which I *won't* do & sending a fine advert, … a front page of the *Bookseller* of the *GR* books…. But putting Margaret Tempest's name in front of mine…. I really ought to do something for my prestige.

19th October
A great thrill when Fabers send a cheque for two hundred and seventy one pounds for *Spice Woman's* accrued royalties. Now I need not sell out to pay my income tax. I slept well.

1st November
The Book Circle say my books are to be shown in USA…. They invite me to the authors' day of the show in London. I am glad, I thought I wouldn't be noticed.

3rd November
MT sends pictures for the book [*Little Grey Rabbit and the*] *Weasels*. I want tinier weasels…. A lovely review of *CC* from the *Irish Press*, the reviewer says, 'How has this jewel of a book escaped fame for so long? Who was Alison Uttley?' I felt pleased.

7th November
Faber will publish my play if I will wait for a year…. a forty pounds advance…. LM writes of the treachery of Russia over Poland, – quite true.

8th November
Last night a dream, poignant & beautiful…. I saw my mother in bed with John in her arms, & both were smiling. John… wore his look of happiness, *security*, as if to say, 'She's looking after me.'

15th November

The first letter from John for six weeks. They are on only half rations.... I was shocked by billetting people and blankets, they are like the Nazis in occupied countries.

25th November

I was amazed, but in a way pleased, that I should be liable for Super Tax. I got six copies of *Country Hoard*, the fourth impression. I discussed tax with bank manager in B.

1st December

I said good morning to December, my month. Off to London.... A very dull lunch at the Stewarts.... I was staggered to see my *Mrs Mimbles* as a book at Medici. I have heard nothing of it. I took the [*pirate*] publishers name.

17th December

[*Her 60th birthday*] It is incredible... I can feel 10 years old easily, but not 60. It has been so grand & exciting, all these years. I hope I will have lots more left, to write books, to play with grandchildren, and to enjoy the sun & moon & earth.... I opened GL's parcel in bed, & found a 10/6 book token. Dear Gwladys, she is a marvel of a friend, my friend since I was 18, just at college.... Listening to Dvorak's *4th Symphony*, lovely music, reading a little & sewing.... Oh John, I do pray you are safe. The Germans have pushed us back into Belgium today. When will it all end?... I've said Happy Returns to the rooms & the air.... & garden.

21st December

A card from Harry – best wishes, no love! He behaves as if I were the merest stranger.... All his life Harry has been cold and calculating with me, and I keep getting hurt against his hardness. A lovely parcel from Ronnie, very different from his father. *Housewife* [*magazine*] wants the serial rights of my next book. I will wait until after Christmas for a decision.... Awful news about the German counter-offensive [*the Ardennes offensive*].

24th December

Christmas Eve. A lovely frosty morning.... I hurried round, got ready for church.... I thought it would be like [*Christmas*].... Not at all. Dull hymns, which I didn't know, a dull psalm.... dull lesson .... & a dull sermon.... Why do they do it?... I won't go except for special days, I can't get any consolation or help.

~ *1945* ~

1st January

I said a little prayer, and as it is New Year's Day, I went through that prayer that Mother always said at the New Year. I remember so well when she and Father went into the drawing room to be quiet....

A lovely frosty day. I did the housework & carried coal & wood, and filled oil stoves. It took most of the morning. Then I suddenly decided to snatch a walk, & out I went in big boots, coat.... under the wires, up [*the*] hill. Remembered the grand old oak tree there, magnificent, & the masses of berried ivy. I got some... ivy boughs. I thought how Hamish used to go up there with me. I remember the last time, how he, very tired, got up [*the*] hill, bless the darling dog. The ice, the blackthorn closely clustered.... really black.... Lunch on chicken soufflé & then plum pudding & a big wash up. I rested a short time & got up & saw some lovely birds, red heads, pink fronts, blue round neck, & black under bill like a tit & the bills very pale creamy yellow. I thought they were redpolls, but I feel sure now they were Hawfinches from all their lovely colour and the blue necks. They were eating & separate on the lawn. Dorothy Collins came to tea... [*she mentioned*] that at GK C[*Chesterton's*] funeral the *servants* were actually in the front seats. 'GKC would have wished it'.... This year I must finish the new *Country Hoard* Tale & also the *Fairy Tales*. Also I must do as much as possible to the book on Bucks, visiting places near.

3rd January

Bliss. Two letters from John this morning.... 'Reading Toynbee's History has helped me to think things out on the truths of simple Christianity seem fundamental'. How I thank God for John, that adorable babyhood, the little boy I took for walks. I talked to MR about *Alice in Wonderland*. Then Lulu Lanigan tells me her daughter was married. She never mentioned it. Well, well ! Neighbours!!

4th January

[*I became*] very anxious about Red Cross information about the hardships of prisoners of war in Germany. But a delicious lunch with Margaret R....I packed up the play and sent it to [*the actor*] Robert Donat.... Oh John, my darling, my darling child. Can I get thought messages through to you? I shall try tonight.

12th January

To London. I enjoyed it tremendously. I *do* love going to London. I always feel excited & happy as I walk there.... Then, Ah then to the Sydney Lee Exhibition. Such woodcuts & prints. Glorious....Then on to the Dutch Exhib. Well, it caught my heart.... .the Breughel sold for 350 guineas, lovely. No words for it. Then the ice skating scene…. a girl & I stood there entranced for a long time. My goodness. Pictures do get me.

16th January
'Life is not a joy-ride, it is a try-out.' The Brains Trust, Barbara Ward was brilliant: life is an adventure. Listening to one the best Brains Trusts…. [*Professor*] Joad at his worst and most pessimistic.

18th January
[*Mr*] Stewart says *Tim R* will come out on Feb 17th. Debate today on Greece. The attacks on Churchill make me sick. That [*Anuerin*] Bevan man, oh dear, he is vile.

23rd January
Letters from CWS saying the lawsuit [*over pirate publishing*] is settled, [*and I*] am to have £62.15s.0. I wrote music for the *Hedgehog* play for the BBC. I find it difficult to write this diary, my heart is so sick and full of anxiety.

24th January
Also letter from M Tempest with suggestions for pictures for play (last woman, she wants to use old pictures!) So I've written a long letter with suggestions, and also said that we ought to ask for decent royalties now. We are being defrauded by Collins.

30th January
The Russians are 95 miles from Berlin… I wonder what is happening to our men out there? Thousands of them, in the snow. Oh God, take care of them and protect them!

1st February
Letter from *Good Housekeeping* says that the *Attics* [*article*] is delightful…. Then to Mr. Dowsett [*her accountant*] whom I asked if he would go through royalties, as I must tackle Collins.

14th February
6 guineas – for the share of *C Hoard* story very little…. I do the house…. To lunch at Puffin Books…. Bill and Jane Wig come. I give them ice cream. They bring me a Valentine, a bouquet or purple and red anemones, snowdrops, jasmine, with a lace cut paper frill, below that a crimson heart, most lovely!.

20th February
A lovely letter [*came*] from Walter de la Mare. How I wish words could tell you my admiration for John's endurance…. Mrs. Allen [*her cleaner*] comes at last…. Oh dear, Nuremberg – bombed – very near to John's camp. I get so frightened.

23rd February
Proofs of *Sam Pig* came. I worked all day at them, and posted them tonight, late…. Mrs. Allen was vacuuming…. My broadcast at 11.00 on *Hedgehog*. Very good. They sang my own music! The first I have written music for BBC.

8th March
[*Allied forces are*] across the Rhine, tonight's news…. Nice letter from [*Mr.*] Stewart… saying he & Agnes [*Stewart*] think of me…. Also a delightful letter from the Marine saying he reads Jane Austen, Nancy Mitford, Adrian Bell & me, in the Pacific.

10th March
1st butterfly [*of the year*], a Brimstone. Song of a dove…. Then I thought of the evil done by HG Wells, all his life. That kind of man is always a C[*Contientious*] O[*Objector*], so they never get killed in battle & more & more of them are left to poison the country's life.

14th March
First galley proofs of *When All is Done* came! What a task lies before me! I am glad I hurried on with *Country Tales*. M. Tempest sent the pictures for the book, the play. I am so bound by all Collins does. I don't care about it at all.

22nd March
Margaret Rutherford told me tonight she is going to be married on Sunday to Stringer [*Davies*] (Lt!!)…. Bless her heart! I am so glad. She is such a darling. So that is why Stringer came here for his leave. And they have but 3 days honeymoon for he returns to France on Weds. What a romance for her in her middle life. A busy day, glorious sun but early mists. I worked in bed with typewriter & went though half the book. Then at 12.15 got up, got lunch and did the second half, and posted it to Stewart…. [*Went to*] a very good interesting film. Leslie Howard quite delightful. I enjoyed it tremendously & his words were so amusing, so witty. On the way home I met Mr Wood & Robin who had been here with a beautiful green glass paperweight and the tray. I think I must give the paper weight to MR. She loves green & it is a beauty. We are nearly all up to the Rhine. Thousands & thousands of prisoners taken.

29th March
We are rushing on in Germany. Out to tea at the Wigs, the first time for three or four years. It was really charming, a nice welcome. Her house lovely and warm, her children smiling, an excellent tea. Mrs Wig talking about the house she was getting in Cambridge – just the same. In fact even her aggravating talk was the same. Home, had supper. Then worked with KS, working hard till nearly 11.00. We laughed till we cried over our dates and the confusion.

1st April
A windy wet day, – but the loveliness of spring & the feeling of Easter and immortality in

the air. Blossom on plum trees, no leaves, only the white flowers along the branches – I kissed them today. Some flowers on the wild cherry in the garden... & many flowers on the cherries hanging over the hedges. Beech trees bare, but *all ready*! A mist of green in the wood, for the hornbeam is covered with tiny leaves and the wet trees are happy, rose leaves all green, a blackbird calling.... The daffodils most lovely, so beautiful I can't write about them, all across the lawn, facing this way. Apple trees with leaves unfolding and flower buds moving. In the flower bed the maroon.... & blue primroses and the anemone, the Pasque Flower, with its delicate mauve cup and furry leaf, the exciting Auruila, which catches my heart. The house too, lovely with flowers and ornaments, & colour. To church this morning, to St Michaels, a beautiful service. People walked out halfway through – rather noisily. Were they protesting? I went to [*Holy Communion*] & prayed for John at the altar. In the corner a garden of flowers for the Garden of Gethesemane, 3 crosses in one place, a shrine of white violets with paths leading to it, through bowls of flowers, a lovely thing. A butterfly flying near, beating at window, so I captured it and carried it out, but it escaped as I spoke to Father Nicholson.

14th April
To B, Old B, when I sadly fell in my resolves by buying a tortoise shell teacaddy for £8 at Mrs. Woods! [*shop*]. A lovely thing, but I ought not to get it. I'm going off the rails [*with*] money, – can't buy a cake or food, so off I go! But I think, a blouse is £7, so why not get this beautiful thing which will keep for ever, which will always bring its money back? I saw a dark green box with lilies of the valley painted on the lid, just like one of our boxes when we were little. Then to B for a bit of slab cake, & home. A lovely day, my knee aching badly. KS called & I gave her a copy of *Candlelight Tales* for her kindness in working at those proofs. M. Rutherford came to tea & we talked of her dresses in *Perchance to Dream*. I talked of James, his sweetness, goodness, & of John.

15th April
To church, just in time, & on the way I heard my first cuckoo. Great happiness to hear it.... Jane Scott came, her first visit for ages, & sweet she looked. I thought she was improved, her face thin & beautiful. She is 54 she told me, slim and lovely – in her grey dress and her hair slightly grey & bluish black. She thought it was beautiful hair & indeed it was. We sat out in the sunshine & talked. She told me how the people in her next flat, a 'child psychologist' ousted her to make room for a friend.... by doing all kinds of despicable things, wireless always on with open doors, kitchen filthy, using her things.... We talked of the war, the awful future of Europe, Roosevelt. David Payne [*sic*] phoned 'I left a foot in Normandy,' said he calmly. Poor boy! But he has an artificial limb now. He asked after John. Picked flowers for Jane, & rhubarb. She told me the tale of the Sitwell's flat. Edith with silver nails. Jane went into the flat & was covered with fleas, 26 fell off into the bath. Later a workman was attacked by them, & he complained, & the flat was fumigated. Tonight [*on the radio*] Edward Morrow told of a concentration camp, so terrible that I cannot write it down. Last night I thought I was tortured by the Gestapo.

20th April

How can I write it? Charles Stewart is dead, killed in a tube accident on Weds morning. G[*Geoffrey*] Faber wrote to tell me. I feel most desolate, most unhappy & distressed. I had the deepest affection & esteem for him. I really loved him, he was such a happy good nice man. I always wrote *for* him, imagining his pleasure in what I had done.

23rd April

St George's day, but I felt depressed, unhappy about Stewart and anxious about John.... I got a cheque for £286 from Collins, but I don't care a button for it. Reading *I Married a Russian* getting all worked up, infuriated. My goodness, to think she is a modern product – her poor parents. She is over 40, about 46, so she ought to be doing something original and good, but she talks about abortion quite commonly.

27th April

The Allies linked up around Berlin.... good old Churchill's voice which always gives me confidence.

2nd May

At 11.00p.m. a phone call from John Brooke-Taylor, saying he had seen John a fortnight ago, he was well. He had been machine-gunned, but was alright. They were in the Bavarian Alps.

8th May

Victory Day. After a wild night of rain and lightning and thunder as if Hitler [*was*] having a last fling at us. I put up the flags, in line of 15 flags across the house and 2 larger flags at corners and a big flag dipping from the bathroom window. Young John Wigg helped me – I wasn't pleased to see him, but I had him help [*me*], – his affected, superciliousness depresses me. When we had finished I said, 'Doesn't it look nice?' 'Well – er yes – er' he replied hestitatingly!! Churchill. 3 o'clock striking. Millions listening. Oh my darling, darling John! Unconditional surrender of all German air, sea, land forces'. Ratified today at *Berlin* 1 min after midnight tonight ceasefire. Ceasefire today . Our dear Channel Islands to be free today. The German war is at an end. Advance Britannia. Long live the cause of freedom. God save the King. I went to St Michael's to pray for a few minutes. Fr Nicholson was praying then. Afterwards he spoke to me, invited me to tea on Thursday. I went to the Parish Church and service there but the usual dull service. Thanksgiving, joyfulness. Church at night, a moving service of dedication.

10th May

Thus John came home. Oh, how wonderful it is! [*On the*] phone at 12. 0 saying 'Is that you mother? John speaking'. He came & I flew to the gate & saw him alight from a lorry with a smiling driver, & then I was in his arms. Brown, thin, very happy, half in a dream of surprise. I made a feast, we had port wine and coffee and chocolate. How we talked as we washed up & set the table or walked about the house. I can't write about it it is so wonderful. He told me how they had been machine gunned and that the gunning had broken the nerve of some of his men, especially those who had been a long time in the camps. 16 killed & about 40 injured. Also the plane of POWs that went down in the Channel, all drowned. Such disasters, bringing grief.... they have suffered. I went to H.C. today, Ascension Day & prayed for John. Fr Nicholson said he would say a special prayer of thanksgiving tomorrow morning.

22nd May
John [*goes*] to Eton to see Mr. Elliott.... John came back to say he had been given the post of form master at Eton, to teach History, or Classics and English.

30th July
I feel we have betrayed the lion-hearted Churchill. [*Labour has won the General Election*]. It is awful to think Attlee and Bevin are at Potsdam instead of Churchill and Eden. Railway workers striking in order to compel the government to nationalise the railways. And then, where will they be? Still striking?

1st August
To see John.... Tomorrow the operation. Dear God, take care of him... & make him quite well again.

12th September
John's 31st Birthday.... Oh darling John, what a happy day for me that you were born, in 1914.

19th September
I felt truly depressed, but I have tried to help John.... John told me some of his difficulties & I suggested ways and means for his teaching of English, no books! 'The best school in England & no books,' groaned John.

22nd September
Letter from Margate Librarian, urging me to give lecture, offering hospitality and a fee of 10 gns. It ended, 'Please come'. So I think I will.... John says he couldn't do his work, he has no memory, he felt ill.... I was terribly upset.... A ton of coal came today!!

29th September
An exciting day, for I called by chance, the merest chance, at the garage to ask if they could hold out hope of a car, – and Mr Timpson said one had come in. I went to see it and liked it. Others coming to see it, he said, so I suddenly decided to buy it. A Morris Twelve.... costing £225. John drove it home.

18th October
Another panic [*at the Corner House Hotel in Amersham*], but not so bad. I felt so afraid of fire.

19th October
Wretched breakfast [*at the hotel*], and then out on a lovely sunny day to Weston Turville.... bought a map of Bucks, 1665, for 50/- [*for her history of Buckinghamshire*]. The great news that *When All is Done* is out. [*There was*] a request for *GR*'s Washing Day in Dutch.

4th November
I sent for the doctor. John so strained.... John told me he dreaded each day.... he has no confidence left. I cannot write about it. I was so troubled

10th November
Barbara Healey, Andrew and Lady Wrigley come to tea. The little boy running about all the time, wouldn't sit down, crawling under the table. No wonder people don't want these badly brought up children. The mothers never stop the children.... At night John and I reading proofs, doing [*cross*]word.

24th November
To B for food. [*There were*] the usual insults at the butchers. I felt infuriated. I get quite sick at the fuss each week..... John came.... looking pale, saying that it had been even worse than ever at Eton.... A robin sang to me. It caught my eye and sang.

25th November
John went to the Psychoanalyst.... He says John is suffering from acute nervous strain. John correcting papers for VI Form, I helping him. I noticed one boy was Bowes-Lyon, nephew of the Queen. (His paper was poor!)

2nd December
Here is only 2nd day of my month & I am feeling awfully depressed. Worry and anxiety about John, the psychotherapist visits, the silences, the odd feelings. Worry about *When All is Done*. The news rotten, the depression we all feel through this government's stranglehold on industry.... I went down & down in my depression, – queer, wrong of me.

4th December
Tonight I spoke to Fr Nicholson about John, he will see him tomorrow. He too doesn't like these psychologists. 'Is he a Christian?' he asked.

5th December
Awake for a long time, weeping, actually tears. A charming appreciation from Nan Duncan, saying she likes *When All is Done*, the best of my books.... This cheered me very much. *Punch* too was extremely good this week. Then off by bus to Windsor.

16th December

A talk on Rutherford. Rutherford like Faraday is [*a*] genius. He inspired others.... I went to St Michael's this morning. It wasn't very inspiring, but Fr Nicholson is never dull. I wasn't very High Church today, I fear. I thought, 'Priests should go the people more – this is all too grand, with purple silk.'

24th December

Christmas Eve. A lovely day.... In the afternoon... John put up holly while I did the little tree & strung up gold & red balls.... It looked most beautiful.... Tea with one of the iced cakes. Then we sang carols, all the old ones we love, for hours.... I loved today.... Oh, my broadcast of *A Fairy Ship* too, to add to the joy.

29th December

In the afternoon I hurried off at 2.15 to see *A Tree Grows in Brooklyn*, beautiful and moving, very good.... I loved it. It is a film to remember, and in England, we not do this because we are too sophisticated.

31st December

The room is beautiful, this last day of 1945.... mistletoe hanging from the beam, & the red cyclamen under it, the red apples & holly & silver balls over the William & Mary chest.... Oh God thank you for all these blessings, the war over, the Germans defeated, John home.... Let us never forget, but let us go on travelling to freedom & to love of God.... Goodnight dear room. Goodbye dear 1945.

❧ *1946* ❧

1st January

Said welcome at the door to the quiet world.... Then there was a silence and I prayed for John, for me, for England, for the world and I thought of the new year fluttering – wings above us.... Twelve copies of *Grey Rabbit to the Rescue* arrived. Stringer Davis [*Margaret Rutherford's husband*] phoned up with good wishes.

2nd January

Suddenly discovered a review of *C Child* in *Punch*, very good for Tunnicliffe, not so good for me... A charming letter from Ethel Makins [*a friend*], telling me of the beauties of Somerset. She can't write short letters, she must see a Psycho-whats-its-name about it.... Now my plans. To write the *Bucks* book, – I have to do this! To do the *Fairy Tale* book, and the 3rd *Country Hoard*, and to plan out and do a tale or so of a new *Sam Pig*.

3rd January

The wood with lovely blue mist through the trees, the colour of violets, most striking. A tom-tit, the queen of tits, an exquisite fern. Sprays of ivy hanging like a fountain from an oak stump. An old man with a spade on his shoulder like Time himself, walking with wide slow steps down road near Penn. Catkins on the hazels in a layered hedge.

6th January

In bed, in blue dressing gown, hole in elbow, with white scarf-shawl over my shoulders, my grey hair tumbled, as I sit here, a sore throat, but not so bad.... John has been working in the next room at the Empire for next term [*at Eton*].... I can hear him bumping below.... Night.... feeling rather wretched, John very silent.... A pain in my head, still 100°.... John's monosyllables are so disconcerting. He seems dumb, poor boy.

8th January

Really I'm worried about John. The doctor came, peeped in at me, said I must stay 'put' till temp goes, & then saw John, who told him he still felt he wasn't right for a teacher, a square peg in a round hole. But what job could he fill? A delightful letter from H Glossop, a fighting letter infuriated with the review in *Punch* for saying my book is not as good as Tunicliffe's work is.... A very jolly letter.... But I begin to feel I can't write.... in fact I prepare for the sneers and snubs from the Bloomsbury people.... A few notes on Christmas ingratitude! My darlings, my dear friends wrote and were so happy, but GGU never bothers to acknowledge my book as usual, so why do I bother?.... Harry sent no ack[*acknowledgement*] of my cheque to Ronnie.... I must cut out the Uttleys in future, they are jealous as always, cold as always, unkind as they have been for 40 years.... no, poor GGU lost his mother in law at Christmas so no wonder he didn't write.

9th January
Temp down...feeling much better..... John rushed off to the dentist, the first time for ten years..... [*He*] cooked a good lunch of mince and pots & carrots, with raspberries to follow. Then he hurried off to work, and my depression came on.... I felt miserable, deserted, unable to work, doing nothing worthwhile, forgotten, sneered at by critics, ignored by people..... a silly ass really, but it was the flu for in good health I wouldn't have felt this weakness.

17th January
Off we went in the morning.... To Speen first – but on Penn Hill a bird struck the car like a stone, it must have been killed.... I felt very sad, Later on we saw a magpie, so we said, 'Good Morning, Sir!'

24th January
Awful night last night.... pain and pangs – but I managed to pull through!.... Mrs Nicholson and Fr N. coming. Fr N was rather odd, restless, shuffling in his chair, going to the book cases.... He said he was overworked – I think he is miserable because his congregation are falling off?.... He is too self important, too, alas.... He actually went to the lavatory before he left! At afternoon tea! Perhaps he is falling in love.

3rd February
John came home late last night, excited, tired after an evening with [*his friend*] Sam Cope, who has come from Burma after incredible adventures.... John rushed off for medicine – car wouldn't go, no petrol.... In the meantime I rose from my bed, dished up vegetables, finished meat, brought a tin of soup & some raspberries upstairs in pans to heat them – & set trays, so when John returned, wet through & anxious for his precious dinner, & all was ready. John said he had quite enjoyed giving the English lessons, which delighted me.

9th February
I lay in bed longing to stay there. I longed to stay in bed, tired and throat not so good. Last night was awful, – such wild screaming winds and a continuous roar like thunder.... Floods everywhere.... Mr. Faber has sent back John's book, alas, but I expected it. [*She had encouraged him to write a book as useful therapy.*] Not original & big enough I think, bless the child.... Tonight a warning about coal supplies, very bad. Everything is bad. This government cannot manage, all they can think about is to nationalise and restrict & stop things from moving.... If you earn money, you pay extra tax.

12th February
Charming letters from E [*Graham*] Wilson, who tells me how she has loved *When All is Done* [*saying*],.'You have a lovely gift of words and such a wonderful power of observation and memory'.

17th February

Slept well, so awoke refreshed. I got up late, reading all the awful news in *Sunday Times*, most depressing on every page, strikes, depressions. I really feel that now England is on the down grade, lost. They say that 600 millions a year [*is*] needed for Social Services. Who will pay for it? I wrote 3 letters, to Miss Granside, Miss King (about dedication of *Country Things*) and to *Farmer's Weekly*, refreshing work.... Finished the *Bear* tale, sent it off.

18th February

No letters, except one from [*her nephew*] Martin Byers, a charming one, telling me how glad he is to have my book, saying the shops in Mombasa full of *Grey Rabbit* books.... Dreamed of seeing a dirty pool.... my goodness – my blood ran cold.

22nd February

Lovely letter from Walter de la Mare saying how pleased he is to have *Country Things* dedicated to him. A dull cold day, but I decided to go off with KS and make a start with factories.... So went off to High Wycombe after filling up with 3 gals petrol at 5/9.... At Nichols and James, we saw Mr James who talked to us in his room, spoke of his craftsmen, showed us chairs.

3rd March

Cooking happily while John sat in here reading.... Then he poured it out, his feelings of inferiority at Eton. 'I hate Eton,' said he.... 'Do you remember when you were an Apache at Cambridge?' I asked. 'I cared nothing for anyone. I felt free. Now I am no longer free', said he.

4th March

Lying awake for hours worrying about John.... I can't understand why [*he*] is so unhappy. After the war and all the horrors, surely the horrors of facing some snobby young Etonians shouldn't matter! Lovely letters to cheer me.... one from the BBC accepting the *Flower Quiz*. MR phoned, telling me about the big operation from which she is recovering.

14th March

Cheque for £440 from Collins! I decided to get up at last. Then I made myself go to B.... just to see Dr Wood's barometers which I feared I had missed.... all but 1 bought by a dealer.... Then I looked round saw the blue tea-set.... I would like to buy Chippendale chairs for 200 or so.... Tonight a letter from Mrs. Tout of Man[*Manchester*] Univ[*University*], saying they are proud of me. Staggering.... A bit late though!

21st March

Cheque for £1,153 from Faber. Marvellous. Mostly for *When All is Done*.

24th March

To Hambledon, by Marlow, everywhere glorious although no sun. I got out at Hambledon

& went down an alley, which opened onto an amazing scene, a great wild stretch of water, reminding me of George Eliot's *Mill on the Floss.*

1st April
Went off to vote in [*the County*] Council elections in Mrs. Holloway's car as I couldn't walk. My bones hurting. We had a talk about socialism & bathrooms & cottages.

16th April
Glorious country, & we rejoiced as we escaped and rushed off.... Then to Tintagel, & the sea. Glorious! Glorious!

7th May
Mr. Coleman called to ask me to join the Conservative Party Organisation, which I did. He said it augured well as Westfield Road had nearly all joined. I [*replied that*] if he had said a poor quarter had joined that it would have been [*better*].

12th May
I was so happy, for I realised he [*John*] is getting his confidence – again.... After a time he got in some good bowling. I fielded for him & enjoyed it very much. I adore cricket, it never bores me.

16th May
A dull gloomy threatening day. A woman came from *Treasures*, I don't like a woman who comes [*about a cleaning job*] rather a go-getting [*person*] & when she left she said 'Bye-bye' in a familiar way! So I am not having her. She talked of getting the sack because she had hurt her fingernail at her last place. I felt rather worried, thinking she was coming, but rejoicing I was free from her.... Worried about my book, bothered over copyright of *Hans Andersen*, thinking I must do income tax & expenses and crowds of things all hanging over me!.... Oh, slow, silly billy. The blackbird is on her nest, lilac and whinberries are out, the room is lovely, the war is over. & darling John is here. So thank you, God.

29th May
Managed to get off to London.... better after my disaster. First to Faber, to see [*her new editor*] Mr [*Peter*] du Sautoy, a nice young man, about the Hans Andersen play, copyright, in [*Mr.*] Stewart's room, I hated going in. Then to see Miss King up on top floor – and I saw the new book, advance copies of *Country Things*.... it is coming out on 15th June. Lunch with Joan Dobell at Fortnums, – it was 23/-.

4th June
The Eton Day, to which I had been looking forward so much, & it was a deep disappointment.... I couldn't hold out against [*John's*] depression [*and*] pessimism.... No laughter or amusement. Even when we got in the enclosure next to the Princesses.... in

boats.... the glorious sight of all the boys arm in arm singing *The Eton Boat Song*, carrying the coxes across the meadow. In the car, caught in a traffic jam, John said, 'This *is* the end of a Perfect Day', his face white & strained.

8th June – Victory Day
Listening to a wonderful broadcast [*Victory over Japan*], so clear I thought I was there.... For lunch we had American soup (*from parcel*). Chops (from Eton), cabbage (from garden), cream, cocktail, coffee and chocolate, our Victory lunch.

29th June
To B and Old B, for pie and fish in queue, so most of morning taken up.... John came at 3.0 & we talked, he said he had been to Leeds to see the HM of Leeds Grammar School. I was deeply disappointed because I felt that he wouldn't be happy in a great school [*with*] very hard cramming, no culture, he would loathe it. To give up Eton for that seems extraordinary. Lovely old school, lots of friends, beauty and happiness for Leeds!!

30th June
My father's birthday, – and what a marvellous day we had. Off at 11.30 to Claydon House.... the long drive with 2 gates.... The house, Ralph Claydon coming to meet us, his nice sister Mary, Edmund his brother... 8 of them in all, he said.

7th July
I wept in bed last night. I could not sleep for the misery. What is it? So many joys and blessings, delights, sunshine, flowers, fruit, & John like a mask of misery. I felt ill, I took a Veganin, slept at 2.a.m. and awoke to a fresh knowledge of unhappiness. I was *afraid*! Old Fear got me.

9th July
A nice but pathetic little letter from John apologising for his behaviour, for his black cloud of gloom. Yes, but it does not move that blight of never using my name, he gives way too easily but never to call me Mother or Mimbles, just to speak abruptly & rudely is too much.

13th July
Little depressions, – no letters from anyone about my book, no notices or anything. I might as well do nothing.... Deborah Collins bought it, but never mentioned it. It is insulting. Also a book of snapshots of *Country Things* came from that Mrs. Green, with the coldest note, never a word about my writings or her enjoyment of reading the books, but sending & asking for their return. Such snobbery.... I long for a friend, like GL or LM or W Armitage, or Mrs. Edward. I seem to write for nothing, & nobody now [*Charles*] Stewart is dead.

28th July
Off to Stowe for John's interview. I could see he was very nervous, & when at Aylesbury he

had a cocktail he caught his glass, spilled it all & just as we were drinking good luck.... I hope John gets the post, I think he will like it [*at Stowe*]. None of the stiffness of Eton, although I prefer Eton. We are hoping he will get the post.

7th August
Off to B. For fish, & tomatoes at Ardwill. Had coffee and sat by the Kings.... Then raced home to the little dog. The puppy adorable, but he *does* wet the carpet.

10th August
Taking out the little dog for short trots, pools in the road, & he sat down in one. Playing with some silver birch bark I picked. I wrote names on it. Angus, Andy or Macduff. I like Macduff for him!

24th August
Letter from John, saying he is engaged to Helen Paine. Well, I didn't like her when I met her, too painted, rather 'fast' I thought – she took John dancing when there were all the wonderful fireworks to see in London. I think she is a town type. But I foresaw it would happen before John went [*to Guernsey*], yet I couldn't mention it. Sweet darling, I do hope he will be happy with her. I adore him & I know his goodness. I've not felt upset, only resigned. At any rate, a nice family [*the Paines*]. I can't write about it, my mind is so tired & so beaten down.

27th August
I wept in bed last night, sorrow & loneliness & distress. Poor John. I fear he is throwing away all his chances, the fun and joy of life.... On the way to Windsor I found I sat dumbly looking, not seeing.

29th August
Suddenly a phone call, John's in London, coming here at 10.30 p.m. – I was very much surprised and got ready for him. He came, smiling, very brown and happy. I felt queer & glum & very sick.... that queer sickness that comes over me. We talked a little and he said it was only an 'informal engagement' – both of them not decided. However, I fear she is. I am sure John is not in love, but he has been deluded.

7th September
To Old B for 1 egg, (which I only got by my chance appearance).... Revised and wrote several pages of [*first*] Chap of *Bucks* book.... GL sent plums and two pounds for the puppy, her share! O joy, the Lanigans have gone away & it's quiet. It is bliss without them.

8th September
Working all day [*on Bucks book*]. But enjoying it as I did it quietly, & chapter 1 is done. Reading the *Fairy* book, which is excellent. I think there *must* be fairies. It makes me want to write more.

10th September

Went with Mrs Wardle to the Thames Valley.... and when we got [*home*] Harry and Hilda [*his second wife*] waiting in the garden. They never told me the time, or even if they were coming.... I was very tired & rather sick. Especially when Harry talked about Downs House & round & round, – John 'If he wants to do a James, you can't stop him' kind of stuff. I said he didn't want [*to*]. He didn't know what he wanted. Harry gave a long lecture on enjoying yourself not doing work you don't like.... but changing 'Look at the James I know, working and sweating all night, & I can go when I like to the pictures when I like. I just enjoy myself,' said Harry. He asked what paper I took. He wanted the *Daily Mail*, for the football pools. He had won £50 by then. I liked Hilda very much.

11th September

He [*Harry*] went out to clean his shoes, so I gave him mine too, remembering before when he did nothing but his own. Then as Hilda & I were washing up, he said, 'Are you coming now, Hilda?' I said 'Oh no, I can't manage alone. Hilda will help me.'.... John came, very brown and fit – he whispered, 'It's all right, Mimbles' but my heart ached horribly. We went off at once to the Thames Valley again & had a torpid wretched lunch.... where we were despised, looked down upon. It was extraordinary, the snobbery, as we sat in the room with great old pictures. 'They all look alike to me,' said Harry loudly.

6th October

John phoned & I re-iterated my anxiety that Rosemary [*the fiancée of Martin Byers, John's cousin*] will *not* like J to be married first. O dear. It is extraordinary. I seem to be going twice through his business.... Why on earth can't he wait! Crazy, all of them.

21st October

I love rain, wet leaves and clouds. Now I am going to put no feelings or personal things in this book, for my heart breaks with grief. I will just put in little things like robins & flowers & keep my sense of proportion.

6th November

I met John & Martin Byers and Rosemary, a darling pair, and we all had lunch at White Hart. John in his Eton clothes, looking so charming & good looking. My heart suddenly ached for him.

7th November

Still a little depressed from yesterday, but a jolly thing, – the BBC: they want me to broadcast to *Overseas at Christmas*. That will be fun. I am delighted. Wrote a note to John thanking him for a lovely time at Eton.... When John is at Stowe I will never ask to go there for anything, only Eton is so traditional and exciting, and I have missed nearly everything [*there*] already through John's diffidence and refusal to invite me.

20th November
Awake for hours, very miserable.... [*took a*] Veganin & slept. Suddenly today I threw off [*my*] misery and felt gay. Nice things, – a crazy dream about mislaying a baby for 24 hrs, & wondering where I had put it as I was busy with my book. So I hunted all over. Sweeping up leaves. Giving coupon for tea to old man. Getting some 'cookies'.

23rd November
A devastating day. Theatre [*with John and Helen*], lovely ballets, but I suddenly collapsed with nervous tension, the snubs of John, the slights.... I sat weeping in the theatre!

24th November
Eton, the lovely Lower School service.... the Bishop in gold.... My questions to [*Helen Paine*] – not interested in poetry, books, anything.... 'What is the Eucharist?' she asked? Oh Dorothy Parker!.... Nice things: To be alone when she is gone. The quietness of the flickering fire.

1st December
Darling December, do bring us joy & kindness and bonds of love again between John and myself.

6th December
I suddenly decided to go to London, to shop. Phoned John at the flat and invited him to lunch. He met me & was sweet. O God, I *do* feel happy when he's there.... so fresh and gay and youthful. Oh all you mothers who can always have this fun.

12th December
[*A letter from John*] reprimanding me! Saying I must rely more on myself. It makes me laugh. Fancy John telling me to rely on myself. My God. But I am laughing, – I won't care. For I know how weak he is and always has been.... I hereby swear I won't ask him to go anywhere or do anything – again.

14th December
The BBC said, 'It's a lovely script, absolutely lovely, I couldn't be more pleased.'.... Thinking of John. He has never been a jolly companion, shopping with me, sharing things. Always reticent & cold, telling me nothing. Showing me no letters.... So this final blow is only part of it. I shan't lose much. Sometimes I feel my heart is broken but it must not be. There are so many things, & human love is not all. There is the companionship of sun, trees and grass and the feeling of the earth.... He drinks too much. And he has been so cross with me, never calling me mother, or darling.

17th December
My birthday, 62 today. My goodness, sometimes I feel about six. A jolly day frost &

sunshine, with a tiny…. wind, when John hurried me rather roughly, so that I felt a panic. John [*is*] going to Guernsey, & I will be grateful when he has gone…. I must go bravely on, not relying on anyone. Yes, I can do it, as I have always done it really.

31st December

[*I*] managed to get rid of most of the cold…. Then to see [*her neighbour*] Mrs. King, who looked sweet with her lovely old dress…. Stars shining, air like ice. My darling John [*is*] with Helen. I pray you two will be happy, a lovely married pair at peace and unity together for many years, my dears & I hope I will fit into your lives, & make you even happier. So ends a year of anxiety, hard work & worry & hope.

1947

1st January

I got the usual work done, & walked to B. then to Old B with MacDuff. I can't do it often, too wearying. I feel utterly done up, as he tugged at the lead & went for women's boots.... Mrs King brought a cake.

Now for good resolutions:

    1. A new *Country* book.

    2. Finish off the *Fairy* book, nearly done.

    3. A *Sam Pig* book.

    4. A *Grey Rabbit* book.

And of course all the alterations to the *Bucks* book, & [*the*] proofs. My life, and I must not feel alone, but I must be aware of God's presence. Besides I have so many friends, seen and unseen.... John will never be the same now, he says so.... Yet we are tied by bonds which will never break, & in years to come he will remember and understand, 'I prayed, and will pray for you, yours. Please pray for me and mine,' says HPE. The old pieties will reassert themselves.

6th January

A busy morning, snow falling fast, icy cold, but I had to wrap up, go out for coal, anthracite, wood, & paraffin, all empty. The snow is lovely.... the silence. Twelfth Night.

17th January

Another lovely day of sunshine. Glorious. We turned out the larder to celebrate.... Thinking of John sleeping in that woman's flat again tonight.

4th February

Letter from John, saying.... he wants to be married at Easter. Coming home on April 7. Married on April 10. I am very glad. It relieves my mind.... I have felt excited & happy all day because of John, knowing his joy.... It might have been more rapturous joy if it had been a girl, & not this [*previously*] married woman. How one wishes it had been different for him. He is missing so much.... rapture & [*the*] beauty of young love with this sophisticated person. Ah well, God be with him.

12th February

John's engagement announced in the *Daily Telegraph*. I was staggered to be called on the phone [*by journalists*].... to be asked questions, – which day will he married on? A Wedding Bureau [*Registry Office*]? etc. Before 9. 0 [*a.m.*] comes another London call, & they said I would have a dozen! So I cut off the phone.

17th February
Delightful letter of 8 pages from John…. Telling me of the choir which he is joining…. but Helen has written twice saying that I haven't replied to her letter. Blast her! Her colossal self-importance is staggering. I loathe getting a letter from her.

18th February
Letter…. saying…. I must be sad John is going to be married. No, I'm glad. I feel I would like to hurry it on. I was thinking, 'My heart was broken that night in London, when I wept in the theatre & said my prayer all the way home', – but with a broken heart I keep very cheerful. No not broken, only a realisation came to me, & all changed.

24th February
News so awful, I won't tell it. Felt… sick with tiredness in bed.

5th March
Oh! Oh! Bliss after an awful walk in deep snow. KS came in morn to type.

20th March
Off to London by the 9.30, so up early, hurrying – and I slept badly last night, too…. Called at Stewarts for coffee, & then on to Mr Collins. He was delightful, just the same. He says the books are selling very well, 100,000 last year and & a target of 150,000. We talked of the little Valentine Mrs. Wig made…. Lunch at F & M [*Fortnum and Mason*]…. To the BBC, where I saw my broadcast, – thought I was rather dull but they seemed to like it.

30th March
[*We went to*] church at St. Michaels, but it was a long, Popish service, kissing [*the priest, Father Nicholson's*] hand, – John refused…. The gate at Hampton Park would not fasten. 'Come on,' shouted John roughly…. why does he do this? I feel like weeping. I might be a horse, or a servant.

7th April
At 5.0 a.m. lying weeping in bed, with sorrow at the rift, at the anger & the silences and the lack of sharing fun and talk. I think of this short holiday, John here for the last time unmarried, the son for whom I have done so much all his life. He came home & I gave him the Oak Bible cupboard for his wedding. The next day to B & I bought the lovely table for him, £36, & found the mirror for Helen, & got the pendant for him to give her. Yet he was angry because I kept him waiting while I shut a gate, & he drove in long bitter silence, unanswering.

12th April
John's wedding day. I [*got up*] at 8.45 & we had a prayer at St Stephen's Church, & lovely little time which helped me all day. The wedding, lilies of the valley. John looking very sweet and loving. A nice plain service very short. Poor reception…. I felt lonely & queer, waiting, to get away from the Paines. But so thankful they are married.

22nd April
K Sibbring called, with the baby, adopted, little red screwed up face. She is brave taking it on.... They have come, Helen with her hair up, looking about 40, John looking older too. I feel rather queer, hoping for the best!! I must get a good holiday, let the beauty of it soak in, and not mind the rubs. So goodbye, my diary for a while.

23rd – 30th April
Wild journey in rain & wind but glorious, and I enjoyed the visit very much. I sat at the front of the car, so I saw the scenery, & I felt grateful to Helen & John for letting me. Helen slept or read the paper at the back.... A lovely holiday.

23rd May
Off to London to see the Chelsea [*Flower*] Show with KS by car.... lovely show, the Tulips, especially 'Beppy' [*for*] 6/- a dozen.

20th June
The month of June has been a lovely month. I enjoyed it so much I didn't write my diary, for I wanted to get away from my sad remembrances. I recovered my senses, & my strength, my vitality this month, and cut away the agony of the past months.

23rd June
John came with Helen for me. Drove off quickly, hardly seeing the house. To his flat. My heart sank. The 20 ointments & bottles covering his little table.... The 5 bottles of spirit, liqueurs on the table, I thought of mother, of James especially, John as a little boy, all my love & care, to end in this.

15th July
To B, standing in long queue for fish, then in queue in Sainsbury's [*for*] eggs, and another.... To W de la Mare's, I only had a tiny rest first. I was worn out.... W de la Mare was delightful.

20th July
Worked in bed, feeling weary as up with Macduff [*who*] was howling in night. Then getting ready for John & Helen, & feeling anxious. They came, John very sweet and lovely. Yet it was not a happy time really. We had tea in the garden, very jolly out there, & I talked about the Russia book.... When they had gone I wept.... I felt so unhappy.... Very depressed, especially with John's.... irritation.

22nd July
A pile of answers about the secretarial job.... Then to B to the bank to arrange transfer back of shares & wrote to John. I hate doing it, but I have felt some discomfort & fear with nothing behind me for the dim future, & dependent on Helen perhaps.

31st August
A glorious sunny day, – in garden all day. Correcting type of the *Country* book. Mrs Lidell [*her typist*] offers to help, so I gave her some pages to retype & now I have finished the book.... She is queer, uninterested in anything, no comment on what she types, or on the garden, or house or anything.... Slept well last night.... pleasant, – because I feel free again. I made nice meals, but it's a queer life.

28th September
Harry's birthday. I send him £3.

2nd – 23rd October
At Tintagel, lovelier than ever, so beautiful, it was a dream.

30th October
Dentist, tooth out, I've dreaded this for weeks but it was most pleasant.

10th November
Margaret Stewart came and typed the nursery rhymes.... A lovely day, – after lunch I went out down Broad Lane, & there was old Norris talking to a roadman, so I went along with them. 'There's a thousand acres all going to ruin round here,' said he sadly. 'I don't know what the world is coming to.' Alas, it is true. I bathed Macduff, his first bath.... Sent a wire to Collins asking for the *Grey Rabbit* books for the Princess [*Elizabeth*].

14th November
Broadcast on *King Arthur's Country*. A good broadcast, I read it well. The young man in the other room burst in to congratulate me. I heard the water rushing under BBC House, an underground river in London, lovely.... Lunch at Antoine, very good.... Bought a blue umbrella, pair of lizard tan shoes.... for all these things will go up in price soon. Princess Eliz's present came, & I unpacked it, autographed the works & packed it up.

17th November
Mrs. Drysdale [*her female residential companion*] came, elegant in pink dress.... Why, Oh why?

30th November
Mrs. Drysdale.... said she must have Freedom, to think, to act, to do. So I agreed. She spoke interestingly. I was touched by her manner and what she said, but after a time I found myself thinking, 'Here is a crank, so set on self-development and freedom that we shall never get on.' .... If she can say, 'I want spectral children, not flesh and blood' then she is beyond my comprehension.... She said.... that illness need not be, [*that*] one could use spiritual means and dispel it, illness through spiritual means.... After lunch.... I asked her to go up to [*the*] wood as I had washed up. No. She couldn't till she had changed!

5th December
She gave notice, – & was I glad! Yes I was indeed, it couldn't go on. No companionship or

help. She knows no poet or writer, no music or art. All her thoughts on (1) Make-up, (2) Divinity!!!!

17th December
A lovely birthday, much nicer than last year's. A heap of letters…. a long, rather dull letter from Winnie Stocks…. [*Mr. Ongar comes from the motoring school.*] So off we went, & I enjoyed it very much.

18th December
Stopping [*a filling*] out of tooth at breakfast, to my horror, but I managed without going to the dentist…. It rained, but I had to go to B for fish struggling in the rain with Macduff…. but decided on cookery. I made mince pies…. Cheered today by a phone from Brown's to ask if I still wanted a little workcase I saw long ago. 'Oh yes,' said I. Well, I can have it for £7, they said. So I am thrilled, for it is a really lovely and perfect workcase with little bottles…. & about 1780 I think.

19th December
A most loving letter from Miss Oakley [*Warden at Ashburne Hall when Alison was a student*], sending a Metaphysical article which I simply cannot understand, bless her, she over-rates my brain…. I feel very Christmassy today, and very happy. Sometimes I feel so happy I could burst, just thinking of trees and woods, wet earth and stars.

25th December
Early service, all of us in a crowded church. Then home to breakfast & presents…. John gave me a cigarette lighter…. Mrs. King a fairy 'for a fairy'…. At night [*I worry over*] the goose and the plum pudding! I keep doing do some small wrong thing!!

27th December
John brings up our breakfasts, – he always takes up Helen's & does all the washing up & fires & waits on Helen, who wears his pyjamas!

31st December
John & Helen left,– a great hustle to get off…. John very sweet to me…. so could truthfully say I was sorry they were going…. I am glad however they have gone, it has been a great strain. Helen isn't like ordinary nice girls – she is different, older, and she offends my eye by her ugly face and queer eyes. However, when she smiles, which is seldom, she looks different. Castle Top would not like her.
Goodbye, old year, which has been nice and better than 1946. 1947 has had John's wedding, & my flying back over the sea. The visit to Tintagel especially in October. The misery of those secretaries. The loveliness of the hot summer days and LM's visit. The bliss of driving my own car. The visits to the ballet.
So welcome New Year, & God be with us & help us always.

~~ *1948* ~~

2nd January
Letter from Princess Elizabeth, very charming, thanking me for *LGR* books.... Listening to Cello concerts by [*Kachachurian*] which I like very much.

16th January
I collected pictures for Tunnicliffe, such lovely memories of C Top.... and charming pictures of James, and John when he was little. Very, very, happy feelings of those times. [*I got*] a cheque for eight pounds one shilling from *Farmers' Weekly*.... A primrose out in garden! Yes, my darlings must be immortal, all of them.

21st January
To London in my fur coat and navy hat.... feeling gay *because* I was so thrilled with the book *Do I Wake or Sleep*.... reading the book all the way [*on the train*].... To Liberty's where.... I saw my ideal tallboy for a 180 gns like [*the*] Castle Top dresser.... Lunch at Stewarts'.... then raced off to the National Book Exhibition of Shakespeare's plays and pictures. I liked best the *Folios*.

22nd January
A bit dashed because Margaret Stewart can't come today, and can't come any more because [*she is*] starting a secretarial course on Monday. I must settle down to do *Grey Rabbit* tales, two of them. *Sam Pig* book. Try to get a gardener and extra help. If I want to cheer myself up, I remind myself of: the *Fairy* book in the press, wire netting in garden, I can struggle along with the gardening, I can do the typing if I get nobody. All the jolly daffodils [*are*] coming up, the apple trees are pruned.

24th January
Collins want me to be photographed with Margaret Tempest at the office for a publicity photograph [*about*] planning a new book. Well, I never plan one, I do it alone, but I will go. I have been writing a *Grey Rabbit* book all day, listening to *Odes of Horace*, Dvorak's Fifth Symphony, the rugby match, Scotland versus France, very exciting.

3rd February
Nice things: a load of manure spread. A fan letter from a nice, illiterate woman. I have been doing galleys of *Wandering Hedgehog*.

10th February
Off to London, in blue frock & fur coat.... I went see [*theatre agent*] Eric Glass. I hear, 'Yes

darling. Don't be so downhearted darling.'…. Glass [is] a fat Jew, very flamboyant & rich – but a nice clever man…. I enjoyed the talk. We spoke of films too, & foreign countries.

25th February
Writing Christmas tale tonight, for the future. Castle Top so near to me I feel sick with longing for the past, just to kiss them & speak to them.

29th February
A day of extreme beauty, I saw 3 *Brimstones* [*butterflies*] flying like primroses in the air.

9th March
I learn from an American fan that Beatrix Potter had sent one of my books to her. I was so glad.

17th March
Lots of things: proofs of *Carts and Candlesticks*, a copy of Austrian *Sam Pig*, pictures by Tunnicliffe, programmes of *The Washerwoman's Child* (first part on 13th March) the Lord Chamberlain's licence, Faber's say Penguin have asked for *Traveller in Time*.

24th March
Joyce types slowly as I dictate. A charming letter from Morley Kennerley, saying he is looking forward to *Carts and Candlesticks*, as I am. I phoned Faber because I was worried about a letter from the acting people to Eric Glass about me…. I can't handle these actors, a horrid money-grubbing set.

1st April
Eric Glass says he's sent *Traveller in Time* to Hitchcock for a film. Hoorah. John home, looking well and jolly. I cheered up because he seems happy.

8th April
I am staggered by Collins' cheque for £1,375 for nearly a quarter of a million books. I felt queer, though not elated because it complicates my income tax, – surtax. I felt dizzy.

17th April
Devastating news that [*the*] type[*script*] and proofs of the *Bucks* book have been destroyed in a fire at the printers. Somehow I'm not surprised, [*I had*] a queer sinister feeling about the book. Robert Hale are a sickening lot. I feel very depressed.

19th April
A cuckoo! Hoorah. I said a little prayer and went up to Hamish's grave to remember him. Russell of the *Saturday Book* is so delighted with her story. I feel touched and thrilled. [*There was*] a nice rejection letter from *Twentieth Century Fox* about *A Traveller in Time*. I am delighted that [*Professor*] Joad is out of Brains Trust, [*he is*] unendurable.

5th May

In London a nice waitress gets me my lunch, although [*it is*] late.... I think I am extravagant in what I buy.... I went to Slatters for a glorious exhibition of Dutch and Flemish paintings. I realised that my own painting [*the Brueghel*] is important.

15th May

Gardening and doing proofs hard. Glorious beyond words, such exquisite days.

20th June

Helen's private conversation. Oh dear. John looks so handsome, nay, beautiful and young & Helen so old – pouched under [*the*] eyes. I think of the unborn children who might have been born.

23rd June

I make a mistake about the day to meet Margaret Rutherford for lunch at the Ritz. I waited and waited.

27th June

Off.... to see John. John not quite smiling, a constraint. Helen looked so ugly.... Suddenly I began to feel ill, and want to go home.... Helen always starts a loud secondary conversation whenever I speak, or John speaks to anyone. I think my ill feeling was sheer hunger.... War is near with the Russians [*over the Berlin blockade*].

15th July

Mother's birthday.... Mrs. Smith [*her home help*] breaks the tortoiseshell workbox, I console her.... I enjoy speeding through the traffic in my car. How I love driving. It makes such a difference to my life.

22nd July

Off to Faber's At Home which was delightful. The great room with panelled wall & lovely ceiling & sparkling chandeliers. The people in charming clothes.... Then on the concert, divine singing by Robert Irwin [*the Schubert song*].

5th September

O magical life, – how lovely it is! Please God let me keep and remember all the beauty for eternity, I know Mother would have loved it too. I thought of Castle Top vividly tonight, feeling it was my mother on the hearth-rug looking up at the picture, at CastleTop years ago.

20th October

Took my [*Driving*] Test, & to my unspeakable joy & surprise I got through. One moment of panic when I could not get the car round.... But the corner, reversing for several yards was awkward. I couldn't keep straight by [*the*] pavement…. 'I am going to give you the benefit of the doubt and pass you,' said the examiner. I could hardly believe it.

23rd October
With joy driving all alone for the first time, to B. and then on to Penn to see Mrs. King, singing as I drove, under the golden trees, happy and excited…. £100 from Faber.

8th November
Awake at night, worrying about [*having*] no gardener! How silly of me…. A sweet letter from [*her cousin*] Sissy. I am anxious about the [*impending*] reviews of *Carts and Candlesticks*. What horrible things will these hard reviewers say?

19th November
To [*Twickenham*] to see [*Walter*] De la Mare. His charming voice & warm hand & smile. How lovely it was, the dim lights, the fire (with a china cat, I thought it was real to his joy)….then the boring Mr. Powys came, snow-white hair, good looking, dominating and very talkative. De la Mare showing me the contents of the bureau bookcase.

17th December
My birthday, – such a happy day. Saying a prayer early, and welcoming the day & thinking of my mother. Off to London with Olley [*her part-time chauffeur*], I driving part of the way. Then to Harrods where I got the white coat with hood lined with scarlet…. Then to the Medici where I rather recklessly got table mats with music on them…. Then to lunch with Mary Treadgold, of turkey, plum pudding & cream, & coffee…. To Fabers, [*where Peter du Sautoy*] told me the *Country Child* wanted for Germany, & [*Richard*] de la Mare who was most affable, telling me of his 4 children, the boy at Eton, Giles de la Mare.

18th December
Phoned Olley to ask if he could polish my car, – he couldn't, so I did it myself, very nicely…. Parcel from GL with [*prints of*] Churchill's Paintings, delightful…. Made plum puddings & Christmas cakes (2), working all afternoon & evening till 11. 45!

23rd December
Two lovely things, a poem, *Solitude*, (written for *me* by Walter de la Mare, & sent with his love)… A little pink Pig (*Sam*) came from Wigs. I put holly sprigs over the Breughel.

25th December
Up early to church, Helen stalking ahead never heeding anyone. I feel nervous, but I put my trust in God.

28th December
I was thankful to go home, I had a little weep in the night, knowing John has left me. [*Helen*]

is frightening, strong-willed and devouring, & I feel her influence. In the car she filed her nails all the way from Aylesbury.... I felt sick as I heard the sound of it as we drove through lovely country – I can do nothing.

31st December
A lovely day, sunshine & colour. A nice post – with a beautiful needlecase from Lilian King, and a *Book of Flowers* from Gertrude, & letters, a sweet one from John, bless him.... Now it is New Year's Eve & I say goodbye to a lovely old year. I have had all my books, 4 published this year, & the driving & passing the Test, & 2 visits to Tintagel, & reading *The Happy Issue*. Please God, take care of us & help us always, & especially bless John, & make his marriage a firm happy good marriage.

1949

1st January
[*Walter de la Mare's Christmas present of a poem written for Alison*] with love and good wishes:

Solitude
Space beyond space; stars needling into Night;
In wonder and love I gaze from Earth below.
Spinning in unintelligible quiet beneath
A moonlight drift of cloudlets, still as snow.

5th January
Walter de la Mare, Florence Thompson and Julia came to tea. Mr de la Mare sitting in the armchair, talking of a book he was reading which gave new [*scientific*] theories for the origins of man. We discussed lead and its instability and splitting up. Man, Homo Sapiens, said to have originated in Mesopotamia, in Garden of Eden. The aliveness of nature. Musical box. 'This is worth all the orchestras,' said he as he listened. Macduff playing ball, looking round at him with bright eyes.... 'How is it that animals cannot speak and we can't understand them after millions of years', he asked. I said I always listened for Macduff to speak and sometimes I expected him to whisper in my ear.... [*We talked of*] fairies. (He asked the time of day of Miss Wood's vision, and time of year. I thought it was about 10.00 or 11.00 and spring. 'Height?' [*I said*] 18 inches).... Mr de la Mare looking around: Here's a subject for a novel. Write about this room, go into corners, tell of all the lovely things in it.' The enchantment of the Breughel. The exquisite Christmas roses in the old glass. The tiny ring of mixed primulas from the garden.

9th January
Tommy Handley [*the radio comedian*] dead, poor man.

11th January
Linda told [*me*] how much de la Mare loves coming here & he loved my Dutch pictures. Talking of me, De la Mare said, 'I think she also has a very real music of her own, not cultivated, but a gift.' I was delighted.

14th January
Decided to go to the WI pantomime. Joan Dobell came and stayed three hours.... so tiring. However, I went off to the panto.... It was amusing in a heavy way, but I did not really like it.

1st February

To London.... Mr. Collins complimented me on my appearance.... Then on to...Miss Gibbs [*at the BBC*].... a lovely time.... talking of pictures.... London and country life and broadcasting. Decided on April 4th , 1.45 [*I*] of Country Things.... Then to Irene Hawkins [*the illustrator*]. Her welcome, a pretty room – the new wording of *The 12 Days of Christmas*.

3rd February

I was angry that the gardener washed the car and then it would not start. Then, with the handle, he turned and turned and got the engine going. [*He is*] a marvel of perseverance & patience.

10th February

Wilson [*her gardener*], cannot come again, he is going to Devon where his father is ill. I felt devastated.

13th February

To church at Penn, driving fast & glorious. But the service dull. The [*priest*] apes the R[*Roman*] C[*Catholics*] & is so *refined*!

14th February

A busy morning as the Hoover man came to mend the hoover and to demonstrate. I told him how my fringes went into it, I nearly lost my rugs!

15th February

Letter from Hatchards, Wolverhampton, asking me to speak to children. No!

19th February

Proofs of *Farm on the Hill* came. I went for a longish drive by myself. It was perfection. [*She speaks on the phone with a Miss Wood, who had seen fairies.*] She saw them at 8 pm on a summer night when she opened the door to shake the supper cloth.... She stood watching them. Holding hands as they danced. Their faces indefinite, not strongly featured, but pointed faces, and radiantly happy.... About 2 ft high. Suddenly they disappeared.... Not a sound.

17th March

Gardener here, putting down lawn seed.... Kathleen [*her daily help*] turning out the box room. A woman for interview, a nice person. Man putting in new electric stove, Mr. Norris to tea, telling me many tales.... The BBC have chosen *When I am Alone* for the title of the broadcast.

22nd March

John's letter, going to Guernsey for hols, – I am glad, it will do him good. [*The Wigglesworth*] twins are at Eton.... I bought lovely books, *Ireland*, for LM.... one volume of

Dutch paintings and two volumes of folklore.... Remembered the hawthorns green in the hedge.... I feel so excited in this day.

23rd March
Worried because £3 gone and bag stolen. The girl [*a home help*] is a thief. Have my gloves gone too? [*In pencil, added later, No.*] The CID came about the man I saw in the lane.

4th April
[*Off to the BBC to do her broadcast on When I am Alone.*] Broadcasting in *Woman's Hour*, the guest. First a practice.... my voice was right and I spoke as if I was completely used to it. Then the real thing.... sitting at the Mike with Olive Shapley.... Then the [*gramophone*] record of *Greensleeves*.

18th April
E.Graham came and we went to Jordans [*a Quaker community near Beaconsfield*] to lunch. Rather constrained. I am no longer under her spell.

29th April
Driving to Eton.... [*I was*] nearly in tears as John spoke to me. [*He had been on a three-day visit to Thackers.*] [*In the*] beautiful old church... a little angel's head consoling me.... I was dazed.... hurt.

30th April
Recovering. Mr and Mrs. Walter Rose came, and a bit of a strain.... He asked if I got my characters for *High Meadows* from [*Thomas*] Hardy.... He asked so many questions, I did not enjoy it.

5th May
A garden mower came, a treat to see the smooth grass. And a garden seat from Harrods, very fine.

6th May
Cambridge, I driving 60 miles in two hours.... The Wiggs were in great form.... I thought of John, my hopes for him when he was at Cambridge.

17th May
Letter from the income tax [suggesting] an auditor. Panic.... Off in rain to Forty Green – to look for Fly Orchids, but found none. The Pusey baby, a lovely little pink rose of a child to whom I gave a new 1/-. Milkwort out and my first nightingales singing in the rain. Glorious, – the sky stormy blue and purple. A double rainbow.

18th June
Secretly I buy a scarf, as I feel unhappy. [*She goes to Bowdon, with John, to*] make my will

there. What about Helen? Yet I cannot leave all to her [*if John were to predecease her*].
20th June
John and Helen came. I must go off at once [*from Bowdon*]. So I obediently came.... Driving fast, [*then a*] breakdown at Towcester.... At Padbury a cup of tea and cake which I praised. 'If you bought the [*Daily Telegraph*] cookery book, and made an effort you could make cake yourself instead of buying it,' said Helen sourly. 'I haven't time with my writing,' said I. 'Of course you have.... You make cakes for us when we come.' She is insufferable.... At last! Free from her rudeness.

28th July
In the morning I phoned [*Heinemann*] who promised royalties on *GR* books when Miss [*Tempest*] does them. [*There was a disagreement over the division of royalties.*] Lovely letter from Mrs Wig, saying she will do the new books, sending some 'mice' pictures....Letter from Sugden saying 25% dividend [*is due*].... Off with Olley... to West Wycombe, where I bought a little round snuff box.... To Great Hampden church and the memorial to John Hampden [*the Stuart Parliamentarian*].... [*I saw a*] cornfield by the churchyard with sheaves all piled up ready.... Home past red and gold colours, absolute beauty.... corn sheaves against the blue sky.

5th August
Interviewed a [*new*] gardener who wants 22/6d per day.

7th August
To the Kings to discuss proofs, – but when Mr. King came in he made it all uncomfortable. He is a prickly man.... [*We*] went to the Knoll to meet Lord Curzon [*later Earl Howe*], a delightful man, a joy to talk to, and how we talked.

30th August
Went to the Gurneys to go through the *Bucks* portion of the book.... Mr. Gurney was querulous. 'How you have the nerve to write it,' he commented.

6th September
Off to London. Coffee and cake at Stewarts, [*then*] to Heinemann, where Dwye Evans and I discussed the books. Suggested Mice for the subject... KW to do pictures by November 8. [*Evans says that when he comes back from the USA*] He will send me some nylons! Oh how funny! [*Then she did a great deal of shopping.*] I've been thinking of Walter de la Mare, praying for him [*on the day*] of his operation.

17th September
John is in the garden, [*I*] reading proofs all day. I am feeling the great strain of Penn Fair [*part of the book on Buckinghamshire*]

21st September
Summoned for jury service on the fifth October. Doctor [*Milner*] says I have acute nervous exhaustion. I knew it! He gave me a certificate [*to excuse her from jury service*].

16th October
To tea with W de la Mare. Met [*Pat Hickson*] who talked of Yeats and her mother. Yeats [*was*] intolerable & awful in his late phase. ...Coming home with the wretched driver, who got lost.... swerving at cars and 2 buses.... A miracle we were saved.... Sick and half fainting, I came home and had a brandy. After my illness, it was too much.

The 1949 diary ends on October 23rd.

1950

1st January
I enjoyed the service at Penn church. Two vital thoughts: one, during the hymn *Christian Awake*, where I know that 'the heavenly babe' shone with luminosity, like a star. The second was that bread and wine are symbols of life and eternity. So much real beauty.

2nd January
Harrods phone, asking for an interview and a photograph. If only they knew that I was struggling with fire and rugs, and kitchen floor, all dusty at the time.

5th January
I go to Harrods, where I am entertained to a lovely lunch, interviewed, photographed, and then speak to a smiling crowd and autograph lots of books.

8th January
I drive to Walter de la Mare in the dark and fog, [*in*] third gear most of the time. My first, longest drive [*of the year*]. I enjoyed it. Macduff was out all night.

11th January
Writing a little of the new tale of [*the mice*] Serena and Snug. I filled in contract for the *Cobbler's Shop* [*and Other Tales*].

15th January
Face still aching [*from the dentist*]. To church to help and [*for*] inspiration…. I was bored by Mr. King telling me that vitamin B is good for toothache.

25th January
D Evans at Heinemann accepts the second tale, but doesn't like the title, *Snug and Serena go Cowslipping*. So I must think of another. Rather bored by the film *Whisky Galore*. I don't agree with LM's choice in films.

2nd February
To B to order a new radio and to pay in Sugdens cheque for a hundred and eighty pounds. Two more teeth filled at the dentist's, [*now*] he's finished for three months. We had a grand talk on birds, especially bitterns. Quite a mild letter from MT.

10th February
Letter from [*someone on the*] *Derby Advertiser*, telling me of her visit to my mother long

ago.... Faber ask me to write a biography, but I refused.... BBC send contracts for broadcast in March and television on Sunday. I mistake the date of going to the book [*event*] in High Wycombe!

12th February
To Penn at night to see the television [*version*] of the *Knot Squirrel Tied*. Quite well done, puppets much better.

14th February
Valentine, lavender bags from GL, a painting of a robin from KW [*Katherine Wigglesworth*]. A stiff note from MT, who detests the puppets, as I knew. I wrote to MT asking about a woman who wants to make toys, and telling her proposals for the contract. Olley is annoyed I don't want him tomorrow.

17th February
Letters. Harry's sketch of *Meadow Wood* [*arrives*]. M Tempest's letter saying she wouldn't agree to any of my proposals for [*the*] Collins contract. So that's that. Instead of feeling downhearted, I sang as I came downstairs, for I don't care now. A marvellous day of sunshine, & all the little rock crocuses came out, & the yellow hyacinth is blowing.... The Rossfield field glasses came, and as I looked through, I was thrilled as if I saw a new world, the beech buds, the bare trees, the robin in the fir tree.... I bought a Tunbridge box with blue velvet, and inlaid edges, for Margaret Rutherford, & ordered a copper 'flour dredger' for perhaps Margaret.... I changed and got ready for High Wycombe, but Olley never came, I am not surprised, taking it out [*on*] me.

20th February
Reading Jane Carlyle's delicious letters.

21st February
I run through the wood with Macduff in the bright sunshine.... Delightful tea with Rev. Muspratt [*the new vicar*] and Mrs. Muspratt.

24th February
Listening to poll [*the general election results*] until 3 am, – Labour getting so many seats I felt despair. However this morning it improved, and this afternoon I was thrilled as I heard the distance between Con & Labour go down, – but it rose again, & Labour is in by a small majority. As for those crazy Liberals, messing up everything, I've no words. I went to B to hear the [*declaration of the*] poll.... Bell got in.... Now we shall see, – I'm so thankful the margin is small. I feared it was another debacle like last time [*1945*].

25th February
Writing, reading. Mary Treadgold came and we discussed books for [*Heinemann*] and for

Collins and all [*the*] complications. She advised [*an*] agent, but I think not, as I shall not do outside books.

12th March
John and Helen come for a lovely short visit. [*I*] will give John two hundred pounds towards his beautiful new car.

13th March
I feel put off by Gwen [*her help*] rushing in, saying her hands were stinking of fish. A heavy clumsy woman, like a horse.... Collins cheque for £1,236. Eureka! I send John two hundred pounds, and Harry fifty.

18th March
[*A*] large pineapple from Ethel and Agnes Stewart – the darlings. Not so well today. Good review from Australia for *Farm on the Hill*. Also pre-notice of the [*Brown*] *Mouse* series, exciting and frightening, – Collins will be so cross, and so will MT.

21st March
Charming letter from W de la Mare. Proofs of new *Mouse* book. Request from Robert Hale for galleys! Collins sent proof of blurb for book jacket. I deal with all this in the morning.

23rd March
Awake all night, feeling ill and troubled. I cancel broadcast, lecture, cocktail parties and all. Pay big cheque into bank, driven by Gwen, who is rude to police.

25th March
Hale want twenty six pounds for printers' expenses. The secretary I was going to interview never arrived. The pictures of [*The Little Brown*] *Mouse* are too loud and crude. I am disappointed.

8th April
I heard the cuckoo at five am in the dawn chorus. It touched my heart, as it seemed to question. I nearly wept with joy.

13th April
A rude letter from MT [*Margaret Tempest*]. Heinemann tell me not to worry.... Miss Collins comes and discusses it. MT's awful jealousy and spite. Charming letter from de la Mare, proofs of [*Little Grey*] *Rabbit Makes Lace*, John's proofs for the *Fairy* book, I also sent a tale to [*Uncle*] Mac, and [*an*] article for *The Saturday Book*. Tonight I should have given my lecture!

14th April
Miss Collins brings draft of reply to MT.... I mustn't do any more books with her, I couldn't bear it. I hate her to touch my sweet little people.

18th April
Cheque from BBC for 15 guineas for broadcast. Letter to MT sent on to me, – Collins actually asked her to correct my proofs, 'the proofs of her book,' they said. I wrote an indignant letter to Glasgow [*and*] one to Miss Snow, protesting.... Miss Collins [*is*] most indignant, says I should threaten her with the law. I told Mac. I thought he ought to know, and also Dwye Evans.... And I've been reading my 2 new *GR* tales, lovely ones, which won't be printed now, for I won't let Collins have anything. They are so sweet, – but I'm thinking of Snug & Serena [*the Little Brown Mice*].

21st April
A strange dream, I was unhappy and lost. I got out of a train at Cromford.... I didn't know where to go. I had no hat, no coat, a thin dress, no shoes or stockings. I knew I couldn't go home, or who would shelter me.... I ordered a rather awful seat at the antique shop.

6th May
I tried to write, but no good.

10th May
The doctor says I must go slow. Although I am much better.

The diary ends on 14th May.

~ *1951* ~

4th January
Sent a wire to Richards to come, – 'Please come. Ill and alone. Uttley.' He came, roused from sick bed, & dug out paths, filled all the buckets of wood…. a terrific business.

6th January
I took down the holly and ivy, which no-one has seen but *I* have seen it & all the invisible ones have had its joy…. Singing carols tonight, happily & easily, & I invented delicious tunes for some.

7th January
[*This year*] I want to write: 1. a country diary book, 2. Another book of essays on my own life, 3. two books for Heinemann, & perhaps a *TR* or *Macduff* book.

24th January
I meet the gypsies and talked to the boys. The little dead gypsy aged 10 [*had*] died of pneumonia.

26th January
A flock of hawfinches in garden. Rude letter from a man most disappointed over *Bucks* book…. a peevish silly letter which I couldn't bother to read so I burnt it. Writing and revising the Christmas tale of *Snug*.

28th January
John & Helen came. A lovely visit….Talking of Korea, & flying saucers

4th February
Reading the *Flying Saucer* book, nearly unreadable, but in part very exciting and strange, – about 2 pages of the little men & their saucers.

14th February
[*Valentine*] card from Mr. Norris and one from John: 'I've always been so fond of you. To me you're just divine.' So I was charmed.

6th March
I sent off a letter to the bank about not paying Sissy's money [*a regular payment to her cousin Sissy*]…. Ivor Novello [*is*] dead, alas.

1954

7 JANUARY — THURSDAY

Enchantment. Snow on the ground, streaks of blue shadow across the lawn, the beech tree now bare of snow but radiant, glowing = sunshine, the boughs red... as-... such persistent truck. Birds flitting = the snow... ...... = little... hopping... swooping = ... pink ups scarfs. Silent, but heads raised ready to fly off. Two peaks of the plum... A blackbird on the stump. The long row very busy, + a network of footprints. The light down is golden, - + the trees are shining with reflected light. No picture could give their beauty. No memory retain it. The snow, streaks... cut ... shadow, the pied beech, in its... grey-purple trunks, + all the net of twigs... some dead leaves, rich light brown, + the bare top bou... + blue sky.

The Partridges came, - + we t...
Cavalican... Borme des... ...
the purple flowers. The cork trees
+ the... in the sea, +

EVENING APPOINTMENTS

FRIDAY — JANUARY 8

Snow, snow, + ice. 1pm Alice would not come, so I went on happily + carried coal + did the work. I drove to B to meet Linda, - she looked nice, + in had a good meeting + talk. Because... pill slipping, I... the road very carefully, gingerly + drove slowly. Linda told me of the King Arthur film done at Tintagel. The castle at K.A.C. hotel, paying 15 p... week for 3 weeks, Robert Taylor (!) in the village, all the villages paid £1 a day to... about in... as hordes of Britons, - this raised to £2 as they did not get enough, + 60 horses. props, + splendid costumes. The Goldwyn Mayer Coy. Why did the news mention it in the most dull letters? How depressing deadly note? The husband of the new "owner" of K.A.C. hotel goes off... bought to the Fish + Chip shop each night for supper for the guests. Dear old Linda, she keeps up. Very cold outside, Jupiter shining, + Sirius sparkling. How lovely it is.

EVENING APPOINTMENTS

All of the *Diaries* are written in hard backed books, often with one page for each date. Alison nearly always uses blue ink. Sometimes the writing is extremely hard to decipher.

Alison at sixteen, in what she herself described as 'a proud pose', c. 1900. She was by then a bright 'scholarship girl' at Lady Manners School, Bakewell.

The chemistry class at Lady Manners School; Alison is second from the front of the right hand row. She was already fascinated by science.

Students and Staff at Ashburne House, Manchester University, 1903-06; Alison is second from right, fourth row back; her great friend, Gladwys Llewellyn (the 'GL' of the *Diaries*), is last on the right third row back; the Warden Miss Stephen is in the middle of the second row back.

The Manchester University physics set in the Coupland Building. Alison (front row, second from the left) was one of the few females studying the subject.

Castle Top Farm, near Cromford, Derbyshire, Alison's fondly remembered birthplace set high up overlooking the River Derwent. The Taylor family had lived and worked at the farm for some two hundred years when Alison was born.

The Uttley family at Bowdon in 1911. Back row (from left), Alison, James and Alice Uttley. George Uttley is seated at the front on the ground. Middle row (from left), George Harry Uttley, Mrs. Uttley, Gertrude Uttley.

Another view of Castle Top Farm.

Alison on Wimbledon Common, in the late Edwardian period, photographed by her fiancé James Uttley.

Gertrude Uttley and Alison share a picnic at Patterdale.

Downs House, near Altrincham, Cheshire. This was Alison's home for almost the whole of the inter-war period, where she first began to write and where she endured James' suicide in 1930.

Alison when first married to James Uttley. She was a hard working and committed wife, although already hankering after a more creative life.

James Uttley as an officer in the Royal Engineers during the First World War.

James about to 'take a spin', soon after the First World War.

Alison and John (with James) camping at Tenby, in the early 1920s.

Alison and John at the seaside at Tenby, in Devon

Alison and James' son, John with his grandparents, Henry and Hannah Taylor, at Castle Top Farm, Derbyshire.

John (right) playing with his cousin, Martin Byers, Emily Uttley's son, at Downs House.

Alison's son, John, good looking and smartly dressed, as a public schoolmaster.

John and Helen Uttley on their wedding day, 1947. Helen had previously been widowed in 1941 during the Second World War.

John at Stowe School, with Lord Louis Mountbatten, the school's guest of honour, inspecting the cadet corps, in which John was an officer.

Alison as a young wife and mother. After her marriage in 1911, Alison gradually found being a housewife insufficiently satisfying, and by 1929 she had written her first *Little Grey Rabbit* book.

Alison while being made an Honorary Doctor of letters, Manchester University, May, 1970. She described it as 'a marvellous time, the best of my life.'

Samuel Alexander, who was Professor of Philosophy at Manchester University for 31 years. Alison saw him as a scholarly and kindly father figure, who encouraged her to begin writing,

After she moved to Beaconsfield in 1938, Alison developed a close friendship with the celebrated author and poet, Walter de la Mare (seen here in 1925), with whom she discussed the significance of dreams, time travel, the possible existence of fairies and much else.

Alison outside 'Thackers', Beaconsfield, in her 80s, busy in the garden. Although she often complained about her several gardeners' work, she was herself a gifted and energetic gardener, who tried to go each year to the Chelsea Flower Show.

Outside 'Thackers' in the late 1960s, towards the end of her life. She called the house 'Thackers' after the name she gave to the home of the Babington family in her best-selling 1939 novel, *A Traveller in Time*.

'Thackers', Beaconsfield. From 1938 until her death, Alison lived in this pleasant and leafy suburban Buckinghamshire town.

The headstone marking Alison's grave in Penn Churchyard. It describes her simply as, 'Writer, a Spinner of Tales.'

ALISON UTTLEY
1884 – 1976
writer
a spinner of tales

Alison in old age, as a grande dame of literature. She revelled in her widespread fame as a best-selling author – including the good deal of media attention she attracted towards the end of her life – despite her general unwillingness to suffer those she saw as fools gladly.

Margaret Tempest, the illustrator of the vast majority of the *Little Grey Rabbit* tales, with whom Alison had a tempestuous, though creative, relationship.

The cover for *Little Grey Rabbit's Christmas*, published in 1939, and illustrated by Margaret Tempest, beautifully sums up the quintessential charm and traditional appeal of this best-selling series of books.

Cecil Mary Leslie created this original artwork for the cover of *The Sam Pig Storybook*, the 1965 collection of more lively and dreamy tales of the mischievous Sam Pig and his long-suffering family.

The child Alison on a swing, looking down on her beloved Castle Top Farm, as imagined by one of her favourite illustrators, Charles Tunnicliffe, for her book *Ambush of Young Days*, 1937.

8th March

Many apologies from the [*bank*] manager, little wretch. I arranged for 2 accounts, for monthly statements.... [*A*] broadcast of the *Musical Box*, charmingly done.

9th March

I invested £1,500 in Defence Bonds at the P[*Post*] O[*Office*].... [*I listened to*] the broadcast of *Tim Rabbit Goes Hunting*.... I liked the pathetic music as the rabbits went into the house defeated.

5th April

First Brimstone [*butterfly*].... Cheque for £1,064. 10. [*from*] Collins. Paid in Barlays, & meet Mrs. Butterworth and Lady Curzon. Mrs. B told me with such joy that Lady B had lunched with the Queen and highly recommended my lovely *Bucks* book. The Queen wished to borrow it. 'I'll take good care of it,' said she, but Lady B went out to Windsor and bought it.... George Uttley! & Doris!! came.... [*I had*] not seen George for 20 years, Doris for 30.

11th April

The Washerwoman's Child chosen for television. Hurrah! Hurrah! To London with K Wig...my ring valued for insurance for £245.... And KW gave me a bunch of roses which I carried all day.

16th April

A little rabbit in the wood.... when I said 'In the wood' to Macduff, he looked in the woodbasket.

17th April

Pictures from Kennedy for *Yours Ever Sam Pig*, – very jolly. Cuckoos calling, an owl in the wood.

28th April

John and Helen came, – a happy visit & a grand lunch.... Cheque from Faber for £438.... I *think* I bought an Ambrose Breughel for 400 guineas, but I fear this was a mistake. However, everything most beautiful.

1st May

Yes, I have the [*bought*] Ambrose Breughel. I saw the little owls sitting in the tree, two little heads, big eyes, fluffy grey hair.

5th May

Joan Dobell came [*to stay*] with no rations, so I had to provide.... [*Joan*] talked for hours of the iniquities of her husband, so that my head whirled.

6th May

I went to Penn church, & left Joan [*here*].... All day the unhappy story.... I said, 'I wouldn't mind what kind of husband [*I had*] if I had a walnut tree'.

10th May

Gave lecture on the poetry of W de la Mare to the High Wycombe Book League. Only about 20 people there – a great deal of preparation for very little. I never felt I had got the audience, as they were dispersed round the room. Lilian King was there. To [*Betty*] Fairbairn in afternoon, & the wood-seller [*came and*] said I collected Breughels – I said Macduff collected Trousers.

6th June

Antique Dealers' Fair [*where I see*] Princess E[*Elizabeth*] in lilac dress.... her sweet face and nice manner.... I bought a diamond brooch (for £75) & a Queen Anne chair (for £135).... K Wigg came home with me to see MT's [*latest*] illustrations.

11th June

Infuriated by [*a*] letter from a school which had visited Castle Top [*Farm*] & wrote disparagingly.

12th June

Even more infuriated by letter from Dwye Evans [*of Heinemann*] criticising my two tales & asking for more plot. I feel I cannot write for him.... My lovely [*Queen Anne*] chair came, – but very late.... The diamond brooch came too & I have worn it.

14th June

A great gardening day.... Walter de la Mare sent his lovely *Winged Chariot*.

17th July

London [*to*] the BBC, to hear songs sung by Diana Maddocks.... I got my picture [*by*] Ambrose Breughel.

20th July

The odious accountant came.

28th July

My awful fall on the glassy sloping stair at Padbury.... I lay in agony.... To Stowe, dressing slowly. Notes. How did I walk back to Stowe? I do not know.

29th July

Wells drove me home.... I crawled to bed in much pain.

30th July
Agony all night.... Phoned doctor.... Taken to Windsor for X-ray.

31st July
Rib broken, muscles torn.... I had a lot of pain, & also from this Dermatitis which covers me.

1st August
K Wig came & looked after me. We went through the drawings.

2nd August
Specialist examined me [*and diagnosed*] a kind of Dermatitis brought on by hard work. [*A condition*] peculiar to intellectual people(!)... Nothing to do for at least 2 months.

10th September
I wrote a review of the *Herb Garden* for the *Sunday Times* & posted it, – a great effort.

12th September
John's birthday. I am sitting in the garden, the first time for ages for the sun at last shines. I had an autumnal tea out here, with a dragonfly on the table. Roses cream & yellow & pink & crimson, & gladioli, apricot, purple and carmine, so many colours.... My hands bandaged but I can write & I feel more cheerful today.

13th September.
Phone call from L Russell [*editor*] asking me to write a poem for GO [*Sunday Times magazine*] for the Xmas number for a children's page. Also he asked me privately if I would take on a gardening or flower column in the *Sunday Times* each week, like [*Vita*] Sackville-West's. I feel flattered and honoured but refused, – no Botany or Latin. I suggested Wilfred Blunt.

14th September
The doctor came, – my hand still very bad. To see the *Wandering Hedgehog* on the TV – I liked it.... Sent John £50 for [*his*] birthday.... Sleeping better but always tired.

18th September
Today I felt depressed, because it is the Anniversary [*of James's suicide*], because John isn't coming, because Macduff climbed the fence & disappeared.

19th September
Cheering up after a rotten night, no Macduff.... howling on the doorstep all night.... I got my hair cut in Penn.

20th September
L Russell phoned to ask me to write an article of 1,500 words for *GO* on the Language of Flowers... .I walked to Forty Green [*and*] talked to the young farmer Brown.... He said I was the first person he had seen all day.

15th October
A moment to remember. 6.30, dusk, lamps lighted, fire burning, wireless playing Tchaikowsky's [*sic*] ravishing music. The western sky banked with red-purple clouds and the tree pointed to the blue. White tobacco flowers in the garden, below the window a lavender coloured gladioli.... A short time ago David [*Davis*] read most beautifully *GR's Washing Day*. Diana Maddocks' sang.... All this should make me happy and thankful.... a feeling of beauty and bliss.

20th October
The Saturday Book published. A lovely book with pictures of roses, my article nicely done. I went to see Miss Collins to ask advice about MT. [*She is in dispute with Margaret Tempest about the latter having offered the Little Grey Rabbit stories to television for adaptation without consulting Alison first.*] Decided to phone Watts the [*literary*] agent [*for advice*].

25th October
Election Day. St. Crispin's Day. I walked to the poll, no-one else there when I voted.... The carpenter came.... I put down poison [*for rats*].

26th October
To London.... [*the literary agent*] D C Watts heard the tale. Sent me to a lawyer.... & he said I ought never to have signed, & it was blackmail.... Then to Faber for Peter du Sautoy.... Then to see the BBC.... Then to see David [*Davis*]. Then to Walter de la Mare. What a day.... Thrilled with the Conservative majority [*in the general election*]. *Ambush* [*is*] published today.

27th October
Recovering from yesterday. Letter from lawyer advising me to cut my losses, and sign no more [*contracts*], good advice too. Shopping & sleep, & listening to wireless with all the grand news. It cheers me very much. Winston supreme again. (a letter from Harry... telling me that CT is falling to decay, [*and*] suggesting I buy it, and he will put it in order!!.... Never a word about my broadcast, or my letter.... nor of the money I have sent him.)

31st October
Letters from [*a*] lawyer, from Walford at BBC, & from MT.... At night Mrs. [*Del*] Anderson came.... & we made draft replies. Oh, how it worries me.... But I worked happily at Christmas Toys all day, & tried to forget.

3rd November

A glorious drive with D. Anderson…. Notes. At night toothache worse and worse. Also my knee gave way. K Wig's lovely pictures came today for [*Little Grey Rabbit's*] *Spring Cleaning*.

4th November

To dentist, at 2.30, & he drew my tooth.

6th November

Worried about the letter to lawyers & M. T. which are too much for me. Posted review of B Nicholls' book to the *ST* [*Sunday Times*].

7th November

Cheque from *ST* (5 gns) for review on *Herb Garden*. Australia wants to broadcast the 2 *Brown Mouse* books. Emlyn Williams [*the actor and author*] wrote a charming letter…. I went to dentist, and he put in penicillin.

9th November

Letter from MT, – but still I do nothing. Washed Macduff…. [*Churchill's speech*] at the Guildhall banquet. The greatest man. The P[rime] Minister!

22nd November

M Tempest wrote & told me her story of her brother and husband. So now we are at peace – I give her equal rights in all TV [*the proposed television adaptation*]. Gardener here at last…. K Wig came, & we went through the pictures.

23rd November

K Wig & I… discussing a book of short tales for Faber, the new books, – a tale of Pin Hedgehog and his gypsy wife, & Snug running away to live with them. Also a tale of Serena who goes in [*her*] caravan harvesting. Planned a postcard painting book yesterday.

29th November

[*Shopping in London*] A good day, my first shopping day since July! 4 months away…. I asked for a picture by A. Brueghel to come on appro (only £65) & I bought a diamond brooch, simple & nice.

1st December

My lovely month. A few days of glory, mild, sunshine, heavenly shadows, blue sky, gold trees. Today fog has settled down, a grey fog hiding everything. The trees in my wood just visible, dark lavender against the pearly grey. I sit here in my room, close to the fire, for it is very cold. The room is gay with flowers. White Roman hyacinth came out last night, all the buds opening at once. Tall ones at the back…and all the different sizes in front. One of the best bowls I have grown because so diverse.

11th December
London. Bought 2 Davis Cox [*paintings*] from those I chose & settled on the Brueghel.

17th December
My birthday. A pile of letters, & a heap of parcels…. A happy day this.

18th December
To the party at High March [*School*], where I judged Fancy Dress, & gave prizes to: 1. A Coal Black Mammy, 2. A Victorian girl, 3. A Hawaian girl (adorable), & a little schoolmaster boy

20th December
Reading the letters of K[*Katherine*] M[*Mansfield*] which are awful, so sentimental, & toshy & sickly.

25th December
Midnight Mass, – chattering people, Helen whispering and grumbling, which spoiled it for me…. Oh my darling Christmas.

26th December
To the Meet at Winslow…. After lunch, to Stowe Park…. Helen [*was*] in a temper which alarmed me, her face big & ugly, & ominous for John. Poor John, he looked old & worn, I thought he looked about 50.

28th December
Mrs. Allen here, – & all cleaned up….I felt so tired. [*There was*] a rude letter from the 'Band of Hope', complaining of the [*Brown*] *Mouse* books and drinking!!

~ 1952 ~

4th January
An owl calling, [*a*] welcome sound at home. I drove home [*from visiting John and Helen*] 250 miles.

14th January
To London, for a television interview with Mrs. Kennish. Tea with David at BBC.

19th January
Very cold, a great frost last night. Sunshine. I made a huge bonfire…. feeding the flames. Picked a little red rosebud.

24th January
4 or 5 owls calling at 5.30, darkish, wet, sounds of rain dropping in the trees, pitterpat of drops, & all the owls in different voices. One was a gurgle like water in a bottle, bubbling out. Weird cries and hoots.

6th February
Death of the King [*George VI*]. [*The words went*] like a sword through the heart…. All quiet, frightened, bewildered.

8th February
The Queen [*is*] proclaimed at St. James's [*Palace*].

15th February
The King's funeral.

19th February
Nursing Home.

1st March
St. David's Day. First bee (honey) hovering on rock garden, and it flew to my yellow apron as if to find honey. A weak little bee.

30th March
Deep snow everywhere. A great astonished silence. The birds did not even come for crumbs until midday. Drifts piled against doors, snow covering trees. Torrents & wind but sunshine

after 1.0. So I planted Gladioli, 6 groups of Rose of Lima, Gen Eisenhower, Ostara, Snow Princess & Sweet Seventeen, – & separate groups of Puccini.... Picardy (?). Very very tired.... Good Friday. I heard a dove as I knelt in Church. Woodpeckers singing & laughing today. Lots of daffs out.

31st March
Mrs A spring cleaned my bedroom, – put up first summer curtains, but I felt quite ill today. Cold & windy & wet. Tree trunks green & gold. Hail. Great clouds. Writing *SP* tales. Greater spotted woodpecker in garden. Robin in kitchen, a rather draggled shy little bird from the front garden.

2nd April
I heard a turtle dove in our wood. Saw a tiny yellow hammer, the loveliest thing, could only just fly.

8th April
To the RHS [*Royal Horticultural Society's*] exhibition, [*where*] I order camellia, polyanthus, many rock plants.

19th April
At 3 a.m I heard the nightingale singing. Four flowers coming out on Magnolia.... All the wood a mist of green leaves, as it is so hot.

21st April
Rain. John came. Writing tale for BBC.... Tea [*in*]... wood. The geese, each with 2 wives, one a favourite wife. The tale of the goose whose wife went to another. Turned out gardener's shed, – a great upheaval, & a splendid clean as we threw things away.... Men moving old fence & putting in new.

22nd April
To Burford, Bibury, Roman villa, Cheltenham & back to Winchcomb.... An owl in apple tree at dusk. Leslie here digging some of the garden. Icy cold winds, & frosts every day.

4th May
To Penn, to tea with Walter de la Mare [*who has been ill*]. He was leaning on a stick, [*talking in*] his warm, vibrant, happy low voice.... We talked by the fire of dictionaries, and his illness which he saw off so brilliantly.

31st May
[*She writes some notes of cuckoo song*] Operation to womb, at 9 a. m. by Dr. Henderson. Injection at 8.0. Anaesthetic at 9 & went straight off for 5 hours or more. Slept on and off all the day & heavy drugged sleep, sick between.

12th June
To the Antique Dealers' Fair, where I bought a (Dutch) Breughel painting of the Virgin, Child and angels. A silver Queen Anne porringer, and two glass lustres, about 1780.

16th June.
Cotswolds with John. Burford – blue geraniums by road, which we picked. Water garden at Burford…. Upper Slaughter, Stow, Chipping Norton.

10th July
Richards came, and a great watering of the front garden…. Mrs. Matthews to tea, – a charming woman.

12th August
Spring cleaned all the books in the drawing room, – & quite fun, but I was terribly tired, & had to go to bed after. Very hot indeed. LM came…. Tea in garden.

16th August
To London, lunch with Margaret Rutherford and Stringer. Then to the [*Royal*] Court, where I sat in the dressing room, & then to see the fantastic play.

17th August.
LM at Mass. I stayed at home. We had a quiet day.

20th August
The Innocents. A wonderful play, very exciting, frightening, ghostly, & perfectly acted by that little magical child.

29th August
Owls hunting very late, both the barn owl and the little owl I think. 'Too-whit-too-whoo-oo' and 'kwich-kiwich'. Hot day. Tea in garden. Torrents so I did not got to the Penn Show today. GL came at tea time.

This is the last entry for 1952.

1953

1st January
Beauty makes us homesick.... [*The*] eternity to which we belong, which is shown in beauty...the feeling, as the eternal breaks through, the certainty that all is well. A secret we carry in our hearts, that at the end of the road we shall hear the music and see the lights.... Peter du S phoned, – he cannot come to my party tomorrow, but will call on Sat. & bring the MSS of [*The Stuff of Dreams*] if ready.... Getting in coal & wood, doing fire, cooking boiled bacon & parsley sauce, & a plum pudding for my New Year lunch. Last night I went to bed at 7.00 after my return from the Children's Party, I was so tired & cold. 'Write a book of *GR and Guy Fawkes*'. 'I know what's in your merry-go-round. There's some magic in it,' shouted a little boy to me.

3rd January
[*Manuscript of*] *The Stuff of Dreams* sent to [*Faber*] today. Very tired in the night, [*I saw*] phantoms through seeing so many people, although there were only 10 guests.... Lovely review in *Truth*.... & the full page quote in *Farmers Weekly* for Xmas.... Letter from Harry, [*talking about*] our mother's potted meat.

4th January
Reading *Space, Time and Deity*, & thinking of my beloved [*Professor*] S. Alexander.... Space and time imply each other mutually.... I drive the car [*for*] the first time since November 29th [*1952*] when I had that skid. I enjoyed it.

5th January
12th Night I think. I wrote to Irene Hawkins and LM in bed after breakfast.... I drove to B, [*put*] £650 in Barclays [*Bank*] for income tax, alas.... [*Barclays*] smiling, Lloyds glum. [*I find it difficult to get insured for driving*] because I learned to drive late in life. So, I must go on, uninsured & not care.... The room is now saying Goodbye to Christmas.

6th January
Twelfth Night. Snow! I saw it falling, twinkling & sparkling last night.... I wrote to E Wilson (I fear she may be dead), to Ethel Herdman (why, oh why!), to Harry.... a letter from John. He had seen snipe, partridge, hare & duck on his walk, & he brought the New Year to the village inn!

9th January
Slept badly, I felt sick today.... Mrs. Allen [*can't get through the snow*] so I ordered a taxi for her.... The carpenter came and cut the bottom stair, great discussions.... Sandwich lunch

& a rest. [*I listened*] to MR's *Desert Island Discs* broadcast. Good but too serious.... I rang her up, and she says she thinks of me every day.... My leg is swollen & a running sore and the Dermatitis.

10th January

[*My*] roast lamb for lunch, with onion sauce.... makes me think of *Wind in the Willows*.... [*I listened*] to the *Second* Borodin, with that ravishing fall of a fifth. Nowadays [*there are*] so many luxuries, even hot water from a tap is a luxury, – music of Grieg [*from*] another tap, & my blue irises which might sing if I could hear.... I thought of Mother so clearly as I lay down, I felt queer.

11th January

Alas, – sick all night.... never have I had such an attack!.... Macduff knew I was ill & I was comforted by his presence. Yet [*only*] one's *mother*... could have helped.... In bed all day. I was letting Mac out & there stood P du Sautoy on the doorstep. I dashed upstairs & gave a brush to my hair & put on a ribbon, then invited in the party of 5 [*the du Sautoy family*].... The usual debunking reviews [*in Sunday Times*], Raymond Mortimer sneering at Carlyle, [*Cyril*] Connolly sneering at Bridges.

12th January

[*I have been*] working at a *GR* tale – 'at the Sea', & when, if ever, will it be published? Still I must have a tale in reserve.... MR cancelled lunch.... She says she is concentrating so hard on her new play she must keep her mind on it.... It is absolutely right.... It is what I try to do.

19th January

A foggy day, very thick fog.... I saw the fog swirling up to my windows like smoke. A queer quiet 'contained' day. I am living in a box in the fog. It makes one realise how precious is light & sunshine.... my first Folio [*Society book*].... I don't know whether I like it.... This morning in bed my conscience pricking me as I thought of all I might help & here I live alone in luxury. So I packed 2 boxes, one for Hilda, one for Sissy, wrote to them, & to Joyce Holt & Teresa Hooley, – I began to write soon after 7 o'clock. Yet I can only write books by living alone, & I have to earn my living.... After lunch I listened to the *Elderly Woman's Hour*, which was comforting. I liked the clever woman who can live on 15/- a week [*for*] food.... so could I if I wished. Sleeping, overcome with tiredness at 4 pm, – so I nodded for over an hour, & then began to work & got on well.

21st January

I felt sick as I read of the Sitwells & Nicholsons [*sic*] & all that crowd of arrogant intellectuals, especially Edith Sitwell. Somehow her world is crooked and evil.... I had to cheer myself up. I put on the Light Programme [*but*] it was so awful I [*turned*] it off.... [*I liked*] Vaughan Williams's *Sinfonia Arctica*.... although the critics hedged.

27th January

A grand day to London.... to the dentist, where I autographed books as I waited for Mrs. Wig to come out.... [*I found*] the Dutch Exhibition a wonder.... I could *live* there. Really, I would mortgage everything to buy pictures.... So much pure beauty. [*The faces of the old women reminded me of my*] childhood, Mrs. Fox, Eliza, my mother, and women in [*the*] cottages, all were there.

28th January

Letter from Mrs. Carver, telling me of the joy in *Plowmen's Clocks*.... 'It was so beautiful, I nearly bursted.'...[*I was heartened because*] it comes with a dull review about my nostalgic memories and regrets, which annoys for I am not nostalgic. I much prefer the present.

29th January

Books I am reading, *Living Time*, by [*Beverley*] Nicholls, Carlyle's Letters (just come), and *Shorelands* by Tunnicliffe.

30th January

The 'cataclysmic' music of Sibelius *Second Symphony*. Primitive & natural & supernatural. The power of nature in it. I was awake last night, irritating dermatitis, & feeling worried about little things, especially all the manure covering the garden. This morning I determined to 'lay my worry', so I set to, in mackintosh and in rain. I raked off the manure, & exposed snowdrops and bulbs & lots of lovely things.... I am really fed up with Richards [*the gardener*] and his bad work.... finished the tale of the *Red Fox*, which I began last night. A book to review, – *Where I Live* by Robert Duncan.... Hilda at last thanks me for my lovely parcel.... K Wig writes to say Heinemann want 2 [more] *Snug* books, a nuisance indeed for I don't want to write any more of them. Also they want a larger book, but I *will not* do it. No time.

1st February

Frightful news of floods on the East coast and the Netherlands, the sea entering towns, houses falling, people drowned.... I wonder if it is something to do with the change in the moon's tidal power.... such strong winds, I wondered if I can drive [*in them*].

2nd February

The story of the floods is appalling.... It makes me realise how Atlantis was lost, & how a land might disappear.

3rd February

Letter from USA, telling me as a friend of S. Thomas of Tommy's death. I think of her long ago.... when we were bosom friends and she was not a Communist.... [*I travelled to London*] to dentist.... Now for the bill! Met K Wig for lunch.... to BBC to discuss the song books. I have proposals to put to Collins and Faber. I met Mary Treadgold by chance near the BBC, & we had coffee thrilled to see each other & a great chat. She is writing a book.

5th February
Packed off 5 pairs shoes to Flood Relief. K Wig came, looking very rosy and excited, in a green suit…. A high tea of finnan haddock, most delicious, & cake & ginger. We talked of books, & the *Brown Mouse*.

6th February
The sweep came (4/- + tip). And we spring cleaned, K[*Kathleen*] went…. I gave KW a blue rest gown, and she looked like a buxom Dutch picture…. I called her Catherine Parr [*the sixth wife of Henry VIII*], & we laughed till we cried.

12th February
Snow! Drifts of 13 feet in some places…. Snow here all day…. & I walked out with Macduff in snow, – icy cold & wet slush…. Jan Bussell and Anne Hogarth came, – a delightful pair, she in a scarlet coat, he in a kind of fawn Eskimo coat with hood – in the snow they looked like Explorers. We had tea by the cosy fire & interesting talk [*about*] puppets & books & pictures & the TV series. Anne Hogarth says Annette Mills is like MT. The same kind of attitudes, difficult to work with. They dislike intensely the woman head of TV, who is all for Education and never for Art…. [*Jan Bussell*] told me they had had complications with the BBC over some of my *GR* tales. *Toad* & the bottle of venom, – *Hare* & cowslip wine! The word 'swig'…. A very good man is doing TV & radio in USA…. & he may do the *LGR* if he can buy them. £500 should buy the set, he thinks. We must all wait & not rush or prices will go up.

13th February
The Stuff of Dreams is formally accepted, to my joy…. Usual terms, all very charming, & a lovely letter from du Sautoy…. Heinemanns [*like and will do*] the *Mouse* book. George Uttley wrote, explaining the business crisis [*with Sugdens*] & young [*Tony*] Tolson also wrote with a form for me to sign. 'A plague on both your houses,' say I.

14th February
[*She quotes from John's Valentine to her*] 'I'm neither Oak, nor weeping willow'…. Bless him! KW [*sent*] daffs by telegram…. This morning a scene of great beauty outside…. I have slept better, because I keep on the [*electric*] fire, which comforts me.

20th February
No Richards so I went out in coat…. & raked off manure from the beds, masses of it…. I began to revise the *Dream* book, which Faber sent [*back*] at my request…. very exciting to get into it.

23rd February
My hair waved, – I was shocked at my white, drawn face in the [*hairdresser's*] glass…. I went to Elizabeth Coatsworth's tonight, suddenly feeling gay with music, fire & cyclamen & light.

1st March
March, and a cold, icy, sunny day, a delight.... To Penn Church – & I felt sudden joy & thankfulness for the porch with its carved timbers over door, the alcoves in the whitewashed porch, the stone benches – & a blue flower. All peaceful & plain inside as if in [*the*] heart. They sang a hymn I noticed last week, words by [*George*] Herbert, I was happy to sing it. I must find the words. Sermon, alas, not very exciting for [*the*] heart.... My Dermatitis is bad, I have bandages on [*my*] arms and legs, and patches all over, but I go on, wondering what to do.... it gets worse.

4th March
K Wig wrote to say Heinemann want both books this year.... They are really inconsiderate, only K Wig could work at such speed.... My spots so bad, so I rang Dr. Milner.... [*I was angry with Lloyds*] for leaving me overdrawn on 2%.... to Amersham.... I promised [*a blind basket maker*] my book.... [*Little Alice Montgomery*] reminds me of myself at that age. She said she would like to stay here all night.

12th March
Feeling grey & ill. Doctor did not come as he promised.... If I were not ill, I should be happy, gay, jolly, for I am so excited, with Spring coming, daffs in bud, *Dream* book in the press, tulips coming out soon. And now I can only anoint my 100 wounds.

13th March
Mrs. Allen [*and I*] put on clean linen sheet. We wondered if the Queen has clean sheets every day, & we think she does.... The D[*Dermatitis is*] so bad I am going to stop the treatment. Coughed all night too

22nd March
A frightful night of irritation. At 6.0 I arose, made my troubled bed completely, – I had tidied it & swept up scurf and scabs all night, but I had a great upheaval. Then I got in, & fell asleep, & I didn't wake till Macduff's little whimpers called me at ¼ to 10. I could hardly believe my eyes.... I went for a little walk in the newly discovered Burke's Wood, quite lovely and restful, & I saw a large horse-shoe lying on the verge of the ploughfield but I left it. The trees.... the twigs & the peace of the wood made me realise the dream Beaconsfield must have been 50 years ago.... K Sibbring's puppy darted out, with her 2 little adopted girls. Such sights they looked. I wonder if KS finds it too much to keep them neat, or is it because they are adopted?

23rd March
A charming letter from Georgina Jenkinson, saying, 'You are such a lovely person'.... Yes, but I am not at all a lovely person, I fear.... The doctor came just as I was listening with joy to Victor Sylvester [*leader of the dance band*]. He agrees I may stop the F99 pills for a week.... I have felt better today.... After my rest, off in the car to Penn Bottom.... I felt I wanted to write about these beech woods. I was absolutely happy as I walked on the soft grassy path.

25th March
[*She recounts Churchill's speech on death of Queen Mary*] Men & women of all lands have sorrowing hearts…. Queen Mary was loved and revered far & wide. Her grandfather a son of George III, yet she lived in this atomic age. 1867-1953. [*Yet*] she moved easily through the changing scene…. A sad day, – the tolling bell in the night, & again this morning before the news. I think of her saying she liked my books & wanted to know of all that were published. I think of the young man who cheered so wildly at the coronation procession, 'I'm a great admirer of Queen Mary,' said he…. Macduff bit little Malcolm [*Montgomery*]'s finger, but the child was brave…. The Dermatitis is bad, but I've half forgotten it today.

31st March
Slept badly last night, tearing off all [*my*] bandages, & scratching the horrible places, as I groaned with pain…. I am invited to open Holtspur church fete…. The day of Queen Mary's funeral at Windsor…. Mrs. Allen spring cleaned…. I had to do a long criticism of [*K Wig's pictures*], for the *Chimney* book…. Some lovely things, – the stars tonight, Orion and Cassiopeia & [*the*] Pleiades.

1st April
I felt cheerful and gay because it is April, the month of the Cuckoo and Spring. I went to B in the Montgomery's car…. I bought my record, which I played this afternoon…. I played Lindy Lou…. *My Blue Heaven.*

3rd April
A wonderful little sermon by the vicar of St. Martin's. I thought of Good Friday so intensely that for a moment I was there…. Finished the great book, *Under the Sea* by Cousteau. A marvel.

5th April
I had a bad night…. at 3 am…. I took a 4th sleeping pill and managed to escape my torments…. I came down and welcomed Easter…. It took ages to dress…my nightdress is in rags. I cooked a chicken, & managed a nice lunch.

7th April
Very ill in evening, I swelled up to a huge size, with throbbing pain, & rather frightened I phoned doctor…. Dr. came at 11.0. Complete rest, no medicine. [*Get a*] nurse, or go to nursing home…. I looked like somebody else, big face, big neck.

13th April
John came…. looking gay and happy & bringing an atmosphere of calm and joy with him. He has this power. He cooked the chicken, – I had doctor & nurse upstairs but got up.

15th April
A lovely sleep last night, – I put on no ointment…. and slept. John got breakfast trays, &

what a joy it is…. We drove off to Amersham…. Aylesbury…. It has been a grand little holiday for me in spite of pain & irritation & agony.

20th April

This morning a phone call from Del Anderson…. asking quite calmly if I could lend her £300. I was staggered…. She spends to the hilt…. Not on country life…. but on showy places…. Doctor Milner says I have improved.

22nd April

Letter from Georgie Jenkinson, very sweet. A glorious day…. I naughtily went in the garden in my nightdress…. Tonight a little owl sitting in a little apple tree by the house! I could hardly believe my eyes.

27th April

Specialist came, a charming young man. He says my illness is through over-stimulation, overwork, [*and*] I ought take a real holiday…. He gave new medicines…. I feel rather shy to ask [*may I*] go to the Chelsea Flower Show. He said No! No!

1st May

Rain, – but I had a good night, after listening to Churchill at the RA dinner. The speeches were great fun, though Harold Nicolson was rather portentous…. Not depressed yet! Lots of people far worse off…. Oh darling month of May, do see me well again…. Why *does* Mrs. M[*Muspratt, wife of the vicar*] phone at 3 pm?

4th May

At 11. 0 Mr. Muspratt came for Holy Communion. I had put the Charles II table ready, with a fair white cloth, candles & 2 silver candlesticks, mother's cross & a glass of gentians…. He talked so nicely of Christ's breaking the bread…. Then I read aloud 2 or 3 verses of a poem by George Herbert…. I could feel the presence of God. All day I felt very happy…. I gave 10/- for the offertory, and said I would like to pay for the painting of one of the shields on the roof for [*the imminent*] Coronation (5 guineas). I shall be very happy to do this for Penn, for I love to think of Penn Church standing there on the hill, century after century….

9th May

I picked big bunches of lily of the valley. This is one of my heart's desires, – to have lots of lilies. They have a strange effect on me, I am enchanted, & lost & intoxicated by them.

18th May

Writing in bed tonight…. [*I*] enjoyed *20 Questions*…. Exciting cricket, both MCC & Australia out in a day…. A charming letter from Georgie Jenkinson…. Mrs. Montgomery came, and she talked of Del A[*Anderson*]…. most difficult now…. I don't like Del…. I am a poor judge of character, except that my *first* impression is usually right.

20th May
A long letter from Argentina [*beginning*] 'Dear Alison' and went on to wonder whether any nice boy had ever married me. I read no more…[*I was*] amazed by his casual impertinence.

2nd June
Coronation Day. I put on wireless at 7.00 am & enjoyed thinking of everyone in London & imagining what they were doing…. I went… to Joyce Kann's. Lovely decorations & flowers. The dining room like a theatre & curtains drawn & TV set before them, with 3 or 4 rows of chairs. It was quite wonderful. I won't try to write down what I felt, of its beauty, strength and spirituality. I felt very proud of England, & so thankful to be English, & thankful for this Queen.

6th June
I decided to go to the Coronation Fete at Penn, at [*Lord*] Curzons. Drove there…. a great welcome from Lord & Lady C, – the babies playing with dolls, & a boy with them. He smiled & I held out my hand… 'Lord…', introduced the nurse primly. But all great fun. Lovely singing & glorious view. I sat with the Wailes, [*but*] Mrs W is not quite my [*sort*], too something, too…. I talked of ghosts. Lord C does not believe in them but she swears they are there & I know they are. I drove home slowly... as I am not really up to driving yet.

10th June
My great day. London with Reeves [*her driver*], – to see the decorations. We drove up the beautiful Mall, like a fairyland, to the Trafalgar Square…along the Strand to Fleet St, Ludgate, all so lovely I was amazed…. to Berkeley Square like a French fairy tale…. Antique Dealers Fair. Princess Margaret, very charming, prettier than I thought, in navy blue silk with white flowers embroidered, & a gay little hat with tulle veil. She spoke well, a sweet voice, & lovely manners. I bought a glass, about 1730…a beauty, for £17…. [*and*] a nutmeg grater, £8…. A marvellous day of sunshine.

14th June
Yesterday Walter de la Mare, speaking of reincarnation [*said that*] I was born with the power to write…. I had a special virtue or grace [*with music and literature*]…. We spoke of where was the essence of ourselves…. I said in the air, a little above me

17th June
I sent off £450 half-yearly tax, – a frightful lot. I can't believe I ought to pay all this.

18th June
'Time is measured by the intensity of emotion.'

22nd July
I put on my best grey silk frock…. and went off to Westminster to the cricket match between the Authors and Publishers. My first visit to London by train for nearly 6 months…. most exciting. I met a lot of people there…. Mr Crawley [*of Faber*] asked me to

write a *Traveller in Time* book, – if only I can write another *Time* book! Also a new *Sam Pig* & a new *Tim Rabbit*, and a book on Bucks. All these I promised ruthlessly…. I met Mr. [RAB] Butler, Chancellor of the Exchequer, [*and*] Compton Mackenzie, whom Joyce later called the epitome of snobbery, – true.

28th July
I had [*an ill*] Macduff in my room all night, gave him brandy & kept the fire on.

1st August
Mr. Desborough came… to bring the Jan Breughel windmill picture…. Sir George and Lady Simpson came…. I found him dull, & moulded into science, – not the quicksilver man I once admired…. I find that these men who go to the smaller universities are narrow, in spite of travel.

10th August
The doctor came. Agrees that I try a little Iodex for a time…. He says I ought to have a new treatment…. [*Perhaps*] scrap it all & try a Homeopathic drug…. My wedding day, and I forgot it. Ah well! A lovely long letter from Georgie Jenkinson in Italy… suggesting we both go some day. *Yes*!

12th August
John's sweet letter [*comes*] from Guernsey. He is sketching, bathing & reading…. [*LM arrives*] looking tired and grey but smiling…. A gay & joyful occasion…. Sent off income tax [*an*] extra £75, or nearly £1,000 altogether! I never save a penny.

28th August
LM went. I gave her *Ploughmen's Clocks*, & I sent a book for little Lucy…. I *have* enjoyed having her. But I fear I've been impatient quite often, rude – rushing about. She is so *patient*… but slow as a snail. There is so much to do, that I rush on to finish, exasperated by her slow motion. Dear old Lily.

1st September
I was up in the night with Macduff, who was not well…. I lay in bed listening to the silvery song of wrens…. exquisite and magical…. After lunch I went to the *Kon Tiki*, a very good & moving film…. I took back Belloc's poems to Miss Collins…. I don't think Belloc was a good poet at all.

14th September
John came! What a joy it was. Macduff wild with joy. So he drove me to B to get my hair done, & he looked after the cooking of my dinner.

17th September
A lovely fairy tale book to review for the *S Times*, – translated by Desmond McCarthy. (*Nutcracker*). Three new books out, 2 *Mouse* books & the *GR* book. I felt tired and rather

depressed, because I'm not so well…. Patches of red spots…. An interval in the Third Programme. 'I will play 2 Chopin *Nocturnes*' said the man. I sang one & then scolded myself for trying to 'get foreknowledge'. The music began. The same *Nocturne*. The same key and the same pitch! I was rather alarmed.

22nd September

Invitation to speak at WI meeting, Tyler's Green which I refused. Invitation to open Woman's Exhibition of Art, which I accepted for 10th October…. The accountant came…. Not as bad as usual, but he is a sententious bore & I dislike his grin & his facetiousness. He really is an awful man to know one's affairs.

24th September

To Brighton. Sitting in train to London with Miss Prescott…. Her fat legs covered with dark hairs, exposed to the knee…. I scribbled in my diary to avoid her, & then she began, thrusting a book of Prayers under my nose for me to read. One was *Cromwell's Prayer*. Oh dear…. She is *so* ugly.

25th September

Sat on beach, weary & forlorn, overwhelmed by all the people. 'A sign,' said I, 'Send me a sign'…. I found a cowrie, a lucky shell of long ago, and I thought of Tenby, & James & John, & all the happy days. I cheered up.

11th October

Peter du Sautoy came, & we had a happy little meeting. He said that 'Everybody' (?) wanted to have an article on me…. Secretly I always wonder why anybody honours me, reads me. I hide here quite unknown, forgetting the world in contemplation.

19th October

Three long letters. One from [*Margaret Tempest*]. My heart sank. I barely read it, & sent it to John to answer. She will only allow Jan Bussell a year to decide. Very well, I will be obstructive if he doesn't get it & won't let others have the film. She is absolutely awful! He has done all the work & put us on the TV map, but she won't forgive him for not asking her permission to use the *GR* tales originally [*for the BBC television adaptation*], when he asked me…. A letter so gushing, so flattering letter from [*Katherine*] Carver I feel alarmed. 'Dear Enchantress'. A poem to me, my eyes and my hands. Tells me of a dream of a filly with a rose, which is me. I am really alarmed by her…. this is ugly. One of those overbalanced females. Oh dear, what shall I do? A sweet letter from Georgie Jenkinson, so sane & good & true…. Tonight a pretty young girl came… with a pile of drawings & paintings, for advice. I was pleased with her nice work.

21st October

A big shock this morning. A Mrs. Black says that I gave permission & she is selling *GR* toys to Harrods!! I wired her 'Stop Production'…. shades of M Tempest…. I cheered up and droves to Jordans…. I began a *Sam Pig* tale, and forgot all the Tempest worries.

3rd November

In London.... Lunch at the Stewarts!... I wrote to Katherine Carver asking her to stop [*writing to her*]. A letter came today saying 'most blessed and enchanting one'. She is quite crazily psychic, I will not have it.

4th November

A glorious day of beauty, glitter of frost & sunshine. But I had a batch of worries which I have to set aside. Letter from Collins about the Jigsaws.... Horribly rude letter from accountant saying he has tried to get my expenses by saying I am old, nearly 70, & take no pleasure in travelling or anything! Still they won't accept it, & no wonder. It infuriates me. No pleasure!!..No letter from W de la Mare who has not acknowledged the *Dream* book sent 4 weeks ago.... [*The*] postman said he could kill Mac[*duff*], who guarded the way as he brought parcels.... [*The book*], *Flying Saucers Have Landed*, came.

7th November

In bed with sore throat & temperature. Reading the exciting statement of George Adamski, on the meeting with a man from space.... It has the ring of truth. Yet I dare not say so as English people will be most scornful. It agrees with my dreams too.

11th November

[*A catalogue of why she feels sorry for herself*] ....the cruel words of the accountant, the gushing sentiment of the Carver woman, my Dermatitis.... the feeling of illness & weariness which has assailed me since the accountant's depressing letter. So I turned to the wireless for *Lift up your Hearts*.... It spoke of the lonely, the really lonely, – & told them to smile & a smile would be returned, – of the men who only put in screws day after day.... And I thought of all my joys & excitements.... A new moon, & I made a wish to it.

14th November

A better day, although I was kept awake by falling logs and rats racing in the woodpile.... I went to B to Barclays Bank (where I saw Sutton from Lloyds Bank, so I was discovered red-handed!)...for Surtax.... At night to a cocktail party at the Colemans.... It was nice, not noisy.... Mrs. Gurney asked how I managed when I was ill. 'Oh, Macduff brought up trays in his paws!'...Well, they never come near me!

16th November

A dream, [*which I noted down at*] 5 am as soon as I had recovered my powers.... I dreamed I was in a little old house.... footsteps... began to come downstairs.... There was no escape.... We were in Scotland... – Doctor came, says I'm much better, and he wants me to go on with the powdering.... Lovell's men came, put up the fence [*and*] stripped the Virginia creeper from roof.

29th November

Eureka! A good review [*of The Stuff of Dreams*] in the *S Times*.... I was astonished &

cheered immensely .... I feel stupified during [*the*] sermons as [*the vicar*] muddles along with clichés & mistakes & contradictions.

5th December
A review from *The Psychic*, something which horrified me.... I felt sick all day [*but*] I must not care. Nobody was less of a spiritualist than I. It fills me with loathing, the whole subject. It is Dunne's theory I follow.

8th December
Letter from Hill, solicitor, saying he has the deeds of Downs House.... I have written asking him to transfer the house to John.

12th December
Letters in the *S Times*. Mothers are now blamed for all the wickedness of youth and grown ups. In my childhood the Devil was blamed, and we had to strive to conquer him. Now children blame their mothers, and it is a legitimate excuse for all evil.

17th December
Birthday, – I awoke feeling much better, ... No letters or cards for my birthday, forgotten by LM, Harry, and GL is far too busy with her invalid.... I went to B... to sign the deeds of Downs House for John.... *The Quiet Man*, I didn't really like it [*the film*]. It was phoney.... Tonight a little dinner of soup... sole & coffee. John phoned birthday wishes, bless him.

25th December
Church at Maids Norton, which I love, – the little boy, his collection. The crib. The Xmas tree. A butterfly; Church and Carols.... Christmas dinner. The Queen's moving speech.

27th December
John & I & Helen go to Stowe..... As Helen leaned over gate to say goodbye in the dark, she whispered she was sorry she had been so rude to me but [*that*] she was tired.... my heart ached but I had said nothing.

30th December
[*To London*] to the Academy to the Flemish Exhib[*ition*].... I went off to the Stewarts.... Home feeling rather depressed.... Perhaps due to the crowds [*or*] a review in *Truth*.... or perhaps learning [that] Collins were selling *GR* toys without my permission.... or perhaps overtired.

31st December
A day of marvellous beauty.... I drove to Old B. Then to St. Michael's, smelling of incense, very lovely.... Then to Penn Church.... off to see *Fantasia* at films. V. good, but such noisy children one could hardly hear the music.... Home with one star shining. Now goodnight dear year. I have been out to look at the stars this starlit night.

~ 1954 ~

1st January

A lovely day.... I went to B to get car license £12.10, & a dog license & petrol & a red azalea 8/6.... The [*living*] room pretty & cosy & happy.

3rd January

A green woodpecker climbing up an apple tree.... but I disturbed it.... [*I find*] the Montgomeries.... really very dull, dull but good.... The Fairbairns came at 8.30.... Lovely songs.... Elizabethan airs. Enchanting. I really felt drawn out of my body away to Eliz[*abethan*] days. RF [*Richard Fairbairn*] sings like an angel, BF [*Betty Fairbairn*] like a disembodied spirit.

4th January

[*The*] Chester Wilmots came, and I made a party table.... I gave [*the children*] *SP in Trouble*, but Caroline wanted all the *GR* books. I would have said, 'There are shops, you know' – I calmly refused to give any more. They have not bought any [*of my*] books, I think.... Still, it is their loss.

7th January

Enchantment. Snow on the ground, streaks of blue shadow across the lawn, the beech tree now bare of snow but radiant, & glowing in the sunshine, the boughs sending shadows across its greenish trunk. Birds flitting in the snow, running on little feet, hopping and swooping as they pick up scraps. Intent, but heads raised ready to fly off. Two pecks & up they glance. A blackbird on the stump.... The light across is golden – & the trees are shining with reflected light. No picture could give this beauty, no memory retain it.

10th January

Music. One of the first musical memories of music was the *Thieving Magpie* by Rossini in the musical box [*at Castle Top farm*]. I must have heard it thousands of times in my life but I never tired of it.... all mingled with flames of the dining room fire, the candlelight.... I became dumb & tired [*at Penn Church*] as Mr. M[*Muspratt*] maundered on in his sermon.... Those boys at [*her friends, the Kings*] are like robots of tin.... Awful news tonight of the crash of the Comet, & the death of Chester Wilmot.... [*Margaret Rutherford telephoned me to say she*] loves the dream book.

11th January

I lay awake most of last night thinking of Mrs. Chester Wilmot, and the terrible & sudden news of the crash, – & it made me think of my own grief long ago, – & that night alone. I wrote to her in the morning, trying to help…. [*There was a*] robin in the kitchen when I brought down my breakfast things – it is always in the house.

16th January
A glorious day of sunshine, high winds & great beauty. I went off in morning to B for bridge rolls & cakes for tomorrow's party…. To old B. to take [*the*] *Connoisseur* to Mrs Brown who is ill. Talked to Mr B…[*and*] he told me of his difficulties [*in*] finding capital to pay for things, – banks not allowed to lend for luxury trades… *Perfection*: a magpie flew across from the trees…. The silver moon, a silver birch tree & a plane against the blue countryside.

23rd January
Such a day! The circus! [*I went with the Fairbairns*] to Olympia. Glorious. The swinging trapeze [*performer*]… in his white silk flying and whisking up the young boy of 15 who did such dazzling feats, the shapes of bodies &…. limbs, the beauty of perfection. The cream horses & Shetland ponies…. Sealions and chimpanzees, elephants and a little dog, – most delightful and thrilling.

25th January
I got up late, after writing letter to Peter du Sautoy in bed to ask him for advice about scientist's questionnaire [*which she had been sent*]…. I did the review of *Children in the House*…. I wrote the review about 10 times to do it. The D[*Dermatitis*] rather bad. I have scratched my leg until it bleeds, alas.

26th January
Gardener here & raking moss from lawn…. John's nice letter, – he has had the Athays to dine on pheasant he had shot in Norfolk…. A queer rapturous joy with this snow, the ice-cold air & the pretty house.

27th January
I didn't go for a walk, tempting as it was, for I must stay here & work, but I went in [*the*] wood & made a bonfire up…. Peter du S wrote a draft letter which he will send to this Dr. C who asks so many questions [*of Alison*], – very polite but firm. I am so thankful…. I wrote to GL thanking her for a dozen eggs.

1st February
Icier than ever, the coldest day…. I have done only 1 page of *S Pig*…. [*It is so*] cold I wonder about atomic disintegration, and the unknown causes of this for Rivers freezing now.

6th February
Shandeloes, – the lake with [*a*] fringe of beige and brown, seeds, bushes, & the lavender trees beyond & the ice itself, steel blue with snow on it. Sunshine [*and*] shadows, brown,

crimson, scarlet, blue, boys & men women & children in the sledges, all very gay, & a mouth organ playing in the distance. I sat on a fallen tree with a rug over it & [*then walked*] on the ice – under an alder tree…. [*the*] ice was cracked in places, very clear & we could see down [*through*] it, 6ft deep, they said. The cracks sounded ominous but we did not mind.

7th February
News of immense crowds at Sydney & great heat for the [*visit of the*] Queen…. thousands of staring people, – the strain it has been. Poor child!

9th February
Quote from MT. A grandmother reading *GR* Makes Lace to a 2¹/₂ year old child…. He said 'But you haven't started at the beginning…. *Little Grey Rabbit* makes lace by Alice Utty, pictures by Marga Tempy.'…. A broadcast on Chester Wilmot tonight. What a genius. What strength & courage & vitality. So much you feel heaven wanted him to help up there.

10th February
A lovely note from Mrs. Chester Wilmot about my letter, & the *SP* book which has comforted her little girl who could not sleep for grief. Poor little one.

11th February
A letter from David [*Davis*] of the BBC wanting to broadcast tales beginning in April…. To Penn to tea with L[*Lilian*] King, a marvel of charm & beauty & goodness.

13th February
A dream, too long to relate, when I slipped into a narrow, reedy channel and climbed out wet dripping from clothes to the bank…. I awoke suddenly & was rather dizzy when I got up.

15th February
A Valentine from John, and an absurdly delicious poem…. To the cinema, *The Third Man*…. and the *Little World of Don Camillo* – excellent, French with captions, but it was easy to follow in French.

21st February
Slept well, 4 hours deep sleep…. [*I am*] reading *The Golden Honeycomb*, – lovely prose. Listening to a blackbird calling in its Devonshire voice, 'Where be ye going now?'

22nd February
Letter from [*a*] Mrs Ham remembering that I used to stand on Cromford bridge and look at the river…. Letter from [*Cousin*] Sissy saying she has now 7 cottages left to sell. She is quite wealthy. I had no idea! She must have 9 or 10 houses, and I gave her 20/- a week!

23rd February
I always feel I must be very careful about these [*Stuff of*] *Dreams* fans, they go haywire.

28th February
[*John and Helen arrive*], John in his green tweed country suit, Helen in dark red cardigan. A nice visit. Chicken for lunch, sherry, cranberries & apple, cheese & coffee, I feeling rather dazed and muddled. John did some gardening for me... while Helen slept by the fire.

2nd March
My windows fruz!.... Snow all over the ground. Gardener didn't come... Mrs. Allen bravely came.... [*K Wig can't come*] flu.... £22 returned from Income Tax!.... The lorry with the leaden figure, & the bird bath. The figure is really charming, & it looks as if it has always been up by the wood. I like it very much & think I must keep it.

9th March
Lovely letter from John.... Note. a broken rainbow denotes broken weather for a fortnight. Country saying (& Ireland too).

13th March
K Wigg went home.... [*To London*] Lunch at... the National Book League, but I shall not go there again, sitting with others at the table & poor cold food.... Taxi to Covent Garden. 3 Ballets...I did not really like [*some of the costumes*] ....the men looked like hikers on Derbyshire moors, disporting.

15th March
I felt rather worried by the shivering.... I wrote most of an *SP* tale after a struggle to do more than one page.

16th March
A big bill for electricity – £14, & I have never had more than £7 before! Lunch at the Hadows... [*where*] we talked of Beatrix Potter, – was she really unhappy in childhood? And [*of*] the Brontes.

19th March
A moment's rest in a busy day.... I washed Macduff, who is black with coal dust, hunting the mice, & gave the gardener his tea & 24/-. Lawyer Hill [*writes*] to say Downs House is transferred to John.

20th March
Lunch at the Fairbairns. Talked of Augustus John. RF [*Richard Fairbairn*] says he lacks character in portraits, some are caricatures. I said No. Collins wants to put *GR's Xmas* into a school reader for Cassell.

25th March
I did a long *SP* tale…. MT[*Tempest*] sent a model of *GR* for me, quite a nice small one. Contract came from BBC. [*But*] I lighted the fire with it, – couldn't find any paper! And then I discovered my mistake & had to write for another.

27th March
A day of such beauty, such ravishment… I was amazed at the mystery & beauty & excitement of the world.

3rd April
Then came a huge document from Mr Muspratt about more subscriptions [*for the Church*]… I do not wish to do much more. I was rather upset & worried over all this.

4th April
To the Kanns…. Leonard great fun and quite crazy as he kissed me and joked…. He said he gave £50 [*to the church*], as I did.

5th April
H[*Harry*] Glossop sent a Quiz about me in the *High Peak News*…. Another day of writing letters to Muspratt…. Lilian [*King*] took me to… meet Lucy Geddes, who was one of M Tempest's friends. Somehow these stalwart women of ladylike mein in cottages always make me feel uncomfortable. They are so out of place, so big.

6th April
Posted letter to [*Mr.*] Muspratt, saying £7 covenant. Decided to resign from the St John's Ambulance [*Vice-Presidency*]. I am not good at it, and I hate uniforms. They all frighten me by their efficiency.

9th April
I went to Bank for statement, – only £154 left out of £500 or so…. I walked through fields & I picked primroses in another wood…. I met 2 girls riding, with hound following. They thought a fox was in the wood.

21st April
Feeling better in spite of the grief of the broken Passion flower tree…. [*The workmen*] dropped a bucket of white lime on a [*flower*] bed, all over a window, and had to wash plants and side of house & window clean.

25th April
Icy cold, shivering. I lighted fire…. The sun came out in afternoon, so I gardened, watering some dry plants…. & tied up some raspberries. The cuckoo called, & I rejoiced.

26th April

Cuckoo calling, filling me with bliss. ...To B...& moved £200 in bank for part of [*the*] Breughel [*purchase*].... I was looking at rock plants [*when*] a screaming woman ran across the road, yelling at me. [*MacDuff*] had made a little pool near her door. Such vituperation, that raucous voice. I apologised & went in & bought my 3 plants, but it shook me that she could behave like that.

27th April

I am always too busy to write, with gardening, housework, shopping.... I rushed to B with my broken clock.... I could not prick [*the seedlings*] out and I threw most away.

28th April

Exciting day, Faber royalties £274, not too bad, but not good. A review of [*Hare and the*] *Easter Eggs*, & a notice of *GR* games. Off to London, reluctantly, but what fun it was!... to the Slatter Gallery. I saw the Exhibition, all set out. It was ravishing. I went round with Mr. S[*latter*] & he talked about each picture & I discussed it.

5th May

I stayed in bed till late, – then rushed off to have a 'curl up', for my hair was hopeless & Sheila did it for me in about 5 minutes.... A cold gloomy [*train*] journey.... went to [*Flemish*] Exhibition.

6th May

Collins cheque came for £632, – and I get 1d a book, so it shows how many [*have been*] sold.... I agreed with M Tempest on 6d a toy, as made by Mrs. Nesbit.

19th May

The Queen's at the Guildhall, & her fine & moving speech. She is a wonder-girl, & a great example, a fine character, brave, lovely, good. May she be spared for many many years.

22nd May

Another cold gloomy day, I got sticks in my wood to make a blaze. [*I answered a*] questionnaire from a young man on children's books. Do I try to be Didactic, which I am answering truly, – for I just write with *no* notion of making the young better.... I loathe being preached at & always have done.

3rd June

To London.... in the train with 2 hard lower-class women who talked like Gert and Daisy, very loudly.... to 115 Chancery Lane. Such a narrow lane, & lawyers about & typists. Mr Carpenter a nice man, went through my bundle of accounts, such a confused lot, I guess I shan't get so many expenses, but.... I would rather pay more & be free.

5th June
[*Cashed*] a little cheque for two pounds. I read the delightful book [*by Iris Murdoch*] *Under the Net*.... witty, original, gay.... No letter from Harry, after mine sent May 17, saying I would help [*with*] John's fees & sending money for stone-mason. No acknowledgement at all. 3 weeks. He always destroys my desire to help by his ungraciousness.

16th June
Such a day of excitement and happiness... [*a visit to the author*] Eleanor Farjeon. Such a welcome.... Eleanor talks of her conversion to R[*Roman*] C[*Catholicism*]. A moving & beautiful experience.... we kissed fondly. I love her deeply & wish I had known her years ago.

17th June
I was bored [*at the cinema with Lilian King*], and shut my eyes.... Poor GL's brother has died. I wrote offering GL a home & yet I know I do not want her to come. I could not write or even keep straight. She won't listen to music, she has no religion, no newspapers, never reads, will not go out, does not cook or sew – poor darling G. She would hate my active life, & I should hate her passivity.

24th June
I saw Mrs. M[*Montgomery*] mowing lawn in red shorts & a hanky round her breasts. She was embarrassed.... she looked an awful sight.... But she is so self-consciously trying to be 'modern'.

30th June
My father's birthday, about 115 years ago. That sounds odd.... [*To*] Mr. Slatter's Gallery [*where*] I gave him £250, & he gave me a glass of Bristol Milk.

1st July
I was insulted at a fish shop in B when the fish woman told me to stand in the queue and then when I walked away, said 'She doesn't like standing in the queues.' I swear I won't go there again.... I went to see GL's cottage, which I found charming, and wondered if I will buy it.

14th July
To see W de la Mare, with Joyce Kann driving .... I was shocked to see how he had aged. His face had a transparency, he looked peaked & thin. I kissed him in the doorway & he was led to a chair & settled.... We talked of life after death.

20th July
[*She describes a visit by GL.*] She is so changed. Poor GL. Her face red and healthy, but her eyes so staring and her voice quite different.... She is still very obstinate and won't do

things…. she is still the schoolmistress. It goes to my heart to see her stooping and old, but she has none of the sweetness of my mother…. I pray I shall be patient and helpful.

22nd July
[*More difficulties with GL*] I asked GL to phone station about train & she shouted so crossly, 'I won't use a telephone. I won't; I can't.' I nearly wept…. She really looks half crazy sometimes…. she makes such noises, like a horse…. Horrid to hear her.

27th August
LM went, – I was sorry to say goodbye. She has been a brick, patient & kind & sweet, although I got weary of hearing of her dog, and of the Peacock family next door, – they come [*into*] every conversation, their T.V., their food & talk.

1st September
The hottest day of the year. 84 [*degrees*] in shade…I sat out from after lunch till dusk, lying in the long chair, looking at the trees, and reading & sleeping. I had tea outside & then began to type a *Snug and Serena* tale.

14th September
[*After a trip with John to the Cotswolds*] Home to devastation. Floods [*pipes had burst in her house*], & much spoiled. Can't write of it.

17th September
More resigned to the awful house and mess, but really I feel like running away, if I had somewhere to go! I hate houses.

22nd September
I went through old letters, from me to James, & James to me. Some touched my heart deeply, but I felt that James's letters were very dull, often, and often censorious, urging me to my duty, full of politics and HG Wells and Socialism. I strove to keep up, & fairy and magic and joy kept coming in. I [*was*] always the optimist, James the pessimist. I don't know how I kept up my heart. I worked very hard, and did many things, and I saved pennies, and lived on the minimum. Why I didn't injure my health I don't know, saving on meals, living so frugally. No wonder my mother said I was thin and ill when I got home. Yet James urged me always to do without, and to keep strict accounts to a penny, and always my letters brimmed with devotion.

23rd September
I continued reading & destroying letters. Again, my own were gay & sweet, & surprisingly cheerful as I tried to help him, ready to sacrifice…. How different we were! How wise to cut away from the Uttleys after James died. That same spirit pervades them all. No simplicity, no real love, no religion.

1st October
A cobweb glittering in the hedge gave me private joy. A terrific day, cleaning up & going all over the stained walls with wet cloths, polishing all the furniture.

5th October
Letter from GL. People are calling on her [*in the new cottage*] & she has been out to tea. They think she is an author, they've got her mixed up with me & she is resisting their advances. It is good for her. I laugh with joy to think she *has* to meet people.

1st November
My heart [*is*] warmed by Eleanor Farjeon's [*letter*]. 'Lovely dear, brave, gay Alison'.... she says she will join me in my hollow tree, and squat beside me... 'with a clay pipe in her teeth'.

23rd November
[*Harry writes, asking her to live with him*] as we are both getting old. But I cannot as we should neither of us enjoy it, too different. I would have him here, – much easier. No use to ask for disaster.

28th November
To Penn, [*for an*] informal concert.... The Bach *Cantata* was ravishing, and so was *On Wenlock Edge*, tears came to my eyes. I was lost in time.

16th December
A lovely letter from John for my birthday tomorrow.... One from Walter de la Mare. He says I am composed of the Essence of England. Most flattering.

17th December
Birthday, – Seventy! I cannot believe it. I feel as I did at 20, only more carefree, but more tired!.... I got up early and looked at the adorable bare trees, and gold light and mist and sun, & I thanked them. John phoned.... yet I wish he had sent a letter to get here with the morning post, & no birthday letters came (except a card from K Carver!!) I felt a little sad, nothing from GL or John or Harry or Ronnie on my 70th birthday. However, Freesias came from K. Wig, lovely, & a telegram from Margaret [*Rutherford*] and Stringer.... I was touched nearly to tears by this.

20th December
A drawing from Peter Ustinov, whom I don't know. How sweet of him.

21st December
The party at the National Hospital. [*I met Alicia*] Markova, the lovely face & great eyes.... I told her [*sister*] that when James died, Pavlova died soon afterwards, and I rejoiced he would see her then dancing for the angels.

25th December
A lovely day, & I didn't wake till 10. am.... John came with Helen at 11.15.... They got lunch, & then I came down in my dressing gown, & sat at the table, & ate a bit of turkey, sprouts, most delicious, in fact most things. Then back to bed after a sit by the fire.... A really delightful time.... The room is charming, John's decorations, mistletoe hanging from beam, holly sprays over pictures in lovely flight, everything done beautifully.... I heard the really lovely broadcast of *GR's Christmas*, & it made me so happy & so proud.

29th December
Feeling a bit depressed, – this dull corner of B, the dirty boys racing about.... & the suburban feeling. I drove to Penn, – & it is heavenly.... I met a woman, red-cheeked, carrying a bundle of fire-wood from [*the*] wood.... I was depressed with letter from GL saying was I sure that she had sent me the same calendar, grumbling about the man cutting down trees.

30th December
To John's, – not feeling very well. The sweet little house.... Luckily I refused to go to a film, & we sat there, – I reading bits from the animal book. But I should not have done so. [*Helen*] not interested. She read a catalogue all the time. I *cannot* fit into life [*with*] them, – a tension.

31st December
Going to bed, rather sick, very tired, cold filling me, & flu still here. So I cannot do anything. Goodbye 1954.

~ *1955* ~

8th January
Suddenly decided, quite late, to go to Rosemary Baird Murray's cocktail party, because Richard [*Fairbairn*] was driving me, so I had no worry & I have a dress, & I am interested to see the house.... I enjoyed it very much – especially Dr Maxwell & various people whose names I have already forgotten. These rich people. I look around – but it was fun and nice. Richard arguing that no one is *content*. I say *I* am..... He says he is filled with melancholy.

25th January
Second day up. I did a little rose pruning.... The Dr came – I am better than he expected. Ironing finished with success. Very tired after it...White face, & white hair! Golly! Dream of an Italian showing me the most gloriously coloured clothes of softest silk, I bought a pair of knickers, partly deep heavenly blue, partly a kind of red like a fuchsia, slit and lined with the different colours, and I looked at the marvels of silk, texture and shade, petticoats very low and frilled, shot silk, & dressing gown of silk, & vests etc.. I wanted a vest like the knickers. Medici colours. 'I've got the sun in the morning, the moon at night'.

3rd February
I felt flat after yesterday, but P du S. sent the book on *Talking to Animals* and the *Cookery for One* for me to read. I went up the road with MacD & spoke to the watchman in his hut with the cat, saved by the men from drowning in the river.... Tonight I listened to part of the *Confidential Clerk*,– easy, clever, and interesting, and then suddenly got sick of all their confidential disclosures but they were bastards, one after another, absurd and unreal. It abruptly bored me & its artificiality made me turn it off.

5th February
A lovely sleep last night, so I feel refreshed. I had a dream, a delightful one, about James, which I forget, except that he was coming through a door to another room near it. & I stood firm, waiting to surprise him, and as he came I saw *my shadow* on the wall, & knew if he saw it he would know I was here. So I pressed very close to the wall, & the shadow of course got less. He came through, & I awoke, excited and interested about this real shadow – caused by sun or a light, on my left. Dr M. came, – gave me Vitamin C (2 capsules) to have with Vitamin B.... The WI. College want me to give my lecture at 11.15 on Weds. March 9.

6th February
A long good sleep. Macduff helps me I think, his presence in the room, a mutual confidence, & I feel *proud* to have an animal with me.

9th February

A gay little Chelsea clock from Margaret Rutherford, bless her. I hung it in the kitchen, & I hope it will go! I drove to Penn…. Home looked beautiful when I got back. I made 10 short précis of *GR* books, for Collins. Finishing *Pleasures of Light*. Colour in garden, – in the trees, in the sky. More and more I am charmed by the windmill of Breughel. Oh how lovely are some things, music, light, sky, trees, pictures by Breughel, – a little Scottie.

10th February

Found…. one of the lovely blank books with cover of true calf, – one of James's prizes. What shall I put in it? Nature notes I think – I wish I wrote poetry for it. I planted the thyme (4 at 2/-. a swindle), 3 Palsatilleas, & 3 Meconopsis, I'm afraid it is too cold for them. To see *Aunt Clare*, MR's film. Very good indeed, but I felt sick, it was really a mock at the 'sweet old lady's innocence'….. Letter from BBC contract for *GR at Sea*, on March 5.

11th February

I had a happy breakfast with nice letters, – one from Linda, one from Tessa Hooley , & …. Linda said she had a letter from Rosalind Vallence saying 'I have just finished *A Traveller in Time*. How is it I have missed this most beautiful, moving and accomplished book…. Will you please pass on my most humble thanks and my appreciation, in the strongest possible terms of her achievement?' How marvellous to have such a message. It is my book of my heart's secret.

12th February

Snowing, – snow all over, very cold, very beautiful & sunshine. Green woodpeckers calling. Owls hooting. Yesterday a thrush singing in the beech tree at the Partridges…. Ludwig Kock's record of Robin singing. I opened the French window & in came a robin and listened. It hopped out while he talked, & then came back for Thrush & for Dunnock, head cocked, listening and looking at wireless.

14th February

Valentines, – one from K Wig, exquisite painting of a little boy, little girl, he offering her daffodils…. Lovely letter from John too, thinking of me, & one from M.T, telling me of changes made in pictures…. I bought 2 little Azaleas [*for*] 5/- each but they are so small and meagre, with 3 or 4 flowers. I dare not give one to Betty Fairbairn so I have to keep them, in the bathroom.

15th February

Interesting letters, from G.L. Who has been to her first ballet, *Les Sylphides*, at Stratford on Avon, – from W de la Mare inviting me to tea, & thanking me for violets, from David of BBC thanking me for my 'shower of sunshine', from child for autograph telling me her great-aunt & her mother also enjoy the *LGR*.

17th February

Snow, quite deep snow of marvellous beauty, sunshine, glitter, the wood very beautiful….

My tufts of unpruned privet looked like a row of little white heads on pikes at London Bridge. Writing again the tale of Churches (Christmas in Church) which I finished last night.

22nd February
No Mrs Allen & no letter & no nuffin!

23rd February
I dug coal out of shed.... A miner, yet I do not mind at all.... I began Essay on *Scents & Smells*. I am managing quite well alone, getting on with the Essay book.

5th March
Dermatitis very bad, great patches all over lip, on arm, breast. I've been writing & trying to forget.

12th March
Mother's wedding day, bless her at Castle Top long ago, yet I know it all, its joys in the beauty, & its thoughts of God.... John's lovely green tray with Stowe came.... I drove to Jordans.... Yet I do not like Jordans, it is unnatural like a Communist state.

16th March
A lovely sunny day, glorious. So after the morning's work & letters, & doing some writing too, I set off for Amersham.... Mr Baily told me of 3 sisters.... Very happy old women. I think I must ask to talk to them. Writing after I got home. A letter from.... Miss Robinson sending letters from children, speaking so warmly of GL & saying she has now the telephone. Somehow this infuriates me. I think how she behaved over the phone, making me weep, so angry I used it [*the telephone*].

25th March
I found water dripping last night, I came down at 1.30 to adjust buckets. It is a leak in copper cylinder. I [*went to the Kann's*] but Joyce looked so smart. I felt she was incongruous or I was, in such different society. I belong to the old fashioned lot.

30th March
I was awake till 4.a.m. – worrying over trifles because dead tired with working at E[*Eleanor*] Graham's Puffin book [*A collection of Alison's writing*].... Then I phoned Peter du S. & he is coming out on Sunday to help me.

2nd April
Letters.... One from K Wig & very complaining about *Red Fox*, sales poor. Heineman not bothering, & she feels like not working for H any more. So I wrote, said she doesn't work for H. she works for herself, for her own pleasure. She must not go to shops and ask about

sales.... I feel very sick with her. Her work isn't wonderful, the sales are good, she has half the income. I feel that I shall refuse to write these books, I am infuriated for she grumbles so much, not only in letters, & she boasts so much.

3rd April
Just heard 5 caprices of Paganini.... so marvellous I am even more convinced that those peasants had to get supernatural help. Music so fast it was like beating of wings of insects if they could send out musical tones.... I was more than enchanted. I was lost in delight.... Peter du S. came & we discussed the Puffin book & the cover, illustrations and various things. He admired my lead figure.... P du S. says Heineman a good publishing firm, & it is silly of KW to object, to show them how to do their business. Great competition nowadays too.

10th April
Easter Sunday. I got up from my sick bed, slowly, set off early & got to church. A full church, – lovely decoration. The old familiar hymns. Queer sermon from Bro. Edward's cousin on disbelief of the Resurrection, – a mistake I thought. But all else was good. These clergy are queer fish.... there was a happy feeling, almost festivity about Penn, smiles & joy, & all so lovely. Poor Lord C had the wrong page marked for his reading & we all breathlessly waited while he hunted through the Bible, – unflurried. 'Sixteenth century worm muddle' said [*someone*] later.

15th April
To London, to see Private View of Mr Slatter's pictures.... Also I went to Leger to see Paddy Carstair's gay pictures. The assistant there said how lucky I had been to get my pictures when I did as prices are soaring.

16th April
So thrilled by yesterday, I could not sleep.

18th April
Kathleen [*her new home help*] scrubbed garden seats, I emptied car radiator & refilled it. [*At*] 4 came [*the*] Mathiesons with 2 children, most sweet. I gave them hot chocolate, cakes, & showed the treasures.... Macduff ill, writhing & leaping with pain. I sent for the vet who found a bone lodged across his mouth. Poor little Mac.

24th April
Penn church, – I nearly slept in sermon, but aware of the beauty & presence of God and happy.

25th April
John came in morning, – I had made 2 beefsteak pies, rhubarb tart, and done [*the*] bed – so all ready. He was tired too, & after going to garage and doing his shopping we both lay down, – John fell fast asleep, he had travelled for nearly 30 hours from Germany.

26th April
We left about 11.a.m. – a dull morning but later it changed. A drive by Lugdon (and that really was dreamlike) to Thame, joined the Oxford Rd, to Witney & Burford. Lambs in fields, herds of Friesians, white blackthorn, young green leaves…. We suddenly saw GL's pretty cottage…. I had been telling of flower paintings, & she said Gilbert [*GL's brother*] had done some. I dare not ask to see them, – but she suddenly produced the most beautiful paintings, about 50. I was amazed beyond words. She said she knew nothing of them & found them after his death. Yet they had lived together for 70 years!! They were so lovely – why didn't she put them out.

16th May
Colder and colder. We got K Wig's room ready, blue sheets on. Then to have hair waved. I saw the article of Proust, which I borrowed to read here. It thrills me, it is my own thoughts, my own way of seeing life.

24th May
Chelsea Show, – glorious day. Haemorrhage at night, alas.

25th May
Doctor came. Operation. Stay in bed.

27th May
To go to Princess Christian on Monday.

31st May
Operation. Drug at 8.0. Operate at 9. Awoke at 2.0. 'I've had a lovely dream', then asleep on and off. Sick. Flowers come.

3rd June
Got up, bath, dress.

2nd July
Geoff, gardener came. Again he flared up when I asked him to weed the path. I was so surprised, I asked so sweetly & his eyes flashed with anger. I retreated, trembling. Lay down for afternoon, didn't see him. The next morning a note saying he wasn't coming. Thank goodness, I cannot stand his rows & rudeness.

6th July
I haven't done too much today & take it easy tomorrow. Thinking of 'bridges' and typing in garden, but I [*can't*] carry the heavy typewriter.

5th August
To Windsor, to the specialist, who passed me as quite well. I felt very thankful indeed.

1st September
Marvellous gold light on the trees, & I got up early & looked out, & said welcome to the golden month I love.... GL & I walked in Timmins wood fields. Then her lunch, & off to B with her. I was more thankful than I can say to see her go, – a queer feeling, like a lost hope, for it is sad a friend is like this and yet I see it always, this streak which is now so pronounced.

7th September
Off to Torquay, Torbay Express. I felt quite ill, but I slowly recovered, a kind of sick nervousness. The frightful porter at Torquay, who scolded me because I kept him waiting. Imperial hotel, its lovely position & view & comforts.

20th October
To W. De la Mare's.... He sat in a wheel chair, in dressing gown, looking very sweet & jolly.... as I kissed him & held his warm hand.... We talked of rainbows, how long did they last?

31st October
Princess Margaret not going to marry [*Peter*] Townsend. A great relief, weight off our minds. Thankful she has made this fine decision.... Feeling happy about the Queen now, who has her sister.

7th November
Can't remember: yes, I felt ill all day.... Sent evening dress to Hilda.

10th November
Marvellous day. Lunch at Henley. The Old White Hart. Then on to Dorchester.... The antique shop where I bought nothing.... To the church, the Abbey, to see the window.

11th November
KW went home.... I mentioned Beatrix Potter book. K said she had it, *given* to her by Deightons the Cambridge bookshop.... She said she had helped to choose the pictures for it. Can I believe she has it? Why didn't she mention it? She said she didn't think Beatrix P. was a great artist, she was limited & couldn't draw people. But she could and did. Picture came. I like it, but??

22nd November
To London, to *S Times* Book Exhib.... Also nice Kathleen Lines – who says she would like to publish a book of my fairy tales. I went quickly on, – saw none of my books at Collins but said Nowt. None at Robert Hales. Only Faber & Heinemann.

27th November
Stay in bed late, but got no writing done. To Penn to Music Informal Meeting.... A lovely

concert, the Bach *Cantata* was ravishing, so was *On Wenlock Edge* (Vaughan Williams). Tears came to my eyes. I was lost in time.

14th December
A horrible day. International Club, – my worst fears confirmed, nay far worse. The cheeky young man came with a car.... to collect me. We sat under platform where a band played raucously and horribly, a saxiphone [*sic*] blowing roof off, a man singing into microphone, terrible, a man shouting into micro nearly blew us away. Never have I heard such a din.... The horrible young man calling me Dear, – photographs.... It was a nightmare, & my head ached & my heart thumped after I got home. I was sick, retching in the night.... The awful young man trying hard to persuade me to go to a dinner on Monday.... Never, never again.

16th December
A lovely letter from John for my birthday tomorrow, & one from W de la Mare saying I am composed of the Essence of England, – a most flattering, moving letter, of beauty. I am so grateful, so happy.

17th December
My birthday, – I looked out on bare beech trees & said a prayer of gratitude for life.

29th December
A marvellous day of sun & colour. I picked yellow jasmine, & some red primroses. I bought grapefruit (only 6d) and some pears. I took my present to the Montgomeries & they gave me Creme de Menthe sweets to my astonishment & pleasure. A blue anemone is out. A robin has looked at me, yesterday not today. I feel happier, resolved not to mind. And there is good news. Income Tax demand has dropped £200. Amazing. So now I shall not be stoney.

30th December
Christmas, – unhappy & bewildered, – but I remember these – the week at Stowe, under the stormy sky.... The short walk before Sunday dinner, – when we stopped on the bridge & watched 2 swans try to get across a barbed wire which hung low.... Driving very fast in unknown dark country, voices buzzing and I unhappy, tired & bewildered, on Boxing Night, & then I saw the cold bright design of Orion in front of me. I recognised a friend who helped me and, like a chattel, I was borne along with loud chattering talk all around me, – not their fault, mine, sick & tired.

31st December
A lovely day, – for the first time I felt better, for I slept well, in bed over 12 hours last night.... Goodbye old year, year in which I've been shaken & afraid & yet inexpressibly happy. Goodbye old year.

1956

1st January

This afternoon, a lovely fire, the lamps shining on the pictures, and the wireless playing *Alone*, which makes me think of a young workman on the roof of a Bowdon house, tapping and hammering the gables, singing *Alone* very loudly, and my secret joy and laughter as I heard him perched so high. A wet day, with brilliant sun between, – and I am the same, depressed still by the tension at Christmas, and yet full of joy and life and beauty and 'Here's a New Day'. The trees, especially my beech, so glorious, so immortal in spite of immortality, the lead boy shining in the wet.... I drove to church, elated and happy.

15th January

Marvellous day after the rain, – woods all glowing, grass sparkling like emeralds. I drove to church feeling this is really perfection. Why do I wish for Switzerland, when there is green and gold and brilliance and such a morning, and a rapturous scene? Church very nice, but the dull sermon when I *nearly* fell asleep. Most painful to keep my eyes open. I don't know what he said.

21st January

To Bertram Mills circus, – very late, I sat waiting from 12.00 till 12.40, and we got there late and missed items, alas. How I love every moment, and grudge missing the parade, the preparation, the announcing trumpets. The seals, three of them, sleek, clever, intelligent, one clapping his fins after each performance.... Midgets which did not enthral. We were so high up and so far away, one felt they might be grown up people.... Twelve horses – the best turn – scarlet and white dancing horses, and a fairy horse at the end, leaping through hoops, a blue silk coat upon its back.

16th March

Thrilling dream, – a crime had been committed in a university, I think. No-one knew who it was, but I had an idea, and I wrote it in this book. The criminal read it, and decided to annihilate me before I told anyone. Suddenly I realised I was shadowed, very frightened as I fled. A long dream, exciting, and parts of it beautiful. A *story*, but I refused to get my pencil, so I lost most of it.

25th April

A lovely day, but icy. I went off, with the car, to Narram Bottom, and walked there with Macduff, and found some primroses. Oh bliss! I got a few little roots, and some buds in my basket, and some woodsorrell flowers. Blue violets out. Wild cherry blossom out, and a lime tree so full of flowers I stood under it, – this in a road in Beaconsfield.... This is W de la Mare's birthday. I sent a cloth for washing his face! (But so pretty, green edges and a rose on it, and a card and letter). He is 84, dear W de la Mare.

27th April

A wonderful box of the Peggy Foye models, all charming, but even better is a model of Grey Rabbit's cottage, windows open and door space through which I could see Grey Rabbit, Squirrel, Hare, with a table and a pot of flowers. There was a fireplace with two dogs and a clock, a window seat and cushion, a rocking chair, and a warming pan all on a minute scale, so fascinating I could hardly bear to put it away.... Cuckoo calling, garden looking lovely.

28th April

6.30 a.m. I have just returned from a rendezvous with a cuckoo, – and what bliss it has been. It came back to my beech tree, and I watched it. As I looked, three wood pigeons flew to the tree, and sat near it, one of them cooing Coo-roo, Coo-roo, as if to listen to the cuckoo. Then the pigeon was quiet, and the cuckoo went sweetly on. I looked through field glasses and saw it so dearly in the tangle of branches, near the summit. It stayed a long time, even when the pigeons left.... From this high place it could see over the country. It must have been a surprise for it to see all the new houses. The leaden boy below also listening, and the earth listened. There is something primitive here, just as one imagines the earth listens when a lion roars, or an elephant trumpets in a forest.

5th May

To Missenden Abbey, – where I met Ruth Pitter [*the poet*]. Very correct and strong-looking, not like a poet. She might be a secretary, or head of a school. We talked of poetry and 'things', and I liked her very much. She lives at Long Wendon with Miss O'Hara (??). I gave my speech, which I think they liked. I looked white and felt very tired before I began – all last week the cleaning and the painting have been too much.

9th May

I feel troubled about Cyprus, – we have not been tactful. To sentence this man to death, and he did no murder. And now reprisals in Greece and Cyprus. Also there are a lot of questions to Eden about the mysterious death of a 'frogman' [*Commander Crabbe*] and Labour suspicions that he was doing some damage to the Soviet ships when Khrushchev and Bulganin came. It sounds crazy; it can't be.

31st May

To Walter de la Mare's, after a busy morning of polishing and cleaning; for the weekend.... W.J. talking to Sir Stephen Tallents.... We talked of dawn and daybreak, which comes first. I thought dawn, but WJ thought daybreak was earlier. WJ spoke of my letters, which are so often written at dawn. We spoke of birds and flowers, and what is the soul?.... After S.T.

left, he went to bed, and I went to his room to talk to him. He had blue pyjamas and a blue cover, very pretty. He looked so smiling and gay. He talked quite seriously about royalties. (He used to have 25%!) He thinks publishers should not claim part of broadcasts or anthologies.

2nd June
Jordans' Music Club. Peter Pears, charming, good-mannered and quiet, and Julian Bream (lute and guitar) in the Mayflower Barn.... The singing, with a trill like a bird, and the lute, and the great dark barn with its mighty beams, the wooden walls with the gaps in the timbers.... and the two men, one singing and the other with the lute, all made a time out of this age, Elizabethan, so that my mind went to 'Thackers', and Anthony Babington.... Richard Fairbairn came up; and at once, oh alas, he spoke bitterly of Pears' singing. It was like an icy douche. It was like the bitter words that some man might have spoken three hundred years ago.

5th June
Letter from Sissy [*her cousin*]. My heart sank. She had been to Castle Top, and she sent the inevitable two or three pressed flowers. She found devastation, – yet the old beauty, the house empty, hikers living in Father's Chamber. She wrote nicely, but it grieves me and upsets me. I can do nothing. All these people write to tell me. They are tactless.... It hurts me so much I put it away; it is inevitable, change and decay, which began thirty years ago, when we left the house. Mother made it, and on her departure it went.

6th June
A letter from [*her builders*] which amazed and delighted me, in answer to my angry letter complaining of their big charge for extra fencing.... They had really sent me a stiff letter in answer to my protest, so I wrote saying I was an author, Fellow of the Royal Historical Society, and had bought many things from them. This is the letter: 'Water Rat, Moldy Warp, Hare, Fuzzypeg and Squirrel present their compliments to Little Grey Rabbit, and being aghast at the abominable depredations of the weasels, beg to enclose an amended account.' (A bill, with £2.17.0. taken off!) I replied as from *GR*, thanking them.

19th June
To London, the dentist, two teeth stopped, and the usual feeling of awful misery tempered with faith.... Then a taxi, – and such fun! The taxi man spoke of the cold and lack of sun, and said we were never grateful to the sun. We ought to worship it when it appeared. I told him I always throw a kiss to the sun. He was delighted. So on we went, and he recited a poem he loves (as we dashed through crowded traffic), and he talked of the people now-adays, all miserable and discontented. 'Educated beyond their means,' said he.

22nd June
The saddest news. WJ [*de la Mare*] died early this morning. I can't believe I shall never see

him again. I went there last on May 31st. What a blessing I went!... I went into the garden to think, to pray. The cuckoo was calling in my wood, over and over. It seemed to me immortal, and it brought WJ to me.

2nd July

All day I have felt unhappy and depressed, – partly the effect of Katherine Wigglesworth, and partly Kathleen [*her daily help*] who is really too rough and rude. I asked her something, and her speech was queer. 'I never! I never done it. See? I never done it. See!' Like a tramp, and really she is akin.... Really I am dead tired, – I must avoid KW. She saps my strength, disturbs me. It is the old feeling of distrust in her speech, when she is untruthful. *Lesson.* Do not go to Cambridge. Do not take KW to any friends, or she says 'her stuff' and throws out grappling irons.... Do not go into any antique shops. Sit in the car and read, or wait outside. Do not speak if she is half an hour turning into traffic, or parking. Never share a room.... Never have tea, if it can be avoided, – I never want it, and she says she doesn't, and then she grumbles, and wants it. Really, she wants me to say I want it, but I can always manage.

24th July

Margaret [*Rutherford*] came to me, her eyes suffering, pouched. She looked shrunken. She told me much, incoherently, trying to compress much into little. It is a breakdown due to Malcolm [*Sargent*], whom she looks on as the spirit of poetry and music. I was amazed, – but I understand. It is how Sand adored Chopin. Stringer knows, he is faithful, loves her, but she has hurt him. What can she do? I said stay on, put it behind you, – it is music and poetry you love, not a human being. You have strength. You move thousands.... thousands love you.

29th July

Margaret [*Rutherford*] – says she goes to a psychiatrist, and he says she ought to leave Stringer. I don't agree. I argued against him.... She says she would like to stay with me.... yet I think she would find it too enclosed with me, too tiny. She had a message from Ivor Novello (through a medium) saying she must not take drugs, and other advice which I forget.

8th August

Lunch with Margaret Rutherford and Stringer. They are keeping on the flat, and have a Scottish housekeeper who lives in. Margaret said she (the housekeeper) ought to give them a meal at night. Stringer said No. She was up at 7.30. Too long a day. I agree with M, – the woman has a lot of free time, with no supper to do. Stringer suddenly angry. He said to me, 'You've spoiled all I've been building up'. Margaret left to be made up, and Stringer attacked me fiercely, didn't give me a chance to explain, so I sat there as he burbled on, and let it flow over me, not caring. A queer man. He told me I must not tell M. that *he* likes to cook her meals.... Margaret told me of an American offer of a play in

New York, – she is to be a Princess. Is it too much for her? She isn't sure yet whether it is her part. Stringer is deadly dull, no doubt of it, and he is on the defensive, – but such a bore.

17th August

In the afternoon a gleam of sun. I suddenly went off to Penn Bottom, and walked in the wood. Marvellous. It is delicious. I felt part of the trees. Not caring for man at all. I notice that the firs have branches perpendicular in every case, – sharply at right angles. Larch branches down by about sixty degrees. Beech, up, and then curving. Oak out.... I could judge the trees from the angles of the branches, and I was surprised at the symmetry of this. Picked a bunch of harebells, – I loved them, and Jarrow.

19th August

A rather frightening day, – Margaret so tearful and unhappy, so intense and so miserable. I could not console her. She cannot bear to be with Stringer. She feels she is disloyal. Should she go to the U.S.A. if anything comes?.... A film offer – shall she take it? I said no, a poor part ... we went to church, – an awful parson, terrible. I heard grunts and mutters and moans from Margaret. She wanted to go, and I was very glad to go. So we rose up and departed.

10th September

John came, – very busy getting ready for him. We had lunch and drove to Henley, and then on to Dorchester. The Abbey. A bat on the floor, and John picked it up. It lay squeaking loudly.... A haunted feeling in the church. Very queer. One magpie on the way.

27th September

Lunch at the Savoy, 'Women of the Year'. Edith Evans excellent speech. Sabrina [*the glamorous TV personality*]. Markova, like a Mermaid, her oval face, and large round hat. I talked to Edith Evans, whom I adore. Her voice so rich and resonant and full, her spirit so vital. Rosamund Lehman rather cheap, 'fast' and 'prepared', – I didn't like her.

24th October

Called at the Globe [*Theatre*] and had a good talk with Margaret [*Rutherford*]. She is going to Liverpool in December.... Two bouquets came in the door for her.... M. told me she wants to get away.... for a time, – to be free. I said, 'Be free, for this fortnight.... and see how you get on.' Theatre packed, and very long queues, they said. It could go on for a long time but they are tired of it. I had a glass of Dubonnet and a cigarette, and saw M make up, and have her wig put on.

1st November

All Saints Day, and a day of cold and sunshine and colour. Most beautiful. A day when I got Faber royalties and a new car. But much apprehension. Fighting, bombing, in Egypt; all against us, and rightly so, all hating England, alas. [*The Suez crisis*] We are quite wrong, and what will happen we know not. Eden ought to resign.

3rd November
All day I felt worried about our [*Suez*] war, and it is so frightful. A week ago we knew nothing. Now bombing all the time. At ten o'clock Eden's broadcast, – a serious voice, but I disagreed all the time. We did *not* go in because of the little raids between Egypt and Israel over the last ten years. Lots of places have raids. We went in to seize the canal, and to fight Egypt, and we are the aggressors, attacking a country that can't fight back. Horrible! And poor Hungary, struggling against Russia. Why didn't he go to save her?

4th November
Tonight Gaitskell's speech. Absolutely true. He did not rant, or exaggerate. I thought he might have been more firm, but every word told. He implores the Conservatives to back him, to turn out Eden. It is the only way to save the country. He made good points, – Eden not 'policing' but at war to get the Suez Canal. Colonies are being separated. Only Australia and New Zealand with us. The British Commonwealth being destroyed by this man's pride.

18th November
[*A visit to John & Helen's cottage near Stowe School*] John so thin, so worn, I could not believe it. And a queer, a terrible depression settled on me, like a weight. It never left me. I have seldom felt so crushed with apprehension and trouble.... Helen chatting about the babe-to-be, I feeling frightened for John.... We walked among the spindle trees and gathered boughs. Then John showed me his study, – very nice – the same depression, and he told me later of the two masters and the house, who are inimical.... the feeling of sorrow overwhelmed me. Why is it? I must overcome it. I am too psychic. [*Helen was to miscarry a few weeks later, and Alison never became a grandmother.*]

25th November
To Penn, not wanting to go, and it was glorious, one of the best concerts.... I wept; tears filled my eyes, I was enchanted and lost. Bach, magnificent and powerful.... Chopin, so sensuous and so lovely, and so tragic in the last movement. I thought of him and of Poland now.

28th November
I felt well, and drove off on a bright cold day to Joyce [*Kann's*]. We sat talking of the Industrial Revolution. I got so sick of her talk, which is: 'I don't blame the working class for revolting and wanting higher wages, when you think of the Industrial Revolution and all they suffered. No wonder they don't forget and forgive'. I want to say, 'Well, we also suffered this, I could tell you tales of our country people in 1840, but it is past and over.'

26th December

I didn't sleep. I lay awake till after 4.00 a.m. in misery. [*She is spending Christmas with John and Helen.*] Only angry looks and disdain. But I won't write it.... At night I went into the kitchen and asked to wipe the pots. 'You must be very tired,' I said to John, who had driven 120 miles on icy roads. Helen turned on me in fury, 'And am I not tired? Nobody thinks of me. I have to stay in and cook the turkey, while you go to church. You leave it all to me!' 'Well, let me do it all,' I said. 'I shouldn't mind staying, in and cooking the turkey.' 'You! You!' she spluttered. She banged and yelled, so I retreated. I slipped up to bed at 10.00 p.m. She never spoke again to me that evening. I wept in the night.

31st December
The watch night service. Bless them, guide them, help them,
Save them.
The lesson of Jesus rebuking the winds and waves.
'Where is your Faith?'
The hour of darkness, with storms as nowadays,
Hungary... the fierce beast has caught it.
The strains and stresses of our lives. The blue skies of
childhood gone, the dark clouds of frustration.
'Master save us, we perish.'
And he storm was quelled. He only can bring peace.
The final word of history does not rest with Paris or Moscow
or New York.
It rests with God.

$\approx 1957 \approx$

1st January
Resolution: to be patient and kind, – to keep my own council [*sic*] and to be careful what I say, especially to John and Helen lest they think I boast. To look for the hidden marvels, the beauty of the world, the secret Heaven. To laugh, to dream and not to care too much.... A lovely New Year present was petrol coupons from the State enough to give me nearly 200 miles per month extra.

6th January
The Stewarts came.... Frances played the piano after tea.... but it was boring.... we all sang Gilbert and Sullivan.

9th January
To London to see Mr. Collins, where [*we*] talked a great deal about whether MT's better than K Wig.... I praised her [*MT's*] colour, said it was better than K. Wig. But her drawing not so good. Lunch with MR at The Ivy.... John and Helen came to the theatre.

10th January
No *GR* to be done this year. [*The next was published in 1968*] No *Mouse*, because KW hasn't drawn pictures.... More news of Eden's resignation.... He will be sick at heart. Macmillan is the PM.

15th January
[*I spent*] 30/- on stamps.... [A] letter from KW saying she had given up *Mouse*, as no-word from Heinemann. I doubt part of her story.

17th January
[*Review of*] *Here's a New Day*.... rather patronising in tone [*I am*] too domestic, I suppose.... I don't dare start my proofs, too tired.... [*I spoke at*] a children's home. Many of them Negro children, – but jolly little people.... I broke my specs!!

23rd January
I cut up oranges for marmalade.... Stars brilliant. I stood out to look at them & now sneeze & sneeze & sneeze!

24th January
A mixed day. Marvellous light in the wood early, gold light shining through tree trunks, quite wonderful.... Kathleen up to her bad tempered tricks, worse than usual, for no reason,

shouting & insolent. Angry because I asked her to get a basket from the cupboard! 'You give me all the dirty work'. Is she crazy? The nice clean cupboard! I left her alone the rest of the time.... I made 16 lbs of marmalade.

25th January
[*She likes her home help*] Nice Mrs. Allen with her country face & good manners.... I think I must get rid of Kathleen [*her other home help*], too uncouth & awful. Mrs. Allen says she hasn't slept a full night since before Xmas, up with her husband, giving him sips of water.... Lunch at Ruth Plant's, I stuck on the hill [*in her car*], could not start, I don't know why, road wet, I even went backwards.... So I reversed, into bushes, started & got off hill.... It was an excellent lunch, mushroom soup, macaroni & something, tinned strawberries.... but the house was icy. Only a small [*electric*] fire, – 1 bar in sitting room, nothing in dining room. I was frozen. Pouring rain.... came home ice cold, feeling ill.... I was as cold as ever I have been, chilled through completely & dead tired. Ruth talks too noisily, too confusedly. I am bewildered by the racket.

31st January
To London, took *A Year in the Country* to Faber.... P du S was very kind and helpful. We discussed pictures, head piece & shape.... to be different from others.

1st February
Sad news. Mr. Allen died at 7 am today.... I wept for a nice man, gone.

4th February
[*After a row with her home help Kathleen*] I was...uncommunicative, not much fun for a happy person, but it is necessary to avoid a showdown.... The piano tuner came [*again*] for final tuning. I took £3 & two weeks wages to [*the recently widowed*] Mrs. Allen.... On the way down the sharp narrow lane I met a huge tractor. It came dangerously near.... 'I am not a good driver,' I called out.

16th February
P du S wrote saying he thoroughly enjoyed my book, he thinks it is one of my best.... Great thrill! Rather long, can we do [*it*] without cutting it?

17th February
[*I cooked*] an enormous boiling fowl [*for Peter du Sautoy's visit*]. We discussed my book.... Peter does not think I would like Justine [*in The Alexandria Quartet*] by Durrell, we all laughed over the implication. I asked Peter to be my literary executor (but perhaps I should say with John, or after him).

21st February
Letter from Peter du Sautoy, offering any help or advice. He said contract enclosed, but nothing there unless I lost it.... My egg fell off my breakfast tray, and rolled under the bed.

I chased it with a *sword*, couldn't reach it, and Mac[*duff*] thought I was playing ball. Hilarious as he dashed about, and the egg rolled sideways.

25th February
Cleaning drains, I did most of it myself of course, so it's well done.

28th February
We dusted the dresser. Quite a strain working with her [*Kathleen*] as she argues each thing. I was worn out by the struggle. She must always have had to stick up for herself.... Drove to the new Library, to be opened on Saturday, a very nice place.

1st March
I welcomed March this morning, a lovely golden lamb.

5th March
To the Bring and Buy [*sale*] for Mission to Seamen.... I took a new *GR* book but nobody noticed it. I must never do that again.... I called at the new Library and got out the *Silence of Heaven*, a book on inn signs, one on Durer (which I do not like).

7th March
I was determined to enjoy the day in spite of the awful Kathleen.... But she is quite cracked.... I long to get rid of her, the fool.... Violet Helliwell came and the deadly, deadly Miss Maxwell, so boring.... [*she*] uses old clichés.

12th March
A marvel of a day in every way.... To London. I went to Selfridges, asked for the book department ...(I saw my *GR* and meant to ask how it was selling). The [*sales*] lady was charming. She had always wanted to meet me.

17th March
To Stowe to see John...I felt they were not happy, [*there is*] none of the elation I feel.

19th March
Mrs. Allen's day, so [*it is*] more cheerful.... Letter from LM saying she is still ill with rheumatism, and must have operation.... poor dear.

20th March
A thrilling day, – wild rain & wind so I decided not to go to London as I had my breakfast at 8.0 but it cheered after brilliant sun, so I went by the 11. 30 train.... a woman [*on the train*] ....talked all the way, – interesting but I was tired – but a nice person who wants to come south to be near London for Art. Taxi to RHS [*Royal Horticultural Society*] & of course it was lovely. Soon I got caught up, & ordered [*lots of plants*].... Lunch at 2.0, restaurant

closing & I alone. Taxi to…see [*the*] Koetser Gallery, – & such a treat!… I loved his gallery and his son took me round…. Then… to Slatter's [*Gallery's*] opening. Mrs. S very sweet in blue silk…. Then a taxi, luckily, & I caught the 5.40 home. Rain poured in torrents…but I escaped. The Tang horse was here, lovely, & this morning 2 books of poems from Mr. Clark whom I met (& forgot!) at…W. de la Mare's exhibition at the NBL [*National Book League*].

22nd March
Mrs. Allen here. [*I*] making my last apple tarts with apples six months old. At night I gave a lecture at High March [*School*], my heart was low as I looked at the audience, [*but*] I forgot it all when I began to speak, and enjoyed it. [*It seemed*] absurd talking about rabbits and magic to these businessmen and sophisticated women, but they enjoyed it.

26th March
I finished the revision of *Year in the Country*…. then did spring cleaning…. I went to post my MSS…. [*then*] walked in a lovely garden [*but*] I came home happy with my tiny plot…. Letter from John, still depressed. Why can't he take things? He's got his desire, a housemaster's job.

27th March
Today came a blue wool dress, cheap (12 guineas).

28th March
Letter from P du S saying he approves of all my alterations. Also letter from Heinemann, not liking *The Queer Visitor*. I don't like Queer, it always gives me a shiver, but I can't think of anything else. Kathleen here difficult and gloomy, – so I kept away & did nearly all the work, not caring to ask her…. I am *dead tired* after she has been here…. I picked white daffodils & took them to the De Hirsh's, – nobody there & put them in kitchen. Then Donald came along the lane, so I turned back, & had a glass of sherry & a nice talk with him. He said T.S. Eliot had called at his Embassy, & he asked him about inspiration. TSE said he just sat & sat, & thought a bit, & sat. Sometimes he waited 3 weeks to get the thing. Then D asked about the…. *Cocktail Party*. Eliot said No, that came at once. He said Eliot was like a Civil Servant, a businessman, not a poet. I agree but he must be alert and alive, not dreaming at all…. I came home & read again Eliot's [*Four*] *Quartets*, which I love, marvels.

29th March
Bumblebee on the rosemary blue flowers. Bluebells out. Wood anemones out…. A busy day. Mrs. Allen springcleaned [*my*] bedroom, & I turned out all the drawers in 2 chest of drawers, & gave curtains, silk & red dress to Mrs. A. She *is* a nice woman…. After lunch at 2 p.m. I gardened until 6.30 except for Grand National…. very exciting…. I moved my old viburnum which was sick & ill in damp patch. I planted 2 roots [*of*] pinks by steps…. I tended all the camellias…. I tied up lilies, the Crown Imperials…. I put a poor old azalea in a good place on edge of wood. Bought box of lettuce today to be planted tomorrow. So I was weary, 4 solid hours, & I had a good tea, & soon I will go to bed, 9.30.

31st March
Mothering Sunday, but not for this mother.

5th April
John came.... I had to ask poor John to help rake up the leaves.... [*He*] told me some of the boys have been drinking.... He is unhappy.... I cannot help.

10th April
A poem to me, called *Old Roses*, from [*Mr.*] Clark. A lovely poem too.... Also several more poems from him, all of them beautiful. I feel touched & honoured for I love his poetry. I had a queer night, – deep sleep, the cavern deep, – & then a dream of old came up – about Stowe, John, Reynolds. It was so distressing, & I could remember it. I *would not* take notes because I wanted to forget & I have quite forgotten, except the misery which kept me awake for some hours, the anxiety for John.

11th April
A walk at last, – on an icy cold but radiant afternoon.... rejoicing in snowdrifts of stitchwort.... violets blue on the banks...and cherry blossom, with sunshine falling through the orchards & the light golden. It was a marvel, larks singing.... peewits calling. Old Dene is ploughed, but I found cowslips, my first, on the lower edge. I walked a long way. [*The*] sky darkened, very gloomy & theatrical.... Letter from Kay [*Katherine Armfield*] Watson, [*Gertrude's daughter*], & Oliver (7) & Rowan to invite me to see them at Kew. What a surprise. Somehow I felt the children would read only Communist literature.

14th April
I overslept, not knowing its summertime, so I missed church.... I loved David Jones's Ancient Mariner pictures.

22nd April
'Let in the green weeks of April
Cuckoo call cuckoo up the wood.'
Cuckoo calling near house for 1st time, about 6 a.m. Yesterday I heard a green woodpecker as I sat in the packed little flower-filled little church at Penn.

23rd April
Comet at 10 pm [*the Arend Roland*] – such a thrill as I saw the light of the tail – a lighthouse in a great tree, for the comet was almost behind a bare tree & the light shone through it.... the comet.... much brighter & more luminous than I imagined. All week I looked at dawn, but no wonder I couldn't see it.

25th April
John came, – looking better I thought. We went off early.... Poor lunch [*at Burford*] bad

waiting, cold food, & not good.... [*We*] tried to get tea at Stow on Wold, – hopeless; & raining & cold. So we got in car & drove off, said Never again. To see the Rollright Stones. Thrilling & lovely & strange, & numinous in the stony light, blue & black sky & falling rain. Man ploughing a field near by.... The solitary stone. The faces in the stones. Home. En route I told John of the ghost tales...A lovely day. But icy cold.

30th April
A blissful drive with a comet hanging above us.... I lay in bed, thinking of all my pros and cons. [*A long list of her blessings, including*] birds, flowers, the Puffin book to be published, the comet, nice friends, Joyce, Lillian, MR, Georgie [*Jenkinson*], the Wailes, Del Anderson.

3rd May
God has a purpose for each of us – we are led to people to help them.

15th May
Eleanor Graham's proofs [*of Magic in My Pocket*] came. Her Foreword is insulting, referring to *CC* as 'so long ago'. I wrote to P de Sautoy about it.... Lillian [*King*] & I had a phone call, – bliss.... to hear her voice again.

4th June
John's letter very depressed, saying he cannot make contact with boys, that there is a bad influence there undermining his presence. It is sinister, horrid.... I felt unhappy all day.... The baby robins are killed. A cat must have found them.

12th June
My leg swollen and matter oozing, all in a mess. I felt better because the sun shone all day. I said No to University of London wanting a bit of a tale, which they have spoilt. No! I suddenly got my wits and finished a *TR* tale. Working swiftly, enjoying it.

17th June
[*To*] London, to Solicitor to make my will. It was quite fun, no depression, in fact I enjoyed doling out my jewellery to dear friends. Mr. Swart, a nice capable man.... whom I like very much. He said.... Peter & John for [*literary estate*]. He knows P du S, so that is lucky. I must put in Oakdene School & K Wig (a small jewel)... Joan Dobell (But she has everything). Afterwards lunch at [*Marshall & Snelgrove*], then I tried on summer shoes... (I won't go there again, too dear), – [*and thereafter*] to Debenhams. Ordered yellow shoes. Also a nightie & 2 petticoats.

19th June
To RHS [*Royal Horticultural Society*], then to the author's cricket match.... Nice P du S loved it too. At lunch I was alarmed by sitting next to Mrs. [*Richard*] de la Mare. She feels worlds away, a kind of inhumanity. John Moore made a very funny speech.

30th June
My father's birthday, and I think of the little fat child born at Castle Top.... the youngest of seven. William, John, Selina, Susan, Mary.... not sure, and he was Henry, the youngest.

1st July
Harry's letter.... 'You are looking older than me'.... he has *no* feelings, blank as a wall, as he always has been, when he used to sit reading the paper when I came home.

23rd July
My usual busy Tuesday with Mrs. Allen.... Then I went to Windsor with Miss MacFarlane, who is a wholesome, good, cheerful companion.... Downs House has been sold for £1,650, only three hundred more than I gave for it, thirty years ago.

29th July
Kathleen [*her home help*] has departed, thank goodness. For 18 months she has been moody, rude. I hope I will now find writing easier.

30th July
Mrs Allen here.... I am rejoicing I have no Kathleen.... I easily did the ironing.... [*Later*] feeling so lost in B's crowds.... Sometimes I wonder what I'm doing here.
Notes. Bought £200 of Premium [*Bonds*] on the 19th July, gave John £10 of Premium Bonds.

6th August
[*She meets the maker of toy models, Peggy Foye*] A great discussion on characters. I told them about *S Pig* whom they did not know. I said I did not want a *cat* in *GR*, nor three year-old-mice in *Snug and Serena*.

10th August
Up all night giving Macduff brandy.... He is so much better.

12th August
One letter from John in script like a little boy, very jolly, – he is resting at Guernsey.... Today Harry goes to C Top to find spring water in the hillside.

14th August
Last night a vivid dream of John, a baby of five years old, most poignant and extraordinary.

20th August
Staggered today to receive a letter from George Uttley, calmly asking me to lend £10 thousand to Sugdens to guarantee their borrowing for trading purposes. Colossal cheek – nay, it is incredible. I haven't the money, and I would never lend it to that crazy firm which has squandered a fortune already and gave me no help in my direst need, when I was penniless.

23rd August
Indoors working at a new *Red Fox* story.... Poor LM wrote, saying she is really worse, poor thing.... I refused George Uttley's request.... I said I could not do an article for *Derbyshire Countryside*.

27th August
Mrs Allen here after ten days of my being alone.... I discussed the legacy part of my will with the bank manager.... I gave John and Harry each a ten pound premium bond.... My Dermatitis is troublesome.... Letter from John telling me of visit to Dinard. It made me long to go there again, I felt the carefree happiness of la plage.

14th September
To Woburn Abbey. We ran over a young turkey and broke its leg.... [*Woburn*] was all a 'show' which we disliked.... In the house a great raging mob of people.

16th September
John on a special visit.... He looks so well & cheerful.... I read the proofs of [*the*] *Mouse* book. We discussed two proposed little books, *GR*'s *Shoe* and *Fishing*.

5th October
Thrilling news of the Russian satellite [*the sputnik*].... Gardening

6th October
I called to see Joyce Kann & I had a great welcome. She is a sweet girl.... I have a psychic link with her & [*we*] know each others thoughts.

13th October
To Penn church.... a dotty sermon.... [*In the afternoon*] the du Sautoys came & we discussed my will and my books.... But then I quite forgot my sherry & biscuits & chocolates & let them go away without a drink or a bite. I felt so cross with my careless self.

16th October
Miss Foye [*maker of toy models*] is indignant about my complaint about the badly coloured models of *Grey Rabbit*.... I must give up *The Times*, as the [*cost of*] postage is huge.... I finished *GR* [*and the*] *Shoe* [*sic*].

23rd October
W. Collins phoned to say MT has been asked to do a TV lecture on *GR* books & the drawings. Do I mind? I said [*I was*] delighted.... I don't think I am very pleased. MT is such a grabber.

8th November
Day of [*publication*] of *A Year in the Country*.... [*She prepares her house for the launch party.*] Moving furniture, – couch across window. My table & typewriter upstairs. Mrs. Allen made

sausage rolls (tiny), & pastries, which K filled. Rolls cut in two &... meats & things put on them. Crab, shrimps. Devilled ham.... Wine poured out ready, decanters filled. The room very pretty.... Hair waved, quick lunch.... A lovely party, drinking healths, & Rex [*Wailes*] made a short toast, & I answered for the book. 17 guests – & plenty of room. I showed some of my treasures, watch, patch boxes...Lilian [*King*] & Joyce [*Kann*] stayed until 11. 30, – very happy.

9th November
Bed at 1 a. m. & didn't sleep till after 3 a. m. Cold too & great frost. A marvellous day of sun & frost. £110 for adv[*advance*] royalties, & a nice notice of Puffin [book].

19th November
I lay awake till 3 a.m., thinking of Scientific work, the urge and thrill of it. The bliss when we calculated the number of atoms in space.... So I lay awake, thinking of what I might have done, yet might have found it sterile, and my life is human now.... I took a sleeping pill.... The robin came in the house again.

21st November
Sorrow, – the little friendly Robin killed, caught in mousetrap in my bedroom. I am very unhappy, – such a marvellous friend who met me several times a day, at door, at gate, entering the house, calling to come in & then walking about serenely, looking at things, never making a mess. Perched on calendar on my walnut desk & surveyed the room. Flew to a chairback & stared around.... Sometimes it perched on a flower, on the lampshade, watching.... I felt really ill, my heart sick & lonely. The words 'Here lies the little friend of Man' came to my mind as I buried him.

23rd November
Three Reviews came, – 2 delightful, 1 from the *Times Literary Supplement* very sneering and sarcastic – so hurt I felt unhappy.... my [*latest*] book was that of a townswoman living in the country. (Really [*I am*] a countrywoman living in the town!) Obviously written by an angry young woman.

27th November
At night I pondered [*the request, from Tony Tolson, to contribute to*] George [*Uttley's*] pension, and looked up my diary for 1932, seeing his refusal to help us in our awful difficulties.

28th November
John writes, saying he is going to help George.... So I will do the same.... H[*Harold*] Armfield writes, the first time for 27 years, saying he will lend £1000 for the fund.

9th December
What a day of trouble.... letter from John. Father Paine is dying. Helen has gone off to

Guernsey, poor girl. John loved him too. He went on to tell me of his despair, he cannot teach, no grip, no interest, no contact with his boys, his memory gone. One of the most unhappy letters I have ever read.... A feeling of evil.

14th December

I felt miserable, – so off I went to the Byrd Mass at the Penn concert. And it was divine to hear. At last a letter from LM.

16th December

I received £403, from Sugdens for shares. A covenant has been formed for George Uttley. A queer business.... Would they do it if anybody else was affected, – if Tony [*Tolson*] went bankrupt for example?

17th December

My birthday. [*73*] Nothing from John, which made me sad.... Then at 3.30 the phone went.... John wishing me Happy Birthday. Mr. Paine [*Helen's father*] died today.

20th December

Letter from Helen written before her father's death, a nice letter, showing real understanding of John. The nicest letter I have had from her.... She thinks John should not change, not give up but face it. I agree.

24th December

I slept like a log with my grief. I really don't know what to do.... I am glad [*John*] has gone back to Guernsey, I could not lift his burden & perhaps they can. Del Anderson came & I discussed with her. She says a doctor, a psychiatrist, & a doctor as soon as possible. Here I am in the midst of beauty.... We seem to have our heart's desire, and John has collapsed, lost his nerve. God help him, & give him back courage & laughter & a Quiet Mind.

25th December

A nice day – I slept well last night, thank God, & awoke early & got my presents & breakfast in bed. Opening up the house was a pleasure.... I was glad to be alone, & I listened to the wireless. To church – crowded but I got my usual seat. A fierce clergyman whom I don't like, so I did not listen to him, but the best hymns & the lovely reading by Lord Curzon – Joyce smiling at me quite near. I prayed for John.... Home for lunch of fruit & cheese & dessert & wine.... To [*Joyce's*] to see the Queen on TV – very good but we were too far from the screen.

31st December

I love the change of year, the feeling of movement in space. I went out to see the stars, Sirius and Orion.

~ 1958 ~

2nd January
To London, – undecided until this morning.... Fantastic feminine shopping. Then a framed map of Derbyshire, a beauty showing all my county in 1821, when my great-grandfather lived at C Top.... I bought a yellow pullover.... for John. Quel jour! Nothing to eat.... I forgot all my anxieties in the sun, [*amid*] smiling people.

5th January
I wrote to John, revising my letter, omitting casual gossip and incidents.... Later I wrote to the TLS [*Times Literary Supplement*], a second letter on my review.... I posted the [*Neville*] Cardus book, which bores me.... I could hear terrible shouting noise...from the wood. [*Little boys had*] made a bonfire.... but easily it could have spread to my fence. I called them.... I insisted. The two letters & John's illness, [*this was*] the last straw. Finally I invited the 2 boys [*and their mother*] in for chocolates. So all ended amicably.

7th January
Income tax, only £121 for the half year, so a good drop.

9th January
Sometimes I think I withdraw from this Life, seeking something in the Future Life, seeing it here around me, half visible.

10th January
Lumbago.... I had to stay in bed.... Mrs. Allen very busy.... Heard the Jodrell Bank telescope talk very good & even *Any Questions* was good because the exhibitionists were not there. So scientific work did me much good, mentally, as I knew and remembered all the answers.

12th January
John and Helen came.... John pale but better than I had thought, Helen very well and sympathetic.... I hunted out some books for him. I made suggestions for lessons. He has no time to read, go out, to meet people.... We are hoping for an easier timetable & if only he would delegate some authority, get some time to prepare lessons.

15th January
I signed the transfer of the Sugden shares, now finally gone.... [*A lot of*] terrific cooking, oh dear, what a waste of energy.

17th January
Tonight in the darkness I stood in the dark with Macduff, who is ill.... Wonderful to feel a kind of power or strength & comfort going between us, I am sure it can physically help.

26th January
The Vet has been, – Macduff is fading away, he says. He is in no pain, he will probably die in his sleep, perhaps tonight.... A nice sympathetic man. I could see that he wondered whether I would ask to make the end short & he was relieved I wished Macduff to die quietly & peacefully.... So now I thank God for the blessing of this tiny life, which has been so much to me, since he was a clinging morsel, holding to my chest, the tiniest pup I had ever seen. Full of fun, trying to talk, deeply curious & interested, game for anything.... And tonight, 2 or 3 hours later, he died. God bless him & keep him. I prayed over his little black body, stretched out peacefully sleeping.

27th January
Macduff buried, – a misty day but the sun shone warmly. Last night I put him in a linen shroud, in a box & today I placed sprigs of rosemary over him. Picton [*her gardener*] came at 12.30 and dug his grave under the hornbeam, – rich brown soil where Mac often buried a bone.... After he had gone I returned, – & a robin was singing on a twig over the grave.... Such sweet low song. I was helped by nature.... Poor darling baby, I feel so unhappy, I cannot do anything.

29th January
Too sad to write, I must get through the day.

5th February
I invested £500 at 6% in stock of the LCC (I will probably only get a fraction, ought to have asked for more and risked it). It's chiefly from the Sugden share money, which I felt I ought to invest. I have been reading the wretched modern *Children's Guide to Knowledge*, some of it excellent, but a lot is crude propaganda for the Socialist State. It made me angry.

7th February
Sad news...of the [*air*] crash with members of the Manchester United football players [*the Munich disaster*]. I prayed for the sad distressed relatives.

14th February
Valentines from John, Georgie, Oakdene [*school*], a little girl.... & later flowers from K Wig.... Off to the ITV after early lunch. [*Ruth Plant drives her*] I felt depressed when I went into the big gloomy building, – but when I met the people I liked them. I had a cup of coffee.... [*Then*] Mr. [*Steve*] Race joined me, my compere in the show. A rehearsal, very easy, – I read poems & so did he in turn. 2^1/$_2$ min. too long, so we cut our talk. 2 poems.... then Mr Happy but his talk not very well done (*he* was good but script not clever) then a band with Mr Race

playing piano, & he turned to me.... Then we read poems, & he held up my books for prize winners, *C Child*, *Traveller*, & *SP at Circus*. Next a rapier fight, quite thrilling.... I was fascinated by it.... Two rehearsals then the real thing. All went well & I enjoyed it very much.

17th February
[*Letter*] from M Tempest saying she likes the new *GR*, but it is very much like her own tale, *Curly Cobbler*. My goodness, what tripe! She remarks that but as *Curly* is out of print it won't matter. Also she raises objections to the *LGR* models – so I wrote pointing out that fairy shoes was an ancient tradition, but I wrote *TR & the Shoe* 20 years ago.... Also I told her to write to Miss [*Foye*] & object as she wished. Really I wish Miss Foye did not make the *GR* models, they will be nothing but trouble. I shall make strong objections to the TV [*televising*] of *LGR* if she changes the words.

25th February
Deep snow. Astonishing! I could scarcely believe my eyes. All night thuds & bangs of rain I thought, but it was snow. Trees thickly coated, the fir tree hanging down to the windows, the spyrea a white thick clock, no branches to be seen. Apple trees with great lumps of thick white fur on boughs. The snow 5 inches thick, or more, like huge blossoms all over.... The fine wire of the wireless like a thick heavy rope of snow.... But all day the snow has fallen (Now I hear this is the worst for 10 years. Trains 11 hours late). The trees wonderful, & I notice that the Hornbeam is like a great fern.

10th March
The new, very sweet puppy arrives. I was worried about the icy cold for such a baby.

17th March
Again I saw the Sputnik. It seemed to go by Cassiopeia, shining out.... a yellow little star.

22nd March
Concert. Nigel Coxe played *Sonata in D major* Mozart (rather dull).... Liszt [*and*] Bartok (Both these marvels of brilliance).... Then.... Lute. Alfred Deller (Counter Tenor). Songs by Campion. Arne & Dowland. (Have you seen the white lily grow).... I did not like the Lute solos, – too thin for the great room, & not like [*Julian*] Bream's playing. The songs, lovely & yet, yet.... queer as if 2 people sang, one with real voice, one with false. I hurried back to MacTavish [*the new puppy*] & had hot tea. Frozen.

24th March
Tired & depressed, struggling on with the puppy, who hides under the chests – then making pools on the floor.... But he is so sweet, and it is I [*who am*] too tired.

9th April
The doctor came, [*because*] my knee was wrong...the cartilage slipped.

12th April
I lay awake because…. It is no use worrying, I am sure. John is troubled about money dissipating…. it is a pity I did not keep my [*Sugden*] shares & Downs House, & have money in trust for them. I have nothing left now…. [*Helen*] will dissipate a fortune.

25th April
To Burford, – but oh! John drove with one hand [on the wheel] nearly all the way…. Lunch at the Plane Tree [*Hotel, where an*] awful young man, a common fellow, talking of cars [saying,] 'I have only one criterion when I apply for a job. Money will decide matters.' I bought E Farjeon's *The Glassy Floor* (lovely)…. Home, but unfortunately we missed the way. I said, 'This is wrong' but John goes on.

26th April
Helen came at night & we had a party [*a gathering at Thackers*]…. I realised John feels *out* [*of it*] – too self-conscious, too sensitive. I felt troubled. Perhaps Helen talks too much, in a lay down the law way.

12th May
My depression was lifted by finding a beautiful cowslip ball with blue ribbons at my door…. I wrote to John, offering him the oak settle and other things…. [*I got*] a crazy letter from GL, a nice one from LM.

19th May
I am glad that John is enjoying his work, thank God…. Should I go to a London specialist?…. Gertrude writes a nice letter acknowledging mine, which enclosed a letter from Connie in 1908 at Oxford.

20th May
In such pain that I phoned the doctor at midday having hurt my knee getting into my car.

22nd May
I was cross that MacTavish made a pool on my white rug!

23rd May
Specialist came at 9 a.m. I was awake at 4 in a panic of forgotten things, lest I should be whisked into a nursing home…. "How old are you?' '70,' said I boldly (a small white one)…. [*The specialist*] said, "I think it is old age', but I need an electric massage.

27th May
Letter from John…. He sounds cheerful & enjoying his work. Georgie [*Jenkinson's*] letter full of fears, and underlinings. She's a nervous woman, timid as a hare. She asked me to remember her in my prayers…. Sissy [*sent a*] letter, I wish she wouldn't write so often. We agreed that we would write less often.

28th May

A lovely day. I made the most of it. I determined to get on with the *GR* book about the May Day festivities, & I paced about and wrote & waited & wrote & gardened and wrote. Suddenly [*I*] got it & rushed along hard till I was dead tired but happy, & finished it. (Rough of course, & a bit long).... I was tired & hungry with writing, & I made a supper, a delicious meal. I grilled, no fried, a chicken leg, with bacon, got it just right.

2nd June

A night telephone call from Dorothy Clayton, GL's friend, worried about GL acting queerly, [*and*] should she have extra help?.... I said I knew nothing of GL's finances.

19th June

A letter saying that GL went home from the nursing home, they couldn't prevent her. Soon she will go to live near Bessie in Cornwall.

20th June

I paid Mrs. Allen £1.13.0, an unsolicited rise in wages. She looked surprised. I made a note of how the sum was made up.... A BBC cheque for £17.10.0.... A Canadian fan letter.... Poultice of kaolin on my knee.

23rd June

The New Zealand test team are badly down, no wonder with that soft wicket.

24th June

A letter from Mrs Spencer [*wife of Stanley Spencer*] saying that he used to make sketches on a toilet roll.

25th June

I am delighted that [*AE*] Kennedy will illustrate the next *TR* book. Ruth [*Plant*] drove me to Longdown.... Walking in woods with wild roses, yellow rock roses & deadly nightshade.

27th June

The wettest June since 1903.... I wrote six or seven letters, including one to P du S about the music.

29th June

Writing a *Mouse* story [*Snug and Serena*], botheration. I am sick and tired of them, and yet I have to go on. *GR* goes on easily, so does the *Fox*, but these bore me.

9th July

A tiny naked girl called to me, Karen, Karen, a sweetie pie.... I got a phone call from Margaret R at Brighton. I nearly rushed off & joined her company. She told me [*that*] I must have a London doctor

23rd July
I posted two MS to Heinemann, *School* and *Toadstool*.... I was driven to give a talk at a school in High Wycombe, but the children are really too young, they don't understand my talk.

24th July
[*To the Andersons*] Only Rosemary there in long dress going, off to a cocktail party. She is 17, a sophisticated Miss, alas.

28th July
Letter from a librarian at Marylebone saying she wants write an article for the 21st anniversary of the *GR* books, & asking to come out & see me.

2nd August
A 20 page letter from Mrs. Clay, Harry went to CT but never told me. She tells me such interesting things, & she loves the place.

4th August
I turned out the cupboards and made a bonfire of lots of manuscripts, copies of *T in T* etc.

7th August
Miss Bewick came, of Marylebone public library. She is writing an article about me.... She does not like the KW's pictures [*of the Mouse books*], too muddy. She likes MT's clear, pure colours.

9th August
I was irritated by [*various*] reviews, one saying that when I was at Manchester University, little did I think I should get fame by writing about rabbits, three million or so. Such cheek! Cheek!

13th August
Saw Lewis King [*Lilian's husband*].... I said I hope you are enjoying your nice little home and your sweet wife, he said yes. I don't really like him, he spends a lot of money on rubbish, on aeroplane travel.... What does he want? He wants to make Lilian miserable.... A letter from Heinemann about *Snug*, might go into a bigger edition, like *Red Fox*. I said couldn't write another book to go with *Mr. Toad's Toadstool*.

18th September
Doctor came.... He doesn't want to get me cured. He reaps too much out of my illnesses.

26th September
A letter from GL saying she has had her long hair cut and permed. Eureka, a brave hairdresser.

30th September
John's nice letter, – but the new Head Master has been too devastating.... too severe. I went

off to Oakdene [*School*]. At first sight I did not like Mr. Clark. He looked like a plumber not a poet. He kissed me, confound him, in pure happiniess.... 'Have you thought about doing your [*auto*]biography,' he asked.

5th October

To Penn Church Harvest Festival. Most beautiful. I feel privileged to go there. I was amazed as I entered. Masses of Michaelmas Daisies, blue, purple, red. Lavender all mingled, by chancel rails & pews, – so many glories of these, in deep windows, in vases. The pulpit gold & red with chrys. & dahlias, & golden rod, scarlet, tawney, breathless. The old church a dream of beauty & colour.

9th October

At 6.00 am I put on the radio, and heard that the good, great Pope Pius XII has died. I said a prayer for him.

10th October

Delighted that the specialist, Dr. Sklatz, will see me. So figs for you, Dr. M[*Milner*].

14th October

I went to London to see the specialist.... He talked too much of his position.... & he had his face too near to me &.... an odd feeling like this, too familiar.

17th October

My hands are much better, so Doctor S[*Sklatz*] has some effect. But my ring makes a green and black band. Frightening.

19th October

To the Penn Mission service.... [*She is impressed by one missionary*] who felt that people have too much luxury.... that birth control is necessary, that imperialism is a problem for the helpless.... I came home [*and*] was met by a barricade of shouts & yells as boys sprang from a bush. I was infuriated but they ran away.

21st October

Broadcast on, speech: – to prepare. The right length. Know when to stop. Time it. Write it out word for word. Make it sound as if extempore & *from the heart*. So write for reading, – to be spoken. Slower than ordinary conversation. *Go slow*. Speak out of your own experience, a picture in words, – you are painting a picture. You must be absolutely sincere. A little humour if possible. Some detail the audience does not know & some details they know.... Today a policeman came, young, good looking, – to ask about the children who caused the upset. He went to the houses, – I felt glad, yet sad. For they make far too much ugly racket, quarrelling & fighting & they do need keeping in order, having some discipline.... They are rude & cheeky, – yet I like them.... John's letter, still unhappy. I cannot help him. It is most strange this heavy cloud. It reminds me so much of James, alas.

24th October

A lovely Autumn Day, – mists & gold & red, cherry trees red, beeches partly gold, the sound of acorns dropping, such a rattle in the branches as they come down, & leaves drifting most marvellously. I felt happy.... [*She meets a new neighbour, 'the author'.*] I said I loved Autumn, he said, 'Except for the leaves.' I said I was thrilled by them. He said he had been sweeping his up, & had cut down 3 trees so they wouldn't leave so many! I said I loved sweeping up leaves, & I chose a fine day & went out. It shows how people differ.

31st October

All Hallows Eve, I think of CT, apples, chestnuts etc.... I wished I had refused to give books for the Conservative Bazaar, I was confused. I must write tomorrow, get down to it.

4th November

[*Katherine Wigglesworth comes to stay.*] Up at 7.30, made toast & tea alone, wishing KW would do it. After breakfast we finished the book. KW said she'd go on holiday with me to the Lakes. I laughed to myself. She has been saying it for 10 years. MacTavish tore the jacket of a book of K's. I will give her mine.... John very miserable.

21st November

A letter from John from the Warnford [*hospital*], saying he [*has*] had ECT. I was much relieved to get a letter from darling old John. Proofs of *TR and Company* came.

14th December

Lunch at Datchet with the du Sautoys. I felt ill, slept badly.

24th December

A marvellous day of sun on Christmas Eve. Kept wishing I was going to green & gold Stowe, yet I think it is for the best for I cough a lot.... In bed all day.

25th December

In bed all day, & very happy. Opened parcels.

26th December

Doctor came, says I am much better. I got up. Blissful when John and Helen come. I think John is improving.

31st December

In bed all day, reading, resting, sleeping, coughing, feeling so tired after the 3 days holiday [*at Stowe*] . A nice day & I enjoyed the comfort of my room & the little feasts.... This has been a sad year as well as a good one. John's illness, my own knee trouble, the dermatitis, & now the Bronchitis.... Very wet year too. Let us hope for better health, strength & finer weather.

1959

5th January

Letter from John [*in*] Brighton.... New Year resolution, to write, say 1000 words a day. Otherwise I shall do nothing.

9th January

Still sleeping badly, partly because the bed is so heavily warm & comfortable, so I cannot sleep as I savour the bliss! I feel I'm hibernating.... John has walked miles on Ditchling Beacon.... I feel so happy as I know.... it will do him good.... Called to see – Joyce [*Kann*].... Michael & his kisses.... It thrills me to start a book again.

11th January

Slept better because [*I kept the*] fire on all the night. How guilty one feels. I did washing up, dusting & fire, feeling it to be a great effort.

12th January

Hair waved [*for*] 10/- + 10/- tip for Xmas.... Reading the excellent book, *The Bell*, by Iris Murdoch. How brilliant it is, characterization, punctuation, perfection, – but too much homosex, [*she is*] obsessed by it.

15th January

Found the lost painting of me, lost about 16 years ago! Also found the MS of that old book I wrote [*that was*] rejected by R[*ichard*] de la M[*are*].... Also the book I wrote for John at Castle Top. Most interesting stuff, and good I think.

17th January

Rugger international at Cardiff, – too thrilling. 'Space-men covered in mud'. Plastered from head to toe in mud.... Most interesting broadcast, very funny indeed, with brilliant commentators, – & the cries & roars of the crowd, & the songs before they began. I have seen it all the time in my mind, & been thrilled.... Wales leading 5 points to 0. Terrible conditions.... Welsh hymns rising, '*Land of our Fathers*', I think it is, as the game gets to the end. Victory song, most moving, slow & grand voices, great cheers.

23rd January

Lovely post, – the catalogue of Diamonds from Christie's. The new Folio [*book*] on the death of Charles I.... Mrs. B & I did the end of the MacTavish chapter [*and*] a part of 'Picking up Stones'.... [*Joan Dobell came.*] She told me her sorrows.... troubles. She expects too much from those she loves.... she says she is penniless, – but she about has £950 a year. That is marvellous I think.

31st January
I am glad the cold month is done.

1st February
[*Another account of MacTavish escaping*] I must accept these disasters with animals whose life is so different from ours.

3rd February
Letter from Gertrude Uttley, very nice, saying she had seen H[*High*] Wycombe with banners of my name when she drove through & she would like to see me.... but I think of the complications. She is a Rationalist, a follower of Bertrand Russell.... But it was a kindly letter & we are all getting old.

6th February
James's birthday, bless his soul.

10th February
I forget it's Shrove Tuesday, so had no pancakes! Oh dear.... Mrs. Allen here & she works so well.... Mrs. B here [*typing*].... We did the Chiltern Woods chapter about Stowe.

16th February
John's letter, – alas still sad…. says his lessons are failures. I do not know how to help him.... MacT[*Tavish*] slept in my room.... tied to a stool, so he was quiet & good bless him.

18th February
To Brighton for the... Toy Exhibition. Fog & fog! But away we went.... The dolls (I kissed one, secretly) – the Bride, the Dutch dolly.

21st February
Tonight P du S phoned to say that the MS accepted, – & the title to be *The Swan Flew Over* [*The Swans Fly Over*].... It cheers me up, – in these days, & provides excitement and happiness for so many as well as so much bliss. [*The book will*] start with 'Going to Sleep'.... after [*Peter*] has seen the John book, I will send it to the BBC.

27th February
Tonight Miss Collins to tea.... I feel rather depressed, I always do.... Cheque for £7.17.6 from India – part of *C Child* in a textbook. [*Faber*] offers the usual 10% & after 2,000 copies, 15 % plus a £100 advance. MT wrote suggesting *GR* for Sandersons wallpaper, do I agree? I said yes... that will be nice.

1st March

A day of great beauty, – sunshine & no wind, & a flashing light in the trees, as I walked through the Penn woods [*with*] MacT our feet rustling the brown leaves, – green & grey moss shining but no flowers yet. Mrs. A[*Allen*] told me someone said that a celandine was out at Forty Green but she had not yet seen it.

2nd March

[*John is complaining*] of loss of memory. He is was in charge of a hockey team which lost. He takes it... all to the heart, bless him.

4th March

Letters, one from GL, depressed & miserable.... Letter from CFT[*unnicliffe*] who says Faber's offer [*for illustrating The Swans Fly Over*] is pre-war.... I hope they will agree to give him more, for he is worth anything.

5th March

[*The film*] Henry V [*starring Laurence Olivier*] is a marvel of beauty & excitement. The colours pastel.... like the Duc du Berry miniatures.

23rd March

GL.... unconscious.... Yet what can we do?...Poor GL, I think of her long ago, when she was young & happy. Now she is old and miserable, and no desires or hopes. Life is sad, it has been sad for her, and yet much happiness for her, the school, and the adulation of girls and parents.

25th March

GL still unconscious in the hospital & they don't think she can live long. It seems impossible. My poor old GL.... As I opened [*So Love Returns, by Robert Nathan*] I fell into the old spell he casts, & this is as beautiful as ever.

26th March

Tim Rabbit and Company published today.... I sent [*a copy of the Year*] to the Armfields (Gert & H), as a memento or a kindness.... A bad night with awful indigestion after having Ovaltine so I must give it up.... D[*octor*] Z[*hivago*] came. Oh dear, I don't want to read it.

27th March

£100 [*from*] Faber [*TR and Co*] & £14 [*from*] Hale.

28th March

GL died at 12.30 this morning. Poor darling. This world has been too much for her, – she was a recluse and she got lost in the loneliness she created. She might have had great happiness.... & I wonder how she lost it, & the warm contact of the world visible & invisible.

31st March
[*John, Helen & she go to GL's funeral*].... I kept saying 'Gwladys! GL. Gwladys. Here we are'.... Then we drove to.... the Executor, who said John had [*been left*] £2000 & that I too had a good legacy.

1st April
Letter from LM from [*the*] Devonshire Hospital. Poor LM, – I hope she too won't slip away.

2nd April
Still lost and lonely without GL in the world of men.... Proofs of *Snug and Serena Count 12"* came, very nice indeed.

4th April
After I had told L[*Lilian King*] about GL & all my sorrow (she remembered her at Penn), – John [*Lilian's son*] came in. He flatly contradicted everything. I held out my hand, he did not take it. 'What kind of dog is this?' he asked. 'A Scottie,' said I. 'No, it isn't. I know Scotties,' said he.... & so it went on, rude, abrupt.... His horrid sneering little face.... a ghastly delinquent kind of youth.... I was glad to get away, but before he came [*in*] it was lovely.

9th April
[*I got details of GL's legacies*] This leaves [£]5,300 for me.... Very good and surprising. I can do a lot with this, the income from investment & leave the money to John.

12th April
After tea to the Fairbairns, – Dr. [*Jacob*] Bronowski came in, dark, virile, happy. Just back from Greece & Israel.

14th April
[*Letter from Faber*] saying that the *John at the Farm* book could not be published, – not for children, not for adults. I'm sorry, but I don't care. I still feel in this nether world, not caring about things, material things. [*The book was published by Heinemann in 1960*]

22nd April
[*On to GL's*] little house.... Inside I felt depressed.... upstairs like a slum.... I chose a bookcase, & books which I have to sort at home.... Such poverty of beauty, poor GL.

15th May
Letter from Dr. Kerlan [*from the University of Minnesota*], asking about my books. He has a collection.... he wants [*some of mine*].... He asked if any library is collecting my books here, & if anyone is doing my autobiography [*sic*]. No! No!

19th May

Posted the tape recording to Malta.... Letters from John & Helen.... The letters have haunted me all day. What can I do? Heaven is here, beauty, happiness, – & he is [*under*] a cloud, poor darling, unable to work or to remember.

29th May

Posted one set of proofs [*of The Swans Fly Over*] to John in trepidation, & another letter of encouragement... [*The film Great Expectations*] was very good indeed, but frightening. I think all my childhood fears came from Dickens.

5th June

Cheque for £41 for the Puffin. Hurrah, quite unexpected. Over 3000 sold [*of Magic in My Pocket*]. Doing *Riddles*, rather thin, and *Telling Tales*, which is very good, I think.

16th June

Dreamt of John, an allegory, – a man struggling with a spirit. He was struggling for Life, & conquered by the hundred hands of this spirit.

23rd June

Lovely day, & I put on my silk dress.... Took a bunch [*of roses*] to the [*lady*] greengrocer. 'You've made my day, Mrs Uttley. I've never had flowers given to me, although we sell flowers.'

30th June

The [*Ingmar Bergman*] film *Wild Strawberries* which I detested. I shut my eyes, bored stiff.

10th July

I have inherited £5,685.11.10 [*from GL's estate*].... How kind of her, & how useful to me. I shall use the interest, and leave John the capital.... Wrote article on National Trust and sent it to *The Times*. It may not be good enough, but it was fun to write it.

11th July

[*She arrives to speak at the Little Chalfont Methodist Church Fete*]. We arrived at an army hut in a waste of ugly side shows.... My heart sank, but I kept it up. I liked the people, who evidently know nothing of books or literature.... I spoke spontaneously, no notes. They listened so intently. [*They asked me*] Did I know Enid Blyton?

12th July

Dead tired last night.... Really I should *not* have accepted that Fete, – it was a very poor little Methodist bazaar, & no Fete.... [*later*] I chided myself for being uncharitable for I may have given great pleasure to somebody there.... I thought of the quiet beauty of Penn Church, – but I thought of Jesus in the multitudes pressing around him. I was touched by the ugliness & the effort of uplift, such as the flower decorations.

19th July
[*Interviewed by the Izvestzia journalist, Tatiana Tess*] I have to do house [*work*] in the mornings, said I, but I do letters from 7 a.m. to 8 a.m.. Fan mail etc. Phone calls [*?*] Oh, I don't answer, said I. She was amazed at this. Later she said, 'Of course you have maids to answer.' Oh no, I have nobody. I live alone with a little dog.

24th July
To Wembley to see the Russian Circus. Marvellous!.... The colour especially of the troupe at the beginning.... girls with maypoles & streamers.

30th July
Spring cleaning 4 months late, my bedroom, stripping it, I washing ornaments, wiping walls.... I took until 5p.m.... At 6.10 I turned off wireless, running with no shoes, & stepped on a wasp. Agony! I screamed as I tore it off.

5th August
Phone from Lilian [*King*] telling me how much 'Mrs. Pain' [*Paine*] admired John. She liked him extremely, his simplicity & the way he accepted all.... never a word of complaint.... [*MT has got half of the fee from the Australian Broadcasting Company.*] So I sent a protest.

7th August
News of the Queen's baby [*Prince Andrew*] expected early in year. Jan? Great joy for her, which we all share.... Thank God for this.... To the Andersons.... Rosemary came [*in*]. She had painted eyes & brows. Most queer, like idols or Burmese stage girls.... She is a tart, – a fast young woman, only 18. She astonishes me, – & so do her parents. Are they blind?

18th August
'Heaven is here, if we did but see it': so I describe what I see, this latish afternoon, in the garden.... A chaffinch walked nearly to my feet as I sat here, on the lawn, long shadows on the rich green grass, a rustle of the trees.... plums ripening. Blue & pink petunias are nearly the only flowers, but [*for*] a cluster or two of roses.... The oak tree is pale olive green against the heavier green of the beech.... & the light falls radiating on the lead figure, his face, hair, his right arm, his left leg & the dolphin shines like dark silver.... A nymph might run down through the gap to the lawn.... I feel quiet & happy, – & all day alone with books.

21st August
Dream of the Queen, ill & her death foretold. I was so troubled.... [*The sculptor, Jacob*] Epstein died today. I think of that day long ago when James and I met him in his Chelsea Studio as he was making the statue for Oscar Wilde, a flying Sphinx.

25th August
Nice cheerful letter from John.... glad I will read all the set books. What a task.... A great row with the milkman who shouted & stormed at me.... & is off to see his lawyer, about my

letter to his employer. O dear! I meant it to be private, – but I had to explain what was wrong. The payments never receipted, & charged a second time.

31st August
Delightful letter from Russia from Tatiana Tess [*of*] *Izvestia*, 5 Pushkin Square, Moscow.... I went to Penn to see Joyce [*Kann*] & ask advice about letter to *Science Monitor*, protesting at article on MT in which it was suggested she wrote the *GR* books, – & I did them orally they said.... We concocted a simple little letter of protest.... Very tired today – these things weary me.... I saw on TV the meeting between [*President*] Eisenhower and [*Prime Minister Harold*] MacMillan. 'I'm mighty glad,' said Eisenhower. Delightful.

15th September
To Henley to lunch – not v. good.... Not to go there again. At night we worked through John's set books. *The Tempest. School for Scandal. Caesar & Cleo*[*Cleopatra*]. *The Mayor of Casterbridge. Pilgrim's Progress.* John took notes as I went through.

28th September
How can I write it? MacTavish is dead.... I can't believe it. I said goodbye, – kissed his head.... He is one of the nicest dogs I have ever known, and quite the sweetest.... He is buried tonight in the wood, & a bonfire glowing near, next to Macduff, who will welcome him & show him the ropes of the dog's Paradise. I hope I will meet these two adorables again.

29th September
I took sleeping pills last night, so slept, – but sorrow haunting [*me*] all day, especially in a taxi down Regent St, in the glitter & sun, I thought 'I would give all the jewels & clothes in this street for my little Scottie darling.'.... Then Georgie [*Jenkinson*] met me, with a scarf on her head like a peasant.... Taxi to [*the*] Savoy [*for the Women of the Year Lunch*], – announced & a warm handshake.... I sat at table 2. But first I met MR, kissed her & we were photographed by a Press photog[*Photographer*] who asked my name for his paper.... A Miss Hope came up & talked of my *Dream* book, was thrilled to meet me as she was writing to me. A delicious & excellent lunch. Scampi, veal, & iced pudding.

1st October
A lovely day, but my heart so sad I could not see it.

8th October
Election Day. Mrs. F. drove me to vote for Bell [*the Conservative candidate*] at Holtspur [*School*].... [*I am*] delighted Conservative are in with such a majority & rather surprised.

17th October
I read the God [*Lord*] of the Flies, – which frightens me.... It is terrific & I felt appalled, but it is brilliant.

18th October
Other side of moon photographed…. say the Russians. Hurrah!

28th October
[*To London*]: Debenhams. I looked at black semi-evening dresses. Chose a black chiffon, – too small but to be copied in my size…. [*She admires some Breughel paintings.*] I bought nothing. I had a glass of champagne & went off for my train.

5th November
Mrs Haymon of *The Times* came to interview me, a nice little woman…. dark curling hair, kind, interested…. She asked first why I, a scientist, wrote children's tales, & she asked about my feeling for Precognition, or the sense of time in *T in Time*…. Always difficult. I suggested Physics was a Poetical Science, not alien to fairy tale or my books. An interesting talk, – science, – & *how* I began to write, or how I wrote, swiftly, said I. When I dust…. I often stop to scribble down an idea, I told her.

6th November
Phoned P du S [and] asked for help for a small advert[*advertisement*] of Swans which I want to send to about a 100 [*people*]…. I suggested that the new edition of *Candlelight* [*Tales*] should be illustrated by Pauline Baynes…. Peter told me he likes my 1960 book *Something for Nothing*…. it is as good as any I had written…. To Miss Matheson's bazaar…. A lady came to me in B[*eaconsfield*] to say that in an exam at her school, the question [was posed], Who wrote *Alice in Wonderland*? The little Curzon girl said, 'Alison Uttley'.

2nd December
Another Peace Union letter (via Heinemann) – for waste paper. P du S wrote, saying Mr. Crawley does not like *Something for Nothing* as a title…. I had a nightmare night, – a long frightening dream, – my bag with money, passport, keys…. all stolen in a foreign country, when I was lost & in a great crowd of strangers, all going on and on, & I joined them, looking for my lost green bag, climbing rocks, slipping, & going through doors, on & on. I awoke in panic, & coughed & coughed & feared Bronchitis & illness.

7th December
[*The arrival of the new Scottie*] Dirk, a nice little fellow, brindle, small, sweet, gay. I must keep him, he is so adorable. The house is much happier with a dog barking.

17th December
Card from [*the*] Curzons, Lord and Lady crossed out and Richard and Gay instead, bless them…. My 75th birthday, it seems absurd, – I cannot believe it, for I feel just the same as ever, full of joy and life, only a bit tireder, so that I have to rest after lunch. A pile of Xmas letters, none for birthday. GL [*is*] dead, John [*sent*] wishes earlier, nothing from Harry, of course, although I always remember his, nothing from Sissy. But Dirk kissed me with a lovely red tongue. Mrs W wished me Many Happy Returns.

21st December
Last night a dream, very vivid…. but I had no strength to stretch out to my desk and write it down…. I was in Russia, talking Russian, & I actually used words I had heard (& forgotten).

25th December
The thrill of Christmas…. & the old happiness…. John said [*his*] headmaster was a hard man….. Helen said that when John gets a letter from him he thinks it is a dismissal. We had a difficult conversation, Helen [*was*] very bitter.

31st December
This year has been lovely, except for the loss of my little MacTavish. Now I feel I have really dropped into Old Age. But I can think quickly and manage to do things, and I have written 4 books for next year.

1960

2nd January
A quiet wet day, – no gardener, so I saved £1.... [*I*] saved another pound [*by*] typing [*some scraps of S Pig*].

4th January
Just gone though Russian lesson, – struggling behind. [*There was*] a card from Tatiana Tess [*the Russian journalist*] & she says, 'I fell in love with your poetic book.'

5th January
[*There was*] a letter from Helen, charging 30/- for the 2 wretched lampshades which I thought were a present. So I sent 15/- & shall return one. [*I was infuriated with Mrs B telling me*] 'You need someone to keep your papers in order.'.... John says they were all much impressed by *The Times* article [*an interview with Alison, entitled, 'Poetic Scientist' and published on 29 December 1959*].

7th January
[*Gertrude writes saying*] 'How pleased James would have been [*about The Times article*]....
this touched my heart, bless him.

10th January
I have not gone to Church. Instead I sit here, after doing the housework more leisurely & lovingly than usual, touching things that respond & know. I sit here & look at the garden in winter sunshine. Divine.

11th January
It's the beginning of a New Year [*and*] I am either ill or heavily stupid, & half asleep & lethargic.... Dirk seized a chocolate I dropped but after licking it refused to eat it....
Adorable creature.

15th January
I find [*that*] I like doing nothing, lying on the couch gazing at the lovely pink azalea....
Letter from K Wig saying *The Times* had not done enough justice to the poetic [*part*] of my person.

22nd January
I had such troubling dreams last night. I always feel weary if I have rushed about in dreams & I had a busy night.

23rd January
A wet day, but off to the circus at Olympia – a wonderful adventure for I adore a Circus.

25th January
Reading Kipling's Ghost.... stories in bed.... I don't think I like Kipling. He reminds me too much of H[*Harry*] Glossop, and of the days when I read Kipling, puzzled except by *Kim* & others.... I made a list of my books. 83. Imagine it!!

26th January
Fog.... so except for a little walk, – indoors.... Outside I heard the first yaffle of the woodpecker this year.

28th January
Decided not to go to London.... the lazy part of me couldn't make the effort.... [*There was a letter*] from G[*Georgie*] Jenkinson.... she saw *The Times* article, [*saying*] it 'failed to convey your wonderful aliveness, and joy in living'. I feel humble & touched by G.J's insight.

8th February
[*She is shocked to hear of the death of LM at Preston on 7 February.*] I am so grieved. I loved Lily and admired her for her courage and bravery in [*the*] face of many difficulties.... I first showed LM the manuscript of *The C[Country] Child*, the first to see it, and she liked it, and then we timidly showed it to James, who didn't like it at all.... Shall I ever forget? She encouraged me with my writing, she brought sweets and good things and flowers in our poverty when J died. I was always excited to open the door at Bowdon and see her, pretty blue dress, gloves, carrying a pile of parcels and her suitcase. And the cricket matches we saw together. Poor dear Lily with her er...er...er... that annoyed me a little.... dear Lily. I shall think of you always.

13th February
Letter from [*Lucy*] Meagher, telling me of LM's last days. She looked beautiful after death.... Poor darling Lily, I did love her & I do miss her. She was a saint indeed.

19th February
The good news of the birth of a prince to Queen Elizabeth, – and delight must fill all hearts [*at the birth of Prince Andrew*].... This afternoon to see *The Devil's Disciple* which I disliked, – the usual mockery of Shaw.

23rd February
A package from the Lloyds Bank executor. He says: shares £4,701.16.11. Cash £538.6.2. I do not understand it at all [*it was LM's legacy to her*].... Miss [*Susan*] Dickinson from Collins came. She is the grand-daughter of H W Tomlinson, whose books I admired. A nice girl. I told her all about the *GR* books...and MT...[*and*] showed her my little Nativity Breughel.

2nd March

Letter from P du S accepting *Sam Pig goes to the Sea*, but no comments.... 2 quotations from *Here's a New Day* and *Ambush* [*are to be included in an*] anthology.... Last night a ravishing dream, which I tried to memorise, but [*there was*] no paper in bed[*room*], it has gone, alas, alas. It was so interesting and original.... Pearls I throw away.

5th March

Also finishing [*preparing*] the talk on Buckinghamshire.... Lovely review from Belfast [*newspaper*] saying I am one of the most delightful of all living writers of essays. O thank you!

7th March

Two dreams, one frightening, one good. [*In one*] I felt something was in the house trying to get into the bedroom.... I whispered, 'Harry I'm frightened' [*to the little boy in bed with her, asleep, aged about six*].... [*In second dream*] I was in a bus going from earth to heaven, but we were quickly there, – & with us Churchill as a passenger.

16th March

[*She sends a copy of Grey Rabbit Finds a Shoe to the baby Prince Andrew*] 'For the Baby Prince with good wishes for happiness & delight in simple things, from Alison Uttley & *Little Grey Rabbit*.'

19th March

Letter from the Queen's Lady [*in-waiting*] saying how much the Queen likes the *GR* book which she accepts, and will read to the baby Prince. A charming letter which gave me joy.

22nd March

From Library has come *Literature and Western Man*. Good, but I find myself preparing for some of old [*JB*] Priestley's propaganda.

24th March

Wild, strenuous dream of climbing down rocks…in Wales, not daring to go. Yet in real life I should have risked it.

25th March

Letter from Collins from Miss Dickinson, saying she loves the *May Day* story, – even more than the *Circus*. Relieved, for…. I thought I was keeping too close to reality.... Sissy's letter, telling me [*Harry*] out of hospital & Hylda his wife has said she won't live with him. Desertion.

26th March

I asked [*the gardener*] if he wasn't afraid of [*smoking and*] cancer. He said he could not stop....

[*The BBC want*] to do a broadcast on my childhood.... Also a lovely book jacket of the *John* book, which delights me.

3rd April
To Church, – a dull sermon, – really I cannot follow Mr Muspratt as he wanders about in confusion.... I began to think of Determinism. The pre-ordained Crucifixion, – and all its implications.

8th April
[*In bed*] I heard celestial music in the air! Most astonished, an effect of wind [*or a*] plane perhaps, but it was like an orchestra.... [*Heinemanns say that*] someone wants to do records of my works, the [*story*] teller [*Vivian*] Leigh.

16th April
Sad news today from John [*telling me that he's been sacked from the post of housemaster of Walpole House*].... a really tough man required. John not up to the test.... I feel most depressed.... It is a tragedy.

25th April
John came, – looking well but thin and anxious.... We talked of many things except the trouble.... At night we talked of the trouble. John hates teaching. He gets [*into*] a panic.

28th April
London, – to keep up my heart, and to see the lovely sights.

30th April
Two good things, – a cheque from Faber for £365, & [*one*] from GL's money for £44, which astonishes me.

6th May
Wedding of Princess Margaret. A beautiful & moving ceremony, & somehow on TV the words came through most forcefully, very reverently, eternal. I was moved by this.... I felt I was in the Abbey.

17th May
Cheque from Heinemann, £126.15.5.... A man wrote.... asking me to join [*the*] Performing Animal Protection Society, – which attacks Circuses....[*I said*] No, too much cruelty elsewhere, – rabbits, horses, calves, hens, – & I [*had*] heard circus animals were well treated.

24th May
[*To Chelsea Flower Show*]. A wonderful show. Of course I bought many things.... Lovely card from E[*Eleanor*] Coatesworth, [*saying*] 'What a lovely face you have.' My goodness, no-one says that to me!

25th May
Reviews came, one with a notice of MT's death, which is untrue. I was staggered.... A nasty thing to happen. [*Margaret Tempest was, in fact, alive and well.*]

31st May
A lovely dream. Tea with W de la Mare. He was as he used to be, moving about, & a great welcome. I knew he had come back from the dead. I carefully didn't ask any questions. We talked of writing.... He read quite a lot, he told me, – & I wondered about the books.

1st June
June the month of roses, & here they are opening their…. buds & showing their beauty.

9th June
MR [*read*] de la Mare's 3 Cherry Trees, [*which*] moved me to tears, I thought of him so closely.

18th June
Thankful [*the gardener*] Picton has gone…. Very hot indeed & my knee ached horribly.

22nd June
[*There is a new gardener, Okell*] An odd fellow but he cut [*the*] grass & weeded under my supervision. When he went he said, putting his face near me, 'So you write books! You'd better write a book about me!' I murmured, No thank you.

23rd June
Remembered the Toad venturing slowly to walk across the road. I feared lest cars should come.

5th July
A quiet day & feeling happier, because I sent for Dr Milner to give me advice. He stayed over an hour.... I told the story of John's illness.... [*Dr. Milner*] suggested John should see Sir John Weir, the Queen's doctor, who has done some wonderful cures in mental cases…. using slow homeopathy.

6th July
[*A Mrs Copper from Cheshire*] called, for an autograph [*and*] to meet me. 'Ah, you are lovely. You are beautiful. I thought you would be, because you write such beautiful books'…. I was abashed, she was so urgent.

7th July
I had frightful nightmare of trying to catch a plane, & nobody to carry my big trunk with all my worldly possessions.... Yet I calmed down by reading Einstein's relativity [*theory*].

8th July
Mr Bevan's funeral today – I always think of Churchill & of Bevan's mockery of him. Great upsets in the Congo, [*which has*] just received freedom.

11th July
John at the Old Farm came.... A nice book, I love it.

22nd July
Dream that I was standing on a great rock.... & I wondered if I dare jump. I felt like jumping, & yet I thought I might damage my feet or legs.

23rd July
Reading *Huckleberry Finn* but now bored with it. Prefer [*a*] book.... on Art & Einstein's Relativity.

27th July
Schubert's 9th Symphony is my adored one.... [*She is worried about getting puppets for the Jordans play.*] Oh dear, – I always fear MT.

28th July
John's last day with boys at Stowe, – and it must have been a very troubled unhappy day.... Yet pray God it may turn out for the best.

5th August
To B. to Bank... & we talked of the confusion caused by Automatics. The machine broke down & printed £ s d one time after another. How I laughed! A fairy tale here!

9th August
A minute of bliss in garden, this late afternoon. Sun shone low through the white clouds & made the illumination that thrills me, a spot light on a red rose, a flame on the statue who holds the rose pitcher in his arms.

20th August
Cheque for £90.1.9 from Heinemann for John [*at the Old Farm*], – 2,200 copies sold. They do not pay advance royalties.... The Country Book Club [*want an*] article for the pub[*publication of The*] Swans [*Fly Over*].

24th August
Penguins want *C Child* for Puffins, so I agree.... P. du S suggests that Faber put *T in T* in paperback ed[*edition*] after 1962. I shall be glad.

11th September
To Windsor, to lunch with P du Sautoy.... R[*Ruth*] Plant attacked English policy in [*the*]

Colonies again, I felt so cross. She would not agree with Elspeth Huxley's book on Kenya, showing all we had done.

4th October
John did not return from the Athays.... till 12.20 & I was stiff with anxiety.... Only the good brakes of the Morris saved a collision. He left for Guernsey today. We had a prayer, as in the old days, at his request, & he told me of his Christian faith after long doubts.... I was most touched, as we knelt. He is more patient & sweet than ever, too sensitive.

6th October
'Women of the Year' lunch.... My new green linen dress.... Reception, all very nice, a special smile from Lady Lothian.... Then home calling at the Tate, very tired & straight to bed.

30th October
In bed. Dr. came, – I am about the same. Memorandum: some titles of books read this year (not in order). [*They include:*] *Dean Inge* by Adam Fox, *Ring of Bright Water*, *The Perfect Wife*, *A New Earth* (Elspeth Huxley), *No Place Like Home* – D Reeves – boring, *The Art of Living* [*by*] F. Lucas (on Burke, Walpole, Franklin).

2nd November
I did not remember one of my favourite days, – but it was a happy day.... Miss Eliz Taylor [*from the BBC*] came.... & we discussed the broadcast. We worked for 4 hours, solid.

3rd November
Lady Chatterley's Lover accepted [*for publication*]. I am sorry. I think it will do much harm to the young, I am glad I did not read it when I was only 18.

4th November
Publication Day for *Something for Nothing* & *Sam Pig Goes to the Seaside*.... I felt happy, relaxed, but tonight I feel cross and [*some*] tension.... [*There was*] a long phone [*call*] from the BBC about the broadcast. So I am weary.... A Greetings Telegram from John and Helen, very sweet.

5th November
£200 from Faber for the 2 books.... Today the [*BBC*] typescript comes, & it was really quite nice, I liked the play.... I phoned the BBC with a few alterations.... the broadcast [*was*] mentioned in *Times Lit Supp*... with an advert[*isement*] of my books, very flattering. I do hope the broadcast will be liked.

6th November
Tomorrow the broadcast. I feel nervous as if my dear ghosts were listening, & myself a little ghost girl too.

7th November
The broadcast. Adequate, but never stirring, it did not give me the thrill of childhood.... I didn't feel ghosts were listening. They would not have recognised themselves at all.

16th November
Gilbert Harding is dead, a fine man, who might have done really great things, but he was a world-entertainer, a figure of sanity in a world of triviality.... I dreamed I was in Russia & going down the Volga with a girl in a small boat, passing great works & buildings.... Men lying in groups, naked bodies.... in heavy stupor.... nobody taking any notice of us for which I was glad.

2nd December
My postponed cocktail party.... Mrs. W and I did trays & plates of nuts.... A happy party.... John phoned at 10.30, – his letter was in a parcel which had not arrived. He wants me to go to Guernsey for Xmas, – but I've still got bronchitis, & it rains & blows.

20th December
[*Harry writes, saying that in the broadcast*] I had not mentioned my little brother! I wrote at once & told him they had cut it out with other things. That's the worst of it, people don't understand the artistic whole.

31st December
News that MR has the OBE.... Bless her. Goodbye old year. I looked at the yellow moon & [*my*] star, so far away, yet so near. They help me. It has been a good year for many things, & I am glad John has escaped from teaching & is free, bless him.

1961

1st January
A lovely day, the bare wood golden for once with sunshine, & a robin on the firtree looking at me. Dirk rolling in ecstasy on the white hard frost lawn, – the first time it has been hard & he adores it.... I meant to go to Church, but I decided to rest.... So I lay, but Dirk got on the bed & walked over me.... A queer content, like a silence in earthquake country. One almost feels guilty of happiness.... Darling John, I hope you are really well, & that life will help you. I shall do all I can to help, thankful he has escaped from the misery.

21st January
Listening to the Rugger match, Wales v England.... Queer how I feel about cricket and rugger!...A lovely review from the *Yorkshire Post*, a treat after some sneers.... A quiet day, after a disturbed night with Dirk calling me to let him out.

24th January
Dreamt that I was reading a book which reminded me of my own childhood.... I looked at the cover, it was the *C Child*, written by some woman, taking out all difficult words [*and*] all dialect words, not well done. I at once wrote to P du S, complaining.

31st January
[*A nice letter*] from Elizabeth Taylor, BBC producer.... I sent part to Jane Wig, who wants to join the BBC.... Arthur Bryant's fine book on the Restoration came.... Tonight: A curious sound in the air, the elements alive and roaring, the sound of the Earth in upheaval, trees clashing and this roar going on.... not close to the earth but high up. I look round the still room, nothing moves, yet it is spinning through space, enclosed in the boxlike house. A miracle.... about 8 p.m.

1st February
I dreamed I was in an opera, [*The Marriage of*] Figaro.... I acted in it. I ranted in long set speeches.... [*But I was*] too weary to write it down.... Letter from John that has worried me. He wrote a protest letter, to the Head of Governors.... because HM [*the Headmaster*] has not mentioned the reason for his leaving Stowe.... I am appalled by the harm he may have done.... I think Helen egged him on.

2nd February
Last night I couldn't sleep for worrying over John's really mad letter to the governors.... this gnawing resentment.... [*Her*] accountant.... thinks I am foolish to lend £2,000 to John at such a low rate of interest.

10th February

A nice visit from Helen & Mary Athay, – cheerful & gay…. Helen looks better, her hair slightly grey…. quieter & not aggressive…. [*Helen*] says John is much happier…. I have sent [*John*] a large photograph & a poem written by James when John was at Prep School.

11th February

I sent off my letter to John with a home-made Valentine…. I think of John, free at last…. [*A*] Cambridge scientist [*claims*] the world & the universe formed by a sudden flare-up [*the Big Bang*], – just as Velikovsky says.

13th February

Packet from Sissy enclosing a MSS from Mary's grand-daughter…. I had to read it. An Allegory, about the Atomic Bomb…. But O dear me…. I wrote saying Propaganda is not Art…. like a horror film.

15th February

[*Her accountant asks what proportion of her car's use is for her work.*] I said …. myself. ….for work, 1,500 miles, a guess. I hope it is right. Nobody to advise me.

16th February

To London, to dentist, 3 stoppings, very uncomfortable…. I got a taxi & tried to find the Courtauld Inst [*in*] Manchester Sq. But it is in Woburn Sq, so I went to the Wallace [*Collection*].

23rd February

Mrs. Walker here, making the house charming, cooking…. Dirk got out again [*a neighbour says*] 'a lady of advanced years, like you, should not keep a young dog.' Confound her cheek.

28th February

An anxious day, Dirk so ill…. The Vet came…. John writes [*saying*] he has bought a house [*in Guernsey, for investment purposes*] for £2,100…. 'I felt sorry for it,' said he, 'for the house used to be pretty.'

2nd March

Beauty! My senses enraptured by the sight of Venus, sparkling in the West. Such extreme beauty. Such a marvel in the deep blue night sky. The moon full rising in the East, with 2 curved lights from planes enclosing her in an archway.

4th March

The first Brimstone [*butterfly*] in the garden…. Letter from W[*Winnie*] Armitage…she is nearly blind…. Peter [*du Sautoy*] came to tea, looking very nice in a tweedy suit…. I [*had*] intended to show him my Will, but couldn't bear to talk of such things…. We spoke of

Adrian Bell who has come to Faber now. He is the composer of *The Times* crossword! Not a good thing for literature I think. To the Windsor Rep. [*in a car with*] that woman Peggy again. My heart sank.... I endured her ugly voice & stupid [*comments*].

11th March
What a day, I drop on the couch, knees hurting horribly, & so tired out. Dirk escaped twice.... I searched with car up the road.... & he turned up.

16th March
John came, a sudden unexpected visit.... I ordered extra food by phone. He brought a box of lovely [*flowers*] from the Paine family.

18th March
[*We borrowed a projector.*] I saw the lovely scenes of Guernsey, photographed with taste.... I could see how happy John is there.

23rd March
Up early, John got breakfast, & he left by early train for London.... He went to his specialist, Helpmann, & then to the osteopath Foster.

26th March
My favourite Sunday, [*Palm Sunday*] but I did not go to church.... [*I went*] to see the High March exhibition of paintings.

29th March
TV put in.... I gazed at the [*aerial*] man on the roof as if he were a trapeze artist. He showed me how to manipulate the TV, but when he had gone I couldn't do it.

1st April
Cheque from Nelson, & a dividend of GL's to help me on.... I had a light lunch of fish cakes, & then watched the TV of the Boat Race. Very exciting to see Cambridge catch up & win.

4th April
Letter from Mrs. Clay [*the new owner of Castle Top farm*]. She has found [*a*] reference to Castle Top 1760, also 1415. Hurrah!

5th April
Slept badly, trying to fix up the Universe & the complex system of mankind after watching TV in bed, [*Professor Jacob*] Bronowski speaking on The Internal Mind, with [*a*] sculptor whose work looked Evil, & a Physicist.... & an architect who had a wonderful USA slickness which might rouse envy in heaven.

10th April

Letter from K Wig, suggesting she should make a Book Plate of [*a*] Unicorn for me.... I don't think she can draw well enough, but, bless her, I must say yes.... [*Geoffrey*] Moorehead's [*book*], [*The*] *White Nile* [*is*] depressing and debunking. Nice letter from Lady Faber saying [*her recently deceased husband's*] mind will find more work to do in the hereafter. True, I'm glad she feels like that. (Later. She never made the Unicorn plate. One of her broken promises.)

12th April

[*News of the first manned space flight by Russia's Uri Gagarin*] 1st Space Man Major Gagarin. 25,000 miles an hour flight. Thrilling, – & very brave to endure the agonies he must have felt. The speed, the loss of gravity – or was he still under gravity?

14th April

A lovely day. Gagarin said the earth was pale blue in a black sky, – this enchants me. I don't think England cares very much, not interested in Science or Astronomy.... Will Gagarin go under the clouds of Venus and return?

19th April

I posted MSS of the fairy book to Faber, *The Little Knife Who Did All the Work*. Too long title?

20th April

Terrific springcleaning day, & we did the bedroom, Mrs W doing walls, & I clearing out the stuff, washing the little china horses, just as I did as a child, – arranging back & polishing furniture.

26th April

A shock, – an income tax demand for [*an*] extra £88. So I will have about £180 to pay in July too.... I have not the free money, I wrote to John to borrow £100.... This is annoying.

4th May

K Wig went home. I feel very lonely without her jolly presence. We get on so well together (as long as I let her have control, I fear).... John sent £100 to me, which I will try to return after I've paid the July tax.

5th May

[*Watching*] the Queen's reception at the Vatican and meeting Pope John, who looks a dear, loving wise old saint.... Reading a book of Autobiography, quite disgusting, sex dragged in at the earliest [*opportunity*].... Letter from Penn Church asking for more money. I do not think I can give it.

13th May

Divine concert at Osterley Park.... the Amadeus Quartet.... The first violin was wonderful, such force, such virtuosity & beauty of tone. Mozart like angel music. All my pain vanished & happiness came.

15th May
Eureka! I won a Premium Bond [*prize*] of £25.... So astonished, – I thought it was a request for tax. A great hunt for the Bond [*finally*] there it was in a tiny old envelope in the Deed Box.

20th May
[*I watched a circus on TV and*] felt sorry for the crocodiles. On TV I felt the inhumanity. 4 cart horses, & I again felt sorry & shocked, so alien from their quiet life they once had before this Topsy Turvy world. I'm old fashioned, I stick to the real things.

28th May
Last night I dreamed that I saw…. GL coming along visiting me…. I asked her if she liked where she was…. She said it was not so bad, – I wondered whether she had got to hell or purgatory.

30th May
Letter & card [*a petition*] for me to sign from the Society for Abolishing Capital Punishment, but I won't sign it in spite of the names of many famous people [*on it*].

5th June
Alas the thrush is dead. I find it lying in the wood border, poor baby, a beauty, – so I buried it & said a prayer & put a rose on its grave. I have fed it for some days.

20th June
[*I saw*] the musical play *Jane Eyre*, wonderful play…. I kept thinking of Castle Top in my grandfather's time. 1857 was the date of the play.

29th June
To London [*for*] the first time for ages, – & I went up in my first Diesel train…. Quite nice, clean and comfortable.

11th July
To Guernsey [*via Gatwick*]…. A lovely plane. I stared down at the fields of England, & somehow I could not feel any motion…. At Guernsey in an hour. John there…. We drove to the Paines, – Mrs. P old & withered, hair like a shock of wisps. Helen calm & collected.

14th July
Wind in the night. I suddenly heard marvellous music, harps and strings, glissando, chromatic, with the smallest intervals, & voices singing 'Alleluia'. It went on for quite ten minutes, ravishing. I was wide awake. I got up at once…it must have been an Aeolian harp

effect, but the words of the singing were human (or divine), as if the spirits of the air were chanting the words.... a magical experience that made me very happy.

20th July
Before flying [*back*], John & I went off to sit on rocks.... I had a plain breakfast, as Helen said I would not eat my lunch at 12.0 if I had anything to eat at 8.0.... I was hungry. John bought me an ice on the way.

2nd August
I wrote, wrote of Witchcraft, thrilled as I wrote, using an old 1613 book.

7th August
In the Psychic book I was struck by the difficulty of the interviewed spirit to remember names. Why should he? Names are nothing.

13th August
Looking at churches with John Betjeman [*on TV*]. Which was very good indeed.... Sundays are too long when I am alone, and when I don't go to church or go out. I can see how old people feel, – lost & forgotten on Sundays! I'm always glad to welcome Mondays, and Mrs. W, and warm washdays! Homely things.

17th August
Miss Dickinson came, I met the train. Great fun, a chatter.... about the change from H[*Heinemann*] to Collins, years ago, & 1st pub of *GR* books.

14th September
Letter from a woman asking for book for the Jewish Bazaar, for Jewish Refugees.... I sent *Plowmen's Clocks* & a letter.... Writing a story for Jewish book.

15th September
Betty Yates came with her nice aunt Daisy Kennedy, over 80.... A nice visit, we sat, & talked of Picasso.... of the Nuclear fall-out. What is Strontium A asked Betty. Alas, I do not know except I think it is the change from lead.

19th September
I have been reading *Fables and Tales*, & *Beauty and the Beast*. Some of the pictures are horrific I think. The beast is a frightful one. It would have haunted me in the wood [*near Castle Top farm*].

22nd September
[*Sissy's letter*] is fulsome, so full of praise for me.... I loathe praise unmerited.... Made scones, in an odd way & they are delicious!

4th October
Last night I wrote my life from childhood to marriage, & sent to P. du S, to fill in gaps.... I hate going back, it is so queer, so ghostly, I think of those I loved long since.

14th October
Tired from tip to toe! Gardening did it. Letter from…. a wretched [*magazine*] asking for a story, no money to pay me.... an article [*in the magazine*] calling cuckoos murderers stirred my wrath. I refused.

30th October
John came, feeling ill. It was gastric 'flu.... I felt very distressed, but glad to have him here. [*He was*] a lot better [*in the*] morning. [*To Windsor to see*] A very good play on Cecil Rhodes.

13th November
Mrs W told me of a woman.…. whose mother-in-law used to lay out the dead. She went to lay out a man & she told his wife the man ought to be shaved. 'How much extra will it cost?' 'Half a crown.' 'Oh, don't bother. He's not going anywhere in particular,' replied the widow.

15th November
Indian [*salesman*] on doorstep.... I told him I didn't want anything. 'Bad Luck,' said he fiercely. 'Bad luck yourself,' I returned.... These men are frightening & one dare not speak.

18th November
[*Collins want*] me to go to this Children's [*Book*] Week.... [*A scolding letter from Mr. Muspratt*] for not going to church very regularly too. Oh dear, I'll send him £1.

20th November
Tonight I made an effort & did my Will alterations in bequests, wiping out MR [*Margaret Rutherford*] and JD [*Joan Dobell*], silly to put them in with diamonds! Better for John to have this.

25th November
A lovely day but a gloomy beginning with large income tax demand, about £220 I think for h/year?.... I sent it to [*my accountant*] Mr. Carpenter..... A letter from lady in waiting to Princess Margaret thanking me for the books for her son.... To Oakdene School bazaar. Ruth Pitter gave only a very short speech.... speaking of making her living by 'art'.

13th December
Income Tax £120, *provisional*, & I sent it on to the accountant.... & wrote to the lawyer, who has had my Will for a month and [*has*] done nothing, I feel much annoyed about this.

14th December

To London, Mrs. Helliwell drove me to the train.... to the Book Exhibition. Georgie [*Dickinson*] waiting for me.... much older and dressed in black.... Many nice people [*there*].... Mollie du S, Ethel Stewart.

16th December
I feel I am nearly born, a babe at Castle Top in Victorian days, all the fuss and preparation.... my father unhurried. Snow on the ground, the midwife ready, no doctor, not necessary. My mother must have been nervous, her first child, but she was always brave, and the nurse was a good, kind little old woman: Mrs. Marriott of Lea. She smoked a pipe in real old age, about eighty five, – I saw her.

26th December
A lovely day of sun. But so cold I had the electric on day and night. What bills I shall get.... Bobbs–Merrill are [*to be*] my American publisher [*for the Heinemann published Little Red Fox and Little Brown Mouse books*].

～ *1962* ～

3rd January
I always feel rather delicious at night, & keep fire on, and light. [*She is ill with 'flu.*]

8th January
Phone call from Miss Eliz Taylor of BBC asking about Jane Wig.... There is possible vacancy. I replied I did not think she was suitable.... I'm not going to bother with the ungrateful Wigs, they are too full of importance and boasting.

24th January
[*A nightmare*] in bed with creatures, ghosts and rats, all surging round me, and I called 'Mother, Mother, Mother' over and over very loud to reach the dead, I was so frightened.... Yes also a nice dream.

29th January
Writing the new *GR* book about the Dumplings [*inspired after Katherine Wigglesworth made them*], & revised [*it*], and started to retype with fresh poems.... A talk with Lilian King on phone, – I said I was sorry [*about*] her husband returning.

31st January
John's nice letter.... Letter from [*someone*] very nice asking questions about the technique of writing.... I have answered it fully.
Memorandum: *The Private Life of 'Walter Mitty'* (alias Mrs. X or Wig). Mrs X when I first met her told me she was descended from one of the Queen of Scots Maries.... Her mother lost 2 fortunes, one of £90,000.

5th February
Slept badly last night, upset by the rudeness & slights of this Mr. Joplings, – an awful man. I realise what many people have to bear from officious insolent men who once had power.

6th February
Pictures from MT [*for Grey Rabbit's May Day*] very pale & dull.... She says her eyesight not so good, & her husband has not been too well. He is 93.

9th February
Two pictures from MT. Both good. A nice letter about her old husband.... She says she is

so thankful for the wonderful time [*she has had*] with him. I returned the pictures with a nice letter to comfort her.... A beautiful poem by [*the late*] Geoffrey Faber came.... I read it at once, very moving & a fine poem which gave me great happiness.

14th February
Letter from MT about the book, O dear, & one from Collins.... [*the Grey Rabbit*] book has to be put off this year. Miss T blamed me for not showing faults on her rough.... For MT doesn't alter, if I tell her her faults. She is a pest, I am weary of her.

17th February
Cross letter from M Tempest, saying I had the finished drawings, I did not answer her questions.... now I won't write [*back*].... To the film *The Inn of the 6th Happiness*. Marvellous most dramatic & beautiful & moving, but too many children in the cinema, bored, turning round.

19th February
Retyped the Russian article [*for Soviet Woman*].... A nice letter from Susan [Dickinson] saying we will keep a lookout together [*about MT's pictures in the future*].... I cannot bear the fuss each year.... she can be so slipshod.

28th February
[*To*] Woolworths where I spent 6d on a small screwdriver [*two and a half new pence*].... Roy Welensky [*Prime Minister of Southern Rhodesia*] flies to England about Rhodesia. We always do too much good and do not stand up against these people, the natives.

5th March
Reading the Soviet paper. They sound so sweet and simple, like people of the country 50 years ago.

7th March
I... sent a map [*to Peter du Sautoy*], feeling sad, as I made it, & know I shall not roam those [*Derbyshire*] peaks again. But one can't go back, – always forward.

8th March
Looked out early, saw the rock garden purple with violets. Extraordinary, – then I realized it was not possible.... Marvel! A light effect, refraction through very small particles. Glorious.

10th March
Pictures from CF Tunnicliffe [*for Wild Honey*] came, & I love them. I am amazed at his imaginative way of entering my stories, as if he really enjoyed them.

13th March
A day of disorder, Dirk leaping from my bed (my breakfast tray sent spinning on the floor),
– milk, bits of pottery, my lovely gold wheat milk jug… tea pot luckily not on tray.

27th March
To London…. to meet P du S. & Mollie. A delicious lunch & good talk. Peter asked John to
do book [*on the Channel Islands*]…. very good for him, & he *can* do it. John is shy and
insecure…. P du S suggests *T in T* for USA [*publication*]. I hope this can be done.

31st March
John's letter alarmed me, – going back the plane…. got into thick cloud. They hovered over
Guernsey & could not descend…. Then the Grand National. I nearly wept with excitement.

6th April
I walked to High March [*to see the Queen's visit to High Wycombe*]…. A flag in Dirk's collar,
and I had a flag too…. we waved as the Queen came.

20th April
Oh joy, the new paper back ed[*ition*] of *Sam Pig*. It is so nice & I read my forgotten tales
again, thinking of children who will read them.

22nd April
1st hearing of Cuckoo. Hurrah!

5th May
During lunch a small crash in the kitchen. I went out & met smoke & flames…. I was
staggered…. Then I remembered 'Water'! Remembering water was a triumph to me…. It
shook me. The electricity was off.

8th May
[*Peter du Sautoy's*] father has died. I am so very sorry. He sent the picture of the Aeolian
Harp by Mrs. Eliot. Cheque from Faber for £316, which is £100 less than last year, but not
too bad…. Lovely letter from John.

17th May
Mrs. W spring-cleaned John's bedroom ready for Irene Hawkins if she comes [*to stay*] after
Faber's party…. In B…. a policeman appeared & reprimanded, parking 2 ft. from the curb
in Non-Parking Place. Oh dear. Everybody looking at me!… 2 women called, Gospellers.

31st May
Very nice party at Faber…. Very noisy, I could not hear & I could not speak, but I enjoyed
it, & the rides there & back.

4th June
Cold, but a lovely day of sun. I sit in the front garden, just had tea on my little tray.... A treat, I seldom manage to get out like this.

13th June
Up early.... for the Antique Dealers' fair.... [*First I saw a display of*] Ceramic birds. English. Lovely creatures so well contrived & natural & beautiful. I walked.... to the Exhibition, marvellous as ever & prices are soaring.

14th June
Yesterday a box of wild lilies came from Cromford.... They touch my heart, they are like a little child, which once I was, shy, timid, intensely alive. They seem to speak. Reading Priestley's [*book*] *Shades of Sleep*, thinking how I would write, if I could, a book on *Shades of Sleep*.

22nd June
Reading *Life of Stanley Spencer*, which I found very interesting. Too much sex, a pity, – for he was a genius.

4th July
To London with a bag of roses in my yellow basket for MR.... Lunch with Susan Dickinson, – & another.... Chateauneuf du Pape to drink. I was short of money, so Susan had to pay the bill & I am sending her a cheque.... To the theatre, Haymarket. Margaret had forgotten to reserve seat. I was staggered, but they phoned through & got the seat.

12th July
To Guernsey for holiday. Up early, a nice day, but I was feeling nervous and queer, as usual before a journey.... John in shabby clothes, just the same dear boy. ... [*Helen*] is a bad hostess.

21st July
The [*potential cleaning*] woman came, rather odd.... Has had 4/6 – [*per hour*] in service, 5/- in office & her fare. I offered her 4/- an hour, for 3 mornings, & she accepted.

26th July
I cannot remember, the days fly past, with housework & garden, flowers, sun & rain, a blissful feeling, as I float along too.

28th July
Reading with joy & bliss Alec Robertson's book on Music – and on religion. He says Music is one of the aspects the light of God, it is the light of God.

31st July

A dream.... I was in Heaven, a golden land full of light.... like an Italian picture.... I wanted to find somebody.... I took.... a sparkling, white, long thin [*loaf*], like a French loaf, but almost crystalline in beauty.

4th August

Many important letters.... The Australian Broadcasting Co. want *Hedgehog and Mole Ballooning* for 1962.... Penguin's new series is Peacock books [*edited by*] Kaye Webb.... Mine is planned for 1963. O dear, a long wait. Heinemanns say Bobbs Merrill want *Wicked Uncle*, $300 advance.... 7 copies of *Unicorn* came.... I wrote agreeing to the terms for the USA books.... Miss Yeatman asks about a lecture on Dreams in 1963.

11th August

I talked to the man who seems to be foreman [*of a big mechanical grab in the road outside*], a thrilling machine which picks up soil.... A first review from USA. 'This reader does not like these human animals.'

22nd August

I feel rather cut off but very happy, dawdling, writing a bit now and then, reading Cymbeline & W de la [*Mare*] & dreaming.... staring at.... things as if newly visible. £38 extra income tax for 1960-61, £17 to accountant.

24th August

Can't remember, – too tired to write. Trying to write a short [*tale*] of Christmas, which the Ed. of *Ideal Home* phoned for today.

26th August

Mr. Muspratt preached against the hordes of blacks coming to England, 30,000 unemployed, bad housing, & our men out of work, – also against mixed marriages. I *agreed*. Miss Mathieson boiled with rage, – she is having two half-castes to visit her.

28th August

A letter from Tatiana [*Tess*] telling me of the two [*Soviet*] spacemen.... [*I received*] the tape recording of my speech to the school, with a voucher of 15/- for a book.... Phoned [*member of the*] Babington [*family*].... Her polite affected voice gave me a shiver of childhood.

3rd September

Terrible disaster, – my two diamond rings have vanished [*the rings were found on the 27th August 1963 by her new gardener*].

9th September

Leonard Kann is dead, – that gay pagan. [*He was*] a brilliant man who tried so hard.... I liked him and admired him. I feel very sad, for Joyce was so devoted.... an ideal couple.

7th October
A dream. I was in a house of many rooms, – with I saw children, deformed, some with no limbs playing in a sunny corridor, rolling laughing & happy.

9th October
Cheques came. Collins for £201.14.3, [*& from*] Heinemann £111.18.10. The 2 new books came. *The Little Knife* [*Who Did All the Work*] and *Wild Honey*. Both very nice indeed, especially *Wild Honey*.

13th October
Two months since gardener here, – the slacker. Well, I have saved nearly £8. [*She notes*]: Rosemary Anderson married [*today*].... Baby born April 26th 1963. O tempore, O mores!

20th October
In bed every day for the last fortnight. I cannot fill in the pages, not well enough.

27th October
Today came £200 from Faber for the 2 books.... 2 nice reviews, the first in *Times Educ. Supp.* I felt anxious, I always do, for I get these stinging, horrible reviews so often.

28th October
Kruschoff [*Khrushchev*] (can't spell it) is most amenable, he agrees to remove bases [*during the Cuban missile crisis*]. The Americans very stiff. Will they remove their Turkish rockets?

31st October
A delightful letter from Ethel Makins [*who she had met at the recent Peacock Books party*].... She told me to have egg in milk, & little snacks to get strong & get rid of cough. She is right.... I felt rather lonely and depressed.

6th November
Last night, I in bed, a phone call from a man asking to come to take photograph of me for *Tatler*. Christmas, in article 'Children's Writer'.... A nuisance.... although I feel honoured.... Reading *By the Shores of Silver Lake* all day, by Laura Ingles [*Ingalls*] Wilder. How good it is. A delight! It ought to sell a million copies.

8th November
Off to B to have my hair waved for the photographer's visit.... I enjoyed it, but felt tired afterwards.... Letter from Kaye Webb asks for birthday essay, which I do roughly.

11th November
A good [*church*] service.... [*but*] it was too wordy. It should be clear-cut, fine prose, good old collects & prayers, not these badly made up prayers full of our sins.... I felt downhearted.

15th November
In the night wondering about my bright blue organza frock, – too bright, too young, too short. But after trying again I decided to keep it. It is pretty, & I can lengthen it.

16th November
Reading *Emma*.... & again I do not very much like it. Jane Austen is witty and delicious, but I can't bear these books about marriage & class.

23rd November
Angela Caccia [*later Reed*] wrote, – charming. Phoned P du S.... to send books to the *Daily Worker* for review by [*Bob*] Leeson.... P du S said he would do biography of me for the *Country Fair* magazine. I am so glad. I wrote to K Webb, saying she can have my tale [*on*] *Birthday* for five guineas, serial rights only. Letter from Eliz. Coatesworth delighted with *Wild Honey*.... She tells me about her nice housekeeper who reads my books.

27th November
Slept badly, with dreams of trying to get over a wall, too high – & then someone opens a gate.... [*An American publisher*] wants *Snug and Serena Go to Town* for 1964. Very good news.... Then to see Betty [*Fairbairn's*] floral arrangements for sale at Harrods. They have ordered 250.... all beautiful.

28th November
Vogue came, its luxury makes me sick. I feel disgruntled in this materialistic world.... Yet [*there are*] many lovely small things, leaves and rain.

1st December
The review & interview in the *Daily Worker*.... a good photograph, making me look much older, but quite a nice working-woman's face that amuses me.

10th December
Still alone to do all the [*house*] work. I awoke stiff with fright. A nightmare in early morning & I was walking in London (?) with a strange woman.... 'I'm lost,' said I. 'I'm in a loony bin,' said I to myself. I got frightened and claustrophobic.

17th December
My birthday, – a joyous day, but I do not like the mounting numbers.... Joyce invited me to tea at Penn.

18th December
I awoke in a fright.... a nightmare had a creature spring onto my back & I yelled in reality & awoke shouting in fear.... Tonight I sang carols, squeakily.

19th December

[*Letter from*] Tatiana [*Tess*] saying she had bought the *Daily Worker* (Fancy! On sale in Moscow!).... It rather shook me, I don't like to be shown in Moscow.

20th December

Taken ill with bronchitis, my cough bad & awful.

23rd December

P Du S called with Mollie, – at 2.0. They made lemon tea for me & helped to do my odd jobs.

24th December

The house all ready for Xmas, & I have to be in bed.... I decorated with meagre holly & mistletoe for which I paid 4/-, wretched stuff.

25th December

Ill in bed. I awoke at 8.0 refreshed from sleep, & coughing less.... Opened presents at Breakfast – such nice ones.

⊸ℯ 1963 ℯ⊸

1st January
Lost my new 'London Diary', so I am writing in this, – the same days luckily. Deep snow....
as if the snow had come from the Ice Age, creeping over England.

2nd January
I awoke, cold, & put on the electric fire. How thankful I am.... I think of Faraday and the old
scientists and their work.... Dirk had to 'relieve' himself on the paper, poor little good dog.... I
felt bewildered with [*all*] the work to do.

11th January
Colder & Colder.
Freezing & Icy.
Snowing & Blowing.
Grey, Not Nicey.
Oh dear. Nobody came, nothing done.... I got a letter from the Council Motor Tax.... to say
my car must be tested.... I swore it was only 2 years old. They argued, I was angry.

15th January
[*Heinemann say*] they cannot afford to do the new *Fox* book like the old ones.... They
suggest a new series, to be done in cheaper format.... I don't mind. I'm sorry to say goodbye
to *Red Fox*, whom I like.... I must think of another, – perhaps *Bear*, perhaps *Hedgehog*....
[*The Doctor*] says I am very different & can have a tonic.

18th January
A. E. [*Kennedy*] is dead & no more pictures by him of *Sam Pig*. [*His widow*] said how much
he loved to do the work for me. I am very sorry, I always liked him so much.

19th January
Gardener came about 1.0, & was as stupid as ever.

20th January
In the night at 1.30.... as I opened the door I heard the roar of water & torrents running
downstairs from bathroom & from ceiling dropping like Niagara in straight silver lines....
The room swam in the water.

31st January
Letter from Mrs. [*TS*] Eliot, telling me the Aeolian harp makes lovely music.

7th February
[*John has*] now gone to London to meet Peter du Sautoy to discuss the book [*on the Channel Islands*].... [*John's book has*] very small crowded type.... & no margins, – but quite good on the 'Stone Age period.'

9th February
[*John has gone*].... the difference he makes to me.... I gave John £100 towards his new car. I feel much better after John & for his conversation & for the little drives.

27th February
A lovely day of sun & beauty and sparkle of snow.... Reading the interesting Nolan book about mid-Australia, the barren God-forsaken land.

19th March
John's nice letter, but one from Harrods saying my name not on their list for a/c & sending bill for 3 dog-wets, 2 of which I returned long ago.

23rd March
[*Heinemann say*] a radiogram firm want to do some of my books for gram[*ophone*] records. The H[*Heinemann*] 4 *GR* books, 2 *Snug & Serena*, & 2 *Red Fox*.... I would like [*Johnny*] Morris [*to read*] the *Red Fox* book.

26th March
Lilian [*King*] told me that John wants to marry a Zulu girl.... We discussed [mixed marriages] & I said they are against our inmost nature.

31st March
[*The clocks had changed, so she arrived late at church, during the sermon.*] Really I liked such a short service.... I agree that the railway plan [*Dr. Beeching's closure plan*] will be the ruin for many.

2nd April
Insurance claim for flood, £34 but.... no word of [*the*] lost rings.... I denounced Mrs Wig to J [*Dobell*], I hated telling it, but it helps me to have a confidante, Joan, as we are always near in our minds.

7th April
A good review, in the *Guardian*, called me the Queen of enchantment, & my stories are for changelings. I like this, – I always felt I was a changeling child, a bit of fairy got into me at Castle Top.... [*In a television programme*] the girl reminds me intensely of myself when a child, such eagerness and seriousness and longing.... but my life was more romantic with its fields and woods and rocky hills – & less happy with the present she got on her birthday, &

the petting from her father. Just as vivid a life, – and the ghosts, and the appearance is if in a dream that I have.

8th April
Two excitements, a green bud shoot on the Bletilla. The other is a cheque for £311.18.2 cheque from Collins, a rise for me.... Last night I saw a film of Michelangelo, – marvellous indeed.

12th April
A brilliant, diamond day, cold & glittering with beauty, frosty air.

23rd April
London, up early luckily, for I found my clock had stopped.... I bought a pair of shoes [*in Oxford Street*] for 10 guineas!!! Never before have I paid such a price.

24th April
Wedding of Princess Alexandra and Angus Ogilvy. [*She is*] the smiling girl with dancing eyes, & he a nice young man.

1st May
Faber cheque for £370.2.8., very good.... The *Little Knife* sold 3,000 copies. Imagine!

5th May
I called to see the old lady Miss Twinch who is at a Nursing Home, her heart very weak.... She was reading *Wild Honey* & liked it. Poor thing, how much better off was my mother in the cottage.

31st May
[*Mrs W hints at a liaison between Joan Dobell and Mr Henriques.*] Confound her bad manners. These women think of nothing but marriage & sex. I should have known better.

5th June
To B.... to put £500 in the Savings Bank.... At Bella the girl warned me the police had taken my car number.... I felt most upset, all day.... as if I was going to prison.

6th June
Dirk barked violently last night.... I think the strong smell of lilies, upset him, so foxy.... Extraordinary political situation, with Profumo confessing he had lied about his relations with this girl [*Christine Keeler*]. She seems a bad lot, – but how could he lie to the House?

15th June
Both hats came, & I kept them, feeling very extravagant, £10 for 2 hats. Never have I been so profligate.

16th June
I saw TV with [*Prime Minister Harold*] Macmillan.... I was glad God gives him strength for Monday's debate.... all the cruelty of the attack on him.

19th June
Oh my! Spring cleaning is very tiring.... [*Russian cosmonauts are*] brave people. I think they will be the world leaders in the future.

24th June
Mrs. Hunt [*her cleaning woman*] says, 'What is wrong with you is that you have too many things'.... Really. I am staggered, yet she said it in all innocence of any rudeness.

27th June
I felt depressed, – & a big parcel came from Fabers...[*the*] paperback of *A Traveller in T*.... I was delighted & I sat down & once felt the spell of time travelling, & swinging back in time.

9th July
[*She travels by plane to Guernsey.*] I always feel bewildered [*flying*].... and unhappy with no Dirk.... Helen [*says*] 'You never believe anything good can come out of Guernsey.' She is alert to pick on something.... Got blanket from Helen after a struggle, – so warm in bed.

10th July
How cold I am ! 'You must have very thin blood,' she sneered. Why do I mind?

24th July
Oh dear! John accuses me of being ungracious in Guernsey, when I tried so hard.... [*Helen*] is a horror, with her sharp tongue. Horse jumping at White City. V. good. I liked the little pony who refused. Quite right.

29th July
The Ward case [*Profumo-Keeler scandal*] Wash day.... goes on & on – such horrors.

4th August
Then I got stuck in a zip fastener, & had to cut off my petticoat. So I had to put on a patch & take the zips off, – can't open [*them*] if.... Twilight gloom, rain falling, but out on the lawn under the dark trees the coloured umbrella, pink yellow, ice blue & orange, shone like a colour from Paris springs.

8th August
[*Betty Yates rings very early, to ask whether she has heard the BBC Radio programme*] *Lift Up Your Heart*. I *will not* answer phone before 9.o'clock in future.... it upsets my morning peace

of mind.... Finished reading *Life of Mrs. Shaw*, & again I feel discomfort with [*the*] thoughts of GBS, & the *harm* he did.

15th August
Letter from [*the head teacher*] of Lea School [*in Derbyshire*], asking questions about dates of the school.... I do not know. I wrote to him and the children, speaking of my schooldays. I wanted to learn French, Latin, Algebra, & Chemistry, Astronomy, but I liked Mental Arithmetic and Geology.

20th August
The new gardener elect came to see me, Mr. Trinfield.... He is head of the firm, but he has only 1 gardener working for him, as men so hard to get.... We agreed a man should come ? day a week [*for*] 10/- an hour, £2 a morning, double Wetherby's money but I think he will do twice the work.

27th August
Miracle, – my diamond ring found by the new gardener.... [*I*] must send back £240 to Ins. Coy.... [*John*] is coming on September 17th. Eureka!

28th August
Down falls my stock! Mrs. W gave notice, [*has*] got a job nearer home.... Alas, she is so helpful, well, I'll manage as I have done before.

30th August
I felt sad to think Mrs. W going today. I hoped for a cheering post. It came! Letter from BBC asking me to broadcast in *Woman's Hour*.... ABC asking for *Tim Rabbit* tale to broadcast in 1964.... Mrs. W said she would come for an afternoon's work if I were in a fix, especially when John [*is*] here.

3rd September
Letter from John who has had a busy time fitting in 3 flats & house, & moving or going & coming.... A dream of walking on a kind of open bridge.... a huge tidal wave across the world.

7th September
I discovered the nice gardener had rooted up my pet plant. I tried to look in the rubbish heap at the woods end, & I.... heard Wetherby at his bonfire. I dodged back but I know he saw me for her made his horrible roar. He is quite dangerous.... I began to write the Woolworth's tale of *Hare*.... will Collins take it? Heinemanns would but I can't give it them.

27th September
Note: sums I have to pay this year. £285 on Oct. 7 for that Bucks Stock. £400 for my road

charge. £200 for the main drainage charge. So this will leave me very short indeed! No pictures, no extravagances.

8th October
Letter.... from *Vogue* asking why I had not confirmed my sub.... Why had I given it up? Because it bored me.... I got so *sick* of *Vogue*.

11th October
£1,039.2. from Heinemann.... I was refreshed mentally by [*meeting*] these people yesterday [*at the Women of the Year lunch*] but the speeches were awful, – especially one by Mary Quant, who looked Beatnik, and stammered and spoke bad English.... Such a jumble, the worst speech I have ever heard in all my life.

29th October
Oh calamity.... A car disaster. I drove extra carefully, a bit nervous today, but happy for a new jumper, jade-green came from London.... I reversed but I must have put [*my*] foot on accel[*erator*] & car leapt forward, pushing car 2 into car 3.... 'It's my fault, I am so sorry,' said I.

31st October
[*Mr. Collins*] is very pleased with Hare's Shopping Spree [*published as Hare Goes Shopping*]... The *Daily Worker* asking for article. I went to London.... I rushed to the BBC, – I was 1¹/₄ hours early! I had forgotten the time.

1st November
A good royalty Fabers today.... of £394.8.6., to make up my balance for all the house expenses, – & now the car accident, – my new coat.

19th November
Nice letter from John, who is rather upset because the Guernsey people do not go to festivals of art & drama & music.... They are not an artistic race, which is partly why I could not live there in happiness.... Fonteyn and Nureyev on TV. *Swan Lake*, divine.

23rd November
Pres. Kennedy [*has*] been shot.... dead. Oh, how terrible is the shock of his tragedy. A man who did so much.... I felt overcome, tears fill my eyes with grief. The TV gave the next programme, Harry Worth. I was sad they should not have music, solemn, or else silence.

26th November
[*John and I think that*] this terrible murder of Kennedy.... is a blow to civilization, a triumph of evil over good.

4th December
[*The*] book of essays [*Cuckoo in June*] will come out in 1964. I am delighted – I always feel a special surprise & joy to think people want to read my books.... John's letter & 3 chapters of Guernsey book, very good indeed.

6th December
Angela and David Caccia came with [*their*] exquisite wee baby.... I like David, fair, blue eyes like a country boy, like... a servant boy when I was a child. I read aloud bits of my diary about John when he was a tiny baby.

17th December
My 79th birthday.... to tea with MR [*at Gerard's Cross*]. A good talk.... A happy day.

23rd December
Glad to rest, – Dirk was quiet, so I did not go down till 9 a.m. I could have dozed all day without food.

24th December
I enjoyed talking to L[*Lilian*]. Phyllis the Negro girl & John go for lunch tomorrow – poor little Negro & poor LK.

27th December
Card from a child, saying that 'Millions of children adore you.' I wonder!!

30th December
I felt ill all day, bad constipation & some bleeding. I took Eno's & got rid of the horrid stoppage, most strange for me.... Peter wrote, – John's chapters to be read by a colleague.... He didn't say much, except that it was an improvement.

31st December
The lights are *fused*, the usual Christmas disaster.... I felt rather shaky after my illness yesterday – but some sunshine.

~ 1964 ~

*'I never found the companion that was so companionable
as solitude' – Thoreau?*

1st January
A lovely day of sun, which began badly with Dirk calling, & with only a candle for the lights fused. [*I hear that*] Susan [*Dickinson's*] baby died a week after birth. Poor Susan. I feel so grieved for her. Letter from GHC [*George Harry Cooper*].... I am weary of GHC.... I am always saddled by these dull men and women too.

3rd January
A sad post, – a letter from Hilda saying Harry had a slight stroke a few days ago, & a fall.... He cannot see.... I can't give advice.... So I sent £10 to help her pay for some help.... I have been [*thinking*] of Harry, who was never very helpful, a saying of mother.

6th January
My first wash day, of this year, – done at speed & quite enjoyed but I'm tired always.

7th January
Letter from EHC. Which is so dull & boring, poor chap.... He talks of lilies of the valley & [*the*] meaning of it in my books.... I ask you! He is sad I was alone on Xmas night – but I was glad!

8th January
Letter saying Harry slightly better, conscious but wandering.... Letter from Marjorie Fisher, wretched woman, asking about my [*animal*] characters.... are they humans dressed as animals.... I wrote a long letter, saying the characters were chosen imaginatively – creations of my own, and not based on children, nor epitomes 'of a wondering child'.... I spent the rest of the day thinking of it.

9th January
Later John said I was too upset [*by Marjorie Fisher's letter*].... [*I got*] Mrs. Eddis to type 3 copies of [*my reply*], one for Fisher, one for Fabers, and one to the USA [*Kerlan*] collection. A good plan, as the woman will return to the attack on my books after I am dead.... She is all out for realism, no fantasy in animals for children. [*LK supports me, saying*] the wedding of fantasy and the familiar makes the best tale for a child.

12th January
I overslept in the dark morning.... A short rest after lunch.... & then I began to write my *TR* tales, revising, doing some good work.

15th January
[*I was saddened to read the obituary in The Times*] of [*Dr. Irvin*] Kerlan. The nice man, killed by a car. Oh dear.... I never wrote to thank him for his present and his letter.

18th January
[*I told EHC*] not to send any newspaper cuttings.... I am weary of his letters & the way he revolves around childhood Cromford.... Today KW will get my tetchy little letter declining to go to Jane [*Wigglesworth's*] wedding. I am rather prickly just now.... I thought how well James used to read and share poetry with me. He was a poet in mind.

21st January
In the morning, bacon cooking on, I fell headlong in the hall, [*catching*] my foot in Dirk's lead which was stretched across.... I fell on left knee.... face to the ground, full length.... after a good long struggle I got up & limped to bed with the Witchhazel & wool.

23rd January
Article on Fords in *The Times*, – & I think of Cromford, the old ford by the Bridge. But what did Crom mean? I don't know at all.... *Crooked* ford. The river curves there.

24th January
MT's illustration[*s*]...came today.... Very successful pictures [*for Hare Goes Shopping*] – [*she*] is very good at creating animals and people.... Her husband died last May, age 94. So he must have been 82 when they married.... [*I hear*] that Prince Andrew's favourites are the *GR* books.

27th January
Letter from a student at a T[*Training*] College, Manchester, a fierce attack.... because in *John at the Old Farm* John [*said he had*] once seen *black niggers* at Cardiff. [*I am told no*] child should read [*this book*].... Also a badly written.... letter from another T. College [*asking about*] my life. No stamp, no good manners, so I won't answer either.

29th January
[*A woman wrote anxiously to tell*] me she had once met B[*Beatrix*] Potter, & was surprised at her brusque manner. BP was a rude old woman, I know.... So I said I would gladly autograph [*my book*], and asked her to tea.

1st February
A lovely day, – I opened the French window.... & said 'A Happy April,' – in mistake for February.... [*met*] John at the station & the drive home.... He brought me a bottle of cognac.

5th February
[*I gave*] a very happy party [*for various local friends*]. John did his stuff well & the pictures [*were*] beautiful. It ended about 11p.m.

22nd February
I write [*and*] all quiet, only the sound of Dirk licking his toes…the elec[*tric*] fire moaning & creaking…. Only the wind. The ticking clock, & these electric noises of expansion & contraction.

23rd February
Sleep:- Last night in desperation I took 2 [*sleeping*] tablets…. slept again till 10 a.m…. All day I have been sleepy & in a dream, a nice dream as if in another world, a world of fantasy & inspiration.

28th February
Harry very ill, – he is suspected of having a growth in his stomach…. Poor old Harry…. He ought to live to 90, to die serenely like our father in his own home.

27th February
[*I was phoned*] by Anthony Derville [*of BBC*] telling me suggested questions…. How many books [*have I written*]? Over 60…. What do I think of authors? I don't like them very much, they alarm me.

9th March
A tragic letter from Hilda. Harry has cancer of the lung & stomach, – no hope…. I feel it intensely…. I have sent £20 towards [the cost of] the Nursing Home. It is £12 a week, – I must send some more soon…. God be with Harry in his pain and take him to our parents in heaven.

18th March
Broadcast at 2 p.m. *Woman's Hour*…. Then to the recording room…. A recording…. I was much longer than the 10 minutes, so we revised & cut & cut again…. At 2 p.m. the broadcast began, I think mine was alright.

28th March
[*I am worried by a rumour that Tunnicliffe dead*] but I am sure he is alive. Fabers would have told me. I hope he will live for years, he is a good man.

1st April
Cheque for a small dividend…. I decided after much thought, not to send the 3 green dishes to Jane Wig [*as a wedding present*] but to send the book Cranford…. Jane doesn't deserve [*them*]. I never see her or hear from her…. Mrs. Wig never writes. So I unpacked the dishes which will be lovely for Xmas presents.

3rd April

A tax demand for £36, but some credits off [*on the Guernsey loan to help John buy property*].... There is no end to my payments, I have continual drains [*for*] repairs & taxes & subscriptions.

6th April

[*Ronnie phones about Harry's death*] he was quietly sleeping, comfortable.... I phoned L King afterwards, for comfort. I felt so sad, my only near living relative gone.... I think his first marriage pulled him down.... I wrote to Hilda & sent £20.

8th April

[*The day of Harry's funeral, which she did not attend.*] I have thought of this all day, – never to see the sun or the brightness.... Goodbye, Harry. Forgive all my impatience.

14th April

Budget taxes on cigs & beer, no effect on me.

21st April

Painters here.... [*I was annoyed by letter from*] a S African, from a black clergyman asking for money for his clinic.... I *will not* send money to these places, when so many societies help. How did he get my name?… letter from P du S saying *Sam Pig's Story Book* now in process of making, & offering £150 advance, a great joy & help for 1965.

7th May

Ascension Day, – & I never know! It has been so busy, with the bathroom spring cleaned.... Paid bill [*for*] £2.6.9 for Harry's wreath.

9th May

A cold lovely day. I think of VE day, 1945, when I was hourly expecting John. I believe he came on the 9th, a marvel, I thank God.... A letter from Eliz C[*Coatesworth*].... I said a prayer in the wood for Bernard du Sautoy's wedding today.

11th May

A big mail on this lovely sunny day. Pictures from M.T. for the *GR* book. Good but not thrilling. Too pale.

17th May

The church lovely but so dim after the bright sunshine.... A woman [*sitting behind her*] with a piercing contralto voice. She reminded me of women I do not like. Some I knew in youth with the same… strong voices.

21st May

A dream last night which is thrilling. I was on a headland [*perhaps in Guernsey*].... saw figures, angels & celestial beings moving up in a stream.... [*Tunnicliffe writes*] saying he had found my sketch most useful.

2nd June
Letter from Fabers suggesting deletion of word nigger, 'black as a nigger was *Sam Pig*,' – so of course I was glad it was found. A nice hot bath this cold day.

10th June
Antique Dealers Fair.... I bought a Hans Bol for £350.... a small picture, with many minute people, a miniature scene, a real treasure.

16th June
John's letter, & some worrying things to deal with. Luckily I cannot remember them.... Posted a letter to GHC. I hope for no reply for a month, confound his dull wits.

20th June
Oh dear! What a sweat to get ready for a holiday! Packed up my silver, listed it.... & hid it away. Also the Hans Bol.

24th June
[*She flies from Gatwick to Guernsey with Joan Dobell.*] John met us. Bliss indeed. His lovely house astonished me.... [*Helen is*] a poor hostess, & this is typical.

6th July
I felt sad to go. It has been a lovely holiday, & I have managed to be good, except when I protested at this acclamation of delinquents on TV. We saw Mrs. Payne [*sic*] is no evangelical.

22nd July
[*A letter from John*] said my letter gave the impression of thanking him not Helen, for the holiday, but she had helped to please me etc. etc. I felt truly hurt, for I had written to both.... I will *not* let it effect me, but keep up my heart in all the beauty I see.

24th July
A copy of my letter to John and Helen – which I should have sent at once.... Thank you both for a lovely holiday.... Thank you Helen, for your nice meals, – lobster and crab and many delicious strawberries and peaches.... love Mimbles.

1st August
The moon has been hit with a rocket, – poor Moon. That is the start of the Moon Invasion. Yet it is thrilling – they find no dust but many volcanoes as we expected.

16th August
Four small irons in my fire, – *Farmhouse Kitchen* to Nelson for series. Refused! *Enchantment*
& *White Mouse* to Heinemann. April 23rd 1963 to Faber. Article on Kitchens old and
modern to *Homes and Gardens* (soon). Titles to be changed.

18th August
MSS returned by Nelson's, as I expected. Too autobiog[*raphical*], they want a real story for
city children…. which has no fantasy or fairy or animals! Can I do it? – feel flummoxed,
because I can't keep out the supernatural which is always present for me and always has
been, even in atomic structure days. I feel depressed, but I have been keeping up my head,
– housework, and to B for shopping.

2nd September
[*My story*] *The Explorers* rejected by Leila Berg [*of Nelsons*], as I expected. She sent pages
of written stuff, with alterations, most disconcerting and rude. So I have written to say I
won't write any more…. I was weary & discouraged, not *free* to write as I wish. P. du S. will
agree.

4th September
Awful indigestion in the night…. & I lay in pain till after 1.0. I am sure it is this worry over
Nelson & this treatment by L. Berg. I took a [*sleeping*] pill…. To B…. but a big crowd…. &
a great noise, & women & babies all eating huge yellow lollipops in all shop doorways. All
looked so ugly, I wondered why I live here.

8th September
I listened to [*The*] *Winter's Tale* on BBC & loved it, but half way through I suddenly felt
very tired. So instead of refusing it…. I turned off light, – unwashed – & fell into deep
sleep…. A copy of the *Tall Book* comes, with my story of *TR and the Cloak* came very
pretty…. I have [*been*] going through John's book, 2 chapters.

11th September
A letter from Leila Berg…. asking why I said she had insulted me (because she scribbled
over the 18 pages of my story, *The Explorers*, all over the margins & text, crossing out lots
of it, mixing it up, changing it)…. She talked a lot of nonsense about children drunk with
beauty tearing branches from cherry trees, pulling up daffs & throwing them away.

12th September
John's birthday. Aged 50 today. I think of the tiny baby, only 4? lbs. and the anxieties of
people, but I always felt confident and at peace and happy, aware of a source of strength and
courage which indeed was needed at that time. He has been a wonderful help and comfort
to me always. I said a prayer early this morning.

23rd September

In my porch I found a packet, with 'A little bowl for a few bird crumbs. Your books are enchanting". Who from?.... How sweet!... I wrote a bit of *Renaissance* and.... a long letter to Tatiana [*Tess*] from whom I had a warm happy friendship letter.... [*She says*] our planet isn't so large as is thought and mankind must be responsible for its destiny, its future, for friendship between people.

24th September

The little wooden bowl mystery explained. A man rang.... he called on me & he wanted to know if I have a walnut tree.... as his dog eats walnuts 5 [*times*] a day.... He went on & on, boring me stiff.

1st October

There are no words to describe the beauty of this St Luke's Summer, each day more beautiful than the last, the sun through the trees, the long shadows, the sparkle of dew, the colour of flower petals.

2nd October

[*A very good post,*] royalties from Heinemann of £281.7.6. (including £225 from Delysé [*the record company*]).... from *Teacher* [*magazine*] saying how much they like my story.... My new book, came, *Cuckoo in June*, very nice.... A hat, – not so sure of this! Letter from Hilda at last, she says she is turning out Harry's books, all mouldy and black. An author's brothers! No wonder we had not much in common, he cared nothing for books.

16th October

Election results.... A great debacle for Conservatives, and now they are OUT and Labour is IN.... We shall see, I think it is better than the Conservatives getting only a tiny majority. Now the Cons[*Conservatives*] will I hope help, and not heckle too much as Labour tries to clear up the mess.... News of Khrushchev's fall from power.... I am sorry indeed.

26th October

News that at midnight a 15% tax on all imports (except food), in force. A good speech by [*Prime Minister Harold*] Wilson. He is tackling affairs in a good manner, & I feel more faith in him than Lord Home [*the previous Prime Minister*].

6th November

A nice post, – a free knife from Persil which astonished me as I never thought I should get it.... Nelson had not sent through royalties for some time, apologies!... We put up Jacobean curtains at end of the room, very warm and pretty.

10th November

Lovely review in *Manchester Evening News*, headed 'Finding beauty in Simplicity,' & beginning, 'In a jewelled collection of essays'.... I feel most gratified.

30th November

Churchill's 90 birthday. The great immortal. I remember seeing him on St Pancras station when I was about 23, up in London.... I looked at that charming.... face & the pretty wife, – I was just engaged too.... The splendid TV *Fifty Years*.... took me back to ploughboys singing songs, and James at the First World War, and all the pain and excitement and bliss.

10th December

Death of Edith Sitwell, aged 77.... A scornful review of *TR* & a long interview with MT in which she practically says she wrote *L Grey Rabbit*.... I felt very sick about it.

21st December

Letter from K Wig complaining of Heinemann giving up the *Fox* stories (I don't mind, I don't want to do any more), – saying that the choosers of children's tales are uneducated and illiterate.... I'm glad I am not doing any more books with her, she interferes too much in bookshops.

25th December

[*She doesn't like John's and Helen's present.*] It was a big hideous bonnet of pink cotton of a Guernsey woman 100 years ago. Helen wrote saying.... I might like to wear this! I felt insulted, it was so ugly & heavy & enormous.

29th December

Letter from John, but no word of the bonnet.... John writes, I am glad.... I can pack it into the depths of my memory, trying to forget the cruelty.

31st December

Still I can laugh now at all the fuss over the.... bonnet. Dirk is adorable.... Goodbye, darling year!

≈ *1965* ≈

1st January
Here am I, sneezing, coughing, groaning with pain as I cough.... Doctor Milner [*came to see me*]. No antibiotic, not very bad.... A card from Peter du S.... 'We went to Castle Top this morning.... Everything looked lovely' I can see it & feel the air and smell the river and rocks. How beautiful.

5th January
Mrs R made some little fairy cakes to tempt me.... We shall see. I detest food.... Today in *The Times* notice of the death of TS Eliot, alas, and of Sir George Simpson, alas again. I feel very sad. I used to adore GC Simpson, who taught me and danced with me. Now he is dead.

16th January
Feeling very anxious about [*Sir Winston*] Churchill all day. Now it blows & howls & rains & I'm going to bed, – fed up!!

17th January
Great gales all the night.... The rain makes a very peculiar noise – hissing and beating with a million fingers, sinister, as if it is trying to get in [*and*] destroy and kill, with hatred of humankind. It is not English rain, it belongs to a foreign country, I feel. I lie in bed, holding tight to [*the*] bedclothes thinking I am being swept away forever, lost in the universe. I know again all the fears of childhood, and they are many. I do *not* know how I endured some things.

30th January
Up early to see the TV of Churchill's funeral. It was most moving & beautiful. The slow march of feet, the 6 or 8 men carrying the great heavy coffin, the sailors drawing the gun carriage, the crowds.... Not a hitch, all so smooth, & yet such a huge spectacle.... the music of the bands & all the time that slow tread of feet.

6th February
A damp day, & gloomy. I got up early to see a man... who once did the drains, & I want to have the paths gravelled. A rough fellow who at once started to point out all defects.... He was doing *me* a favour.

10th February
Agnes Bottomley of Clitheroe writes saying [*she*] would like to write an article on me. I said

NO thank you. Whatever would it be like? She was a stodgy dumpling, & her letter the same.

11th February
Miss W[*Whitehead of Heinemann*] came late.... She said Dwye Evans wants 3 little books, all printed together [*in*] a year. He will do the *Woodpecker Tale*, the *White Hen*, and the very first *GR* again, – with new pictures. I was worried about MT, but he said [*the*] contracts made me safe.

20th February
The moon hit by a rocket which is taking photographs. Poor old moon, man is a nuisance, isn't he!

27th February
A bad post, [*including a review*] from the Australian B[*Broadcasting*] C[*Corporation*], by a woman saying *Tim Rabbit* is Namby-Pamby stuff like all Alison Uttley's books.... I can imagine the hard faced, female. All the letters were bills or something I did not like.... I forgot [*the review*] in the bubbles of rainbow I saw [*as I washed up*].

3rd March
I bought a box of Suchard chocs to have some fun & a sweet taste.... [*I cooked*] a dull pancake, – I am not a good cook.

12th March
Anniversary of my mother and father's wedding day in 1884. I think of them with happiness.... Proofs of *Sam Pig* big book came, – badly printed…. I shall complain. But am enjoying reading these forgotten tales which are *good*. I love the Dragon tale, the Irish tale.

13th March
John came at 7.00 am, – knocking on the door.... I thought it was the police, and my car had gone! I had a lovely review from *The Countryman* comparing my work to Chardin's painting.

1st April
Feeling a little better. I made my bed, but Janice came, and swept the stairs.... In between sickness & swelling & coughing I feel minutes of rapture, bird song, sun, flowers, being alive.

15th April
To B in car, to buy, O extravagance, a box of After Eight chocolates! [*But*] nobody will send me any choc[*olates*], and I feel hungry for a few for Easter Day and after. Yet my conscience smote me.

23rd April
[*She has a quarrel with the new home help about time going slowly.*] 'Your clock moves very

slowly,'she remarked.... I said, acidly, 'Time doesn't change. There are 24 hours in a day.' I was glad to see her go.

30th April
A gardening day.... I planted 50 gladioli.... Fabers good royalties [*of £454.12.10*] have surprised me.
Memorandum: [*She quotes a little girl's letter to her from South Africa*]
'When any of us are sad or lonely.... the best remedy is to take out a *Grey Rabbit* [*book*], curl up, and become enrapped [*sic*] in the story.'

1st May
O dear, I don't feel the old joyful excitement of May.... [*The*] Odes of Horace have come, – to remind me of youth and my struggles in the attic window as I translated. Vitae summa brevis. Ah, it makes my heart ache for all the shortness of life.

2nd May
Peter and Mollie du Sautoy came, a lovely visit.... Peter showed me photographs. Castle Top, looked bleak and bare, all its enchantment gone, like a gaunt ghost house.... [*Peter*] suggested that if MT writes to me, I send the letter to Heinemann to answer [*about the first three little books, including GR*].

15th May
Cheque for £162.2.6. came from Faber – *Penguin Magic* £67.19.1., the *C Child* £34.3.5. and Delysé *S Pig in Trouble* £60 [*for 4,000 records sold*] at 5% of 6/-.... [*MR*] said I had helped her with her indecisions about life, the house, the play.

21st May
Working at Income Tax all day, after doing housework, – so I'm dazed and tired.... The great thing is an egg! In the empty [*thrush's nest*].... I prayed it would return, – & it has done so after 3 days.

24th May
I feel cheered to think of my [*recently purchased*] Dovedale picture [*by Vickers*], I am longing to see it [*next Friday*].... I am glad I am not going to the Chelsea Show, I cannot be made as tired as I was last year.

10th June
Note: Angela [*Caccia's*] baby to be called Arabella Sabina... [*the Caccia*] ancestor came from Italy when he got into trouble for supporting Garibaldi, – what a thrill.... [*Her cousin*] Sissy has left me £500 [*for my*] 'great kindness on the occasion when I broke my leg'. How wonderful of dear old Sissy. How grateful she was always.

11th June
Eleanor Farjeon's funeral, – my darling Eleanor. This year I have lost Eleanor and Betty
Yates, alas.

13th June
Trying to recover from yesterday [*a chaotic church fête*], – but I could not get over the feeling
of stress…. that mob so close. I know how the Queen must feel when people crowd in.

29th June
[*The car arrives late to take her to Gatwick. On the plane to Guernsey, she tells a woman that
her sister-in-law Emily Uttley was at Cheltenham School.*] 'Oh, the same name as the author,'
said she. So I said, 'I *am* the author…. [*In Guernsey*] John seems rather edgy…. No towel
except a rather soiled heavy one…. No soap, but I had a tiny soap.

1st July
[*Helen said*] 'You *were* mean to take my mother's box.' I was amazed at her bitterness. I have
never been called mean before. I explained [*that Mrs. Paine*] had agreed but she turned away
furiously.

3rd July
[*I have*] a great plan. I 'accidentally' dropped my dirty bathmat into the bath, so I scrubbed
at it with the nail brush…. rinsed it. Left it to drop into the bath. Nobody said anything….
The mat was hung out…. & a clean one in bathroom to my joy.

21st July
'We are already in Paradise and we do not know it'…. Pauline Baynes [*the illustrator of
Recipes from an Old Farmhouse, phoned*] asking about things, my brother…. not mentioned
in the C Child…. I fear she won't do the book well, she has no *sense*.

22nd July
Peter Shelton…. suddenly said, 'Why do you always say you can't afford a holiday?' I was
amazed, I never say such a silly thing. I say I prefer it at home rather than go to a hotel alone.

18th August
John worried about a woman [*reader*] for Faber [*criticising his book on the Channel Islands*]….
I too found the 100 years was confusing. John does not like criticism…. he is impatient,
poor boy.

27th August
Can't remember.

14th September
Peter likes my new book. I think he likes the title *The Immortality of Dust* [*published as A*

Peck of Gold]. I feel on air, very happy, excited, for I always have qualms, wonder whether a book is good, & this was so personal.... Miss W [*from Heinemann*] came, looking shabby.... she cannot be poor after all those years at Heinemann. I told her of my worries over Jenny Corbett's pictures [*for the next book in The Little Red Fox series*].

2nd October
On Friday came the pictures of P Baynes, marvels of beauty, which thrill me.

3rd October
Not well, still worried by the main allegation of dishonesty [*over her change, yesterday in the Post Office*].... Pain in bowels etc.

4th October
[*To the*] Women of the Year Lunch. 12 a.m. Savoy. Expenses, taxi £1.5.0.... called at Heinemanns [*and said*] I did not like Miss C[*Corbett's*] illustrations.

10th October
[*Reading about the Rhodesian crisis and UDI*] We are too black prejudiced, I feel. It is like a missionary cell.

30th October
Faber's royalties came, – I had quite forgotten.... of £488.10.2. A nice surprise.... I forgot to go to the Penn concert.

9th November
Letter from John, chiding me for not writing to Helen.... She dislikes being bypassed about anything, said John.... My bank book came, – £1,200 in it – but £500 came from Sissy.... Thinking of Rhodesia [*the UDI crisis*], what will they do? They will split away & so should I. Risk it.

22nd November
Welladay! What a post! A letter enclosing an article on me by Alix Coleman, who did the awful interview [*in the Sunday Times*]. The article was most insolent, vindictive and sneering.... I must forget [*it*].... The article sent by Mrs Lee Smith who remarks that if these are my sentiments (that I dislike people's fan letters [*and*] they bore me with their photographs of relations), she will not buy any more of my books.... What a woman!

24th November
I lay awake feeling ill & depressed.... I read some E Farjeon and longed for her and W de la Mare.... I decided to write to [*the Sunday*] Times' editor.... Peter [*told me*] he was writing [*too*].... I was cheered.... such a good letter. [*She is staggered to find that Collins had arranged the interview with the Sunday Times.*] I told them that she [*the interviewer*] had tried to make me say that I hated children.

1st December
My darling December, but I did not give my usual welcome, as I felt depressed…when I got a cross letter from the Editor of *S Times* saying they had questioned Miss Coleman and did not agree that I had been misquoted…. Rhodesia news disquieting. [*Prime Minister, Harold*] Wilson sending troops [*this did not happen, in fact*].

5th December
Quite a nice interview in *Observer* [*colour supplement*].

17th December
My birthday, – 81 [*and*] I think of the bowed ancients of my youth & I feel so different, yet I am of their age…. [*There was*] a marvellous Christmas cake in the porch when I opened the door later, left by LK…. John's freesias came yesterday.

18th December
I am so busy I cannot write my diary. A parcel with 150 cards came today, so I did no sweeping or dusting, and started off to send the cards…. [*She suspects that GHC has sent her some yellow chrysanthemums anonymously.*] He is really too silly.

25th December
A lovely Christmas. Dark muggy day, but I enjoyed it…. Joyce's party…. very nice.

31st December
I think 1965 has not been such a good year, beginning with the awful sun bonnet from John and Helen for Xmas, going on to 'flu, a bad attack…. and Mrs R leaving. I've had no help. This Autumn the horrid malicious interview in the *S Times*. Then I think of nice things, flowers, some glorious days, writing two books, the holiday in Guernsey and Daphne's friendship. Goodbye Old Year & Welcome 1966, with my new books on TV.

1966

20th January

John went off to London, after a lovely little time here. Nothing to mar it. He washed up nobly & did a lot to help, & we have had drives.

21st January

Mrs M[*Mitchell, her new home help*] is so stupid, like an old cow wandering about, a duster in her hand, but never doing anything. I paid her £2.10.0. for the weeks 3 morning potters, glad to see her go. She says rude things, [*like*] 'I've never been in a house like this before'.

23rd January

Another butterfly came out. I put it in the guest room with some sugar.

5th February

The song of a robin at night, nearly dusk, touched my heart.... I thought of the moon with a piece of earth lying on it, & the moon did not shine down as usual. The robin, & the moon – O God.

6th February

[*I watched with horror a TV programme on Anglesey about*] the building of [*a nuclear*] Power Station in fields.... I thought of CF T[*Tunnicliffe, who lived on Anglesey*] and his birds, his world of peace. Then I thought of God's presence in these works. I used to feel this in engineering works I visited. I feel God there, in great machines as well as in Nature. God on the moon as well as on Earth.

20th February

[*She quotes at length from a letter from Tunnicliffe*] 'Poor old Anglesea! It is no longer the fresh unsophisticated island it used to be. Jet planes scream about the sky, visitors career on water skis behind speedboats, atomic power stations shatter the sky, & great pylons are striding over the land! Yet! There is peace on the walks & more birds than I have ever seen.... The island still holds me.'

24th February

Great news, Nkrumah [*President of Ghana*] deposed. Too good to be true but it is time....I have always dreaded him as a traitor and enemy of his country.

6th March

Penn concert.... Haydn, Beethoven, & Brahms after the interval. I liked all of it, but the Brahms was divine, completely marvellous.

8th March

As I idly turned the pages of [*Blackwell's catalogue*] I saw.... Alison Uttley by Peter du Sautoy, I was staggered.... Peter did not tell me it was done. I feel nervous and alarmed, I hate publicity. Yet it is exciting, and I must not feel frightened. I always feel I am unworthy, – & I want to hide, for it is only ME, a little girl at Castle Top.

1st April

Labour in by 100 [*in the general election*], – but I don't care, I am glad they have a chance to continue for they have made a good beginning.

10th April

A marvellous miracle-day.... This has been a lovely day. I felt helped in [*the*] church [*service*] & I thought of the people 100 years ago, 500 years ago who worshipped there, in the same place, very vivid.

25th April

[*She describes giving a talk at the Caxton Hall.*] I gave my lecture, and they applauded, & listened eagerly. He [*the chairman*] said I had not given details of money received! The cheek! Questions, good ones.

29th April

Cheque from Faber for £723.14.9.... for the new *Sam Pig* book. So I can go serenely on, using electricity as I like, for a time.

30th April

I sent CF T[*Tunnicliffe*].... a picture of the mill at Alderley Edge, as he knows it & loves it. It was the subject of his first picture for his Art Master.

3rd May

Budget Day, – & luckily no increase in income tax.... [*Collins are researching into the first GR books with Heinemann.*].... I told them that Heinemann bought it outright in 1929, but later MT refused to do new pictures for Heinemann and wrote a very rude letter, which finished it off.

6th May

[*To the Royal Academy's private view with Daphne*].... We saw K Wig sitting alone.... I saw this old woman, & I thought the poor soul.

26th May

The first rose & I hailed it with joy.... [*There was*] a nasty letter from MT, really bitter and horrid. I sent it on to Dwye Evans, and wrote a letter to MT, a very mild [*one*], reminding her that she had *refused* to do the pictures for Dwye Evans, – but after phoning Collins and talking to Miss MacRae [*an editor*], I decided to do nothing.... Caught mouse in a trap. The 3rd in kitchen.

2nd June
USA have made a landing on the moon! Oh dear, I don't want Man to catch the Moon....
MT sent her nice pancake pictures, & the usual letter saying I had not answered.... I said I
had sent her letter to Heinemann.

7th June
Letter from MT. Her fourth. I will not answer, – all about Heinemann asking her to do the
pictures over 20 years ago. She had only £60 for illustrating the 1st four little books. (I only
had about £30 for writing them).

17th June
[*Susan Dickinson wrote.*] She told me again that MT was much upset etc. etc.... So I wrote,
going through the whole tale again, pointing out that Heinemann can do what they like &
saying that MT was so rude that Heinemann said, Never again. Oh, dear, 3 pages of typing
when I'm tired and busy.

1st July
July, & my beloved June is over.... A letter from MT was a shock, I wondered whether to
open it, or to send it back. I opened it, – just to tell me she had made a new picture and sent
it to Susan Dickinson.

2nd July
Alas, Miss [*Maria*] Bueno beaten by Mrs. Billie Moffat King, a conceited brat [*at
Wimbledon*].... Mrs. Reece has just been to say that on Monday she is going to scrub the
kitchen floor, & dust & clean ready for [*the visit of*] Tatiana. Really, – how can I thank her,
or even stop her?

7th July
[*The Russian plane is on its way*].... Suddenly... I recognised Tatiana as the special one & we
kissed. She looks the same.... a darling.... I drove to Penn, to LK's.... & we saw the black
babies [*the grandchildren of Lilian King*] to T[*Tatiana's*] surprise!

8th July
[*To Oxford with Tatiana*] Then to lunch at the Mitre.... Then to Marks & Spencer & bought
T a cardigan.... To Ashmolean [*Museum*] but I was dead tired, so many steps.

11th July
[*News that John's Guernsey book has been taken by an American publisher.*] Great news! I am
so pleased for him for he was despondent often, thinking his work was no good.... At night
watched soccer [*with*] Uruguay v England [*in World Cup soccer tournament*]. Brilliant!
Fascinating.

20th July
Watched the exciting football. England v France, which England won, very thrilling & I
loved it & forgot all as I watched.

23rd July
[*Lilian King*] thinks of me at Cambridge, imagines my life there. It was my first vision of beauty of houses, river and architecture and the arts. I felt happy all day.

3rd August
A badly written ill-spelled letter from a woman going to write an article on Beatrix Potter, & she asked me for information! I answered it, pointing to some of the mistakes, and saying I know nothing that is not in the books of BP.

4th August
O, how much the sun means to us. Cares fall away & one feels full of light & happiness. Darling sun! I think of people 1,000 years ago, darkness.... To the film *Mary Poppins*.... The film too long, too much Disney.... But I loved it.

9th August
John's book came... a great thrill to see it, & to read his charming inscription.... I feel so happy.... Also my proofs of *Peck* [*of Gold*] came. So happy over John's book, a great work & a struggle, & I'm so thankful.

12th August
[*Tea with MR*] Really Stringer is banal, he talks in such a silly way, coy and childish.... he has learned it by heart, and is repeating it.

22nd August
John wrote saying I cannot stay longer [*in Guernsey*] than Sept 20th [*because*] Rosemary Athay is going there.... I wrote saying I would change the date of my going, the 12th..... Exciting letter from [*Christine in the Orkneys*], she has found a Stone Age hut underground, with great stone slabs, all complete, with axe heads, arrowheads.... needles & many things.... I am thrilled indeed.

25th August
To London, full of fears, which disappeared like snow. Why these panics? I don't know.... [*To dentist*] 3 small stoppings.... [*I was upset to hear that the waitress Margaret at Marshall & Snelgrove has cancer.*] Poor darling. I will write &.... send her one of my books.

31st August
[*Recipes from an Old Farmhouse arrives.*] I was thrilled to open it, & I love it. So charming & so simple. Yet so fairylike in its pictures & memories.

1st September
John's Guernsey book [*is*] published today. Bless him. I think how loyal he has been, all his life, how good and patient in our many trials, the stretches of poverty we had and the difficulties. Now he is happy.

10th September
The roses seem to be full of light. They are sources of illumination this evening, glowing in flames of red & pink.... & now I sit in peace, with the great.... lily which has 4 large flowers (which I kissed to welcome them this morning, they were not out last night).

18th September
To church.... Harvest Festival.... I had only 1/- in my bag to put in the collection, & John put in £1. I felt Helen's cold disapproval.

6th October
[*I sent a telegram to MR, saying*] 'A thousand good wishes. Love to the immortal Mrs. Malaprop from Alison.' The girl at the phone took this with pleasure!

12th October
Yes, I remember [*Ramsay MacDonald*] well. I used to go to Lincoln Inn's Fields supper with Mr. & Mrs. RM and then to the Reform Society or to meet people.... [*the French socialist leader*] Jaurés, and once to the MacDonalds' cottage at Chesham with [*Philip*] Snowden.

21st October
The tragic news of disaster in a Welsh mining village [*Aberfan*]. I think of nothing else, & feel so unhappy for [*the*] mothers & little children. News coming in all day.

3rd November
To Windsor to see *The Cocktail Party*, which I liked at the time but on reflection not so much. I dozed & fell asleep a few moments in one scene. Very witty & good but I do not understand why I am so worried & bewildered.

7th November
Writing a long letter to L King about her daughter in law [*Phyllis*], who has no sense of Time or duty or work.... If they are not careful their marriage will wreck.

9th December
I mentioned Rhodesia [*to the doctor*] he said that all the people he knows are on their [*the whites'*] side, which cheered me very much. I feel weak.... tired.

31st December
Torrents in the night, frightening, like cloud-bursts.... I wrote to Edmund Ward, publishers who asked me to write a book [*of*] 10,000 [*words*]. I do not think I can or want to do so. Goodbye old year, which has had many blessings but too many days of rain.

～ 1967 ～

'I want to see some small intimate beauty and record it each day'.
(Is this the purpose of diaries?)

4th January

I take down the decorations, except one Christmas tree, – & the room looks better, it was overcrowded.... Sad news that [*Donald*] Campbell killed [*on*] Coniston lake, his boat [*Bluebird, attempting to break his own world water speed record*] shot up in the air & broke.... I expected this when I heard of his racing [*over*] Coniston lake, – which I feel is wrong to do.

18th January

8 p.m. Speech on 'Writing for Children' in Beaconsfield.... Questions: How old were you when your 1st book was published? 30, said I untruthfully, it was 1930, I got mixed [*up*]. One woman said, 'Could I write, if I tried?' I did not answer, she obviously couldn't. But I enjoyed doing it.

23rd January

I came to London in 1909 (I think), occupying a bedsitter in 6 Cheyne Row [*in Chelsea*] at 15/- a week, I had a gas ring and cooked my breakfast, and had dinner at night, of all the food I wanted for 1/6. A charwoman kept the flat clean, I made my bed and tidied up.... I went on top of a bus to the school in Fulham (Sec School). Thrilled by the bus, by World's End and Chelsea.

5th February

At night to production of *Much Ado*. It was terrific, so quick, so lively & so beautiful, I felt I was an [*Elizabethan*] watching it. Beatrice [*the play's heroine, had a*] lovely voice, soft in the turmoil. Enchanted entirely.

8th February

Dream. On a tombstone (a wooden one) in a churchyard, in a dream, I read the epitaph, by moonlight. 'Oh softly, softly, like a white snow-flake he drifted away.'

11th February

A nice warm letter from Tatiana, 'You love works of art as if they are human beings', says she, truly. 'The soul of the artist is in his creation.'

13th February
In bed all day ill with sore throat & cough.

20th February
Dr. Milner came. 'I've just finished dusting', said I. 'You dusting? I thought you would be in bed. I didn't say you could get up,' said he.

6th March
I felt triumphant that I have done so much housework.

13th March
With my letters came one from the Income Tax, telling me to appear before Tribunal on 7th April. No tax [*had been*] sent. I felt frightened and angry. [*I phoned my accountant*] Carpenter…. He said, 'Take no notice!…. he would deal with it.

26th March
The lovely service from King's Col[*College, Cambridge*] chapel today & the feeling of Cambridge comes vividly for me. How I enjoyed it! It was rapture to be at college there…. The very best spectacle seen on T.V. today, – the performance of 'The Dream'. Exquisite…Oh darling Shakespeare, I kept thinking how [*he*] would have loved it.

7th April
I was have been reading the book sent Joyce de Hirsch…. & now she has got on to sex, it is really filthy…. I won't read it…. I may destroy it. Why, oh why? Written by a queer oversexed in every way woman…. It is selfish, wicked & frightening.

18th April
I was turning out the Boxroom for spring cleaning [*when*] I turned out a pile of baby clothing I had kept for a grandchild…. I gave Gwenda [*her home help*] John's blue smock & brown baby boots.

23rd April
Awoke very depressed & feeling queer, so sick…. Dr M came and gave me homeopathic arsenic. I lay in bed all day, nothing but Lucozade & water.

27th April
I rushed off to B to see electric cookers…. I saw a larger one…. Belling, a good make, just under £40. So I decided to have it next Wed.

1st May
Just heard John Pertwee [*born John but stage name Jon*] tell the *GR* tale, *Washing Day*, so delightful, so humorous &, rich and great fun. How different from [*actress*] Wendy Hiller,

her prim voice! He brought us the earthiness of the gipsy, the boastfulness of Hare, and the magic behind the gipsy's singing.

2nd May
I wondered if I could sit for 3 hours with the [*hair*] dryer on, & I thought I might faint.... but later I got calmer & decided to face it. And it was easy & comfortable, I had no big coughing fit. I never felt [*like*] choking. It just shows!

4th May
Posted *The Explorers*, a rotten tale, and *When That I Was*, a good tale, to Kaye Ward, Publishers, of 194 Bishopsgate, EC2, with a little note.

12th May
I found my last year's dresses too long, & I shortened 4 of them. A wearisome job which I disliked. Yet I am glad I can sew.... [*Publication day for the Puffin Fox book*] is June 28th.... L King told me.... that Phyllis [*her African daughter-in-law*] had tried to kill [*her husband*] John, because he came home so late from his work.... We agreed that Zulus have different ideas!!

16th May
A nice woman came to explain the [*new*] stove, electric, & I confess I find starting & stopping the oven confusing.

23rd May
Tonight, a beautiful clean room.... [*John sent me a letter*] enclosing one of my letters to him at school [*in*] July 1930.... 2 months before James died, written in joy and innocence of the shadow!

3rd June
Last night I found a flower, Nellie Moser, on my clematis. I was thrilled! The first clematis I have ever grown.

4th June
To church, the first time since Xmas I think. An empty church, so I sat quietly in my old place & enjoyed the service.... A very dull sermon of course – Mr. M[*Muspratt*] seemed to be comparing Nasser with Goliath, and the Israelites [*Israelis*] with David & his weapons. He was most confusing.

8th June
Writing a prologue for [*a new edition of*] *High Meadows*, the fourth time I've done it.... Difficult.

10th June
Very ill again, a horrid cough, cold, sore throat & all the works.

21st June
Pretending I'm on holiday, feeling so different.

13th July
I have a nagging worry that John is not so well, he seemed on edge, I think he does not get enough food.... We had such meagre meals... vegetarian.

17th July
Daphne's daughter Ann while waiting [*to go to Glasgow University*]... is earning £9 per week by making flowers in a factory.... They are dotty. She should be studying music at home.... not making paper flowers.

2nd August
Letter from Fabers to say the BBC are going to do a broadcast [*of*] *T in T*, beginning Nov 10, 5 readings. Hurrah indeed.

17th August
Waiting for men to discuss the double [*glazed*] windows.... [but] I don't... want to be shut up by double windows, even in my bedroom.... I am struggling with income tax [*returns*]...a fine old muddle of accounts.... I think I shall have the bedroom double glazed for £37.

12th September
John's birthday, bless him. 53 years old, – I remember 50 so clearly, I felt so young, & looked young too except for [*my*] hair.

13th September
The new *GR* [*book*] came, *Grey Rabbit's Pancakes*. Is this the last I shall do? I don't think MT can paint any more, her colours [*are*] very poor & faint. I would go on with the series.

23rd September
Margaret R and Stringer came.... She looked fragile & tired.... We had no private talk. I suggested I would like to join them at Brighton later.... they were delighted.

4th October
[*Feeling*] rather miserable with Stringer's non-stop gabble.

5th October
[*To the Brighton Pavilion*]....I feared SD would make silly remarks, but he was not too awful.

6th October
Home at last, after the nastiest drive I have ever known, – Stringer sending the man [*the*

driver] to all sorts of places…. Making his silly jokes…. arguing…. I suggested we asked the way & he went Beserk…. His eyes were red & he gets a rush of blood…. He was so angry.

7th October
Jackanory on BBC 1. 30th October to Nov 3. *Sam Pig* [*stories*].

15th October
Trying to recover from all this stress…. I've done too much.

30th October
Jackanory Sam Pig begins for 5 weeks. Very well told by Dandy Nichols. A lot omitted, & all the dialect words changed. Washday, wet, & gloomy.

8th November
Mrs Helliwell called & we had a delicious tea… & I read the ghost tales. We talked a lot about Stringer Davis…. [*She*] was worried that he [*had*] an inferiority complex, so he puts up a show off fight of aggression.

10th November
Start of *Traveller in Time* broadcast. Well contrived…. but the reader's voice rough & very inferior, & [*an*] ugly accent for Derbyshire. She must have come from an outer mining part.

20th November
Papers full of pound [*sterling crisis*] & rise of bank rate, & troubles of Old England, beset with strikes & rebellions, people crying for blacks to enter, no wars and no struggles except for their own private freedoms.

29th November
Hilda came – all my anxieties vanished as she rushed to me & kissed me…. I autographed a great pile of books she brought…. [*Hilda*] said Harry had only £70 in the bank when he died.

30th November
I wish I had known [*that Hilda*] was so nice, I would have helped her more than I have done, poor girl…. We talked at night of her difficulties.

10th December
Dr Milner came, with a 2nd doctor, Dr Lister…. Dr [*Milner*] had already booked a room at the Nuffield Nursing Home, Slough, where Margaret [*Rutherford*] went. I must go today, they said, so I raced round…. Tried to stop milk & papers.

11th December

In the night I started to cough & the night nurse came in & I *was* glad to see her. I told her ghost stories & she told me one by Warwick Deeping. She cheered me in the lonely night. I could see a nebula in the sky (East). What is it? A beauty. The moon also rode across my window view.... But I feel like a bird in a cage, captured.... Face washed by nurse! Pill taken. I got up & washed quickly & back to bed. Inhaling. Bed made. Lunch ordered.... Blood test, a tiny tube in vein. Sputum [*test*]. Phone number for John [*required*]. Breathing the inhaler.

12th December

A little happier. Letters came & *The Times*.... Peter's letter with the nice news he likes my book [*to be published as The Button Box*]. I am so glad, for I feel a bit critical of some things. But some is good I know, especially the Dream essay.... Doctor came when I was in the lav[*atory*] & the nurse opened the door & peeped at me. Cheek! No locks on doors.

16th December

K Wig sent the beautiful flower book by Beverley Nichols. The pictures kept me occupied & happy. She thanked me for showing her beauty in the world. How sweet of her.

17th December

Here I am, my birthday, & my first word was Damn, as I put a tea [*cup*] down on another one, luckily no breakage. A lovely day, & the first nurse in wished me Many Happy Returns.

20th December

Came home, feeling much better.... But in the night I felt I would [*have liked*] to stay longer. I do not feel ready to tackle my cooking & house.

30th December

Peter du S came to tea, – with my MS, and we had a good talk, & made several small changes where I was at fault.... He suggests *The Button Box* for [*the*] title. It amuses me, original & good. I only put this essay [*with the same title*] in for fun!

31st December

Oh dear, here I am, ill.... But I am improving & much happier each day, & thankful for the help.... God take care of us all. Amen.

~~ *1968* ~~

1st January

A new year, & I am glad for the last year was not so good with bronchitis & coughing all the time.... food bores me & I want nothing but sleep & bed!

15th January

Nice letter from CF T[*Tunnicliffe*] saying he will illustrate [*my books*] as long as I write.

24th January

Still depressingly ill with much phlegm.... No doctor came, – I managed to eat part of an egg for breakfast.

3rd February

I made a Rice Pilaf, – saw it in *The Times* & made it. But desperately tired as I got back to bed.

4th February

Sunday! A day I don't like in bed but I enjoyed today.... I read the paper, full of bad news about Vietnam & Saigon.

11th February

A quiet day.... Listening to [*broadcast service from*] St. John's Church, Buxton, & remembering that a boy I knew used to be in the choir.... How far away is that Buxton life, how strange it was... a bad influence I think. Reading Proust again.

25th February

Sun shining & I feel extraordinarily blissful; is it the sun? Or life itself?... Fuss about [*the possible*] immigration of 500,000 Pakistanis from Kenya.

1st March

Rats & rats! The rat catcher came – a nice polite man, – who saw all the holes & put down the poison.... The Immigration Bill [*restricting immigration into the UK*] passed, I'm glad to say.

18th March

Letter from Bobs-Merrill publishers, of Indianapolis.... sending on a letter from Ohio asking for broadcasts of *TR*... paying 300 dollars (about £100).... John & Helen came... en route for the airport. A nice chat, cup of tea, off.

19th March
Budget. I sat for 3 hours at the TV.... Very glad [*income*] tax not raised, it is too high already. Car tax & petrol affect me, & of course everything will rise in price. Still it might have been worse. I felt anxious about the £2,000 I gave John.

25th March
The old Rent Day when my father went off with his hard-earned money to Cromford, to a hotel I think where the Rent Dinner was held.... How far away & long ago!

4th April
Sleepless night, thinking of Death, of my father looking so beautiful like a statue, his chiselled face so pure in outline. I remember how astonished I was to see such beauty in death. I thought I must tell John about this.

16th April
[*She is upset by Hilda sending*] a letter to Gwenda, + 5/-. This surprises & annoys me.... It is not done, writing to a maid after a visit. Very queer. I must beware of Hilda's visits after this. I feel nervous & worried.

6th May
I have been reading my proofs [*of The Button Box*] & have taken out some of the overflow of bliss I feel at times!

8th May
Reading K Mansfield's journal & I see how it influenced me & helped me in my early writing days. I've not read it since I began to write & found my own style.

21st May
I heard the cuckoo, it made me joyful.

25th May
Riots & riots in Paris, horrible & frightening. Revolution in our time! One thinks of 200 years ago and France.

31st May
Letter from Leslie Frewins [*publishers*], Mayfair, asking for *Cricket*, which Jim Swanton used, for an anthology on cricket.... I have the copyright.

11th June
Letter from Mr [*Hookham*] of Curzon St saying he wants to make TV films of *GR*.... Tea in garden, & pottering about all day, trying to *think*.

12th June
[*To London*] to see Mr. [*Hookham*].... He spoke of merchandise & the film rights.... Nearly bought a picture [*for*] £750.

13th June
Recovering from the thrill of yesterday. I cannot help thinking of the £60,000 mentioned as a possible bonus from my books (shared with MT, – of course) and the joy of having a large audience. I posted *Sam Pig and the Singing Gate* to Mr. Hookham.

14th June
[*On the basis*] of the TV proposal, I indulged in a tiny carton of the first strawberries [*at*] 1/8d. (Not cheaper till after Henley, I was told). Letter from Mr Hookham, saying he will have some cartoons made to show me.

15th June
Wrote to M Tempest sending news of the TV Plan. Will she at once smash it dead? I wonder!

19th June
Letter from M Tempest, saying she does not wish to have the colours of her pictures changed & making various objections, & agreeing to see a film, saying we should have a lawyer.... [*Angela Caccia writes saying*] she... sat next to the Foreign Secretary Michael Stewart & next to Prince Henry of [*Gloucester*], who had been David's fag at Eton.

5th July
Came home. A lovely flight [*from Guernsey*].... I feel a lot better, refreshed. They were *very* kind to me.

9th July
Angela [*Caccia*] says P du S.... seems to be preparing her for a refusal [*of her book*].... He is always so kind & thoughtful, but I feel sad for I like her book.... The [*garden*] seat is done, I now loll & swing in it, with a blackbird singing near me, & roses in front of me. Bliss indeed!

19th July
Tatiana said that our tea is much nicer than Russian. Why? I said because we insist on boiling water, 537 times as hot at [*Boiling Point*]. She said our birds sing in the rain but Russian birds don't. Yes it is true, birds are singing gloriously on these wet stormy days.

21st July
Last night I listened on TV to a film on the Abominable Snowman, & to a discourse.... on Loch Ness Monster, in whom I believe.

27th July
(How I wish my James had been called Jamie, it would have mellowed him, & helped him in life!)

7th August
Letter from John [*about Mrs Paine removing*] £6,500 which she lent John for his house, – free of interest. [*Mrs. Paine has left John and Helen*].... I've been thinking, & I am going to send £100 a year to him. I can manage. I could even manage £200, but I have lots of big bills owing, Tax, Dr, Dentist.... all so much.

8th August
I felt worried about John.... He will be so unhappy at Mrs. [*Paine's*] departure. She is an obstinate old lady, very one-sided, Cromwellian in the Civil War, & a hater of so many things. These Presbyterians are so narrow minded.

21st August
Bad news on the wireless, Russia invaded Czechoslovakia last night. I am amazed & horrified. Poor old Czechs.

25th August
[*To tea at neighbours*] I went, & hated it. That awful young Italian.... saying I was a Victorian writer. 60 years ago books.... Sheer cheek.

28th August
Mr Hangham (or is it Hookham?).... told me all arrangements for TV to be done in Spain to save taxes.... He would pay us £1,000 in advance too.

29th August
I felt on air, all day, so thrilled with the thought of the films, not the money, for I have enough, but the fun and games of the films for children, & the delight in the colour. He wants them ready for Colour TV.

31st August
I am awarded a bronze medal [*from a German gastronomical academy*] for *Recipes from an Old Farmhouse*.... I am delighted! And Fabers will be glad. It is their triumph, not mine, their lovely production.

3rd September
Letter from MT. My heart sank as I saw the postmark Ipswich. Of course she doesn't like the rabbit, – a Walt Disney one, says she. Head too large. Colour all wrong.

4th September
London, – a terrific day.... I met Mr Collins, who says he will write to Miss T. I told him I would give him a *GR* tale.

11th September

[*I wrote*] to Tatiana, tactfully referring to the invasion of Czechoslovakia, which I *cannot* spell, ever.... [*And*] to Peggie Foye, to ask about.... models as Collins ask about them for this film.

15th September

I read a few chapters of *Treasure Island* in bed last night, – it is remarkably well written. I am amazed how good it is. No wonder we were enchanted & frightened by it in our childhood at Castle Top.

30th September

Wash day, – I discovered [*that*] my dear James's Christening Spoon was missing [*and*] a beautiful Georgian dessert silver gilt spoon, about 1760 was also missing. Is it possible that G[*Gwenda*] can have taken them? She is so nice, she surely wouldn't.

6th October

To Penn, the Music Society.... I did *not* like the Britten. He seemed to create [*these*] discords, & all the instruments seemed to have this one discord & play his loudest. Pandemonium in the music world, my ears hurt & my mind reeled.

13th October

Too many NUDES in the *S Times* supplement. I burnt it up in the wood! Sick of all this stuff. Why, Oh why!!

14th October

[*The Country Child is broadcast on radio.*] The broadcast was beautiful. It brought tears to my eyes, I remembered so vividly my home & parents, the fields, lanes, our road down the hill, – the horses straining and all the difficulties my parents faced.

23rd October

Just listened to [*a*] reading of *The Good Companions* & my admiration of JB Priestley is higher than ever. He is a marvel indeed.

24th October

The beautiful bronze medal from Frankfurt [*for Recipes from an Old Farmhouse*] came today. I feel very proud.

28th October

Harrods sent a new TV by Pye. £74 on [*approval*]. [*Very*] good & I shall get it by 'what's its name', not paying [*hire purchase*].... £2 for my old (new) dog basket, which pleases me in all ways.

30th October

Another busy day, [*the*] sweep... came, – he told me he had read my books, he loved the country, birds, flowers, animals. He talked of the Bucks villages & little churches he knew.

31st October

Phone [*call*] from Mr. WAR Collins. 'This is Billy Collins', – & he told me he & Mrs C love the new *GR* book I sent [*Little Grey Rabbit Goes to the North Pole*] He wanted a small cut at the end & I quite agree. I don't think it is a *very* good story, I must go through it again. Also he told me that the TV people are working hard & have done some cartoons.... He likes the characters very much.... Yet what will MT say? He too is nervous.

1st November

A gloomy day, but I felt thrilled over Mr Collins & the TV. He says he might publish a [*Little Grey Rabbit*] 'cheap' series too. I feel rich & famous on one hand, & tired and stupid on the other.

4th November

The broadcast [*of The Country Child*] was beautiful, – on December, but it brought my childhood & parents so vividly [*to life*] I felt unhappy. Yet it was marvellous. I feel like a ghost, – a queer feeling.

6th November

[*The doctor was*] horrified at my swollen red face. He gave me BETNOVATE ointment to put on every 2 hours.... I felt really ill, & in pain, eyes hurting, as if skin removed & some liquid drained out of my head.

10th November

R[*Roger*] Benedictus for tea. He brought the [*Grey Rabbit*] films.... Weasels too fat and clumsy.... but MT's are ugly too!.... I suggested KW.... for the illustrations of *GR at the Pole*.

11th November

K Wigg left after doing some shopping for me, & I *have* really enjoyed her visit. She laughs and giggles too much, but she is a fine & splendid person, so hard working & good.

13th November

Faber £963.0.1. The largest [*royalty payment*] for a long time.... [*John wants*] to come with Helen for Xmas Day, & he wants me to go with them [*to Guernsey*] for my holiday. Not very keen for either.

14th November

This afternoon I gardened in desperation, about 5 weeks since he was here. Made a big pile of stuff & a bonfire.

15th November

I managed to write a page for *LGR* tale of the Pole, – explaining about the compass.... Also I corrected the script of the [*Little Grey Rabbit*] film, with all its connecting links. Very well done.

16th November

Lovely letter from a girl who knew me at Fulham, – Marie Street.... She remembered me walking with her, both of us late for [*teaching at the*] school, and I too now remember it.

17th November

[*A letter from Irene Hawkins says*] 'I think the reason that your writing so enthralls is that, unlike most of us, you have retained the feeling of passionate wonder of vision of all known childhood delights, and in reading, one recalls so much. You have given yourself time to stand & stare & thus to give us in light & darkness, things growing, those flowers found, birds, trees, rocks.... in *The Button Box*.' Bless her kindness!

27th November

Writing in bed tonight, glad to have my own writing table instead of buying one for £87. Too expensive by half!!

3rd December

Yesterday a man from the *Bucks Advertiser* called to ask me to give some memories of Enid Blyton. I could only say that we only met once, and when I asked her which books she wrote, she replied, 'Look in Smith's window', and turned away, and never spoke again.

6th December

Lovely letter from D[*David*] Davis [*BBC producer*] telling me of the fan mail for *The C Child* – the best reception he has ever had.

10th December

Pipes burst & the men here mending them... working all day.

17th December

My birthday [*her 85th*], a big age. I cannot believe it. I don't feel old, only tired when I do a lot, – and I enjoy doing nothing, just sitting, and looking about me.

18th December

Can't remember, too busy to write in the diary.... Yes, – a lovely day.... I set off with parcels to deliver.... Then off home [*in the dark*] but I felt really frightened, it was sinister like a cruel 'End of the World' feeling.... I prayed to God for help & got home.

21st December

Letter & card from Gertrude, & for the first time in her life she has praised my work.... 'I have much admiration for all you succeed in doing, giving pleasure to thousands. You are wonderful.' I was amazed & deeply touched by this tribute.

25th December
Very cold. The church [*Penn Church*] lovely.... The feeling I was in a Mediaeval Church, such a friendly happy family attitude.

27th December
The [*United States*] astronauts landed, great rejoicing. Amazing that they kept so close to the calculated time. Venus shining like a sparkling jewel in the sky. I thought I saw a firework when I first saw the planet glittering through a tree at night.

28th December
Ruth Pitter's poems came to cheer me. I sat & sewed & patched a kitchen cloth, enjoying the mundane things, thinking of God in all that we see & do, in matter itself, whether Moon or dish cloth. Venus again in night.

~ *1969* ~

Nursery rhyme adapted for my new book of 1970....
A dillar, a doller,
A ten o'clock scholar
Why have you come so late?
I stopped to talk to the fairy folk
As I went through the gate.

1st January

Tracks in the snow in the garden. A round paw mark, – perhaps a cat. Two long spikes, like a bird but so long about 1? inches it must be a large bird. Fascinating indeed.... [*Met*] Joyce Kann, – who said that Helen had whispered to her [*that*] I had given up my bedroom to them. I was most touched by this.

7th January

5 pm – The wood is red gold, every tree brilliant. I feel half frightened, as if the world is burning.... I got up & got my meagre breakfast, thankful for electric fire. Letter from Helen who is…. taking the cure. 2 oranges & ? grapefruit & one drink of water a day. Already lost 4 lbs.

15th January

K Wig did not send the pictures or phone. She is too off-hand, I felt annoyed as I phoned her again today…. Roger Benedictus came, – & he showed me the pictures by MT, both very poor & one of them horrible. I of course said they would not do. We discussed the difficulty... of having a new illustrator [*for the Little Grey Rabbit books*] after all these years.

17th January

K Wig's belated pictures came.... 2 done only, but they are good, & very much like MT's. Children will not notice. MT will be infuriated. I'm fed up with the whole thing.

25th January

Lilian King [*thinks that K Wig*] does not do her best, her painting is muddy, she could do well but she is too involved with household affairs. We both agreed she is *not good enough*.

28th January

To B in the rain to get a cake & vegs & when I got home R Benedictus on the phone. Mr Collins agreed to reject MT's pictures & he phoned her. She said she [*Margaret Tempest*] wanted to do a final sample of her work for him before finally giving up if so he agreed. They all liked KW's pictures v. much.

7th February
Broadcast of *Rabbits Go Hunting*. Listen! Very well done. I had forgotten it. Went to B for the 10/- owing from the bank.

17th February
'You combine fantasy with reality, with the happy result of possibility,' says my typist in a clever epigram that pleases me. And she thanks me for my friendship.... Letter from John, telling me of early arrival of gannets at Alderney, *Feb* 15th.

23rd February
M. Wynzar came to tea, bringing chocolate (After 8s).... A nice person & we had a lovely talk.... She is 62, she told me, – & I did not give my age, I feel so old when I do. I lay awake thinking of Death & Old Age, & it frightened me.

1st March
Can't remember, but I know I enjoyed several small things today. A bunch of snowdrops from the wood & garden. Bread & cheese for lunch, delicious.

3rd March
Collins cheque for £301.1.10., – a small drop from last year.... [*Collins tell*] me Miss Beresford is to interview me for *Woman's Hour* on April 15 (? I forget).

14th March
Today came the horrid interview with the *Daily Mail*, who called me a 'white-haired widow' who wrote children's stories & by a coincidence lived like Enid Blyton in Beaconsfield. He said I wrote *T in T* which was unknown.

19th March
Ill in bed. RB has rejected my new *GR* book which is the best I have written. He does not like humans in it. But I insist.... All the favourite tales of animals have human beings in them, fantasy animals or not. *Alice in Wonderland* & the [*white*] rabbit, *Uncle Remus, Wind in the Willows*.... Mr Collins has always accepted them. Now this young man is showing off his power by rejecting the book. I feel very cross.

25th March
I wrote to Mr Collins.... speaking of RB's rejection. I feel I cannot rewrite the [*latest Little Grey Rabbit*] book at all, & it is good.

27th March
Heinemann [*cheque*] for £97.10.10, BBC £6.... Gwenda posted my letter of protest to Mr.

Collins's home address, marked Private, I hope RB does not see it! I could not sleep for worrying about RB's rejection of the *GR* book on *Snow Baby*.

5th April
I feel rather lonely when P du S is out of England. Yesterday came his Easter gift, *Shadows & Spells*, a lovely anthology of strange poems. I adore it.

8th April
Letter from R Benedictus enclosing copy of his letter to MT & telling her that the proposed illustrator [*Katherine Wigglesworth*] was good and experienced & she would call to talk to MT if she wished!! I phoned RB to say yes, I agreed.... Next came a phone call from WAR C[*Collins*] himself.... He had been distressed by my letter & he was anxious to read the tale.... so I quickly added a changed ending.... and Gwenda's daughter posted it at once for him to get it tomorrow. I think MT will still protest. She had asked about if someone she knew in the village could combine with her over the pictures, but RB thought it was not a good plan. This is her 3rd attempt to keep her job.

9th April
Phoned K Wig about [*her*] seeing MT, & she said Reverse the charge. They said No, it ought to be done by K Wig at the start. The charge would be £1. 0. 6 for the ? hr talking. O dear me! (KW sent £3! How kind).... I phoned WAR [*Collins*] about KW going to see MT when no certainty about her position. It isn't fair & WARC agreed & said he would phone KW.... The interview with the *Guardian* came, – very nice & interesting. I am [*described as*] a large sturdy woman in it. Oh!

10th April
[*Notes of an interview for BBC2 with Miss Beresford*] Little Grey Rabbit, – 35 (?) years ago.... called on me. How I was feeling rather lonely and my son had gone to school, so I set down 3 animals about the same size. I was used to [*Squirrel*] [*and*] to rabbits which played on our lawn. Hare in the top pasture. Not based on real people.... Why do children love them? Because I believe in them. Mine aren't made up. They are real.... I don't sit down to write a story, they come. Hare is a Boaster. [*I have a*] tremendous feeling for country. I was born in a place of beauty. Animals [*are*] more important than man. I talked to all the animals. I don't want to go back. I could live in the middle of London, and I would still feel in the country.

17th April
At last. Letter from Collins WAR himself saying that my story of [*Little Grey Rabbit and the Snow Baby* is accepted, & that KW is to do the pictures for *GR* as Miss T agrees!! I'm very glad.... I felt ill today, & dizzy.

18th April
Letter from Elliott Stocks [*brother of her friend Winnie Stocks*] I've torn it up, – cannot read all of it, he hopes he has not shocked me & he says he is 'psychial'.

9th May

Writing to Mr. Collins about the 4 forms sent to me for cancelling contracts: – to David Davies for music, K[*Kenneth*] Collins for toys, Peggie Foye for china, [*Anne*] Hogarth for puppets. I feel most indignant. I rang up RB [*Roger Benedictus*] & he just made excuses, calling them Merchandise for the future.

11th May

The Stewarts [*came*], after about 5 years... Ethel looking old and frail, but charming with pink cheeks. Agnes... she was so pretty. Janet rather stiff, nice and plain, & good looking Charlie. All in Charlie's car!

12th May

P du S phoned , saying he had read the contracts & letters [*from Collins*] & I must not sign.... Good man! and such a help to me!.... I wrote to Manchester University [*library*] & to Mr Koetser.... saying... I don't want to sell my Breughels.

21st May

Cheque for £1,119. 5. 3. from Fabers. Thrilled.

26th May

Today I watched on TV the return of the astronauts from the moon. A wonderful picture & the shining light dancing in the air.... Marvel to see it & to think about it.

28th May

One of the nastiest reviews I have ever had. I have torn it up, – from *The Scotsman*. My books are imitations of Beatrix Potter, but my writing [*is*] very simple & she uses a larger vocabulary, – my stories with no knowledge of the country, – I think of a *hedgehog*, but she thinks of Mrs Pricklypain [*sic*] & so on, sneering at style & at plot.

6th June

Dr Ratcliffe [*Librarian of Manchester University*] came at 10.00 am, – and I liked him at once, great fun, and a happy man. He enjoyed every minute and so did I, for I felt like meeting a long-lost brother, so in tune with my likes and loves and desires, so happy in the sun, and thrilled with the house. [*He buys various of her books for £60.*] A darling man, whom I wish I'd met long ago. Shades of Professor Alexander too.

17th June
[*She sees on television the story of a Mrs. Brown*] who hears the voices of Bach, Beethoven.... Impossible to make it up.

20th June
Mr K[*Koetser*] came [*to see and perhaps buy her Brueghel paintings.*] At the end he said... only

was up to his standard, the Flower picture by Ambrose Breughel, for which he offered me £2,500. The rest £800 – £700.... they are the Breughel School, he says.

21st June
A letter from [Dr] FR [*Fred Ratcliffe*] which delighted me when he spoke of the dream like visit here which was perfection.

2nd July
[*In Guernsey*] I bought a long dish for Helen to placate her. She never admires a present. She's casual in her thanks & manners.

7th July
I am writing an article for the *Radio Times* [*about A Traveller in Time*].... Then to a garden, public.... But icy cold & I sat 2 hours waiting, in a thin dress. I felt cold & miserable & lonely as I watched the sparrows.... I asked for a cup of tea when we got back. No, said Helen. Too near dinner. But John [*made me one*] & put brandy in it. It saved me but I felt not well.

8th July
In bed all day, after a horrid night of coughing and panic. Helen never came to see me. John did all the trays etc, – I never asked for anything at all

18th July
'Of all our many guests you do the least to help us,' writes John with candour. No apology for H's rudeness. I do little because I dare not interfere. I would love to dust or wash up or cook, but I dare not enter the kitchen or ask for a duster. No, – O, I do not mind, it is so small, so queer a friction.

19th July
The Shakespeare edition came, 1st Folio, £30. I ordered it at once on appro[*val*].... Today polishing off my letter to John. I hope it will not sever our connection, but I cannot let Helen snub me, and to be so cruel for all my life & with no protest.

20th July
I wrote my 6th letter to John, unposted & worried & not wanting to hurt him. 'Life is short, it is a pity to waste it over trifles, real or imagined. I am much older than your many guests & I cannot carry my tray or use the vacuum, but I am always happy to help.'.... Man on the Moon. Thrilled & yet [*to get*] down to earth with no reliance on *man*! What will he do?

22nd July
Trying to keep up my heart, still hurt over John's letter last week. But this is silly, – I have so much love from many, from countless people & I love them all so much.... To B, a big shopping.... I felt rich as I chose... 3 small peaches (8d. each).

31st July
The worst has happened. John has taken offence at my little poem... upbraiding me fiercely, & saying I must not visit him in Guernsey again. He will come here occasionally, – but he won't. This would be the end of Love. I felt wounded & dying, – I wrote a little letter & enclosed it in a long letter of news, – & I sent it. I tore up his, too cruel. One cannot use a poem or a joke & I hoped he would laugh & forget our miserable quarrels.
[*She quotes the poem she had earlier sent:*]

Lament for a Mother in Law
She never did the dusting,
She never swept the floor.
She never washed the linen,
She though it was a bore.
She sat out in the garden.
She read a fairy book.
She ate the wholesome fishcakes
Which she had not helped to cook....
She wrote a little letter
And sent it to her son.
'I'll soon be off to paradise
To sweep in Kingdom Come.'

7th August
John's letter, much quieter and kinder, but rather odd, no list of my faults as I asked but explaining he must play golf & lead his ordinary life. (As if I opposed it! I'm only too glad he plays.) Milk boils over!! What do I mean?

9th August
I feel drunk with music this evening, listening to Beethoven, Brahms, Dvorak, on the wireless.

18th August
Rain. I am watching a pale fawn pigeon, so sweet sitting on the arm of a garden seat.... looking so happy, preening.... A lovely interview.... in Smith's *Trade News*.... It mentions the Ramsay MacDonalds & me in my early days in London & [*the*] many happy things I once did. Oh why did I not continue with the MacDonalds, I just left them, & I loved them so much.

29th August
Awoke early with deep depression. I do get such awful miseries now ever since John sent his cruel letter. I don't think he ever realised, but it has given me insecurity & loneliness in the vast Universe.... Busy rewriting the *Village School* essay, & posted it to Sheila to type.

14th September
The Jacobsons came to tea, & a lovely visit.... I talked of my delight in Cambridge. It all came back to me, – racing fast down the narrow lanes to get back in time for dinner. Going to the Union for debates. To tea at the house of [*a*] Physics man and his wife. Seeing the Cavendish lab.

15th September
Trying to find a title [*for the new book for*] Faber.... I can only say *When that I Was*. [*It was published as The Ten O'clock Scholar.*]

21st September
[*The Du Sautoys came*] I agreed I should give my Library to Man. Univ. I said [*Peter*] could choose any books he wished to have, & so could John.

9th October
Paid in Bank. £50 from Man[*chester*] Univ[*ersity*] for the 4 Bucks books.... Good news. Bill Collins and Mrs. C[*Collins*] both like the Rainbow story very much [*Hare and the Rainbow*], & want it next with the *Snow Baby* following.

22nd October
I wrote to CF T[*Tunnicliffe, about the death of his wife*], poor man, how lonely he must be. I saw an enchanting baby in a pram.

28th October
Gardening, making bonfires of leaves. Writing a *Fuzzypeg's Brother* story.

1st November
I realise that I still like men and women alike, for their aura or what I feel. Never sexually, always as I like a sunset, or clouds, or Brahms' *2nd Symphony*, or that celestial music – is it Dvorak, the [*Song to the*] moon or art. I fall in love with a painting, Van Gogh, or Cezanne or Breughel, and it is the same as my love for the artist. His work is himself. It is the atomic structure I love in men and some women, and poet's words get [*to*] my heart. But women do not understand. They are catching and holding on for the sake of sex. I love the invisible, the secret soul of man.

4th November
The [*Children's*] Book Fair.... Mobs of children in the Hall.... They surged & pushed & shouted like a wild mob. Somehow we got to Collins' stall.... & they surged in, frightening, pushing so close I was nearly pushed over. I kept saying Go *Back*! Back!.... Then to see the film [*of Little Grey Rabbit and the Weasels, for television*] in Wardour St. It was delightful, such fun.... I felt quite happy.

5th November
RB phoned to see if we were well today! Yes, & we loved the film.... Off to Winslow where I got a frying pan, a steel dish & a lovely green glass jug from Italy.... The trees near Winslow! Oh! The beauty of the trees is extraordinary. Yellow & gold glittering leaves, the sky blue with big white clouds, like a fairy tale. We were enthralled by Earth's beauty.

13th November
[*At lunch, with Lady Iris Campbell and Miss Wilson, I am asked*] why don't I wish to find out more about the invisible world. Because it should be inviolate & I don't trust MAN. Don't I like people, they asked. Yes but not en masse. And so on.

24th November
Margaret Rutherford & Stringer came unexpectedly.... Margaret looking so old, bent, nearly stooping & with 2 walking sticks. She clasped me & held me as she kissed me. I felt sad & surprised at her appearance, it was resigned, no vitality or vigour. Her leg still bad & she seems to have no hope. Stringer talked & talked but she was silent.

4th December
Taken ill with Bronchitis. Dr came. Bad cough. To stay in bed.... So no diary. Packed parcels in the bed.

12th December
I felt very ill & frightened, as I paced up & down, waiting for the Dr.... it ws horrible.

15th December
John's flowers came, carnations.... Got out the silver tree & a few ornaments for Xmas to cheer myself.

24th December
Feeling better, & off to the Fairbairns for lunch, well wrapped up with [*Richard*] driving me. The lovely house with its embroidered plaster ceiling, & the room like a 19th century picture as we sat round the fire.

～ 1970 ～

'Each year may be the last, so I must enjoy it, and work hard.'
Alison Uttley. My Motto

1st January
I lay in bed until 10.15, wanting letters & newspapers.

8th January
Peggie Foye came.... I was tired & sleepless but she was imaginative & alive. She brought a carousel of *GR* [*with the theme music of the film*] *Dr. Zhivago*, & also a little night light house of *GR*.... She has a small factory with 8 girls working for her, & all to be done for Easter.

18th January
My faith, which I would like to tell to CF T[*Tunnicliffe*]: 'When one thinks of the many rich compensations that life offers, even after the direst tragedy, & how lucky we are to be given the chance of living on earth, whether rich or poor, – then.... fretting & melancholy seems like a sin against the Holy Ghost.'

19th January
Letter from RB. saying Mr Collins showed him *Fuzzypeg's Brother*, & it is the best I've written but he (RB) does not like the green door & brass handle.... He is the limit! Also he questions whether MT can do the pictures. Of course he must ask KW to do them.... I *know* a gorse bush with a door & a brass knocker.... but I saw this place in childhood, – a patch in our Top Pasture, where I once crept.

30th January
Letter from F Ratcliff, saying no trace of school picture [*of Lea School in the John Ryland's Library archives*] so CF T[*Tunnicliffe*] will manage without it.... [*She quotes from*] John's sweet letter of 9 years' old [*when he was a boarder at Yarlet Hall prep school*]. 'I am John and [*what*] I like best [*is*] to cuddle my Mummy & Daddy.' O, darling James!

31st January
My savings a/c brought in over £200 interest. It amazes me.

28th February
Letter with a proposal for a play [*based on her tale*] 'Holly & Ivy' [*from a*] Mr. Pittfield of

Bowdon, & a prof at the school of music. A nice letter, with a book of his small poems. I am delighted.... [*The*] *Evening Standard* also wants a photographer to come on Friday interview on Tuesday. [*The interviewer was Fiona McCarthy.*]

7th March
[*The recipe for*] Grey Rabbit's Salad [*is given in detail*].

9th March
[*An interview and photograph for the London Evening Standard, when the photographer*] never stopped snapping me. I felt dizzy, it was like mosquitoes biting me, and darting at me.

11th March
Terrible picture of me, all wrinkles & shut eyes & loose drooping mouth, as I held 2 snowdrops. The worst I have ever had, a caricature. It might be spite!! However, I can bear it. I *will not* mind. The world is lovely, and the sky. Ill.

12th March
Letter from Man[*chester*] Univ saying the Senate have passed the resolution that I should have an Hon degree, [*of*] Doctor of Letters. I am thrilled it has gone through & I am rewarded for a lifetime of work.

16th March
Joyce Kann came to tea.... She is a spirit of fun. She brought the paintings & they are lovely & sensitive & decorative. I am excited over them as I am over a *good* picture.... Letter from Tempest saying she was surprised to read my age & I am older than she. She is 77 she said. She is a gloater. I wrote back a nice letter but short & saying I liked KW's pictures, mostly. I will not write to MT. She is a treacherous woman, & her grandchildren must know this too.

24th March
I felt ill all night, & lot of pain, & wanting to be sick.... John & Helen left for Cyprus.... Letter of congrat[*ulations*] on D. Litt. [*from*] WH Perkins, who reminded me that we were both [*once*] County Scholars. It was a nice letter, but he was rather wistful of fame for himself! He was always keen on fame and chose his friends for it, I think.

4th April
Letter from F Ratcliffe with more details of [*the honorary degree*] ceremony.... I must ask if we wear evening dress for the Reception (but I don't think I shall go to it).

8th April
Mrs. [*Barbara*] Lees (Warden of Ashburne Hall) came & I like her very much. Warm hearted & friendly and capable. A good person for a warden. She remembers Ethel

Herdman, Miss M, the gardener, Miss Hughes, dear Miss Conway. She invited us to visit her.... She told me of the queer, hard girls who now, [in] the last few years, go to College... and the goings on at Owen's Hall next door. Poor Mrs. Lees, how worrying indeed.

13th April
I don't think I like Frankie Howard's [sic] Roman plays [on TV] – too mocking, too sexual.

20th April
I gave my lecture on 'Dreams'. I spent hours & days trying to make it perfect. I dressed nicely & Ruth [Plant] drove me.... The big empty room, only 2 or 3 people there at 8 p.m.... More people drifted in, about 30 at most.... I was cold & bored & couldn't see my script. I struggled through it, doing most out of my head & they listened intently, no applause or sound. Questions good.... [But] a silly woman telling us she had a silly dream. No tea or coffee.

1st May
Lovely May Day & F Ratcliffe came visiting for the day. As nice as ever.... 12 ingredients in the salad, he said. We laughed & talked.... He stayed till 8 o'clock, & then drove back all the way to Manchester.... I felt so happy all day for FR does me good, a tonic.

4th May
TV people came [to make a programme for Line Up] – & the most beautiful day of the year.... Mrs. Ingrams was the interviewer, very nice. We sat up by the wood & [she] asked questions while 4 men photographed me. A sudden click of a wooden box & that was the signal to start. I walked in the wood alone.

6th May
I got the 6 copies of *Lavender Shoes*. A nice book. I'm so glad Fabers did it & not Heinemann, and that awful Jennie Corbett.

7th May
Hair permed for the big occasion, but what a bore. I hate it. Such a waste of time.

11th May
Waiting for John from Guernsey & Angela from Italy.... I did my washing and pottered about, for tomorrow I go off to [Manchester] for the degree ceremony, a great thrill, especially to be with such nice people as P du Sautoy, John, Dr Ratcliffe and Joyce Kann. Posted the review to Macmillan... of New York, with a letter saying Do not send books for review as I do not want to do the work [for] free and pay postage & the typist's pay too.

12th May
[By rail to Manchester for the Honorary Degree ceremony] To Euston.... I stood on a platform

waiting, & Angela in a green long trouser suit & no hat came along like a girl out of Hans Andersen. Then Peter joined us.... & we were off! Lunch on train, after a long wait.... Drove to hotel, very nice.... John & Peter went to the party, but first we had a crazy dinner, all laughing in the French restaurant.

13th May
Last night Joyce, Angela & I went to Ashburne Hall.... long talk of old days with Mr. [*and Mrs*] Lees.... Weds. too tired to go to F [*Ratcliffe's*] library, so sorry.... [*She then describes the ceremony after the lunch.*] Then to be robed, a lovely robe of scarlet with pale gold linings and gold on the collar & front. Big black Tudor hat that suited me. The procession, & the presentation. The hall filled with light & brilliance. I could have wept I felt so moved by the beauty. I was presented & I shook hands with the Chancellor & I became a D. Litt.

14th May
This night at 10.55 we saw the film of me on BBC 2 in colour, v. good.... Last night we travelled home.... I must not forget the fun we had in a hired car in [*Manchester*], as [*the chauffeur*] kept asking where he was, as he got stuck in traffic, and downpours of rain. We laughed till we cried! We all felt so giddy as if at a wedding as we drove packed 6 in car with driver [*and*] 2 hat-boxes on our knees.... [*She describes again the scene as she was presented.*] I stood half facing the audience, thrilled. I thought of God, of C Top, and of L Meagher.... At the reception I met Nellie Meagher. I was staggered, like a dream fulfilled. She came all that way to see me in memory of LM. I spoke to nice Duke of Devonshire, who said, 'Bakewell is just as beautiful and happy, and the school very good.' We spoke of various other people. I met Geoffrey Cooper, [*but*] I didn't know him, he looked so old and shrivelled. John has just gone, and I am alone again. What a marvellous time, the best of my life.

20th May
To the TV studios in Wood Lane [*to be interviewed for a programme on her work*]....They liked me & my voice. I felt I talked too much, but it was good, and well contrived with the wood, treetops a rich green & flowers & garden & interior of house [*Thackers*].

1st June
Letter from CPH, who is a bore.... He calls me 'dear' now & then & tells me I was a 'beautiful strong girl at school'.... How can I get rid of him?

6th June
Signing books at the little bookshop at B. Very well arranged & orderly queue. I signed about 100 books. 70 of *Lavender Shoes* & 30 miscellaneous.... I thought the children were sweet.

9th June
I took Dirk to vet, who said [*he*] had a growth & must return tomorrow for operation. On

the way home.... I drove carelessly & found myself stopped by a heap of asphalt I had driven into thinking it was a shadow.... I hurt my breast & ribs, bruised my knee & cut my hand.... I phoned the Council Surveyor to complain of no signs.... Full of pain and shock.

10th June
The doctor came & said no ribs broken, only bruised.... M. Rees drove me to the vet with Dirk for [*his*] operation.... When I got home 2 policemen to make enquiries about the smash in London about a month ago when all we drove up to see the TV [*programme*] of myself.... Fetched Dirk at 5 pm & I felt frightened as he lay so quiet.

18th June
Voting Day. I was taken by Mrs Rees to vote for Bell, the Conservative [*candidate*]. Who gets in? I guess Labour with a small majority. Good letters about [*Enoch*] Powell.... Like Churchill, warning of dangers in near future.

25th June
Off again to Guernsey.... Really, I would rather stay at home with all the roses & books and TV, & writing my book of essays, – but I ought to have a change. The journey daunts me, it is too tiring.... John meets me.... The house looks nice. Helen cool.

27th June
Mrs. Payne [*sic*] in tears over Helen's scolding of her & I comforted her by singing:
O dry those Tears
O calm those Fears
Life was not made for sorrow.
Twill come, alas!
But soon will pass.
Life will be happy tomorrow.
She joined in, & our squeaky old voices sang, a pathetic & comical duet. But it did us good.

30th June
John infuriated by me because in a kind of dream I took something & did not say 'thank you'. 'You behave as if you were in a hotel,' he shouted. 'Where are your manners? Why don't you say thank you? You sit there and say nothing etc etc.' I was quite overwhelmed. Life is queer. I just sat. Mrs Payne in tears over the upsets.

2nd July
Gave a talk on Early Writing to the girls of the Ladies College [*in Guernsey*]. A nice audience & I enjoyed it. The head girl, a poppet, so fresh & young & good mannered.

3rd July
Returned home. [*In Guernsey*] to my bedroom; Helen stood there. She said, 'So you've

come back. Look at the way you've left your room! Flower petals all over. Sheets stained. What are these stains?' She dragged [*the*] sheets to my face, I could see nothing & she said they were new sheets & I had stained them. She was furious, demented, [*almost*] out of her mind with anger. I was bewildered. I cannot write about it. I do not know what she meant. I could see no stain on [*the*] white sheets. But her roughness and fury were horrible. I just whispered to Mrs P[*Paine*] but Helen came in.

4th July

I felt as if I had escaped from a mad woman. It really frightens me. She is filled with hate. Yet I won't be sad.... 'She does not know what she says', Mrs. P[*aine*] said about her daughter.... Only me with an aching heart, so sad for John. Shall I never go to Guernsey again? I do not know. I said to John, 'If you invite me here next year I will bring my own sheets with me.' Dirk adorable, & a good sleep!

5th July

I told Lilian [*King*] about the stained sheets episode. She thinks that Helen is Mental.... filled with jealousy & anger, & goes over the edge.... Certainly it seems so. It is rude even if blood lay on the sheets, nobody should attack a woman or accuse her like this. And the sheets looked to me white as snow! How could John agree with her?

14th July

K Wig came, – and it is lovely to have her, – just the same, stout, limping, smiling, warm-hearted, shedding joy around her.... her new Morris 1000 car, very nice.... we talked & looked at the pictures. I suggested deeper blue skies.

11th August

Rosemary [*Shelton's*] son, aged 11 weeks is the loveliest baby I have ever seen. Perfection of face & hands & feet.... My heart was overwhelmed with his beauty. Like seeing a perfect rose, a picture of great worth.

16th August

On TV the Kirov ballet, which fascinated me, & took me back to my London ballet days, when I went every night to see the Ballet. We were all crazy over it, & no wonder.

21st August

Frightful painting of Princess [*Margaret*] for her 46th birthday. When she was born, I was in Bandol, with James, enjoying the beauty & French life. I walked on the front by the sea, and the news of her birth came from news boys.... shouting it.

23rd August

Margaret Rutherford came.... She was ages getting out of the car.... Tragic to see her, struggling on smiling bravely as I kissed her.... *Very* tired & depressed over MR.

24th August
Why cannot [MR] be cured, or have real help?... She is resigned to Fate, and the act of resignation is terrible. Like seeing a bird in a cage or an animal in the zoo.

25th August
Letter from John. Tired after some visitors had left the house in a dirty mess. After my experience I am sure I should not call them dirty. Rose petals are dirt to Helen.

26th August
[*A visit from Faith Eaton, who brings a collection of dolls.*] Enchanting display.... I gave her some of my smaller dolls, all those from USA, & the wooden doll too. I promised to leave her my own Dolly, which I had when I was about 5 years old.

1st October
To Windsor to see *Twelfth Night*.... I liked the glittering décor.... Songs I didn't like, – ugly music & rough. Nor did I like Maria, too flighty & silly with her orange dress.

13th October
Mr. Muspratt [*the vicar*] rang up [*to say*] I am allowed to be buried in the graveyard [*of Penn Church*]. Very glad, a home up there.

30th October
The vicar called & I signed papers & gave £100 for the grave space at Penn.

17th November
Russian machine on the Moon. Frightening, 8 legs, like a horrible story of science fiction.

21st November
Dr Milner came to test me for the Royal Ins[*Insurance policy*]. He took a Blood Pressure last.... my blood pressure is perfect. He could not believe I was 85.... It cheered me very much.

26th November
To London, – & a great success although I felt nervous after so long. A taxi very quickly, & to the dentist. Not much of an ordeal.... I went to D & F & looked at dresses & chose 2 for appro.

7th December
John came for 6 days. He looked well & brown, & we were happy as we sat & talked.

31st December
Goodbye, dear 1970. A lovely year. Snow here. I'm very tired but happy & I look forward to 1971. Through the kitchen window a lighted Christmas tree here in the garden & the young moon shining in the sky above it. Bliss, & may it always be blissful, this life of ours.

≈ 1971 ≈

[*She writes a list of things to remember for the year, about the compensations of life, beauty, animism.*] The sense of the supernatural in natural things.

1st January
New diary, instead of my old London Diary. Lines too close for me I fear. Icy cold & foggy, – very gloomy. I stayed at home, determined to write part of an essay. I wrote 2 or 3 pages. Then BF [*Betty Fairbairn*] came, to my annoyance & stayed over an hour, preaching at me.

28th January
[*David Caccia*] asked if my scientific career had changed my feeling about the reality of God. I said No, it... had strengthened it.

11th February
Eureka! The book [*Secret Places*] is finished. I managed to tidy up [*chapter on*] 'Weeds', & all is done.

12th February
10. 30. A Mrs. Butt to interview me for the Beaconsfield Society. Bother her. She didn't come, baby ill, I am glad she put it off as I felt very tired.... I actually sat down, doing nothing for a time, listening to Radio 2 & some old songs.... Last night I laughed at an absurd film on TV, the 'Liver Girls' [actual title: *The Liver Birds*], – impossible & silly but very funny.

14th February
Peter & Mollie [*du Sautoy*] with [*some of their grandchildren*]. The 2 boys played Cowboys & Indians in the wood & lawn, – such abandon as they flung themselves down on the grass! I loved to see their joy, I gave them 2 *GR* books & Mollie a little purse.

24th February
To B, for shopping.... & paying with new pence. So dotty. 86 pence! I ask you.

2nd March
St. David's Day festival, – Prince Charles receiving the Freedom of City of London, – procession, speeches. Terrific. [*It filled me*] with pride in England, & all this island stands for in a weary world. It was splendid. The Prince [*is*] ...a worthy descendant of the Kings and Queens of England.... I prayed for him, his future, his safety & his heart. I was most touched.... Snow today, – a big fall in the night.

11th March
Taken to Beaconsfield [*Nursing*] Home, St Josephs. Joyce Kann took me there & settled me in bed. A pale blue room, with a small cross.... Body prepared & shaved.

16th March
A struggle, still bleeding.

19th March
Doctor Milner [*says*] take pills at night & Enos in morning to try to get regular habit & prevent this pressure and bleeding.... paid in Bank £397 from Collins.

28th March
Very interesting interview on TV with [*former Labour cabinet minister*] Lord George Brown. I have always liked him & I admired him still more, a good socialist.

31st March
John left at 11. 30, after putting in a row of parsley in the garden…. & buying & putting on the plug light at end of room.... He told me they cannot have me in Guernsey, too much work. I agree, John gets tired and Helen irritable. They have Mrs. Payne on their hands. So be it.

11th April
Easter Day. Up early, a lovely day, & I got ready for Church.... I could not kneel but I could pray. It was like going home to God.... After I returned I had an accident. I fell on the stairs & crushed my foot.... No bones broken.

23rd April
[*Margaret Tempest says in an article that*] 'Alison created her characters orally, and I visually,' she explained. They [*we*] both took immense trouble over detail. Doctor's bill for £40. Too much.

2nd May
Roger Benedictus [*came with his wife*] Tanya & baby Philip.... big blue eyes & smiling like a cherub in heaven.... (Poor Roger, sacked by Collins, leaving at end of May).

4th May.
Letter from T[*Tanya*] Benedictus [*talking about her visit*] 'I had been more than a little nervous of the visit, expecting someone of your fame to be overawing, – but while, if you will forgive me, the awesomeness is there, it was wonderful to be received with such warmth and interest!'

13th May
Anniversary of [*the award of my*] hon D. Litt. degree, one of the happiest days of my life....

I said Angela [*Caccia*] should accept, & bear it [*David loving a second woman*], it is in his temperament, – many love him for his brilliance.

8th June
I cannot write. I feel a kind of heavy misery, I think it is a Cosmic Misery, with the thought of the people in India and Pakistan [*at war with each other*].

25th June
To London, the most beautiful day.... Then to Collins.... Sir William Collins came in & thanked me for the *GR* books, so I thanked him.

26th June
To Ellesborough to visit Miss Wood at number 3. Her pleasure, nearly in tears. We talked of her fairies & she told John the story.

28th June
I feel so happy with John [*staying here*], a quiet & lovely little holiday.

1st July
Saw [*Wimbledon tennis*] duel between Billie Jean King & Miss Smith & felt glad that Miss S won. Her cheerful optimism & a smiling face & brilliant tennis.

23rd July
Sir Billy Collins wrote: 'Pierre [*Lady Collins*] & I both read your new story [*Grey Rabbit's Spring Cleaning Party*].... We were enchanted by it & very much like the idea of all the small creatures & the nursery rhymes, so it should be a delightful one to illustrate. I have now passed it on to the children's department. Thank you so much. Yours ever, Billy.' (How glad I am about this book!!)

24th July
Found in a drawer with papers.
Last Will. Testament.
This I leave behind –
All that belongs to me.
In the birches a silver wind,
A wave on the shore of the sea.
F. Niven.

3rd August
Dr. Ratcliffe came at 2.00, delightful as usual, & we sat & talked. But Helen Dickens [*her cousin and the sister of Sissy*] came at 4.30. I was shocked at her ugly face, rough dark brown, creased, & ugly shouting voice. I had to ask her to speak softly, I am not deaf.... How can I bear her? A great disappointment to me.

4th August

I went down early & got 2 breakfasts. She keeps shouting at me & declaiming as if teaching a class & I am in the back row. Very stilted and odd.... But O, how can I bear her?.... It never stops.

7th August

Another week of misery with Helen [*Dickens*]. She reminds me of Sissy & her father.

22nd August

Helen left, & we had a nice talk, not so aggressive. I gave her mother's garnet gold brooch which thrilled her.... Her visit a strain & she shouted so often. She queried & argued & pointed out defects, dusty mantelpiece & all small defects.... An unattractive woman I fear, but a good heart.

27th August

Pan books ask for the *Brown Mouse* stories in 1973. The new *Story Book of Sam Pig*.... to be published on 28th Sept!! Took Dirk to vet, a thorn in his foot.

1st September

I am a bad writer of a diary, – days go too fast to write.... Lost latch keys & prayed to St. Anthony.

3rd September

Letter sending me a copy of *Chitty Chitty Bongo* (?), [*an*] ugly book & pictures. Asking for *Red Fox* Puffin book to be put in this ed[*ition*]. I agreed to do so & they will use KW's pictures. They offered £300 between us.

4th September

I had curry from a tin for lunch, a treat – most delicious, – a find for me.

12th September

John's birthday.... Bless him & the joy he has given me. I sent him £10 & he bought some shoes I hear later.

17th September

A fine day. Then came a letter from Alfriston, [*Derbyshire*], the [*Townswomen's*] Guild wish to use my life as a 'project' & write plays [*about*] me.... Of all the cheek! I am horrified. They will make me a country bumpkin, dull and stupid.... All day I felt worried.

30th September

Mary Rees drove me to B. to the music shop, to test some *GR* records. Delightful, but my old records do not play! Shall I buy a record player? – £20. It is a nuisance really.

2nd October
Nigel Hollis, the Publicity Editor, came.... He took me to Old B to the little shop [*where*] I autographed a pile of 10 & about 10 more, a meagre lot but I enjoyed it.

4th November
Home from [*Nursing*] Home, – all so lovely, gold beech trees & garden full of flowers & colour. I feel better already.... Expenses [*of medical care*] about £280.

9th November
The most cruel letter of my life, & a surprise of cruelty, from John who tells me 'bluntly' that I am self centred & selfish, that he dislikes coming to see me at Thackers etc. etc.. All because.... in the [*Nursing*] Home I phoned him to ask him if he would come [*from Guernsey*] & get me out of the N. Home [*and take me to*] Thackers to recover, as the doctor had said I could not leave until I had somebody here to sleep in the house.... Still I have all the beauty of garden and flowers and sun and moon. Dirk my beloved dog. All people have troubles, & so we must bear it & laugh. God help me.... Oh Life!!

24th November
Letter from WAR [*Collins*] accepting the Snow baby [*Little Grey Rabbit and the Snow-Baby*] saying it is is enchanting. So I am delighted.... A nice day, snow melting.

28th November
All day I anticipated trouble but all was wonderful as the nice clever doctor gave [*me*] my [*medical*] test for driving.... This is to certify that the applicant is in full possession of her faculties & the use of her limbs & is able to read a car number plate without the use of spectacles.

7th December
Margaret [*Rutherford*] shocked me. Her face all creased up as she worked her jaws as if biting something. Horrible to see. She cannot go on much longer.

9th December
Struggling on, a lot of pain in the bowels.

31st December
Goodbye old year. I am full of pain in bowels, making me ache all over. I have had this on and off for weeks & written nothing. Still, lots of fun. Today a great work, gardeners.... came & pruned roses.... Well goodbye old year, lots of happiness & beauty & fun. I hope 1972 will be as good.

There are no more diary entries after this.

Books by Alison Uttley

PUBLICATIONS FOR CHILDREN
Fiction
The Squirrel, The Hare and the Little Grey Rabbit, illustrated by Margaret Tempest, Heinemann, London, 1929

How Little Grey Rabbit Got Back Her Tail, illustrated by Margaret Tempest, Heinemann, London, 1930

The Great Adventure of Hare, illustrated by Margaret Tempest, Heinemann, London, 1931

Moonshine and Magic, illustrated by Will Townsend, Faber, London, 1932

The Story of Fuzzypeg the Hedgehog, illustrated by Margaret Tempest, Heinemann, London, 1932

Squirrel Goes Skating, illustrated by Margaret Tempest, Collins, London, 1934

Wise Owl's Story, illustrated by Margaret Tempest, Collins, London, 1935

The Adventures of Peter and Judy in Bunnyland, illustrated by L. Young, Collins, London, 1935

Candelight Tales, illustrated by Elinor Bellingham-Smith, Faber, London, 1936

Little Grey Rabbit's Party, illustrated by Margaret Tempest, Collins, London, 1936

The Knot Squirrel Tied, illustrated by Margaret Tempest, Collins, London, 1937

The Adventures of No Ordinary Rabbit, illustrated by Alec Buckels, Faber, London, 1937

Mustard, Pepper, and Salt, illustrated by Gwen Raverat, Faber, London, 1938

Fuzzypeg Goes To School, illustrated by Margaret Tempest, Collins, London, 1938

A Traveller in Time, Faber, London, 1939; Putnam, New York, 1940; Viking, New York, 1964; Puffin, Harmondsworth, 1977

Tales of the Four Pigs and Brock the Badger, illustrated by Alec Buckels, Faber, London, 1939

Little Grey Rabbit's Christmas, illustrated by Margaret Tempest, Collins, London, 1939

Moldy Warp, the Mole, illustrated by Margaret Tempest, Collins, London, 1940

The Adventures of Sam Pig, illustrated by Francis Gower, Faber, London, 1940; Puffin, Harmondsworth, 1976

Sam Pig Goes to Market, illustrated by AE Kennedy, Faber, London, 1941; Puffin, Harmondsworth, 1979

Six Tales of Brock the Badger, illustrated by Alec Buckels and Francis Gower, Faber, London, 1941

Six Tales of Sam Pig, illustrated by Alec Buckels and Francis Gower, Faber, London, 1941

Six Tales of the Four Pigs, illustrated by Alec Buckels, Faber, London, 1941

Ten Tales of Tim Rabbit, illustrated by Alec Buckels and Francis Gower, Faber, London, 1941

Hare Joins the Home Guard, illustrated by Margaret Tempest, Collins, London, 1942

Little Grey Rabbit's Washing-Day, illustrated by Margaret Tempest, Collins, London, 1942

Nine Starlight Tales, illustrated by Irene Hawkins, Faber, London, 1942

Sam Pig and Sally, illustrated by A.E. Kennedy, Faber, London, 1942; Puffin, Harmondsworth, 1979

Cuckoo Cherry-Tree, illustrated by Irene Hawkins, Faber, London, 1943

Sam Pig at the Circus, illustrated by A.E. Kennedy, Faber, London, 1943; Puffin, Harmondsworth, 1982

Water-Rat's Picnic, illustrated by Margaret Tempest, Collins, London, 1943

Little Grey Rabbit's Birthday, illustrated by Margaret Tempest, Collins, London, 1944

Mrs. Nimble and Mr. Bumble, illustrated by Horace Knowles, with This Duck and That Duck, by Herbert McKay, Francis James, London, 1944

The Spice Woman's Basket and Other Tales, illustrated by Irene Hawkins, Faber, London, 1944

The Adventures of Tim Rabbit, illustrated by A.E. Kennedy, Faber, London, 1945; Puffin, Harmondsworth, 1978

The Weather Cock and Other Stories, illustrated by Nancy Innes, Faber, London, 1945

The Speckledy Hen, illustrated by Margaret Tempest, Collins, London, 1946

Some Moonshine Tales, drawings by Sarah Nechamkin, Faber, London, 1945

Little Grey Rabbit and the Weasels, illustrated by Margaret Tempest, Collins, London, 1947

Grey Rabbit and the Wandering Hedgehog, illustrated by Margaret Tempest, Collins, London, 1948

John Barleycorn: Twelve Tales of Fairy and Magic, illustrated by Philip Hepworth, Faber, London, 1948

Sam Pig in Trouble, illustrated by A.E. Kennedy, Faber, London, 1948

The Cobbler's Shop and Other Tales, illustrated by Irene Hawkins, Faber, London, 1950

Macduff, illustrated by A.E. Kennedy, Faber, London, 1950

Little Grey Rabbit Makes Lace, illustrated by Margaret Tempest, Collins, London, 1950

The Little Brown Mouse Books (*Snug and Serena Meet a Queen*; *Snug and Serena Pick Cowslips*; *Going to the Fair*; *Toad's Castle*; *Mrs. Mouse Spring-Cleans*; *Christmas at the Rose and Crown*; *The Gypsy Hedgehogs*; *Snug and the Chimneysweeper*; *The Mouse Telegrams*; *The Flower Show*; *Snug and the Silver Spoon*; *Mr Stoat Walks In*), illustrated by Katherine Wigglesworth, Heinemann, London, 1950-57

Yours Ever, Sam Pig, illustrated by A.E. Kennedy, Faber, London, 1951; Puffin, Harmondsworth, 1977

Hare and the Easter Eggs, illustrated by Margaret Tempest, Collins, London, 1952

Little Grey Rabbit's Valentine, illustrated by Margaret Tempest, Collins, London, 1953

Little Grey Rabbit Goes to Sea, illustrated by Margaret Tempest, Collins, London, 1954

Little Red Fox and the Wicked Uncle, illustrated by Katherine Wigglesworth, Heinemann, London, 1954; Bobbs Merrill, Indianapolis, 1962

Sam Pig and the Singing Gate, illustrated by A.E. Kennedy, Faber, London, 1955

Hare and Guy Fawkes, illustrated by Margaret Tempest, Collins, London, 1956

Little Red Fox and Cinderella, illustrated by Katherine Wigglesworth, Heinemann, London, 1956

Magic in My Pocket: A Selection of Tales, illustrated by Judith Brook, Penguin, London, 1957

Little Grey Rabbit's Paint-Box, illustrated by Margaret Tempest, Collins, London, 1958

Little Red Fox and the Magic Moon, illustrated by Katherine Wigglesworth, Heinemann, London, 1958

Snug and Serena Count Twelve, illustrated by Katherine Wigglesworth, Heinemann, London, 1959; Bobbs Merrill, Indianapolis, 1962

Tim Rabbit and Company, illustrated by A.E. Kennedy, Faber, London, 1959

Sam Pig Goes to the Seaside: Sixteen Stories, illustrated by A.E. Kennedy, Faber, London, 1960; Puffin, Harmondsworth, 1978

Grey Rabbit Finds a Shoe, illustrated by Margaret Tempest, Collins, London, 1960

John at the Old Farm, illustrated by Jennifer Miles, Heinemann, London, 1960

Grey Rabbit and the Circus, illustrated by Margaret Tempest, Collins, London, 1961

Snug and Serena Go to Town, illustrated by Katherine Wigglesworth, Heinemann, London, 1961; Bobbs Merrill, Indianapolis, 1963

Little Red Fox and the Unicorn, illustrated by Katherine Wigglesworth, Heinernann, London, 1962

The Little Knife Who Did All the Work: Twelve Tales of Magic, illustrated by Pauline Baynes, Faber, London, 1962; Puffin, Harmondsworth, 1978

Grey Rabbit's May Day, illustrated by Margaret Tempest, Collins, London, 1963

Tim Rabbit's Dozen, illustrated by Shirley Hughes, Faber, London, 1964

Hare Goes Shopping, illustrated by Margaret Tempest, Collins, London, 1965

The Sam Pig Storybook, illustrated by Cecil Leslie, Faber, London, 1965

The Mouse, The Rabbit, and the Little White Hen, illustrated by Jennie Corbett, Heinemann, London, 1966

Enchantment, illustrated by Jennie Corbett, Heinemann, London, 1966

Little Grey Rabbit's Pancake Day, illustrated by Margaret Tempest, Collins, London, 1967

Little Red Fox, illustrated by Katherine Wigglesworth, Puffin, Harmondsworth, 1967

The Little Red Fox and the Big Big Tree, illustrated by Jennie Corbett, Heinemann, London, 1968

Little Grey Rabbit Goes to the North Pole, illustrated by Katherine Wigglesworth, Collins, London, 1970

Lavender Shoes: Eight Tales of Enchantment, illustrated by Janina Ede, Faber, London, 1970

The Brown Mouse Book: Magical Tales of Two Little Mice, illustrated by Katherine Wigglesworth, Heinemann, London, 1971

Fuzzypeg's Brother, illustrated by Katherine Wigglesworth, Collins, London, 1971

Little Grey Rabbit's Spring Cleaning Party, illustrated by Katherine Wigglesworth, Collins, London, 1972

Little Grey Rabbit and the Snow-Baby, illustrated by Katherine Wigglesworth, Collins, London, 1973

Fairy Tales, edited by Kathleen Lines, illustrated by Ann Strugnell, Faber, London, 1975

Hare and the Rainbow, pictures by Katherine Wigglesworth, Collins, London, 1975; Puffin, Harmondsworth, 1979

Little Grey Rabbit's Storybook, illustrated by Margaret Tempest, Collins, London, 1977

From Spring to Spring, chosen by Kathleen Lines, illustrated by Shirley Hughes, Faber, London, 1978

Tales of Grey Rabbit, illustrated by Faith Jaques, Heinemann, London, 1980; Piccolo Books, London, 1982

Little Grey Rabbit's Second Storybook, pictures by Margaret Tempest, Collins, London, 1981

Tales of Little Brown Mouse, illustrated by Faith Jaques, Heinemann, London, 1984

Foxglove Tales, chosen by Lucy Meredith, illustrated by Shirley Felts, Faber, London, 1984

Little Grey Rabbit's Alphabet Book, pictures by Margaret Tempest, Collins, London, 1985

Plays

Little Grey Rabbit to the Rescue, illustrated by Margaret Tempest, Collins, London, 1945

The Washerwoman's Child: A Play on the Life and Stories of Hans Christian Andersen,
   illustrated by Irene Hawkins, Faber, London, 1946

Three Little Grey Rabbit Plays (includes *Grey Rabbit's Hospital, The Robber, A Christmas
   Story*), Heinemann, London, 1961

PUBLICATIONS FOR ADULTS

Novels

High Meadows, Faber, London, 1938

When All Is Done, Faber, London, 1945

Other

The Country Child, Faber, London, and Macmillan, New York, 1931; Peacock Books,
   Harmondsworth, 1963, reissued in Puffin Books, 1969

Ambush of Young Days, Faber, London, 1937

The Farm on the Hill, Faber, London, 1941

Country Hoard, Faber, London, 1943; Howard Baker, London, 1976

Country Things, Faber, London, 1946

Carts and Candlesticks, Faber, London, 1948

Buckinghamshire, Hale, London, 1950

Plowmen's Clocks, Faber, London, 1952

The Stuff of Dreams, Faber, London, 1953

Here's a New Day, Faber, London, 1956

A Year in the Country, Faber, London, 1957; Howard Baker, London, 1976

The Swans Fly Over, Faber, London, 1959

Something for Nothing, Faber, London, 1960

Wild Honey, Faber, London, 1962; Howard Baker, London, 1978

Cuckoo in June, Faber, London, 1964; Howard Baker, London, 1978

A Peck of Gold, Faber, London, 1966

Recipes from an Old Farmhouse, Faber, London, 1966

The Button Box and Other Essays, Faber, London, 1968

The Ten O'Clock Scholar and Other Essays, Faber, London, 1970

Secret Places and Other Essays, Faber, London, 1972

Editor, *In Praise of Country Life: An Anthology*, Muller, London, 1949

Stories for Christmas, chosen by Kathleen Lines, illustrated by Gavin Rowe, Puffin,
   Harmondsworth, 1977

Our Village: Alison Uttley's Cromford, illustrated by C.F. Tunnicliffe, selected by Jacqueline
Mitchell, Scarthin, Cromford, 1984

Country World, chosen by Lucy Meredith, illustrated by C.F. Tunnicliffe, Faber, London,
   1984

Index